PHOTO. Richard Walch   RIDER. Dave Downing

www.burton.com

1.800.881.3138

GIVE US A CALL TO GET YOUR OWN NINETY 8 PRODUCT CATALOG

ERIKSSON

ATLANTIS SNOWBOARDS, INC:

PATRIK KARLSSON • AMATEUR

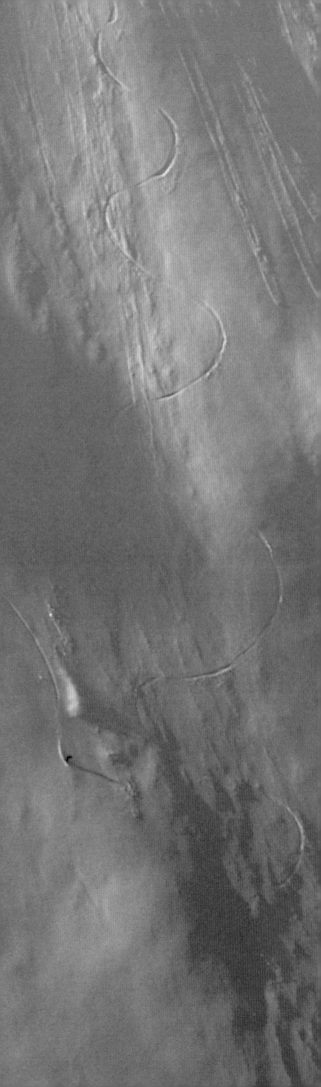

First published 1997 by
Low Pressure Publishing Ltd ©
Unit 21, Pall Mall Deposit
124-128 Barlby Rd
London W10 6BL
Tel/Fax +44 (0) 181 960 1916
Low Pressure Europe +(33) 558 77 76 85

Creation modification of all maps, graphic arrangements
and devices, pictograms, text and index,
© copyright Low Pressure Publishing (1991) Ltd
State and relief maps copyright MapArt by Cartesia Software.

Repro by Aylesbury Studios
Printed by Jarrold Book Publishing

A catalogue record of this book can be obtained from the British
Library.

ISBN no: 9 780951 927533

THE snowboard GUIDE
NORTH AMERICA

LOW PRESSURE PUBLISHING

swatch

6

This book, the third in our four book set emcompassing surf and snow guides to Europe and North America, is the culmination of a vast effort by an international team of riders from as far afield as Argentina, Australia, Canada, England, New Zealand, Scotland, Switzerland, and yes, the US. The information came from a much bigger number of sources, though it's written from traveller's perspective. As such, it has its faults and omissions, however we believe the foreigners' perspective is uniquely valuable. We had help from a million really cool people on the ground right across North America. To everyone who helped at any time, a warm thanks from the whole team.

There is no way we could have covered every resort in North America — that would turn into a phone book and would cost the earth — so we picked 75 of the most popular resorts with a fair geographical spread. There are some notable omissions such as the snow-capped peaks of Hawaii, but we feel we've reached a balance. We welcome contributors comments, additions, notes and observations for our future editions.

THE snowboard GUIDE
NORTH AMERICA

Commissioning Editors
Ollie Fitzjones and Tim Rainger

Publishing Editor
Tim Rainger

Editor
Ali Hanan

Copy-Editor
Gina Dempster

Art Director
Dan Haylock

Assistant Art Director
Gareth Parkinson

Photo Editors
**Tim Rainger, Bruce Sutherland,
Dan Haylock, Gina Dempster**

Project Co-ordinators
Alison Curry and Ali Hanan

Advertising, Marketing and PR
Suzanne Alleyne

Key Journalists
**US West to East: Bruce Sutherland, Tim Rainger,
Gina Dempster, Marc Hare, Gary Johnson
Canada: Tim King, Mike MacWatt**

Other Key Contributors
**Marco Bruni, Karta Healey, Javier Proccacini,
Ryan Runke, Jerry Saunders**

Photographic Contributors
**Bob Allen, Kore Antonsen, Alex Badley, Marco Bruni, Tom Brownold,
Richard Cheski, Jeff Curtes, Gina Dempster, Greg Von Doersten, Bud
Fawcett, Mark Gallup, Gary Johnson, Mark Junak, Tim King,
Ace Kvale, Gary Land, Bill Marsh, Wade McKoy, Mike MacWatt,
Chris Murray, Chaco Mohler, Nils, Nolen Oayda, Tim Rainger,
Quinn Sheilds, Matt Small, Richard Smiles, Bruce Sutherland, Vianney
Tisseau, Sean Ward, Scott F. Wicklund, Tony Welch**

Additional Contributing Journalists
**Richard Cheski, Logan Curtis, Doug Ellsley, Dave Pinkerman,
Jenny Spiker, Ron Simenhouse, Chip Wayt**

Special thanks to
**Bernie Bernthal (Swatch), Steve Klassen,
Nick Clout (Delta Airlines), Paul Eyre (Lloyds Bank),
Gary Lovejoy (Eurosport), Nim Singh (Canadian Tourist Board),
Kathleen Willis (American Skiing Co.), Ski USA, Ski Utah,
Frank Strang (Boston Ski Party), Ski New Mexico, Steven Jenkins,
Kore Antonsen, Neil Stuart; everyone who supplied us with equipment
including Birgit Purrmann (Ortovox), Barry Duggan (Burton),
Sean and Liberty (Mervin Manufacturing), George and David (K2),
Trey Cooke (Switch), Lorenzo (Level), Enich (Arnette), Karrimor,
Paul and Harry (Rad Air); additional thanks to Tom Thibedeau (ABA),
Tiki Yates, David Macmillan; Jevin, Jania and Ginger Ryan, Santa
Barbara Lauren, and as always, to Patagonia.**

**We'd also like to thank all good weather forecasters everywhere,
all the funky lifties, the wild-eyed crazies who rode with us,
and the resorts who let us in on their best stashes.**

**To everyone else who helped out in anyway —
you know who you are — thanks for everything.
We hope the work justifies your faith.**

LOW PRESSURE PUBLISHING®

swatch+

Contents

PACIFIC

MOUNTAIN WEST

EAST COAST

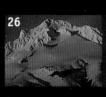

26

78

154

ALASKA

BRITISH COLUMBIA

ALBERTA

WASHINGTON

OREGON

MONTANA

IDAHO

WYOMING

CALIFORNIA

UTAH

COLORADO

ARIZONA

NEW MEXICO

192

206
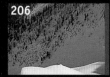

QUEBEC

MAINE

VERMONT

NEW HAMPSHIRE

NEW YORK

1985: Breckenridge, Colorado.
We were there for the world's
first freestyle snowboard event.
Where were you?

1997/8: Europe and North America.
Swatch World Boarder-X tour.
Where are you now?

Steve Klassen, Swatch Pro Team. Big ol' road jump, Revelstoke, BC   Pic: Marc Gallup

swatch®

Time is what you make of it.

MOUNTAIN AWARENESS

'An extreme snowboarder is one who rides the steeps with technical mastery not with adrenaline-based recklessness. The back-country is beautiful but will snap at you when you make mistakes. Respect her and she will reward you with endless powder turns that ignite the soul.'

RIDING THE BACK-COUNTRY

BY SWATCH PRO, STEVE KLASSEN

As a pro-rider travelling internationally, making my living back-country, I have to be aware of the dangers I face every day.

THINK LOCAL

One of the dangers in the US is that going out of boundaries may be illegal. Ducking ropes can get your lift ticket pulled and can even land you in jail. The most important thing I've found as I've been travelling around is to ask the locals a lot of questions. Ride with the locals, talk to the ski patrol and heli guides, and gain your own knowledge. You may be comfortable in your own territory, but as you change locations, mountain ranges and continents, it's a whole new game and a new snowpack.

GUIDES RULE!

I follow the general rule of always going out of bounds with a guide in any new place. My life is too important to take risks lightly. Listen to your guide and learn the area so that you can make your own judgement calls.

INJURIES STOP YOU RIDING

When I show up somewhere new, my priority on the first day is 'don't get injured'. I've found that if you are in some new place for a week, at least 50 per cent of all injuries happen on that first day. The first day should be about getting orientated. Make sure you have all your gear: transceiver with fresh batteries, shovel, probe, first aid kit, emergency blanket, and if you are travelling around glaciers, a harness and ropes.

YOU'RE IN TROUBLE IF YOU DON'T KNOW FIRST AID

Anything can happen in the back-country: cornices snap off, wind slabs pile up, chutes slide and people can get hurt — it could be your best friend. Be ready for the panic adrenaline rush like no other. When your friend is in front of you, bloody and unconscious, you need to stay calm and know what to do. Knowing CPR and basic first aid could make the difference. Feel competent in your ability to save someone else's life.

A SNOWBOARD IS A MAGIC CARPET

Things change fast in the back-country and it's easy to get disorientated and put yourself in a bad position. At the very least you should take a basic back-country course, know your limits and trust your gut instincts when they tell you something is wrong. Have respect for mother nature, and don't push yourself past your capabilities. There has never been a powder turn that was worth a full burial. Remember that the snowboard is a vehicle that can take us into different worlds. It's a real-life magic carpet flying us to different lands and cultures. Temper the buzz with respect and knowledge of nature's laws — each place is unique.

Opposite — Steve Klassen in The Books, Chugach Mountains, Alaska
Photo: Greg von Doersten

Top — Illustration: Kore Antonsen

Middle — Tree wells aren't always a laughing matter **Photo:** Kore Antonsen

Bottom — A snow mushroom **Photo:** Tim Rainger

GENERAL HAZARDS

AVALANCHES

When you're off-trail, keep in mind **avalanches** Ⓐ are the main cause of death on the mountain. Always be prepared when you go back-country and follow the rules. See p.14 and p.15 for more information on how to pick out potentially hazardous situations, and what to do if you, or your buddy, are caught out.

SNOW CORNICES

Snow cornices Ⓑ are formed when wind-transported snow is plastered on the lee side of mountain peaks or sharp ridges. The deposited snow eventually overhangs the ridge. The weight of the cornice can cause stress areas well back from the overhang. Large blocks may break off and crush a rider or release large avalanches.

Never walk out on a cornice as it can break off.
Never stop under a cornice.
Always keep an eye on any threatening cornices. Immediately move out of the travel zone at the slightest warning of any danger or movement.

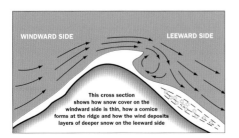

WINDWARD SIDE   LEEWARD SIDE

This cross section
shows how snow cover on the
windward side is thin, how a cornice
forms at the ridge and how the wind deposits
layers of deeper snow on the leeward side

TREE HAZARDS

A **tree well** Ⓒ is formed when the snowpack often doesn't cover the base of a tree as overhanging branches prevent the snow from forming a pack. A rider falling head first into a tree well can be trapped upside

down and suffocate. We often ride in the trees when snow conditions are good but visibility is reduced, and it is easy to lose sight of your mates. When in the trees always ride in full control to avoid injuring yourself or falling into a tree well. Use the buddy system; stay in verbal contact, and preferably within sight of your buddy.

Snow mushrooms Ⓓ are large snowfalls perched on the tops of trees and rocks. They are heavy and can fall naturally or if the tree is jarred. Watch out for, and stay away from, trees with large mushrooms.

HIDDEN OBSTACLES

Rocks, logs and stumps Ⓔ just under the snow can cause injury. Avoid riding over terrain with slight unevenness; it could be a clue to what lies underneath. Be careful on ridges where the snow cover is often quite thin because of the wind.

Deep, uncovered holes may exist in **creek beds** Ⓕ and narrow gullies. These holes are often hard to see, especially in flat light. Not only will you get wet, but you could get trapped. Ride in control and use caution when near creek beds and gullies.

OTHER HAZARDS

Cliffs, Ⓖ **wind drifts, and roads** Ⓗ are all hazards that are often overlooked. If you encounter changing snow conditions, changing terrain or any other hazard: STOP, evaluate the situation and adjust your technique and speed accordingly.

FROST BITE

An oil-based, high altitude cream will protect your face, nose and ears against frost-bite. Boots that fit properly and do not restrict circulation should keep your feet safe. Be sure that your boot liners and feet are dry. Powder your feet with talcum powder in the morning to help keep them dry. Mitts are best on extremely cold days.

BINDINGS

Ensure that your bindings are checked and properly adjusted prior to going into the back-country. When hiking, attach your board to yourself.

BAD WEATHER AND POOR SNOW CONDITIONS

Remember that you have absolutely no control over the forces of nature. Experience and knowledge will give you the greatest chance of staying alive in the back-country, and also improves your chances of finding the best snow conditions on any day.
(See Weather Knowledge, p16.)

CREVASSES

Crevasses are cracks in a glacial ice pack, sometimes hundreds of feet deep. All glaciers have crevasses, though sometimes they can be invisibly covered by snow bridges. If riding in such areas, always wear a harness to aid your recovery.

Mountain Rules

Avalanches

THE RULES

WHEN RIDING IN POTENTIAL AVALANCHE TERRAIN

1. Never ride alone.
2. One person descends at a time.
3. Only one person at a time should be exposed to avalanche danger; in other words, do not enter the slope until the rider before you has reached a safe area.
4. Stay off avalanche paths, especially release zones.
5. Do not make rest stops at the foot of an avalanche path. When pausing for a rest, stop at safety zones such as ridges, rocky out-crops or timber islands.
6. Always wear your Ortovox underneath your clothing.
7. Beware of lee areas (slopes beneath cornices and deep drifts), especially those with a convex profile.
8. Beware of narrow chutes and gullies and steep slopes between 30 and 45 degrees, even if short in length.
9. Do not assume a slope is safe just because it did not slide when the first person crossed it.
10. Do not assume that avalanches are confined to open slopes. Glades can avalanche as well.
11. If the snow acts suspiciously by suddenly settling or fracturing, head to the nearest point of safety.

IF YOU ARE CAUGHT IN AN AVALANCHE

1. Call out so other members of your party can observe your course.
2. Discard as much as you can to prevent you from being weighed down — pack and board if possible.
3. Try to swim in the snow and fight to stay on top.
4. Try to work your way to one side of the moving snow.
5. When the snow slows down, cup your hands in front of your face and make an air space, as your survival will depend on the size of the air pocket around you.
6. If you're buried, don't panic. Your Ortovox will broadcast your location.
7. If you try to dig yourself out, make sure you dig upwards toward the surface. Look for the source of light or spit to get a sense of direction.
8. Do not waste valuable oxygen by shouting. Snow is a very effective sound insulator.
9. If you think you are near the surface, try to reach out a hand or thrust up a foot.

IF YOUR BUDDY IS CAUGHT

1. Do not panic. Check for further danger.
2. Mark the 'last seen' point if it's safe to get close.
3. Make a hasty search for clues such as a hand sticking out of the snow, goggles and hat.
4. Organise an Ortovox search.
5. Signal the nearest guide or send two riders by the safest route to report to the snowcat and ski patrol as soon as possible.
6. Use probes in systematic way to located the buried person. Probes are also handy for checking snow depths and crevasses.
7. Use a shovel or a board end to uncover the person.
8. Administer first aid.

ONCE THE AVALANCHE VICTIM IS UNBURIED

1. Clear snow from airway passage and check for breathing and bleeding.
2. Check and treat for any neck and back injuries.
3. Check and treat for any other injuries.
4. Check and treat for shock.

OTHER ESSENTIALS

Before you head out, be prepared. Always take some food, preferably something with a high energy content; a drink bottle is another essential — there may be snow around you, but unless you have something to boil it up in you may as well be in the desert. A hat is another piece of life-saving equipment as 70 per cent of your body heat is lost through your head.

AVALANCHES

Avalanche's are a rider's main concern. An avalanche is a mass of snow sliding down a fall-line, which can be released either naturally or by simple disturbances such a loud noise. There are two main types:

Loose snow avalanches start from a small point, fanning out as they travel downwards and gain momentum. They can be initiated by a falling rock, an explosion or — more commonly — a skier or boarder, and they can occur in both wet and dry snow conditions. Loose snow avalanches can be huge — the air blast in front can reach speeds of 100 miles per hour (160 kilometres per hour).

Slab avalanches occur when the snow pack is not robust enough to cope with the weight of additional snow building up on top of it. The weight of a snowboarder cutting across a slope of this nature can overload the snow pack, causing it to break away along a fracture line. Slab avalanches come in two main types:

Soft slab avalanches are mostly caused by the rapid loading of fresh snow on slopes with a gradient of between 25 and 45 degrees, and are released during or shortly after a snowfall. They can be easily predicted as they occur at the surface layer of snow, and the attachment of the new snow to the base can be examined with the help of a probe. Wind during the snowfall will increase the risk of soft slab avalanches.

Hard slab avalanches, on the other hand, occur from a well-defined fracture line, which can be deep in the snowpack. A prolonged period of cold weather or any sort of heating beneath the snow pack (for example, large rock bands warmed by the sun) causes the pack to become unstable. Hard slab avalanches are difficult to predict because the top layer of snow can look and feel very safe.

TERRAIN FACTORS AFFECTING AVALANCHES

Gradient: In general, avalanche danger increases with the gradient of the slope, up to the point where the slope gets hairily steep. The greatest possibility of an avalanche occurring is between 25 and 45 degrees. There are exceptions to every rule, but it is rare that slopes above 60 degrees avalanche as the sheer force of gravity prevents snow building up to dangerous levels.

Convex slopes: The most dangerous. On a convex slope, tensions slowly build up along the mild-looking upper reaches of the slope. If a boarder traverses across a stress area, the entire slope can break away.

Concave slopes: These are considered less dangerous for two reasons. Firstly, it is much more daunting to ride a steeper slope where an avalanche run-out zone and/or debris can be seen. Secondly, the volume of snow waiting to avalanche will be slightly less as most of the snow builds up at the base of the slope.

Bowls: They look absolutely fantastic and inviting, but are a potential death trap if conditions aren't perfect. Bowls tend to have well-rounded concave sides and a relatively flat bottom. If a boarder were to start an avalanche in any part of the bowl, the movement and the air blast may bring all three sides of the bowl tumbling down. If this occurs, the depth of snow at the bottom would be immense.

Geographical position: The composition of the snow is also affected by the sun. The sun changes the temperature and the temperature changes the structure of the snow pack. South-facing slopes are generally safer as heat variations compact the snow and the layers combine with each other. North-facing slopes account for 80 percent of northern hemisphere avalanches; the layers do not adhere easily in the shade and are likely to slip.

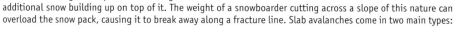

STARTING ZONE

TRAVEL ZONE

A and B are two points on the victim's trajectory

Line of flow

OUTRUN

Probable location of victim

DEPOSIT AREA

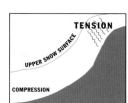 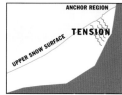 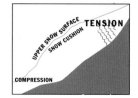

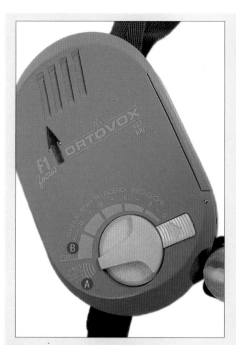

YOUR ORTOVOX AND USING IT

It is crucial that you ride back-country with an Ortovox transceiver. The avalanche transceiver sends out a radio signal that can be picked up by other transceivers, and will hasten the search for the buried person.

PREPARATION

1. Before you go out, CHECK YOUR BATTERIES.
2. Turn your Ortovox onto transmit. Ⓐ
3. Wear it with the cord around your neck, secured inside your clothing.

IN CASE OF AN AVALANCHE

1. All avalanche transceivers must be tuned to receive with the volume at maximum. Ⓑ
2. Systematically search likely areas using one of two search patterns. If there are enough searchers, spread out across the avalanche path 30 to 40 feet (10 to 12 metres) apart. Head down the fall-line in a parallel fashion until a signal is heard. Ⓒ If there are not enough searchers, head down the fall-line in a zig-zag pattern. Ⓓ
3. Mark the spot where the signal is first heard. Ⓔ Now you must begin a fine search. Hold the Ortovox close to the snow in the position receiving the loudest signal.

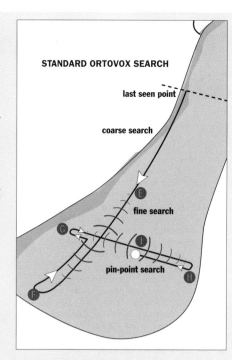

STANDARD ORTOVOX SEARCH

last seen point

coarse search

Ⓔ

fine search

Ⓖ

Ⓘ

pin-point search

Ⓕ

Ⓗ

4. Keep walking in the same direction. The signal will increase in volume then become weaker.
5. Retrace your footsteps to the loudest point. Ⓕ Turn down the volume until the signal is barely audible.
6. Head at right angles to your original path; Ⓖ determine both points where the signal starts fading.
7. Quickly retrace your steps to halfway between the two points, Ⓗ and once again turn down the volume until the signal is barely audible.
8. Repeat the last two steps till you are on the lowest volume setting and have zeroed-in on the signal.
9. The buried transceiver will be directly below the spot where the signal is loudest. Ⓘ
10. Probe with a probe pole or an upside down ski pole to determine the exact location before digging.
11. Dig the person out; prioritise uncovering the head.

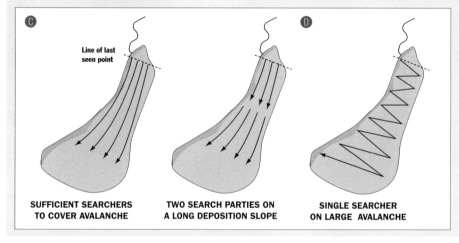

Ⓒ Line of last seen point

Ⓓ

SUFFICIENT SEARCHERS TO COVER AVALANCHE

TWO SEARCH PARTIES ON A LONG DEPOSITION SLOPE

SINGLE SEARCHER ON LARGE AVALANCHE

THE TEN COMMANDMENTS

1. RESPECT FOR OTHERS
Slope-users must always behave in such a way that they do not endanger others, either through their actions or their equipment.

2. BE IN CONTROL
All slope-users must adapt their speed and behaviour to their personal capabilities, as well as to the general conditions of the slope, weather, snow conditions and density of other slope-users at all times.

3. GIVE WAY
People ahead of you have the right of way — it's your responsibility to avoid them.

4. CHECK WHAT'S COMING
When joining a trail or setting off, always look uphill and give way to others already coming down.

5. BE WARY OF WHERE YOU STOP
Don't stop where you block a trail or are not visible from above. If you fall in an obstructive position, move out of the way quickly.

6. THE SIDE OF THE SLOPE IS SAFEST
Any slope users walking uphill or downhill must keep to the side of the slope, away from the line of other users.

7. RESPECT SIGNS ON THE MOUNTAIN
Whether concerning weather, slope or snow conditions, these signs are there for a reason. Keep out of closed areas.

SAFETY MESSAGE
OUR MOUNTAIN IS LIKE NOTHING YOU HAVE SKIED BEFORE! IT IS HUGE, WITH VARIABLE TERRAIN FROM GROOMED SLOPES TO DANGEROUS CLIFF AREAS AND DANGEROUSLY VARIABLE WEATHER AND SNOW CONDITIONS. YOU MUST ALWAYS EXERCISE EXTREME CAUTION. YOU COULD BECOME LOST. YOU COULD MAKE A MISTAKE AND SUFFER PERSONAL INJURY OR DEATH. PROTECT YOURSELF – UNDERSTAND THE TRAIL MAP AND ASK QUESTIONS BEFORE YOU PROCEED. OBEY ALL TRAIL SIGNS AND MARKERS. PLEASE THINK AND BE CAREFUL.
GIVE THIS SPECIAL MOUNTAIN THE RESPECT IT DEMANDS!

8. ASSISTANCE
Any person who is a witness to, or instigator of, an accident must give assistance. Should the need arise, first raise the alarm and then, if asked by the mountain rescuers, help out.

9. IDENTIFICATION
Any person who is involved in, or a witness to, an accident must identify themselves to the ski patrol or emergency services, as well as to any others involved in the accident.

10. EQUIPMENT SAFETY
Lay your board on its bindings when on the snow and be aware of others while carrying your board, especially when in queues.

Above — Dustin Varga, Pemberton Helis in Whistler **Photo:** Chris Murray
Right — Top of The Tram, Jackson Hole **Photo:** Tim Rainger

Weather Knowledge

WHAT IS SNOW?

The Inuit have 29 different words to describe snow. We, the English speaking, mountain-using world have coined our own collection: cement, corn, champagne, gaunch or just plain ol' pow-pow. But what do you really know about it? Snow doesn't just happen automatically when the temperature drops below freezing. Snow is born when ice crystals form in a cloud containing other fine atmospheric particles. Dust is one particle aiding crystallisation. This is one explanation behind Utah's unrivalled reputation for the lightest snow on earth: once the air has crossed the high, dusty inland plains separating the Sierra Nevada range from the Rockies, the ice crystals have a higher concentration of nuclei on which to form.

Snowflakes also increase their size and change shape, as ice crystals bump into water droplets, and fuse with each other, forming bigger flakes. Large snowflakes can mushroom into clumps of up to a hundred crystals. The more motion in the air, the more collisions, and the thicker and more complex the crystals. When cloud eddies hit the mountains after travelling over the sea, the warm, moist air is forced to rise rapidly. Snowflakes bump together and the presence of water droplets help them fuse to each other. All this bumping and grinding is the reason that coastal mountains get heavy, wet dumps. Conversely, when clouds have a smoother ride, finer crystals will form and you get the infamous light powder of the interior resorts.

THE GENERAL WEATHER SCENE

LOW PRESSURE AND THE BIRTH OF SNOW

When the sun heats the earth, hot air rises and is replaced by cool air (Fig 1). The rotation of the earth disturbs this air movement and forms wind. This uneven heating of the planet causes bands of different pressures and winds.

When warm and cold air collide, they form a spiralling, low pressure system. Lows spiral anti-clockwise in the northern hemisphere and clockwise in the southern hemisphere.

If you look at a sequence of satellite images, you'll see a continuous stream of circular cloud eddies spiralling east and northwards, towards the Arctic. These low pressures (also known as depressions, storms and cyclones) continually encircle the globe, becoming more frequent and intense during the winter.

The largest surfaces giving birth to lows are the vast, warm water reservoirs, the Pacific and Atlantic oceans. As warm air moving off these sea masses approaches land, its course is changed by barriers in front of it. If the air is forced to rise it will drop its load of moisture on the obstacle; in winter as snow.

THE PRINCIPAL DEPRESSION TRACKS

The main routes for the depressions causing snowfall in North America run across the North Pacific towards the Gulf of Alaska, and southwards toward Vancouver and Washington, guided by the path of the jet stream, a high altitude, zonal air current. When they hit the mountains of Canada and the northern US, eddies can split off and spin as far southwards as Sierra Nevada. The eddies are sometimes reinforced as they travel eastwards across the Rockies, before tracking across the Midwest. (See photo right.)

Another secondary but consistent stream of weather forms over the Gulf of Mexico and runs up the East Coast, often picking up water off the Atlantic seaboard en-route before joining up with the other systems crossing northern America.

ANTICYCLONES

Also known as highs or areas of high pressure, anticyclones have a different personality to depressions, and spin in the opposite direction. For the most part they are lethargic beasts, often sitting around for long periods. Even in their mobile form (known as ridges of high pressure), anticyclones bring mainly clear weather. Ultimate anticyclonics occur when bluebird days arrive straight after a decent depression. This weather pattern sends snowboard photographers (a breed of notorious weather freaks) into a frenzy of activity.

READING A WEATHER CHART

The lines and number variations refer to the fluctuating air pressure of deepening and stagnating depressions on their travels around the globe to the North Pole. A weather map uses isobar lines to measure the areas of equal pressure, and the air pressure itself is measured in lines of isometric pressure, measured in millibars. Anything above 1000 millibars is considered high pressure, anything below is low pressure. The steeper the pressure gradient, the closer together the isobar lines and the stronger the wind speed.

A decent low will look like a dart board with a series of concentric rings, and warm and cold fronts spinning off the leading edge. It is these fronts in their various forms that bring snow, so to know what's going on, you have to watch the progress of these fast-moving surf and snow-making factories. Consequently all good surfers and snowboarders virtually plan their lives around their movements.

Fig 1: Hot air rises and is replaced by cool air.

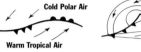

Fig 2: The anatomy of a depression.

Cold Polar Air

Warm Tropical Air

Fig 3: The principle depression tracks.

Fig 3: Flow of air from a high to a low

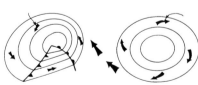

Top — Track the lows to get tracks like this; deep powder, Sunshine Village **Photo:** Bill Marsh

Opposite — The weather channel **Photo:** Tim Rainger

NORTH AMERICA BY GEOGRAPHICAL AREA

WEST: PACIFIC (INCLUDING ALASKA)

This region stretches from Mammoth in the southern Sierra Nevadas to the Chugach Mountains in Alaska. Much of the snow that falls here is wet and heavy, especially at lower altitudes. At the southern end of the Sierra Nevadas, average sunshine figures are around 35 per cent and daytime temperatures are warm. Further north, the weather is less settled because of maritime westerly air flows, which regularly cover Seattle and Vancouver. Sunshine figures are only about 20 per cent throughout January and February. The further north you go, the more extreme it gets. In 1955, Thompson Pass in Alaska got 80 feet (24 metres) of wet Pacific snow, but sunlight hours are woefully short. These mountains are the first obstacle in from of the predominantly westerly airstream coming off the Pacific, and consequently receive the highest snowfalls in North America, no questions asked.

THE ROCKIES

The Rockies are a truly enormous chain, covering ranges from New Mexico to Alberta and including Colorado, Utah, Idaho, Montana and eastern British Columbia. The altitude of the ski resorts tends to drop the further northwards you travel. Likewise the tree line, which starts at 10,500 feet (3200 metres) in New Mexico dwindles down to 6900 feet (2100 metres) in Canada. Low air temperatures mean riding in the Rockies is often down amongst the shelter of the trees, especially in deepest winter. What the Rockies lose in quantity (when compared with the Pacific ranges), they make up for in quality: many of the state's claim the best powder on earth, and they may have a point. The map above shows a low that has spread nearly the entire stretch of the range, producing snowfalls throughout the area.

THE EAST COAST

The East Coast is a meteorological battleground with invasions of intense, cold air sweeping down from the Arctic and colliding with warm, humid air from the north and the Gulf of Mexico. This all adds up to intense climatic variability. Sudden and ferocious storms, freezing weather and plentiful snow can be immediately followed by equally dramatic thaws. For East Coast riders, artificial snow has made these extremes way less intense. Virtually all the mountains lie below the tree line, except Sugarloaf in Maine, which pokes its solitary bald peak skywards.

HOW MOUNTAINS CHANGE THE PICTURE

Similar to the movement of waves passing over reefs, mountains can refract, bend or distort the direction and shape of a depression. The weather patterns in the northern hemisphere are shaped by the location and size of the major mountain chains in Europe and North America. Mountains generate their own weather patterns by forcing moving air to rise, or otherwise change direction, often leading to condensation. They also alter wind streams by compressing and accelerating air as it passes over the crests of the range. As it passes through gaps, the air speeds up and slows down. Once on the leeward side of the range, the air drops in pressure in a wave-like motion. The altitude of high mountains means they experience more intense weather; the peaks are usually colder, wetter, windier and snowier than the surrounding lowlands.

Key

STATE AND REGIONAL MAPS

Orientation

All maps
are oriented
Due North

N

Scale (Grids)

State maps

1 square = 50 miles

Regional maps

1 square = 10 miles

Map Elevation

ft		m
15,000		4575
14,000		4270
13,000		3965
12,000		3660
11,000		3355
10,000		3050
9000		2745
8000		2440
7000		2135
6000		1830
5000		1525
4000		1220
3000		915
2000		610
1000		305
0		0

Land Areas

National forest

Provincial parks

Metro areas

Natural Features

Rivers

Lakes

Glaciers

Roads and Road Signs

Free limited access highways

Toll limited access highways

Other four-lane divided highways

Other through highways

– – – Ferry route

90 Interstate highways

95 **281** US highways

11 **904** State and provincial highways

16 Trans-Canada Highway

Land-marks

1 Snowboard resorts
covered in this book

State capitals

Towns and cities

International airports

Domestic airports

20,320 Mountains

International boundaries

– · – · State boundaries

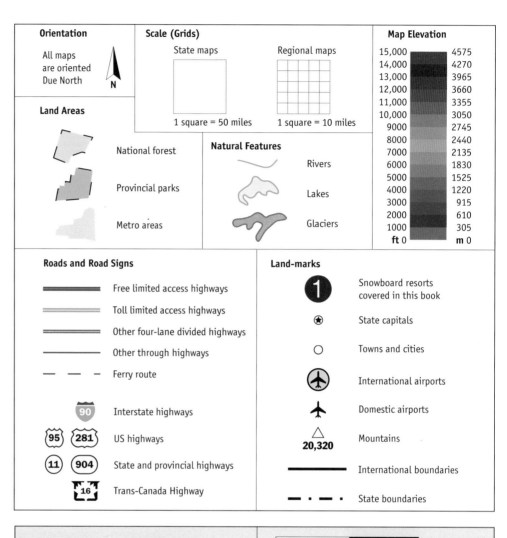

RESORT PAGE SYMBOLS

THE SYMBOLS EXPLAINED

The symbols on each resort review are an acurate
representation of scale. Figures to the left of the
diagrams are represented by ruled divisions.

ELEVATION

feet
13,000
11,000
9000
7000
5000
3000
1000

Summit: The highest point
serviced by the resort's lift.

Vertical drop: The vertical
distance between the
summit and the base.

Base: The starting point
of the resort's lowest lift.

SNOWFALL

inches
600
500
400
300
200
100
0

Average annual:
Yearly mean figure measured
at the mountain base.

Snow-making:
Expressed as a percentage
of the total resort area.

AREA

%
100
80
60
40
20
0

Total area: Area within
resort boundaries.

Difficulty variances:
Shaded to represent a
percentage of area.
Advanced
Intermediate
Beginner

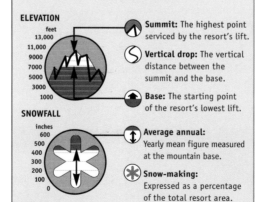

swatch access

Swatch Access is a cool new watch that not only tells
the time, but opens up lift gates. This piece of high-
tech wizardry, developed jointly with SkiData, comes
with a micro-chip and a ring-shaped sensor. The chip
stores details of your pass, and the sensor opens the
gate; all you have to do is point your **Swatch Access**
towards the gate and it's open sesame, even if it's
under your clothes. When your ticket expires, you get it
reprogrammed at the cash desk. The resorts using this
system covered in this book are denoted by the
inclusion of the **Swatch Access** logo under 'lifts and
prices'. Check out the new Palmer signature watch for
something mega funky.

B+B

Abbreviation for board and boot rentals.

PRICES

All prices quoted are correct at the time of writing and
subject to change and seasonal availability.

READING A TRAIL MAP

Northern hemisphere trail maps (also known as piste
maps) are usually drawn so that the shaded parts
represent north facing aspects. Be aware that actual
scale and steepness may vary significantly from the
map representation, and that resorts' interpretations of
difficulty variance symbols may differ appreciably.

North America

Arctic Ocean

150°
135°
120°
105°
90°
75°
45°
60° GREENLAND

Beaufort Sea

Gulf of Alaska

YUKON
Whitehorse

*Juneau

NORTHWEST TERRITORIES
Yellowknife

CANADA

BRITISH COLUMBIA

Hudson Bay

ALBERTA
Edmonton

MANITOBA

QUEBEC

NEWFOUNDLAND

Vancouver
Victoria
Seattle
Olympia
WASHINGTON
Spokane
Portland *Vancouver
Salem
CASCADE RANGE
OREGON

*Helena
MONTANA

ROCKY MTNS

SASKATCHEWAN
Calgary
Regina*

Winnipeg

ONTARIO

NEW
Charlottetown
BRUNSWICK
Fredericton
Quebec
MAINE
Montreal
NOVA Halifax
SCOTIA
Ottawa
Augusta
VT.
Montpelier
Concord N.H.
Boston
MASS.
R.I.

Boise
IDAHO

NORTH Bismarck
DAKOTA

MINNESOTA

Lake Superior

Toronto
Rochester
NEW YORK Albany
Buffalo
Hartford
CONN.

USA
WYOMING

SOUTH DAKOTA

Minneapolis
St. Paul
WISCONSIN

Lake Huron
Lake Michigan

Milwaukee

MICHIGAN
Lansing
Detroit
Cleveland
OHIO
Harrisburg
PENN.

New York
Trenton
N.J.

Sacramento
San Francisco Oakland
Carson City
NEVADA

Salt Lake City
UTAH

*Cheyenne

Madison
Chicago

Des Moines
IOWA

Lincoln

Boulder
*Denver
COLORADO

NEBRASKA

Omaha

ILLINOIS

INDIANA

*Indianapolis
WEST
VIRGINIA

MD. Baltimore
WASHINGTON D.C.
DEL.

CALIFORNIA

Los Angeles

San Diego
Phoenix
Mexicali
ARIZONA

Santa Fe
NEW MEXICO

Topeka
KANSAS

Kansas City
St. Louis
MISSOURI

Springfield

Charleston
Louisville
Frankfort
KENTUCKY

VIRGINIA
Richmond
Norfolk
Raleigh
NORTH CAROLINA
Charlotte
SOUTH
CAROLINA
Columbia

Nashville
TENNESSEE

Oklahoma City
OKLAHOMA

Little Rock*

ARKANSAS

Memphis

Birmingham
MISSISSIPPI
Jackson
*Atlanta
GEORGIA
Montgomery
ALABAMA

MEXICO

TEXAS

Austin
Houston

*Dallas

Baton Rouge
LOUISIANA
New Orleans

Jacksonville
Tallahassee

Tampa
Orlando
FLORIDA
West Palm Beach

THE BAHAMAS

Miami

Pacific Ocean

Atlantic Ocean

Gulf of Mexico

Caribbean Sea

The United States of America

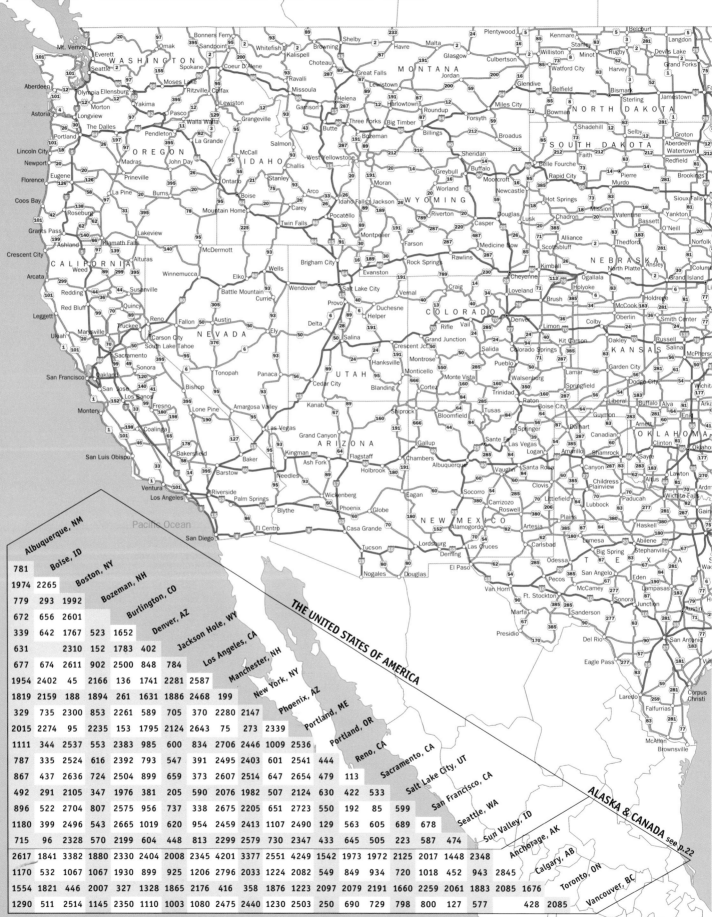

Distance chart (miles):

Albuquerque, NM	
781	Boise, ID
1974 2265	Boston, NY
779 293 1992	Bozeman, NH
672 656 2601	Burlington, CO
339 642 1767 523 1652	Denver, AZ
631 2310 152 1783 402	Jackson Hole, WY
677 674 2611 902 2500 848 784	Los Angeles, CA
1954 2402 45 2166 136 1741 2281 2587	Manchester, NH
1819 2159 188 1894 261 1631 1886 2468 199	New York, NY
329 735 2300 853 2261 589 705 370 2280 2147	Phoenix, AZ
2015 2274 95 2235 153 1795 2124 2643 75 273 2339	Portland, ME
1111 344 2537 553 2383 985 600 834 2706 2446 1009 2536	Portland, OR
787 335 2524 616 2392 793 547 391 2495 2403 601 2541 444	Reno, CA
867 437 2636 724 2504 899 659 373 2607 2514 647 2654 479 113	Sacramento, CA
492 291 2105 347 1976 381 205 590 2076 1982 507 2124 630 422 533	Salt Lake City, UT
896 522 2704 807 2575 956 737 338 2675 2205 651 2723 550 192 85 599	San Francisco, CA
1180 399 2496 543 2665 1019 620 954 2459 2413 1107 2490 129 563 605 689 678	Seattle, WA
715 96 2328 570 2199 604 448 813 2299 2579 730 2347 433 645 505 223 587 474	Sun Valley, ID
2617 1841 3382 1880 2330 2404 2008 2345 4201 3377 2551 4249 1542 1973 1972 2125 2017 1448 2348	Anchorage, AK
1170 532 1067 1067 1930 899 925 1206 2796 2033 1224 2082 549 849 934 720 1018 452 943 2845	Calgary, AB
1554 1821 446 2007 327 1328 1865 2176 416 358 1876 1223 2097 2079 2191 1660 2259 2061 1883 2085 1676	Toronto, ON
1290 511 2514 1145 2350 1110 1003 1080 2475 2440 1230 2503 250 690 729 798 800 127 577 428 2085	Vancouver, BC

THE UNITED STATES OF AMERICA

ALASKA & CANADA see p.22

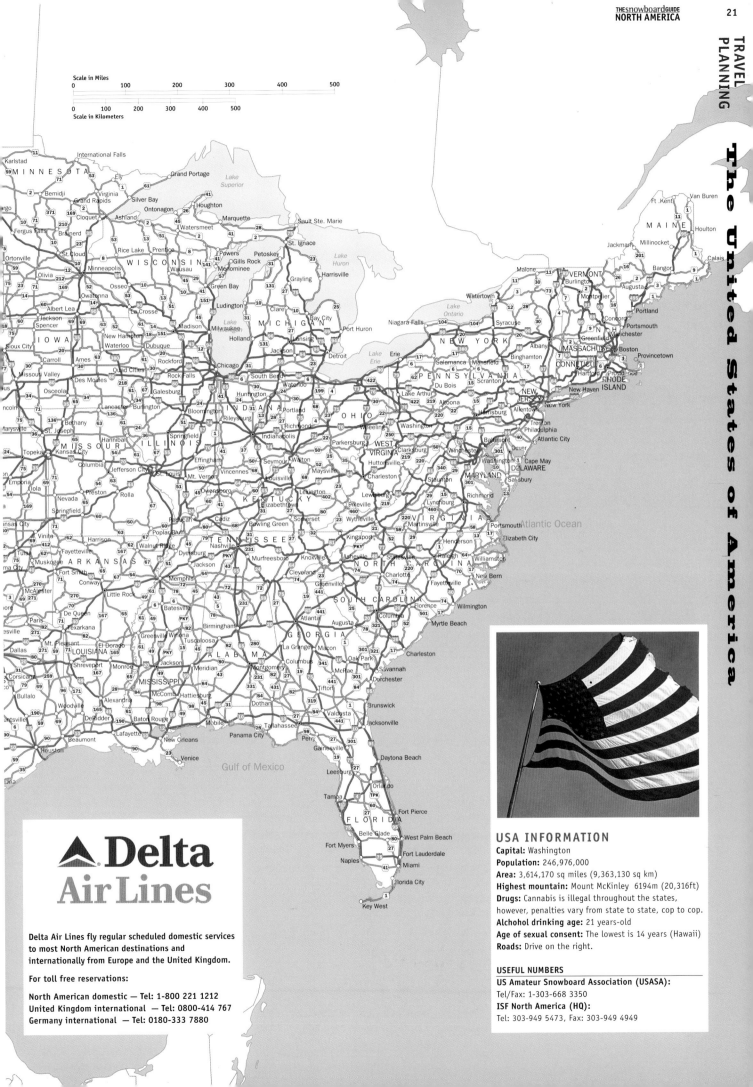

Scale in Miles
0   100   200   300   400   500

Scale in Kilometers
0   100   200   300   400   500

USA INFORMATION

Capital: Washington
Population: 246,976,000
Area: 3,614,170 sq miles (9,363,130 sq km)
Highest mountain: Mount McKinley 6194m (20,316ft)
Drugs: Cannabis is illegal throughout the states,
however, penalties vary from state to state, cop to cop.
Alcohol drinking age: 21 years-old
Age of sexual consent: The lowest is 14 years (Hawaii)
Roads: Drive on the right.

USEFUL NUMBERS

US Amateur Snowboard Association (USASA):
Tel/Fax: 1-303-668 3350
ISF North America (HQ):
Tel: 303-949 5473, Fax: 303-949 4949

Alaska and Canada

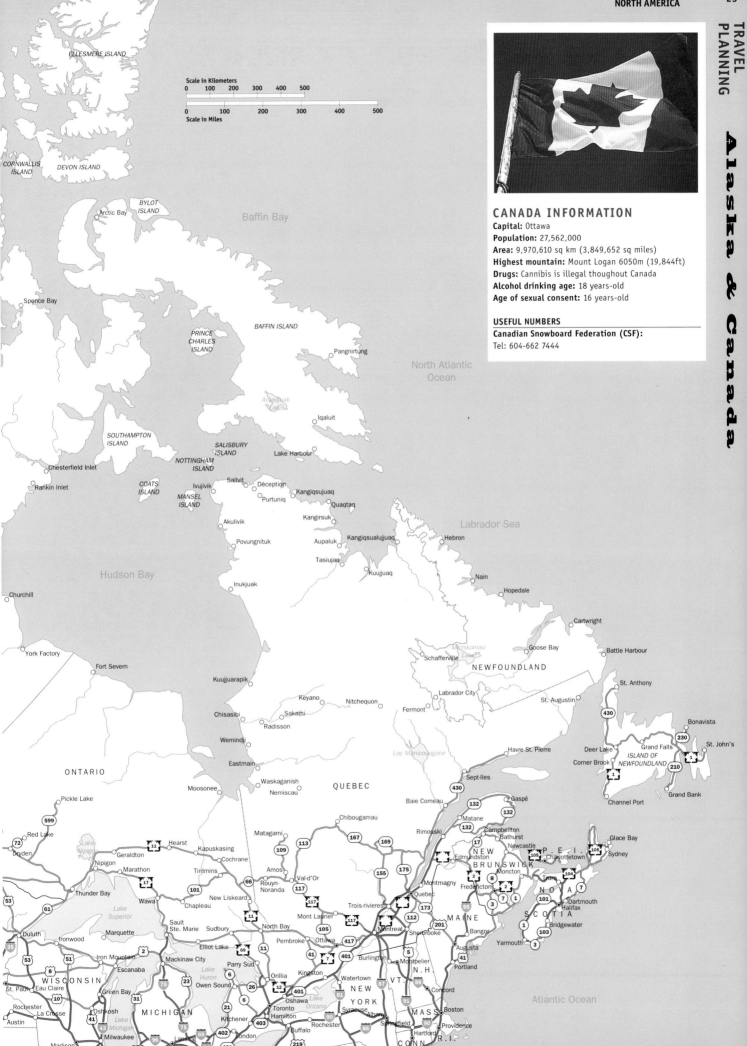

CANADA INFORMATION

Capital: Ottawa
Population: 27,562,000
Area: 9,970,610 sq km (3,849,652 sq miles)
Highest mountain: Mount Logan 6050m (19,844ft)
Drugs: Cannibis is illegal thoughout Canada
Alcohol drinking age: 18 years-old
Age of sexual consent: 16 years-old

USEFUL NUMBERS
Canadian Snowboard Federation (CSF):
Tel: 604-662 7444

AXEL PAUPORTÉ BY HOSTYNEK / ABSINTHE

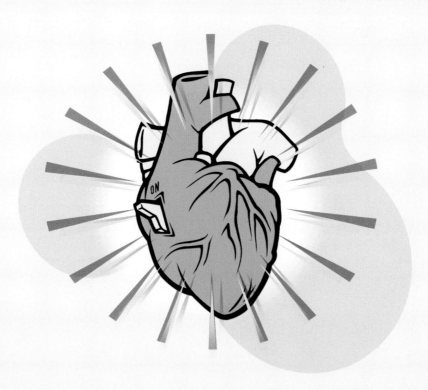

RIDING IS KNOWING.

PACIFIC

Dusk at Mount Hood, Oregon Photo: Bruce Sutherland

WASHINGTON

STATE INFORMATION

Population: 5,429,9000
Time: Pacific Standard Time = GMT minus 8 hours
Capital city: Olympia
Area: 66,582 sq miles (172,380 sqkm)

COMMUNICATIONS

Washington Tourist Board:
Tel: 360-586 2088 or 360-586 2102
Fax: 360-753 4470
Web site: http://www.tourism.wa.gov
E-mail: tourism.wa.gov

GETTING AROUND

By air: Seattle-Tacoma (Sea-Tac) International Airport —
Tel: 206-431 5906
By bus: Greyhound — Tel: 1-800-231 2222
By train: Amtrak — Tel : 1-800-872 7245
Road conditions: Tel: 206-368 4499 or 1-888-766 4636,
Mountain pass reports — Tel: 1-888-766 4637
Web site: http://www.wsdot.wa.gov
Speed limits: The interstate limit is 70 mph (112 kmph).

INTRODUCTION

The north-west corner of the USA provides Washington with the perfect snowboarding environment. Huge mountains like Mount Rainier and Mount Baker can be seen for hundreds of miles but the resorts have sprung up in the lower altitude ridges and peaks of the mountain passes which are more easily accessed. The main resort riding is located in four separate areas in the Cascade Range, all within easy reach of Seattle. Despite the unexceptional altitudes, Washington resorts receive the highest average annual snowfall in the US, courtesy of the jet stream storms from the ocean. Great natural features and sensible boundary laws make Washington a freeriding heaven, but there is enough variety to keep freestylers happy. Bad weather is common so quality outerwear is crucial, along with a relaxed 'whatever happens' attitude.

Left— Seattle from the air **Photo:** Bruce Sutherland
Right— **Photo:** Bruce Sutherland
Opposite— Shuksan Arm **Photo:** Bruce Sutherland

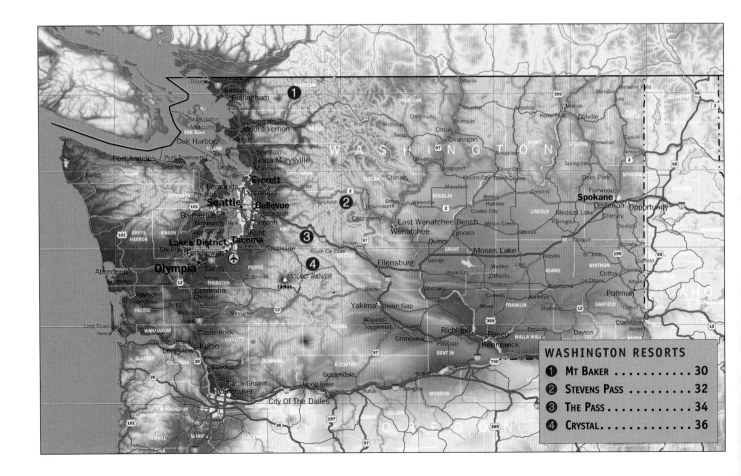

WASHINGTON RESORTS

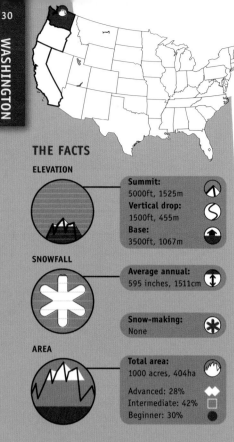

THE FACTS

ELEVATION

Summit:
5000ft, 1525m
Vertical drop:
1500ft, 455m
Base:
3500ft, 1067m

SNOWFALL

Average annual:
595 inches, 1511cm

Snow-making:
None

AREA

Total area:
1000 acres, 404ha

Advanced: 28%
Intermediate: 42%
Beginner: 30%

SEASON

Early November — late April

COMMUNICATIONS

Snow reports:
Tel: 206-634 0200 (Seattle)
Tel: 604-688 1595 (Vancouver)
Tel: 360-671 0211 (Bellingham)
Web site: http://www.mtbaker.skiarea.com
Mountain information:
Tel: 360-734 6771
Fax: 360-734 5332

LIFTS AND TICKETS

Number of lifts:
8 chairlifts, 2 surface tows
Lift pass prices:
1/2 day: $22 (weekends and holidays only)
1 day: $17.50-$20, $29 (weekends and holidays)
Multi-day: N/A
Season: $505
Other ticketing information:
Group rates are available for groups of 20 or more
on weekends and holidays only. Youth rates
(7-15yrs) are discounted by around 25 per cent.

SNOWBOARD SHOPS

Mt Baker Snowboard Shop — Tel: 360-599 2008
Located in Glacier and run by the Dobis family, the
shop is the hub of the boarding scene and they
have all the stuff you need to tackle Baker's
demanding slopes. Their forte is full tuning and
repair services, costing a six pack of Coors in the
local currency. B+B: $28.
Mt Baker Rentals — Tel: 360-734 6771
In the White Salmon Day Lodge. B+B: $29,
performance $36.

SNOWBOARD SCHOOL

Mt Baker Snowboard School — Tel: 360-734 6771
Mt Baker offers a wide range of snowboard lessons:
the Intro Snowboard Package includes a 90 minute
lesson, rental and beginner ticket for $43,
Technique Tuning for groups starts from $47 for
lesson and rental, and a lesson only costs $18.
They also have multi-week programmes and courses
for local schools.

Mt Baker

ON THE MOUNTAIN

Mt Baker (sic) is definitely one of the best places for snowboarding on the North American continent. The early '80s saw snowboarding pioneers like Carter Turk and Erik Janko utilise Baker's early acceptance of boarding to access the incomparable freeriding terrain. They have become the nucleus of the Mt Baker hard-core, a loose bunch that includes champion riders like Jeff Fulton, Eric Swanson and Craig Kelly. The hard-core part is a testament to the mountain and the weather, both being a lesson in extremes. Eight chairs sprawl across Shuksan Arm, a low altitude ridge line. Nestled between the peaks of Mt Baker and Mt Shuksan (sic), you'll find every feasible type of freeriding terrain on the Hemispheres and Shuksan Arm backcountry hikes. The 28 per cent expert rating for Mt Baker would rise considerably if the backcountry was included, and this is why you can bump into some of the world's best riders here.

SNOW CONDITIONS The lift system gets you up to 5000 feet (1525 metres) with a further 500 feet (152 metres) to be hiked. North-facing Mt Baker is notorious for inclement weather and snow that is closer to its watery origins. When the Cascades are unloaded on, Baker gets the deepest drifts of dense wet snow so technical clothing is crucial as Baker exposes pretenders, especially in the outerwear and attitude departments.

FREERIDERS This snowboarding heaven tucked away on the Canadian border offers the best of both resort and out of bounds riding. The gentle slopes in front of Heather Meadow's Day Lodge and the runs off the C7 Quad give beginners a go. All the runs under the C8 Quad have a perfect intermediate pitch with a few interesting banks and hits. Everything gets way steeper when you head to the centre of the resort. Chairs 4 and 5 are flanked by virtually unrideable cliffs to skier's left and drop-offs through the trees on skier's right. Chair 6 takes you to the top of Panorama Dome and the decision about which black run to burn. Huge cliffs and cornice jumps ring the flat section preceding Razorhone Canyon. The fall-line runs under Chair 6 are consistent and long, whereas The Chute and Panface under Chair 1 are shorter but to the point.

The real action begins by hiking from the top of the C8 Quad, where you must ensure you use the gate and read the big warnings. It doesn't take long for a well-defined track of post-holes to materialise, leading to the top of The Hemispheres. Here you'll find wind-lipped powder bowls which roll down to the nasty cliffs above Razorhone Canyon, so keep heading skier's right back under Chairs 4 and 5. The huge expanses of untracked powder beckon hikers out along the ridge line towards Mt Shuksan. This area carries an 'extreme avalanche danger' tag to match the seriously extreme riding. Near vertical chutes run out into undulating powder bowls that hide hits and gullies, some of which end in 40 foot (15 metre) cliff drops. Cut left towards the bottom to cross the boundary at the base of the C8 Quad and scope your lines on the way back up.

FREESTYLERS The Halfpipe is in a natural gouge at the top of the mountain, located just to skier's right of the top of Chairs 4 and 5. It's the site of the Legendary Banked Slalom, where riders perform fast banking turns around flags set high up on the 20 to 40 foot (seven to 15 metre) walls. In big snow years the whole thing can fill up leaving a very unimpressive dish, but there are other natural halfpipes tucked away in the back-country. There is no funpark because there is Razorhone Canyon. This narrow alleyway between vertical cliffs builds up snowy walls with an endless number of regular and goofy hits.

CARVERS Groomers aren't Baker's main attraction. There are some steeper trails like Canuck's Deluxe off the Panorama Dome, but they don't have the width of the trails under Chair 8. Carvers should rent a big fat powder board and learn to hike.

HAZARDS AND RULES When you go through the boundary gate, you're on your own. A former Ski and Safety Manager sums it up: "If there's a place on this mountain where people can kill themselves and nobody else, they can go there. We'll just go in later and pick up the pieces."

MOUNTAIN FOOD The aesthetically pleasing White Salmon Lodge offers the regulation menu. Razorhone Café does burgers, chillies and snacks, or try the Heather Meadows Lodge for more of a selection.

EVENTS AND COMPETITIONS The Mt Baker Legendary Banked Slalom in late January attracts the cream of international competition and is usually won by an all-round rider, such as last year's winner Rob Morrow — Tel: 360-734 6771.

①

Top — Mt Shuksan **Photo:** Bruce Sutherland
Bottom — Chip Wayt, Panorama Dome **Photo:** Bruce Sutherland

ABOUT TOWN

Baker is the classic cul-de-sac resort. There are no hotels, no swimming pools and there isn't even a telephone line to the mountain. This leaves Glacier to provide the services, 20 miles (32 kilometres) down the narrow, twisty alpine road. In this sleepy little settlement, the human population is out-numbered two to one by canines. There are a few roadside hotels, three restaurants with bars, a general store and a snowboard shop. Chalets, condos and houses are hidden away in the forested side streets. Further west on Highway 542 towards the main town of Bellingham, you'll find Maple Falls which has a bigger general store and a petrol station.

GETTING THERE

By air: The closest international airports are Vancouver International Airport and Sea-Tac Airport.
By bus : No services available.
By car: From Seattle: Take Interstate 5 north to Bellingham. Bellingham is 56 miles (90 kilometres) west of Mt Baker on Highway 542. The resort is a two and a half hour drive from Seattle and a two hour drive from Vancouver.
From Vancouver: Take Interstate 99 and Interstate 5 south to Bellingham.
Getting around: Take a car; a four-wheel drive is the best way to go.

ACCOMMODATION Mt Baker Lodgings specialise in cabin rentals which means that group assaults are the way to go. Mid-week non-holiday specials cost $99 per night for two people and an extra $10 per person thereafter. The most affordable cabin goes for $159 a night and sleeps eight to ten people; styling, mod-con luxury cabins with all facilities cost $235 — Tel: 360-599 2453 ext. 3500 or 1-800-709 SNOW, E-mail: mtbaklod@telecomplus.com. The Glacier Creek Motel and Cabins start at $42 for two people per night — Tel: 360-599 29941 and the Logs cost $85 per night — Tel: 360-599 2711.

FOOD Don't blink when you drive through Glacier or you might miss the three main restaurants. El Pavo Real is the ruling Mexican, serving huge portions of freshly prepared food at super low prices. Efficiently run by Kelly-Joe in a historic building full of antiques and relics, this establishment is a must for Baker pilgrims especially if you like kick-butt chillies. Milano's is the best (and only) Italian in town serving average pasta at average prices. The Chandelier Restaurant usually gets the post-mountain party.

NIGHTLIFE The restaurants double up as the main night spots, unless you crack the local house party scene. This all changes during the Banked Slalom when the town bulges with riders, more dogs and the annual police presence.

OTHER ACTIVITIES Golf, hiking, mountain-biking, boating and fishing.

THANKS TO Gwyn and Amy Howat, Barbara Stein, Kelly-Jo, Steve Adkins, Javas Hehn, Leon Fire, Joe and Jason Florence, Adrian Turnbull, Eric Granstrom and all the Baker crew.

Stevens Pass

THE FACTS

ELEVATION

Summit:
5845ft, 1783m

Vertical drop:
1784ft, 544m

Base:
4061ft, 1239m

SNOWFALL

Average annual:
415 inches, 1054cm

Snow-making:
None

AREA

Total area:
1125 acres, 343ha

Advanced: 35%
Intermediate: 54%
Beginner: 11%

SEASON

Late November — early April

COMMUNICATIONS

Snow reports: Tel: 206-634 1645 or 206-353 4400
Web site: http: //www.snowlink.com/steven
E-mail: skistuns@ix.netcom.com
Mountain information:
Tel: 360-973 2441
Fax: 206-292 8584

LIFTS AND TICKETS

Number of lifts:
1 high-speed quad, 10 chairlifts
Lift pass prices:
1/2 day: N/A
1 day: $18 (Mon-Tues), $23 (Wed-Thurs)
$34 (weekends)
Multi-day: N/A
Season: $650
Other ticketing information:
Night-riding goes from 5.00pm to 10.00pm and
costs $12-$20. Board free on your birthday.

SNOWBOARD SHOPS

Stevens' Rental and Repair Centre
Tel: 360-973 2441 ext.222
A large stock of K2 and Sims boards are available.
B+B: $26 day, $23 night.

SNOWBOARD SCHOOL

Stevens Pass' Snowboard School
Tel: 360-973 2508
The snowboard school has a range of programmes.
The First Timers' package includes a one hour
lesson, equipment and beginner lift ticket for $32
week days and $40 weekends. Night-rider lessons
start from $25. Check the list of 24 private
independent schools in the School Without Walls
brochure; the most experienced 'boarding only'
school is the North West Snowboarding Training
Centre — Tel: 360-435 9718.

ON THE MOUNTAIN

Stevens Pass lies at the highest point on Highway 2, halfway between Seattle and Wenatchee. Surrounded by three National Forest Wilderness areas deep in the snow-blessed Cascades, Stevens is yet another great Washington resort. The beautiful view from the top of Big Chief Mountain is matched by the terrain which offers some serious double diamond trails, wide open fields and pockets of insane tree riding. Stevens is split into two areas; the front side is well-wooded with steeps off Cowboy Mountain and Big Chief Mountain while the back side Mill Valley area has some wide open spaces with pockets of trees and a constant fall-line. New quad chairs have improved access to the back side and given Stevens Pass the prestige of having 'the only high-speed quad in the state open for night-riding'. However, there are also a bunch of those typical north-west double chairs that would go unnoticed on the set of Jurassic Park. A long time favourite of Seattle's families, the improvements and new terrain are now attracting snowboarders from the big city.

SNOW CONDITIONS Abundant and frequent snow storms is the call for Stevens. Being on the crest of the Cascades means that cool air can drift across from the east providing drier snow conditions, otherwise it's healthy doses of Cascade crud. The two mountains cover just about every compass point, so almost all snow conditions can be found at any given time of the day.

FREERIDERS Beginners and families will like the bottom of the mountain which is all fairly flat, along with the trails under Blue Jay Chairlift, Brooks Chairlift and Skyline Express Quad. At the other end of the spectrum, you'll find super steeps serviced by the Double Diamond Chairlift and the 7th Heaven Chairlift, with chutes to the right and cliffs to the left. Some of the cliffs are rideable further down near the Meadows area, providing you know your line and haven't eaten beforehand. There are also some adrenaline lines around the Tye Mill Chairlift, like Roller Coaster and Tye Bowl. Big Chief Bowl has long, steep shots and cliffs leading into the expansive powder fields of Showcase. There are some absolutely superb tree runs in the thick forest between Double Diamond and Wild Katz which can be sessioned for hours without taking the same line twice. Over on the back side, similar tree turns beckon around Corona Bowl and in the gullies of Polaris Creek, just over the boundary. The rest of the acreage here is open and fairly steep, producing many a mogul to negotiate. After a fat fresh dump there are screaming speed runs to be had all over the back side.

FREESTYLERS The halfpipe is situated in between Marmot Meadows and Skyline. Minimal vertical and an easy transition make it intermediate friendly and an undaunting practice forum. There is a funpark on the right as you come down Broadway. It's nothing large and has too many skiers. Jibbers should look for the gullies full of soft fluffy and the natural hits that are spread around the mountain, even in the trees. Check out the possibilities in Polaris Creek.

CARVERS The steep groomers get chopped up quickly so be early for runs like Parachute and International. The back side has some wide cruisers like Aquarius and Orion.

MOUNTAIN FOOD The three separate Day Lodges have four restaurants, all serving excellent expresso and good food. The East Lodge has Cloud Nine Pizzeria and a well-stocked bar. If you're driving from the west, check out the Mountain View Chevron just east of Sultan where you can get coffee, lift tickets and updated weather conditions from the electronic information board.

HAZARDS AND RULES Retention devices are required. If you poach the boundary trees on the back side and don't cut right, you'll be post-holing back to the lift. Washington law means that some of the appealing adjacent back-country is hikeable.

The names "Big Chief Bowl", "Lower Rock Garden", "Tye Bowl", "Meadows", "Schin's Meadow" and "Winnie Chutes" are for reference only and are not designated trails or runs.

Stevens Pass

By air: Stevens Pass is 98 miles (157 kilometres) from Sea-Tac Airport. A rental car is your only transfer option from Seattle.

By car: Drive 78 miles (126 kilometres) east of Seattle on Highway 2 along the Skykomish Valley. From Wenatchee, the resort is a similar distance west on Highway 2.

Getting around: The base at Stevens is compact but you'll need a car to get to a decent bed.

ABOUT TOWN

There is no town at Stevens. Skykomish is the nearest civilisation, comprising of a few motels, a general store, gas station and a couple of bars and restaurants. The Skykomish River runs through town. All around there are big views and a real frontier feeling.

ACCOMMODATION There is no accommodation at the resort, other than the RV parking lot which has a crusty community scene. Heading west 16 miles (28 kilometres), you'll find the cosy Sky River Inn at Skykomish which has rooms starting at $50 — Tel: 360-677 2261. Further down the hill is the Bush House at Index with prices from $60 — Tel: 360-793 2312. At Sultan, 40 miles (60 kilometres) down the road, the Dutch Cup Motel provides good roadside motel facilities with a separate restaurant; a one bedroom unit costs $49 for one person — Tel: 1-800-844 0488. For all other reservation information, call Bavarian Bedfinders — Tel: 1-800-323 2920, Leavenworth Chamber — Tel: 509-548 5807, or Destination Leavenworth — Tel: 1-800-962 7359.

FOOD The Whistling Post Tavern in Skykomish does excellent pizza and budget chicken wings. The diner-style restaurant next to the Dutch Cup dishes up large helpings and hearty breakfasts.

NIGHTLIFE Since most riders are commuters from Seattle, there's not much going on. The Whistling Post Tavern in Skykomish has pool, darts and a basketball ring for the competitive as well as a good array of local beer for the thirsty.

OTHER ACTIVITIES There is a hard-core indoor skate ramp not far from Stevens which the local grommies built for themselves. If you're friendly and produce the right bribes, they might let you ride it.

THANKS TO Chester Marler, Eric Vines and the skate groms who hacked with us.

2

Top left — Photo: Bruce Sutherland

Top right — Photo: Scott F. Wicklund

Bottom — Mark Martin, Stevens Pass back-country Photo: Scott F. Wicklund

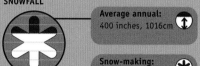

The Pass

THE FACTS

ELEVATION

Alpental:			Snowqualmie:
5400ft, 1647m	Summit		3900ft, 1005m
2200ft, 667m	Vertical drop		900ft, 273m
3200ft, 969m	Base		3000ft, 1183m
Ski Acres:			Hyak:
3900ft, 1183m	Summit		3700ft, 1122m
868m, 2860ft	Vertical drop		1080ft, 327m
1040ft, 315m	Base		2620ft, 795m

SNOWFALL

Average annual:
400 inches, 1016cm

Snow-making:
None

AREA

Total area:
2500 acres, 1010m

Alpental:		Snowqualmie:
50%	Advanced	30%
40%	Intermediate	20%
10%	Beginner	50%
Ski Acres:		Hyak:
20%	Advanced	18%
45%	Intermediate	40%
35%	Beginner	42%

SEASON
Mid-November — mid-April

COMMUNICATIONS
Snow reports: Tel: 206-236 1600
Web site: http//:www.snowlink.com/thepass
E-mail: thepass@ix.netcom.com
Mountain information:
Tel: 206-236 7277

LIFTS AND TICKETS
Number of lifts:
23 chairlifts, 9 surface tows
Lift pass prices:
1/2 day: $24 (weekends)
1 day: $15-$18, $28 (weekends), $26-$28
(weekend swing shift*)
Multi-day: N/A
Season: $485, $400 (12-18 yrs)
Other ticketing information:
* Swing shift is from 1.00pm till night closing
(10.00pm). Night-riding in the weekends from
5.00pm to closing costs $14-$18. The cheapest
rates are available on Mondays, Tuesdays and
Sunday nights.

SNOWBOARD SHOPS
Facilities for rental are spread across the four area
Base Lodges. B+B: $25, demo with step-ins $30.
Extremely Board in Issaquah — Tel: 206-391 4572
Boarderline Snowboards — Tel: 206-646 7547
A large range in Bellevue. Demo B+B: $25.
Marley's — Tel: 206-634 2933
A cool shop with plenty of stuff from the Seattle
based giant Mervin Manufacturing.

SNOWBOARD SCHOOL
Alpental Snowboard School — Tel: 206-434 6364
Snoqualmie Snowboard School — Tel: 206-232 8210
Ski Acres Snowboard School — Tel: 206-823 2690
Hyak Snowboard School — Tel: 206-391 2782
A New Snowboarder Special will get you on the hill,
kitted out and turning for $35-$40.

The Pass

ON THE MOUNTAIN

This aptly named area sits at the highest elevation on the main east-west route in Washington.
Since '37, the Pass has provided Seattle with its closest winter sports playground. This cluster of
four resorts breaks into two distinct areas; Alpental and 'the rest'. At around 3000 feet (1000
metres) Snoqualmie, Ski Acres and Hyak sit on a ridge line of small peaks. Alpental soars another
1500 feet (457 metres) above on a totally separate mountain ridge. Alpental has some of the
steepest and angriest looking snowboard terrain around, lending weight to its claim of being the
resort with the second highest avalanche danger in the US. Experienced freeriders will approve of
the 50 per cent advanced terrain figures, plus the opportunity to ride some hellish back-country
under the Great Scott Traverse. Beginners and intermediates have acres of choice in the other
three areas; gentle, open spaces and crossover cat-tracks link the lower resorts. Hyak has the
halfpipe and Ski Acres has the funpark for jibbers.

SNOW CONDITIONS Most of the Pass faces east or north-east, meaning plenty of those fat, thick north-
westerly flakes will have somewhere to settle when they blow in from the ocean weather systems. Hyak, Ski
Acres and Snoqualmie are fairly open with minimal tree cover for holding the powder, while the back-country
of Alpental is a stash supermarket. The 1500 foot (493 metre) difference in elevation can sometimes affect
snow quality and increases the chance of rain in the lower three resorts.

FREERIDERS Advanced riders will be blown away by the sheer steepness of the rideable terrain at Alpental.
The top half of the mountain is serviced by the ageing Edelweiss Chair which accesses all the main freeriding.
You can take the easier route through the fast powder fields beside Upper and Lower International or try
the extreme lines of Adrenalin. To the right of this area are the trees and glades of Snake Dance which have
some great contours and rock drops interspersed with vertical-sided gullies. The whole area directly beneath
the Edelweiss Chair is rife with chutes, bowls, cliffs and trees with only one flat section in the middle. The
trees of the Fan are steep and well-spaced with the option of a 50 degree exit, skier's left just past the cliff
signs. This leads back to the consistent pitch of the front face and down to the ancient Debbie's Gold Chair
16. For current back-country information, contact the ski patrol at the top of Edelweiss Chair 17. Ski Acres
and Hyak have some short steeps and nice trees on the resort fringes which are perfect for intermediates to
practice on before they tackle Alpental.

FREESTYLERS The only halfpipe is situated at the top of Chair 23 on Hyak. This is Seattle's closest pipe, so
the standards are maintained and night sessions are popular. On the down side, Hyak shuts in early March.
The funpark at Ski Acres is fairly flat and undemanding with a few medium-sized table tops and bread-boxes,
plus an even easier line of jumps and whoopee-doos on the left. There are far better natural hits sprinkled
around the three lower areas to satisfy air addicts.

CARVERS Laying out arcs at Alpental is confined to the front face runs like Meister and Eisfallen under
Debbie's Gold Chair, or the slopes of Lower International which are as high as the cats can manage. Carving
at the other three resorts is fine for beginners, but the lack of long steeps plus the big flat sections
(particularly at the bottom of Ski Acres) means competent hard-booters will get bored quickly.

MOUNTAIN FOOD The Pass offers 12 food and beverage facilities spread out amongst the four areas.
Snowqualmie has the largest Base Lodge, where Webb's Bar and Grill, Stan's Family Pub or Stan's Café can
satisfy most food cravings. Alpental is an Austrian village clone with Tyrolean-style chalets that serve
generous chillies, pizzas and giant hot pretzels to complement the locally brewed beers.

HAZARDS AND RULES The sign 'Caution' says it all. The back-country area outside the designated ski area
boundary is challenging and not patrolled. The terrain is rugged, steep and very prone to avalanche danger
so obey all signs. Ski patrol tours are conducted, weather and snow conditions permitting.

EVENTS AND COMPETITIONS In spring the Pass holds a huge snowboard competition and festival called
Board Stiff, featuring big air, snow-biking and skate ramps. Thousands of boarders foam to great live bands
and check the latest trends at manufacturers' stalls set up at the base of Snoqualmie.

Seattle

THE FACTS
GETTING THERE

By air: Sea-Tac Airport is serviced by the major carriers including Delta Airlines — Tel: 1-800-241 4141.

By bus: The I-90 Ski Bus departs from Seattle, Bellevue and Issaquah from January through mid-March — Tel: 206-236 7277 ext. 3242. Mountain Outfitters run a shuttle bus from Seattle — Tel: 206-409 0459.

By car: The Pass is located on Interstate 90, 43 miles (70 kilometres) east of the Interstate 405/Interstate 90 Junction just outside Seattle. Take Exit 52 for Alpental and Snowqualmie, Exit 53 for Ski Acres and Exit 54 for Hyak. Road conditions — Tel: 1-888-766 4636.

Getting around: A free inter-area shuttle runs every 20 minutes in weekends and holidays.

Top — Seattle with Mount Rainier **Photo:** Bruce Sutherland
Right — Aerial view of Snoqualmie, Ski Acres and Hyak **Photo:** Bruce Sutherland
Bottom — Miles Burgess at Alpental **Photo:** Scott F. Wicklund

ABOUT TOWN

Seattle sits on the central eastern shore of Puget Sound, a vast estuary that extends all the way north of Vancouver Island, BC. This cosmopolitan city is a launching pad to explore Washington's amazing mountain areas. It has its own personality and cultivates artisans, scholars and grungers all at once. Seattle has the hedonistic goods and is a fine contrast to the lack of party potential at the resort areas.

ACCOMMODATION At the Pass there is only the Summit Inn for on-mountain accommodation, sitting on the exit road at the Snoqualmie base area. Offering 80 rooms with all mod-cons, mid-week specials can be as low as $79 for two people including lift tickets. If you are planning to ride the Pass, Bellevue is a good place to stay. The Embassy Suites provide a cushy appliance-packed two room suite for $149. This includes an unbeatable buffet breakfast and evening cocktails when you get back down the hill — Tel: 206-644 2500 or 1-800-EMBASSY. Seattle is a huge city with more than enough beds; the East King Country Convention and Visitor's Bureau can track one down for you — Tel: 206-450 5631 or 1-800-252 1926. For cheap rates call the Youth Hostel Association in Seattle — Tel: 206-622 5443.

FOOD For the low-down on Seattle restaurants, bars and music options, pick up one of the funky free information papers like The Stranger. If seafood is your thing, stroll around the downtown waterfront where you'll find dozens of fish n' chip shops fighting for the tourist trade.

NIGHTLIFE The downtown area between the waterfront and 5th Street has plenty of dependable drinking dens and Irish pubs traditionally popular with the university set. Washington State Laws mean foreigners must carry their passports as the only acceptable form of ID, even if you look 40.

OTHER ACTIVITIES Ferry rides around Puget Sound, San Juan Islands or up to Victoria and Vancouver are a great way to spend the day. Seaplane flights from Seattle to the surrounding areas like Skykomish Falls are expensive but worth it.

THANKS TO John Maulding, Jason Skipper and Sean Donnell.

THE FACTS

ELEVATION

Summit:
7002ft, 2135m

Vertical drop:
2602ft, 793m

Base:
4400ft, 1342m

SNOWFALL

Average annual:
340 inches, 863cm

Snow-making:
1%

AREA

Total area:
2300 acres, 929ha

Advanced: 30%
Intermediate: 57%
Beginner: 13%

SEASON

Mid-November — mid-April

COMMUNICATIONS

Snow reports: Tel: 206-634 3771 or 206-922 1832
Web site: http://www.crystalmt.com
E-mail: crystalmountain@compuserve.com
Mountain information:
Tel: 360-663 2265
Fax: 360-663 0148

LIFTS AND TICKETS

Number of lifts:
10 chairlifts, 1 surface lift
Lift pass prices:
1/2 day: $30 (weekends and holidays)
1 day: $25-$28, $35 (weekends and holidays)
Multi-day: N/A
Season: $695
Other ticketing information:
Night-riding takes place from Friday till Sunday,
4.00pm to 8.00pm until late March, cost $15. Teen
tickets (12-17yrs) cost $30 in weekends and
holidays, $25 on week days. A teen season pass
costs $475.

SNOWBOARD SHOPS

The Sports Shop — Tel: 360-663 2309
The shop is under the Main Lodge with a small
range of new sticks and bits to keep you out there.
A number of knowledgeable staff will help you with
tuning and repairs, plus some inside info if you
smile. B+B: $28.

SNOWBOARD SCHOOL

Crystal Snowboard School — Tel: 360-663 2265
Crystal has one of the best schools in the state,
offering Skill Builder courses to fine-tune your turns
and learn freestyle tricks. Two hour group lessons
cost $25. Lift ticket, rental equipment and two hour
lessons cost $49-$59 (weekend). The same package
with a four hour lesson costs $59-$69 (weekend).

Crystal Mountain

ON THE MOUNTAIN

Strung over four peaks, Crystal Mountain Resort sits under the 14,410 foot (4395 metre) shadow of Mount Rainier in the Cascade Range. Ringed by awesome volcanic peaks, this isolated resort is another gem in the North-West's crown jewels. Once again, the wide expanses of accessible back-country on either side of the resort's lift-serviced terrain are the main drawcard. The South Back Country and North Back Country areas are unbelievably good on a powder day. South Back holds the lease on steep open bowls and chutes, while North Back is lord of the trees. In-bounds has plenty of variety, with fall-line flyers or easier tracks and trails that wind down the mountain. Crystal were bought out in '97 by Boyne, USA who plan to invest $15 million in on-hill improvements over the next ten years. First up is the replacement of the Rendezvous Chair with the first six passenger high-speed quad in the North-West.

SNOW CONDITIONS Crystal gets heavy, wet snow ('guanch' in local lingo) but it is a prolific snow-catcher. Storms funnel down the valleys from the north and west attracted to the hulking mass of Mount Rainier. While most of the resort faces north-east, the back-country areas have a westerly aspect. This means South Back is perfect for morning tracks and North Back holds the fluffy right through the afternoon.

FREERIDERS With over 1000 acres (405 hectares) of back-country, Crystal has some awesome terrain. Starting at the summit of Silver Queen via the High Campbell Chair (C6), you can take the sunless shots of Powder Bowl (skier's left) or the fast lines of Marmot and Exhibition back down to the High Campbell Chair. From the Silver Queen summit, follow the well-used track along the ridge line above Campbell Basin and hike up to The Throne. This is where South Back starts; nasty but short chutes lead into Avalanche Basin. If you keep hiking another 15 minutes to the top of Silver King, you'll find steep, wide open slopes hemmed by craggy rocks up high and nice trees down lower where you re-enter the resort. The runs under Rainier Express Quad (C10) tend to suffer from bumpage but lead into Exterminator, a long, fast blast back to the Main Lodge.

Snorting Elk Bowl has some interesting ways down and a fun cat-track that you can drop off into the trees. Rainier Express Quad (C10) and Green Valley Chair (C3) will get you near the North Back access gate. The top section of North Back is aptly named Paradise Bowl, and will catapult you into the best timber tracks on the mountain. Spook Hill, Gun Tower and Niagaras keep the snow in top condition but there is a price to pay for these powder turns. The torturous traverse back to the main Base Lodge is the pits and even the fittest legs will be tested by the bumpy, flat, narrow trail through the lower trees. The shuttle bus could be your saviour if you take Lower Northway to the road, but make sure it's running before ending up here. The left side of the resort offers some good beginner and intermediate areas under Discovery Chair (C8) and Quicksilver Chair (C4), and more runs like Broadway and Skid Road off the Midway Shuttle Chair (C11).

FREESTYLERS The halfpipe at the top of Rendezvous Chair (C9) is small, flat and usually fills up after a dump. Plans for a real pipe are in the pipeline, so to speak. Halfway up the agonisingly slow Quicksilver Chair (C4) is the Boarder Zone Snowboard Park. A mixture of kickers and table tops of varying difficulty gives intermediates a good go. There's a nice little gully under K-2 Face and Kelly's Gap Road is full of hits.

CARVERS Seventy per cent of the in-bounds mountain is carveable. Speed freaks should head to Iceberg Gulch which is wide and smooth. A good training slope is the short, uncrowded Gold Hills run.

MOUNTAIN FOOD Rafters does everything well with friendly service, great food and beer. The Summit House does basic burgers which come a distant second to the views from the highest restaurant in Washington. For a quick snack, the Snorting Elk Deli/Inn does great lunchtime pizzas to go with their microbrews and expressos. Breakfast downstairs in the Main Lodge will keep you hiking for a long time.

HAZARDS AND RULES Despite avalanche control, the back-country can be closed in extreme conditions.

EVENTS AND COMPETITIONS Mountain Dew Snowboard Festival, K-2 Snowboard Camp which can increase advanced snowboarders' abilities in ungroomed and steep terrain.

Crystal Mountain

ABOUT TOWN

'Town' is a bit of an overstatement with Crystal's one horse settlement at the base of the mountain consisting of two bars and a general store. There is a cluster of lodging properties and a recreation centre for working out or soothing those aching muscles. A few houses for employees are tucked away in the trees, along with old gold prospecting claims dating back to the 1900s. Some of these old miners' huts occupy the trees around the Gold Hills Chair (C7), now part of the Mount Baker-Snowqualmie National Forest.

ACCOMMODATION Crystal Mountain offers six different accommodation options: three hotels, two condo groups and a RV hook-up spot from $15 a night. The Alpine Inn has the cheapest rooms from $40 a night — Tel: 360-663 2262, the Village Inn has rooms from $65 per person — Tel: 360-663 2558 and the Quicksilver Lodge has rooms from $80 a night — Tel: 360-663 2262. The condo options are the Silver Skis Chalet Condos; priced from $118 per night for a one bedroom condo, and the Crystal Chalet Condos; priced from $110 for a one bedroom condo — Tel: 360-663 0145. Check out the Atla Crystal Resort, a few miles down the road from the slopes. Chalets or log cabins start at $69 for one bedroom, self-contained units — Tel: 1-800-277 6475 or 360-663 2556.

FOOD Base Lodge options include Rafters and the Alpine Inn Restaurant which serves tasty but spendy food. The pizzas, soup, pastries and quiche in the Snorting Elk Bar downstairs are quality eats at reasonable prices. The Snorting Elk also does dinner and will deliver great food to your doorstep — Tel: 360-663 0259 or 360-663 7798 to order. The only other alternative is the general store.

NIGHTLIFE The Snorting Elk Cellar is the be all and end all, but it has great microbrews. Employee parties in the dorms are all that's left if you're lucky. Go to bed instead and cut the hiking tracks first thing in the morning.

OTHER ACTIVITIES Pool, gym, spa, saunas, drinking and prospecting.

THANKS TO Kelly Graham, Eric Vines at Action Video, the Cat Crew.

Top left — Silver King **Photo:** Matt Small
Top right — Temple Cummins **Photo:** Matt Small
Middle left — Eric (Heidi) Vines **Photo:** Bruce Sutherland
Bottom right — Elan Bushell **Photo:** Matt Small

GETTING THERE
By air: The closest airport is Sea-Tac, 67 miles (107 kilometres) from Crystal. There is no shuttle service between the airport and Crystal Mountain; the best option is to rent a car.
By car: From Seattle take Highway 410, Highway 164 or Highway 169 to Enumclaw. Head south on Highway 410 for 33 miles (52 kilometres) to the turn-off for Crystal Mountain Boulevard, a six mile (10 kilometre) mountain cul-de-sac.

④

OREGON

STATE INFORMATION

Population: 3,181,000
Time: Pacific Standard Time = GMT minus 8 hours
Capital city: Salem
Area: 97,060 sq miles (251,418 sq km)

VISITOR INFORMATION SOURCES
Oregon Tourism Commission:
Tel: 503-986 0000 or 1-800-547 7842
Fax: 503-986 0001
Web site: http://www.traveloregon.com

GETTING AROUND
Main airports: Portland International —
Tel: 503-460 4234, Eugene — Tel: 541-687 5430, Medford
— Tel: 541-776 7222, Redmond — Tel: 541-548 6059,
Pendleton — Tel: 541-276 7754
By train: Amtrak — Tel: 1-800-872 7245
By bus: Greyhound — Tel: 1-800-231 222,
Trailways — Tel: 1-800-366 3830
Road conditions: Tel: 541-889 3999 or 1-800-977 6368
Speed limits: Other than rural interstate systems
where the speed limit is 65 mph (104 kmph), the
posted speed limit is 55 mph (88 kmph).

INTRODUCTION

Sandwiched between California and Washington, Oregon has a diverse landscape with only one constant theme: trees. From the pristine Pacific beaches to the volcanic peaks of the Cascade Range and eastwards out into the high desert, pine forests dominate the landscape. The patchwork vista is a result of clear-cutting by logging companies who have raped huge tracts of virgin timber. The Cascade Range, home to the monoliths of Mount Hood and Mount Bachelor, reaps the rewards of wet Pacific storms and builds up huge snowpacks which can last year-round. Portland and Bend provide all the necessities if you're riding Bachelor or Hood, otherwise there are hard-core local scenes in the small mountain towns. Oregon has a long history of being laid-back, which is still reflected in the snowboarding scene today.

Right — Mount Hood **Photo:** Alex Badley
Main Pic — Steaming logs after a fresh dump **Photo:** Bruce Sutherland

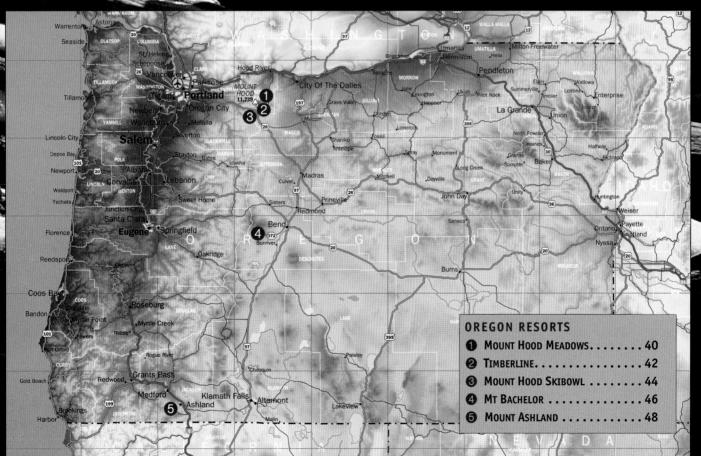

OREGON RESORTS

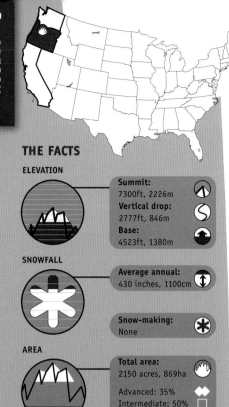

THE FACTS

ELEVATION

Summit:
7300ft, 2226m
Vertical drop:
2777ft, 846m
Base:
4523ft, 1380m

SNOWFALL

Average annual:
430 inches, 1100cm

Snow-making:
None

AREA

Total area:
2150 acres, 869ha

Advanced: 35%
Intermediate: 50%
Beginner: 15%

SEASON
Mid-November — early May

COMMUNICATIONS
Snow reports: Tel: 503-227 7669
Web site: http://www.skihood.com
E-mail: info@skihood.com
Mountain information:
Tel: 503-337 2222
Fax: 503-337 2217
Chamber of Commerce:
Tel: 541-386 2000

LIFTS AND TICKETS
Number of lifts:
1 snowcat, 3 high-speed quads, 7 chairlifts,
1 surface lift
Lift pass prices:
1/2 day: N/A
1 day: $35*
Multi-day: $150 (5 out of 7 days)
Season: $800
Other ticketing information:
* This is for a 'shift ticket' which runs from 9.00am
to 4.00pm, 11.00am to 7.00pm or 1.00pm to
10.00pm. A 10 shift punch pass costs $300. From
mid-March there are big reductions (30 per cent or
more) on shift lift tickets. $20 lift tickets are
available if you stay with participating Hood River
lodging properties. Cat-boarding costs $50 for five
runs.

SNOWBOARD SHOPS
Demo Ski and Snowboard Centre
Tel: 503-337 2222 ext. 327
Located in the South Lodge, the techs can set you
up on rental equipment for $28 (shift) or $21
(nights). They rent good demo models.
Hood River Outfitters — Tel: 541-386-6206
Windance — Tel: 541-386 2131

SNOWBOARD SCHOOL
Mount Hood Meadows' Snowboard School
Tel: 503-246 1810
Beginner specials start at $45 (Buttercup lift only)
including a 90 minute lesson and rentals. The
Mountain Master Programme provides all of the
above without the lift ticket restriction for $75
group lesson or $105 private lesson.

Mount Hood Meadows

ON THE MOUNTAIN

The conical majesty of Mount Hood is home to two top-class resorts: Mount Hood Meadows and Timberline. They are separated by the gash of the White River Canyon which snakes down the south-east flank of this glacial giant. Mount Hood Meadows covers a vast cross-section of terrain, from tasty trees lower down to consistent cornices and wind lips above the tree line. Add the steep chutes of Superbowl and Heather Canyon serviced by the snowcat, and you have one of the best all-round resorts on the continent. There are loads of options when it comes to choosing your line off the ridges which feed into the abundant gullies and bowls, and there are plenty of stashes for the inquisitive. Quad chairs service the important parts of the mountain, spreading out the crowds and keeping lift lines to a minimum.

SNOW CONDITIONS Mount Hood Meadows is on the sunny side of the Hood, facing mainly east. Soft conditions prevail on hot days, except for in the northerly powder-holds of Heather Canyon (positioned on the lee side of the predominantly north-west Pacific storm path). The prolific Pacific storms translate into a good 36 feet (10 metres) of the white stuff from November till May.

BACK-COUNTRY OPTIONS Weather and avalanche danger permitting, $12 will get you snowcatted to the upper Superbowl, 1020 feet (335 metres) higher than the top of the Cascade Express Quad. Once you disembark, a daunting drop-in initiates the 4000 vertical foot (1220 metre) run full of wind lips, a few rock drop-offs and wind-sculptured snow features further down in the canyon.

FREERIDERS Freeriders will be spoilt for choice with just about all the lifts having something worth investigating. Swing left at the top of the Cascade Express Quad and choose from a variety of cornice heights to leap off, or slash the wind lips around Boulevard and Gulch. Elevator also has some nice drop-offs and rocks leading into the trees of Discovery, with steeps at 3-D and O Ring. If steeps are your thing, then Superbowl and Heather Canyon are where the goodies are. Riders once had to do a tendon-tearing traverse from the Heather Canyon run-out, but the new Heather Canyon Chairlift has put an end to those days. The bowls on the main face provide plenty of speed opportunities after a dump, but the main night-riding trails, North and South Canyon, can suffer from traffic overload.

FREESTYLERS There's a lengthy funpark which has the usual hits and table tops; enter it via the Hood River Express Quad or the Mount Hood Express Quad. Under the Cascade Express Quad you'll find some funky hits around Chunky Swirly, and the wind lips around Catacombs and Texas Trail are also excellent for boosting off. There are no plans for a halfpipe so go to Timberline or Mount Hood Skibowl if you're hanging out.

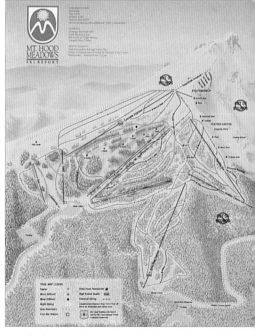

CARVERS Carvers will get some joy on the groomers off the Cascade Express Quad; check out Gulch, Boulevard or Outer Limits down into Middle Fork. The Hood River Express Quad offers some thigh-burners with a consistent pitch, as does the Shooting Star ridge area. The new groomers in Heather Canyon are a great place to lay out some high-speed arcs thanks to winch-cat technology.

HAZARDS AND RULES The usual retention device rules apply, along with a 'no-smoking in the lift lines' law. Firm boundary policies are in place to protect you from some fine-looking, but high risk, canyon riding. Meadows is a class A (high) avalanche area so the ski patrol are serious about pulling passes.

MOUNTAIN FOOD The Alpenstube on the second level of the South Lodge has burgers, salads and microbrews next to Schuss, the fast-grill service. Auntie Pasta's Deli on the third level pumps out gourmet pizzas, or try the pasta dishes in the full service Sahallie Room. The Finish Line Bar and Grill on the same level has the après action, and Mazot at the bottom of Arena is the on-mountain snack shack.

EVENTS AND COMPETITIONS Mount Hood Meadows runs Vegetate, a big snowboard festival in late April which includes boardercross, slope-style and big air comps. The event raises funds for the native wildflower revegetation programme. Freestylers around at that time will have better man-made hits to choose from.

Mount Hood Meadows

GETTING THERE

By air: Portland International Airport is a one hour drive from Hood River on Interstate 84.
By train: Amtrak is tentatively servicing the gorge.
By bus: Bus transportation is available from several Portland metro locations. For the Hood River Ski Shuttle — Tel: 541-386 4202 or 503-BUS LIFT.
By car: Meadows is 67 miles (107 kilometres) from Portland. Take Interstate 84 to Hood River and follow Highway 35 to the Mount Hood Meadows' entrance.

ABOUT TOWN

Hood River is known as a Mecca for windykooks (windsurfers) but also boasts excellent mountain-biking, kayaking and access to several volcanoes with epic back-country. Generally considered a yuppy sailor town, Hood River is starting to attract more visitors from Portland and a younger crowd, stoked on the freeriding terrain at Mount Hood Meadows. The town sits within the Columbia River Gorge National Scenic Area where the Cascades meet the high desert of eastern Oregon.

ACCOMMODATION There's a variety of reasonably priced lodgings in Hood River which have deals, including the $20 lift tickets offered by many hotels. For really cheap lodging, sleep in old classrooms and scale the climbing wall at the Bingen School Inn — Tel: 509-493 3363. For moderately priced rooms ranging from $50-$150, try the historical Hood River Hotel downtown — Tel: 1-800-386 1859 or the Best Western on the edge of town — Tel: 1-800-828 7873. For Ski and Stay destination packages — Tel: 1-800-929 2SKI. Central Reservations — Tel: 1-800-929 7254.

FOOD The Sixth Street Bistro is the locals' favourite for classic north-western cuisine and a full bar. Bo's Bistro is good for pizza, pasta and pool with a happy hour from 5.00pm to 7.00pm every night. Santacroce's on Highway 35, between the mountain and Hood River, has good herb crust pizza and primo Italian dishes. For Mexican go straight to Chili's Cantina in Hood River or cross the river to Fidel's in Bingen. Big City Chicks on the Heights above Hood River has fancy ethnic and vegetarian dishes.

NIGHTLIFE The North Lodge Bar at Mount Hood Meadows usually brings in decent regional bands for the aprés scene on Fridays and Saturdays. River City Saloon down in Hood River has big club acts on the weekends and hosts retro disco nights on Wednesdays. Around the corner the Golden Rose has huge Scorpion bowls full of potent venom, drunk hookah style, for $12. The Northshore Bar and Grill across the river is the hang-out for good vibes, great food, pool and the occasional band. There are a couple of microbreweries in town worth sampling; the Full Sail Brewing Company and the Big Horse Brew Pub are both mellow places to numb the day's ailments in. The Shed is a good hole in the wall for gettin' loaded and lucky in pool.

OTHER ACTIVITIES Thanks to Hood River's mild sea-level climate, world-class kayaking, mountain-biking and windsurfing are available year round for the hard-core. There are also about a dozen waterfalls near Hood River with extensive trails throughout the lush forests of the gorge. Veg out on the couches and bean-bags of the Skylight Theatre and Pub while taking in a new movie and some regional brews. For aching bones, check out the Anne Cruz Spa downtown for hourly massages, jacuzzis and steam rooms.

THANKS TO Chip Wayt, Dave Tragethon.

Top left — **Photo:** Quinn Sheilds
Top Right — The Vegetate Festival **Photo:** Randy Boverman **Courtesy:** Mount Hood Meadows
Bottom — Mount Hood Meadows from the carpark **Photo:** Bruce Sutherland

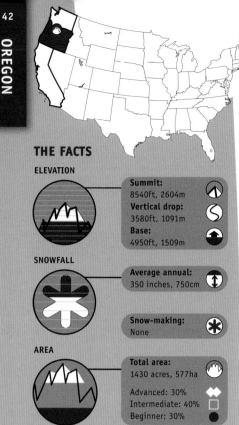

THE FACTS

ELEVATION

Summit:
8540ft, 2604m
Vertical drop:
3580ft, 1091m
Base:
4950ft, 1509m

SNOWFALL

Average annual:
350 inches, 750cm

Snow-making:
None

AREA

Total area:
1430 acres, 577ha

Advanced: 30%
Intermediate: 40%
Beginner: 30%

SEASON

Year round — the lifts close for two weeks in September for maintenance.

COMMUNICATIONS

Snow report: Tel: 503-222 2211
Web site: http://www.timberline.com
Mountain information:
Tel: 503-272 3311 or 503-231 5400
Fax: 503-231 7979

LIFTS AND TICKETS

Number of lifts:
2 high-speed quads, 4 chairlifts
Lift pass prices:
1/2 day: $19
1 day: $32
Multi-day: N/A
Season: N/A

SNOWBOARD SHOPS

There aren't any as such but the Wy'east Lodge rents B+B for $33 and has some emergency spares. Don't expect a huge selection.

SNOWBOARD SCHOOL

Timberline Ski School — Tel: 503-231 5402
Learn to ride the obstacles and the halfpipe. Group lessons for six or more cost $30.

Timberline

ON THE MOUNTAIN

Timberline occupies a large slice of Mount Hood's southern face, offering some of the most spectacular scenery and the best year-round riding conditions in North America. It was the continent's first ski area to offer lift-serviced summer skiing and constructed the second lift in the USA after Sun Valley. The resort is characterised by its main lodge and carpark, positioned slap in the middle of the ski area with lifts above and below. Timberline has two distinct riding areas: the trees and glades of the lower mountain and the wide open fields that stretch towards the summit. It's the home of the famous Palmer Snowfield where intense summer training camps are held for all comers, from snowboard beginners to Olympic skiers. T-line has the most vertical feet of any resort in the north-west and is now serviced by a brand-spanking new high-speed quad, the Palmer Express. The quad has more than halved the ride time and has increased the potential for attaining huge vertical drop figures; the only restriction is how much burn your legs can take.

SNOW CONDITIONS The southern side of the roof of Oregon is always going to be a good snow trap, as it sits at right angles to the Pacific jet stream bringing in dump-trucks of snow which are usually accompanied by strong winds. The precipitation from storms spinning in from the north means Timberline scores heavily in the snow league. When the sun is about, there is nowhere to hide and soft spring conditions can appear by midday.

FREERIDERS Freeriders will be jostling with the carvers for Palmer's crisp corduroy lines which are interspersed by powder fields of consistent pitch and deceptive length, especially if you continue down to the bottom of the Magic Mile Super Express Quad. Along the way, there are usually wind-sculptured lips and rollers with the odd drop. Down the bottom, take Molly's Run into the fringe of the trees then cut across to the steeper lower runs of West Pitch and Cut Off. There are some wild canyons on either side of the resort, but due to the odd inexperienced rider trundling down a canyon into a huge wilderness area and not being found for a couple of days, boundaries are enforced. If you want a long mellow ride down to Government Camp, ask the patrol for directions to the Alpine Trail or go with someone who knows the way.

FREESTYLERS T-line is a freestyle heaven during summer; no less than four large snowboard camps fill the Palmer Snowfield with pipes, parks and the patronage of many an international pro. During winter there is a short hand-dug pipe located just below the Wy'east Lodge next to the Betsy Chair. Big air and obstacle clinics are offered at various times in the winter. The Paint-Brush terrain park left of Blossom Chair has some natural berms and lips that lead to a series of small kickers and table tops, all spaced down a cruisy incline. After big snows much of the terrain park disappears under the thick Pacific powder, but this means some nice wind lips have probably built up elsewhere — look around.

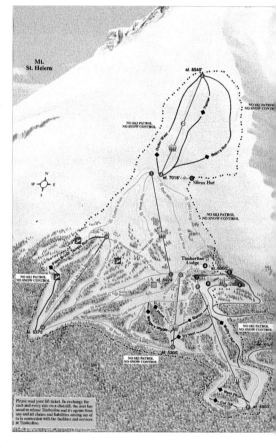

CARVERS Carvers only need to know one word in Oregon and that's Palmer. There are swathes of picture perfect groomers and the new quad chair quickly pumps you back up for more. You are guaranteed to enjoy the consistent pitch and carving surface. If you want to put the pedal to the metal, the top of Palmer to bottom of the Magic Mile will leave your legs and lungs on fire.

MOUNTAIN FOOD Three refuelling stops serving good food are the Timberline Lodge, the Wy'east Lodge and the Silcox Hut. Silcox does unsurpassed chilli and snacks in a traditional alpine hut.

HAZARDS AND RULES It is possible to hike up Mount Hood but serious climbing conditions exist so the right equipment and a guide are a must. If you leave the resort area, you are responsible for your own actions — you'll have a fat search and rescue bill if you get lost.

ABOUT TOWN

Timberline Lodge was built in the '30s depression by unemployed craftsmen using government cash. The result is a national historic landmark that attracts mountain users and tourists alike. If it makes you feel a bit creepy, it may be because Stanley Kubrick used it as a backdrop for The Shining, a testimony to the attraction of the building and the location. The Lodge and Silcox Hut have the only fully serviced on-mountain facilities and accommodation on the West Coast.

ACCOMMODATION The main resort services like tickets and rentals used to all be crammed into the Timberline Lodge until they completed the Wy'east Lodge in '81. This has allowed the T-line Lodge to concentrate on providing great hotel services, with a range of rooms from dorm to luxury. Pool, spa, sauna, restaurant and two bars are some of the facilities available. Prices range from $65 to $170 — Tel: 503-231 5400 or 1-800-547 1406. The recently restored Silcox Hut caters for large groups (16 to 24 people), who are taken by snowcat to the stone oasis at 7000 feet (2135 metres). There you'll eat dinner by the fireplace and bed down early for dawn tracks followed by a huge breakfast, all for $75 per person — Tel: 503-295 1828.

FOOD The Cascade Dining Room is the plush, pricey restaurant situated upstairs in the Lodge. To the right of the 92 foot (30 metre) chimney and huge fireplace in the downstairs lobby and past the many 'objets d'art', you'll find the Blue Ox Bar. Their pizzas are great and go down well with the tasty Mount Hood brews in the Wy'east Lodge. The Country Store does expressos and bakery snacks. The Wy'east Kitchen serves burgers and burritos, or head to the Wy'east Bar for post-boarding drinks and beer snacks with big screen entertainment.

NIGHTLIFE Err... go to Gov'y

OTHER ACTIVITIES Chess.

THANKS TO Jon Tullis, Phil Hetz, Brenda Currie, all the old ski journos at Silcox plus the Hemp boys.

See Mount Hood Skibowl review p.44 for Gov'y and Mount Hood Meadows review p.40 for Hood River.

Top — White River Canyon **Photo:** Bruce Sutherland
Inset — First turns on Palmer's great groomers **Photo:** Marco Bruni
Bottom — Richard Smiles **Photo:** Bruce Sutherland

GETTING THERE

By air: Portland International Airport is 52 miles (80 kilometres) away on Highway 26. Luxury Accommodations can transfer you to the Timberline Lodge for $65 for one person, $35 for two. It takes two hours and you must book in advance — Tel: 1-800-831 7433.
By bus: The Greyhound Bus goes to the Huckleberry Inn in Gov'y — Tel: 503-538 5517.
By car: Tyre chains are a necessity by law, and if you get caught without you may be fined.
Getting around: Gov'y is a few miles up a windy road from the Timberline carpark; it's an easy hitch if you get to the turn-off just east of town.

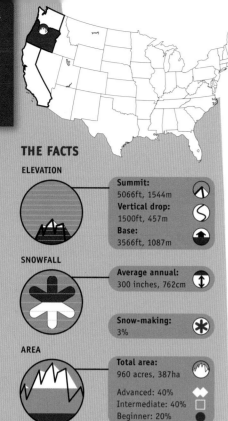

Mount Hood Skibowl

THE FACTS

ELEVATION

Summit:
5066ft, 1544m
Vertical drop:
1500ft, 457m
Base:
3566ft, 1087m

SNOWFALL

Average annual:
300 inches, 762cm

Snow-making:
3%

AREA

Total area:
960 acres, 387ha

Advanced: 40%
Intermediate: 40%
Beginner: 20%

SEASON
Mid-November — mid-April

COMMUNICATIONS
Snow report: Tel: 503-222 2695
Web site: http://www.skibowl.com
Mountain information:
Tel: 503-222 2695

LIFTS AND TICKETS
Number of lifts:
4 chairlifts, 5 surface lifts
Lift pass prices:
1/2 day: $20 (weekends only)
1 day: $19, $25 (weekends)
Multi-day: N/A
Season pass: $395-$430
Other ticketing information:
Night-riding runs from 3.30pm to 10.00pm, a full day and night pass costs $30. A night-riding season pass costs $138-$165. Buying a pass from Ticket Master saves $2.

SNOWBOARD SHOPS
New Release — Tel: 503-622 5363
Located in Zig-Zag (on the drive from Portland) and complete with a drive-through, this shop has a large selection of everything from coffee and smoothies to full tuning, technical repairs, boards and accessories.

SNOWBOARD SCHOOL
Mount Hood Skibowl Snowboard School
Tel: 503-222 2695
The beginner special includes rental, lesson and ticket for the surface tow ($34) or bottom lift ($41). The school has a one hour one-on-one offer for $30.

ON THE MOUNTAIN

Although Mount Hood Skibowl (sic) doesn't occupy a position on the conical flank of Mount Hood proper, it does have some of the most radical terrain in the area. Ask any hard-core local and they'll use glowing terms such as 'rad, killer, or sick' to describe the lines available. On the east side of the circular ridge line is Tom Dick Peak with its bowls, chutes and cliffs, beyond which you'll find the endless freeriding of Outback. Once a great ski jump hill in '28, Multorpor Mountain lies on the western boundary of the ski area. It's short and steep with great trees off the sides. Skibowl is serviced by four chairs, which combined with a bit of hiking and traversing access a wide range of terrain. Add the best winter pipe, one of the steepest terrain parks around and long night-riding hours, and you've got a great little all-round resort.

SNOW CONDITIONS Mount Hood Skibowl is a fair bit lower than Timberline and Mount Hood Meadows; consequently when the snow is a bit lean or the temperatures warm up, it's the first place to show it. On the plus side most of the riding has a northerly aspect and the powder is stashed for days after storms, especially in the plentiful tree areas which catch the precipitation of northerly storms heading onwards.

FREERIDERS Take the frighteningly ancient Upper Bowl Chair and exit right to the easy hike east along the ridge line to Tom Dick Peak. Views of Mirror Lake greet you before you drop into one of the numerous lines of the Outback: glade turns, trees and rock jumps end in a right-hand traverse down to the bottom. There's big stuff to skier's left of the Upper Bowl Chair, but skiers tend to bump out the obvious runs that are steep and close to the lift. The large cliff band halfway down Skibowl Peak is largely unrideable so avoid the area if you're scared of heights. Multorpor Mountain has some good trees on either side of the groomers which can be accessed by a short hike; check your line or you'll be walking out. There is some very attractive back side action that can sometimes be ridden with the right equipment and the OK from the ski patrol.

FREESTYLERS The halfpipe at Skibowl is undoubtedly the best in the Hood, with a good 330 foot (100 metre) length and decent radius allowing for sizeable air to be extracted from the regulation vertical. Situated at the end of the funpark on the Boarder Garden run, it is well-maintained by a dedicated crew of local diggers who excavate in summer, ensuring good dimensions in winter. This park takes the award for the steepest gradient on the West Coast, giving plenty of speed for the main table tops and kickers. It is very compact so overboosting and run-outs can be a problem, although not for skiers because they are not allowed in!

CARVERS Hard-booters can jostle with skiers for the steep consistent groomers off Upper Bowl like Canyon Run. Over on Multorpor Mountain you'll find steep fall-line runs to carve to your heart's content.

MOUNTAIN FOOD Starlite and Multorpor Lodges have all the goodies with hot soups and chillies. For Mexican and microbrews try the Beer Stube Cantina. The historic mid-mountain warming hut does great club sandwiches and fat homemade sausages which you can wash down with some fine, rare German pilseners.

HAZARDS AND RULES You are on your own if you cross the resort's boundary.

ABOUT TOWN

Skibowl is situated right across the road from Government Camp, on a loop road off Highway 26. Government Camp, or 'Gov'y' as it's affectionately known, was born when a bunch of soldiers rag-dolled their supply wagons while trying to get down a double black diamond trail last century. They set up camp in winter and since then Gov'y has grown into a small mountain town, providing essential services for Skibowl, Timberline and Mount Hood Meadows. The wide, quiet main street contains all the hotels, restaurants, bars and shops, giving the town a compact friendly feel. The leafy side streets have nice condos and chalets, some of which are for rent. If you want anything, Geoff Ecker could almost be described as the information centre. You can track him down at Gov'y Junction; he's in the A-frame shop surrounded by his eclectic collection of consumables, nic-nacs and a second-hand book and record exchange.

ACCOMMODATION One of the most convenient places in town is the Huckleberry Inn, which has comfy rooms from $50-$100 plus a bunk-room for groups — Tel: 503-272 3325. The Mount Hood Inn has luxury facilities starting at $105 for two doubles. There are also house and chalet rentals such as Summit Meadows — Tel: 503-272 3403, Trill'am Lake Basin — Tel: 503-272 0151, England's Lodging — Tel: 503-272 3350 or the View House — Tel: 503-272 3295. The Cascade Ski Club — Tel: 503-272 9204 and the Mazama Ski Club — Tel: 503-272 9214 can help with bunks for groups. Central Reservations — Tel: 503-222 2675.

FOOD The versatile Huckleberry Inn has a 24 hour diner that serves huge hearty meals around the clock. Their world-famous Huckleberry pie is legendary as are their breakfasts, particularly the blueberry pancakes. In the weekend the Huckleberry has a separate steakhouse. The Mount Hood Brew Pub, home of the famous beer, has decent pizzas and salads. The Ratskeller does a good, reasonably priced bar menu for those late night eating frenzies, and also has a family eating area for the kids.

NIGHTLIFE There is only one real party place and that is the Ratskeller, providing all the essential elements: good beer, food, pool, pinball and live music. Interesting decor complements the conversations you're likely to have when you drink with the locals, many of whom treat it as their living room. Good live bands, pool competitions and a generally laid-back atmosphere make the Ratskeller a friendly watering hole.

OTHER ACTIVITIES Skibowl has a freefall twin bungy-jump tower over at the base of Multorpor Mountain which will stretch your funds by $25. The tube hill and sled-dog snow skates (like rollerblades on snow) are a blast too.

THANKS TO Ed at the Huckleberry, the Hemp Boys: Richard, Lance, Carl, Timmy (Elvis), Jeremy and Rich, and all the nutters from the Rat.

Opposite — The mosh pit at Skibowl **Photo:** Richard Smiles
Top — Tim Vlandis **Photo:** Richard Smiles

GETTING THERE
By air: Portland International Airport is the closest global entry point. Luxury Taxis run from the airport — Tel: 503-668 7433.
By bus: Greyhound stops at the Huckleberry Inn, right in Gov'y — Tel: 1-800-231 2222.
By car: A mere 52 miles (83 kilometres) of asphalt separates Mount Hood Skibowl from downtown Portland. Follow Interstate 80 east to the Greshem Exit 16A, where you join Highway 26 coming from the south. From Hood River in the north, take Highway 35.
Getting around: A car and feet are vital.

THE FACTS

ELEVATION

Summit:
9065ft, 2764m
Vertical drop:
3365ft, 1026m
Base:
5700ft, 1738m

SNOWFALL

Average annual:
300 inches, 762cm

Snow-making:
None

AREA

Total area:
3686 acres, 1489ha

Advanced: 25%
Intermediate: 55%
Beginner: 20%

SEASON

Early November — late June

COMMUNICATIONS

Snow report: Tel: 541-382 7888
Web site: http://www.mtbachelor.com
E-mail: info@mtbachelor.com
Mountain information:
Tel: 541-382 2442 or 1-800-829 2442
Fax: 541-382 6536

LIFTS AND TICKETS

Number of lifts:
7 high-speed quads, 4 chairlifts, 2 pomas
Lift pass prices:
1/2 day: $31
1 day: $36
Multi-day: $157 (5 out of 6 days)
Season: $750
Other ticketing information:
Swatch Access watches! These are worn on your
wrist as you slide though the electronic turnstile
system; no more grovelling down your clothing for
pass checking. You can buy them for $50 at the
West Village Guest Services building. A mid-week
non-holiday season pass costs $525.

swatch access

SNOWBOARD SHOPS

Mt Bachelor Snowboard Shop — Tel: 541-382 2442
In the West Village Day Lodge, the shop has a huge
range of boards and accessories. B+B: $26.
North Shore — Tel: 541-388 2328
Along with Outer Limits, this shop is the best of
the bunch of board shops on Century Drive.
Outer Limits — Tel: 541-382 4115

SNOWBOARD SCHOOL

Perfect Tracks Training — Tel: 1-800-829 2442
Five High Cascade Camps are run each season.

Mt Bachelor

ON THE MOUNTAIN

Mt Bachelor (sic) is a perfect volcanic cone, rising out of the high desert plateau of central Oregon's Cascade Range. This picturesque peak has two distinct areas: the entire lower half of the mountain is blanketed in Oregon's famous coniferous forest, which abruptly gives way at 7500 feet (2287 metres) to the wide open spaces of the bald upper cone. The trees have some great trail and glade riding while providing protection from adverse weather. The upper half holds steep chutes, open bowls and the wind-shaped snow formations that are common on volcanic peaks. An efficient modern lift system easily accesses 270 degrees of the consistently steep cone. Of the 13 lifts in operation, no less than seven of them are high-speed quads. The new Northwest Express Quad covers two miles (three kilometres) in eight and a half minutes, and the replacement Summit Express Quad (opening in the '97-'98 season) will be equally speedy.

SNOW CONDITIONS With 360 degrees of rideable mountain, aspect becomes academic as daily local conditions dictate where you ride. Storms from the Pacific dump large quantities of snow on the north and western sides, but the wind then transports it around the cone. It's possible to have perfectly sunny weather on the southern slopes while the Outback Express Quad on the north side is completely enveloped by cloud. It's also possible to strike slush, ice and powder in three consecutive runs.

FREERIDERS Freeriding is the essence of the Mt Bachelor attraction. Beginners and intermediates have the whole lower mountain to ride with plenty of consistent groomed trails that cut through the trees. Experts will head straight for the Summit Express Quad, where a short hike accesses the 60 degree chutes of the Cirque. This is the steepest stuff on the mountain and the chutes lead into a massive powder bowl, dominated by a huge wind lip to skier's left. It is quite common for the top of the mountain to be closed due to bad weather and strong winds, but the ski patrol open it at the first available opportunity. There's the option of dropping over the back side from the Summit Express Quad to access the rarely ridden powder fields above the Outback and Northwest Express Quads. This is a joyous run when conditions are perfect, otherwise you'll find wind-blown ice and death cookies. Once you reach the timberline of the Northwest area, the well-spaced trees offer the best lower mountain riding with preserved powder. Cow's Face has some great wind spines and little gullies which continue into the trees, east of the very slow Rainbow Chair.

FREESTYLERS The halfpipe to the left of the Skyliner Express Quad is the best pipe in Oregon. Approximately 200 feet (61 metres) long by 35 feet (ten metres) wide with eight foot (two and a half metre) walls, this immaculately maintained pipe is the creation of Pat the Man, the local snowboard park designer, and that wonderful mechanical beast, the Pipe Dragon. If all the natural hits don't satisfy the jibber in you, then the funpark on Chipper trail definitely will. The line of kickers and berms on the left side are more forgiving, while the right side has some bigger bread-boxes and motorcross rolls. The sequence of large table tops through the middle requires speed and extra boost to make the transitions.

CARVERS Mt Bachelor's high grooming standards will ensure carvers are kept happy. Under the Pine Marten Express you'll find a World Cup sanctioned course, plus a NASTAR course where you can pit yourself against the world's best times. The whole Northwest area is riddled with steep corduroy, and the runs like Healy Heights and Beverly Hills under the Summit Express Quad are wide and consistent.

MOUNTAIN FOOD Sunrise Lodge and West Village Day Lodge both provide good food at budget prices, such as a burger basket for $3.50. Vegetarians are well-catered for. There's a three star restaurant in the Pine Marten Lodge, which is surprisingly well-priced considering the million dollar view.

HAZARDS AND RULES Leashes are required. The ski patrol must be consulted if you attempt the back side. A circular catch trail brings you back to civilisation; going beyond the trail will result in a long hike out of a wilderness area — go for the long, painful traverse instead. Inverts are a no-no.

EVENTS AND COMPETITIONS Bachelor hosts a round of the FIS Grundig World Cup Championships plus other major comps.

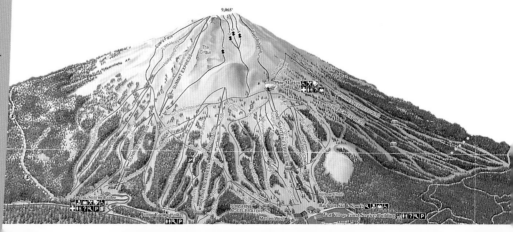

ABOUT TOWN

Bend is 15 miles (26 kilometres) from Mt Bachelor, and like the mountain it has two distinct personalities. The older parts of Bend are nestled on the banks of the Deschutes River, where a tranquil atmosphere complements the beautiful mountain backdrop. The main access road Highway 97 has grown into a light industrial area, including all the modern fast food and supermarket outlets. Central Bend has a range of speciality shops spread out along a wide, unhurried main street. Drake Park, near the town centre, is an idyllic riverside chill-out zone.

ACCOMMODATION The closest accommodation to the mountain is the Inn of the Seventh Mountain. It is fully self-contained with shops, restaurants, bar, pool, spa, sauna and large apartments for groups starting at $50 — Tel: 1-800-829 2442. In Bend, the cheapest option is the youth hostel where $14 gets you a bed. Beware the boot bouquet — Tel: 1-800-299 3813. Other choices include Motel West — Tel: 1-800-299 5577, Westward Ho — Tel: 1-800-999 8143 (both from $25 a night) and the Bend Riverside Motel from $35 — Tel: 1-800-284 2363. Central Reservations — Tel: 1-800-800 8334.

FOOD The places for pizza are John Dough's and Stuft Pizza. Café Baja Norté and the Taco Stand are the goods for Mexican food, and Yoko's has the rawest Japanese sushi. For breakfast Café Sante is a good stop. Beers and big portions of wholesome bar food can be sampled at Deschute's Brewery. If you want something more upmarket, try the food at Café Rosemary; it's spendy but superb.

NIGHTLIFE Deschute's Brewery has the killer local brewskis and is definitely the favoured meeting, eating and drinking spot. Snowboarders tend to hang out at the dingy Evil Sister which has live bands and pool. The Timber Tavern is for red-necks who like to play eight-ball and darts. Monet's Garden has a chilled-out atmosphere and jazzy snacks to complement the live music. There's a ten pin bowling alley off Highway 97. Café Paradiso has live music, poetry and the like for under 21s, who will also find some hang-out stops on Wall Street.

OTHER ACTIVITIES Cross-country skiing, telemarking, mountain-biking, a skate park, swimming, hiking, rafting, horseback riding and rock-climbing at Smith Rocks. Mt Bachelor activities line — Tel: 1-800-829 2442.

THANKS TO Bill Healy (Bachelor's founder) and his grandson Karta, Tiia Sumera, Eric Lilley, Barbara Leppe and Jason McAlister.

GETTING THERE

By air: From Portland International Airport, it's a 160 mile (256 kilometre) drive to Bend. Redmond Airport is 20 miles (32 kilometres) from Bend; Horizon Air fly daily — Tel: 1-800-HORIZON.
By bus: Greyhound has daily services to Bend from Portland and Salem — Tel: 541-382 2151.
By car: From Portland: Take Interstate 5 to Highway 26 and south to Madras. Then follow Highway 97 for 42 miles (68 kilometres) to Bend.
Getting around: From Bend to Mt Bachelor, there's a free all day shuttle service. Schedules are available from the information booth.

Top - Jason McAlister **Photo:** Bruce Sutherland
Middle - Jason McAlister **Photo:** Bruce Sutherland
Bottom - Drake Park at Bend **Photo:** Bruce Sutherland

THE FACTS

ELEVATION

Summit:
7500ft, 2286m

Vertical drop:
1150ft, 350m

Base:
6350ft, 1936m

SNOWFALL

Average annual:
300 inches, 750cm

Snow-making:
Mother nature

AREA

Total area:
110 acres, 45ha

Advanced: 50%
Intermediate: 35%
Beginner: 15%

SEASON

Late November — mid-April

COMMUNICATIONS

Snow reports:
Tel: 541-482 2SKI (Ashland)
Tel: 541-770 2SKI (Medford)
Web site: http://www.mind.net/snow
E-mail: mta@mind.net
Mountain information:
Tel: 541-482 2897

LIFTS AND TICKETS

Number of lifts:
4 chairlifts
Lift pass prices:
1/2 day: $14, $18 (weekends)
1 day: $20, $25 (weekends)
Multi-day: $175*, $215 (weekends)
Season: $325
Other ticketing information:
* Multi-day passes comprise of 10 vouchers which
are each valid for one day.

SNOWBOARD SHOPS

Low Down Board Shop — Tel: 541-488 8969
A hard-core outlet with a good range of
snowboards and skateboards, plus a full body-
piercing facility if you feel like going for a Prince
Albert (piece of iron through the penis). B+B: $25.

SNOWBOARD SCHOOL

Mount Ashland Snowboard School
Tel: 541-482 2897
A cheap first timer package of board, boots, lift
ticket and two hour lesson costs $30. Group
lessons cost $15.

Mount Ashland

ON THE MOUNTAIN

The Mount Ashland Ski Area, halfway between San Francisco and Portland, is in the picturesque Siskiyou Mountains and is known internationally as the alpine gateway to the Pacific. A few years ago the local community saved the resort from closure, and it now runs as a public non-profit organisation. This gives Mount Ashland a close-knit feeling; it's well-patronised by the local community and they give visitors a warm welcome. It's certainly not a large destination resort but Ashland has a cross-section of terrain for most intermediate riders, a nice beginners' slope and a good snowboard school. Experienced die-hards can access some of the area's awesome back-country by hiking up the huge volcanic cones of Mount Shasta, Mount McLoughlin, Mount Bailey or Crater Lake.

SNOW CONDITIONS North-east facing Ashland is in the path of Pacific storms, bringing beer snow that stays in the trees for a good week without being champagne for a day. Ashland's storms are consistent rather than heavy compared to neighbouring mountains, but the resort's snow is generally much drier than other ski areas to the north.

BACK-COUNTRY OPTIONS Freeriders will constantly be gazing at the monolithic peaks of Shasta to the south and McLoughlin to the east, both of which offer some insane riding once you've negotiated the insanely long ascent. There are some incredible shots at Crater Lake — ask the locals where to ride and park.

FREERIDERS Ashland has a consistent and relatively steep pitch making it top to bottom fun after a fresh dump, although possibilities become limited once it's tracked out due to its small size. The short steeps are located at the Circe and Second Circe Bowl. There's a range of cornice heights to choose from before entering a cluster of mellow trees and then traversing right back to the Ariel Chair. There are clumps of trees across the face of the resort, however some are too tight to ride. Over on the right side, there's fun terrain on the Void run which continues down to the carpark. The south face, accessed via the gate at the top of the Ariel Chair, is a good run for finding fresh tracks and hits — don't drop down too low past the warning signs before traversing left back to the carpark.

FREESTYLERS The meagre terrain park is a direct result of trying to do the right thing without the right tools, but considering Ashland doesn't have any friendly Japanese investors, it does have a few decent hits and berms under the slow Comer Chair. The Balcony area of the mountain has some natural terrain that'll keep jibbers entertained with wind-scoured hits and lips, plus lots of rolling steeps for the odd gap jump. The south side also has some funky launches which soften up in the afternoon sun. The halfpipe is maintained for competitions but disappears thereafter, so grab a shovel if you feel like doing community service.

CARVERS Dream and Caliban (off the Ariel Chair) plus Winter and Tempest offer corduroy possibilities for carvers. The resort is a dream for intermediates with cruisy runs, no flats and beautiful views.

MOUNTAIN FOOD There's a good range of food from the one main lodge outlet with some bargain refuelling dishes like stir-fry rice. The open plan lodge includes a cosy bar and a room full of relief maps, models and general area information. The obligatory deck barbecue takes place, weather permitting.

HAZARDS AND RULES Never cut under a boundary rope; they're there for a reason. Keep your speed in check around Lower Juliet.

EVENTS AND COMPETITIONS In January and February, Ashland hosts a boardercross and halfpipe comp.

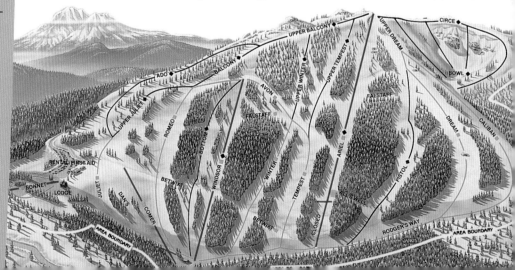

Mount Ashland

ABOUT TOWN

The city of Ashland, located eight miles (13 kilometres) from the lifts, is a real gem of a place exuding both style and history. Internationally famous for its annual Shakespeare festival, visitors come from all over to sample the great works of the British bard. This event has given the town a strong infrastructure so finding accommodation, food and entertainment (especially before March when the festival usually starts) is easy. A visit to the Pacific Northwest Museum of Natural History will educate you on the origins of the mountains.

ACCOMMODATION The resort works with a wide range of accommodation options: there's the Ashland Hills Inn with prices from $41-$49 — Tel: 1-800-547 4747, the Ashland Regency Inn with prices from $34-$40 — Tel: 1-800-482 4301 and the Oak Street Cottages with prices from $52 for a four person occupancy — Tel: 541-488 3778. If you feel like some stylish isolated digs, the Mount Ashland Inn rules. It's the only accommodation on the mountain with superb views and facilities, starting at a reasonable $95 per night. Central Reservations — Tel: 541-482 2897.

FOOD Ashland is a city, so all your city favourites are on offer along with plenty of restaurants for thespians intent on eating their pound of flesh. One place definitely worth checking out is the Northwest Pizza and Pasta Company; create your own massive pizzas and wash them down with a blinding selection of local and domestic beers. Geppetto's aubergine burgers will have vegetarians salivating. Traditional English pub food lovers can relieve their yearning for sausages and chips at the Black Sheep.

NIGHTLIFE Being a university town, Ashland has quite a vibrant party scene. The Northwest Pizza and Pasta Company is a good starting point due to its big beer and screen scenario. The Ashland, down by the riverside, has a nice layout, live music and impromptu jam sessions. It's also the first to go underwater when Ashland gets one of its regular floods. The Beau Club on the main drag is the place to shoot some pool and meet up with the local riding scene.

OTHER ACTIVITIES Siskiyou Adventures do tons of different radical sports year round — Tel: 1-800-250 4602 or 541-488 632.

THANKS TO Gene Landsman, Michael Lip, Scott and Matthew, plus the crew at Low Down.

Opposite — The Circe **Photo:** Bruce Sutherland
Top — View to Mount Shasta **Photo:** Bruce Sutherland
Bottom left — Ashland by night **Photo:** Rick Schafer **Courtesy:** Ski Ashland
Sequence — Marco Bruni **Photo:** Bruce Sutherland

GETTING THERE

By air: Rogue Valley International Airport is 11 miles (18 kilometres) from Ashland with rental cars available.
By bus: Greyhound travel northbound to Ashland from Los Angeles via Sacramento, and southbound to Ashland from Seattle via Portland.
By car: The Mount Ashland Exit on Interstate 5 is ten miles (16 kilometres) south of Ashland city. From the city, it's eight miles (13 kilometres) to the resort.
Getting around: While there is no bus service from the town to the resort, hitching is a cinch as the road doesn't go anywhere else.

5

CALIFORNIA

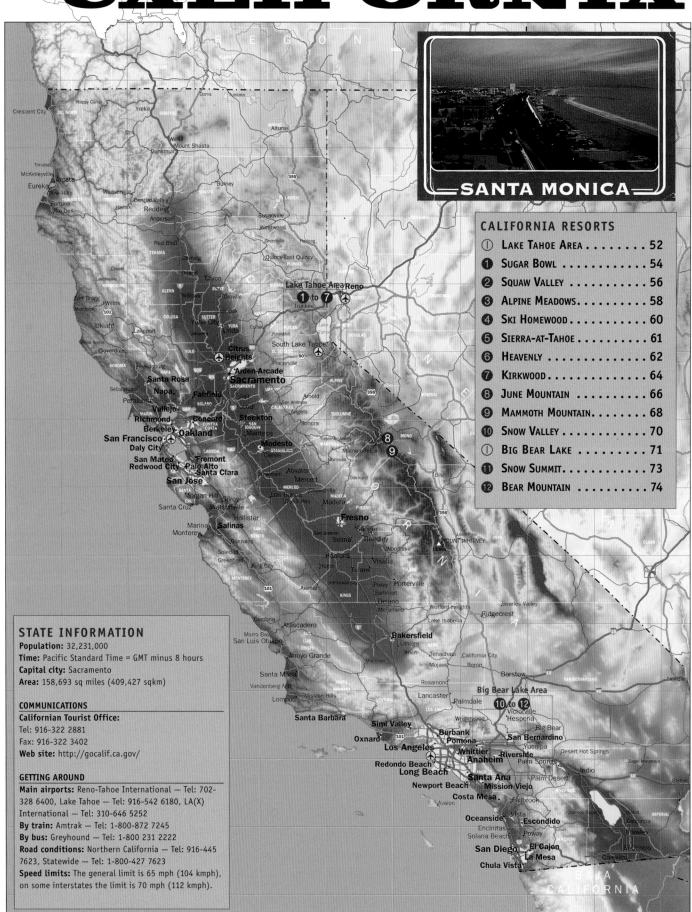

SANTA MONICA

STATE INFORMATION

Population: 32,231,000
Time: Pacific Standard Time = GMT minus 8 hours
Capital city: Sacramento
Area: 158,693 sq miles (409,427 sqkm)

COMMUNICATIONS

Californian Tourist Office:
Tel: 916-322 2881
Fax: 916-322 3402
Web site: http://gocalif.ca.gov/

GETTING AROUND

Main airports: Reno-Tahoe International — Tel: 702-328 6400, Lake Tahoe — Tel: 916-542 6180, LA(X) International — Tel: 310-646 5252
By train: Amtrak — Tel: 1-800-872 7245
By bus: Greyhound — Tel: 1-800 231 2222
Road conditions: Northern California — Tel: 916-445 7623, Statewide — Tel: 1-800-427 7623
Speed limits: The general limit is 65 mph (104 kmph), on some interstates the limit is 70 mph (112 kmph).

INTRODUCTION

California must have kissed butt when the gifts were handed out; how else did it end up with gold, waves, Hollywood and some of the hottest boarding in North America? The powder stashes around Lake Tahoe are legendary, and despite the high profile of mountains like Squaw Valley, the riding fraternity is still way chilled. In the middle of California are the big free-standing volcanoes of Mammoth, the highest resort in the state, and its sister mountain June. These resorts provide a huge range of quality riding for the multitudes beached in the cities of Cal. Just outside LA, the giant snow parks are a lesson in what you can do with a small hill, unlimited grooming technology and urban vision. The snow comes from the Pacific storms in heavy, waterlogged dumps which have the spring nickname of 'Sierra cement'. The state is full of people making a living out of the snowboarding industry: riding, designing funky gear, shooting pics, pressing boards and publishing mags.

Brian Bozack, Sugar Bowl back-country **Photo:** Sean Ward

Lake Tahoe Area

TRUCKEE

Truckee is located just off the main San Francisco-Reno artery (Interstate 80), right on the railway line that runs through Donner Pass towards the Pacific. The Donner Pass was the route taken over the mountains by the first settlers, who managed to get snowed in and ended up cooking each other when the food ran out — giving rise to the name 'donner kebab'. The town still has a rough-hewn wild character, and clusters of weather-beaten shacks give a feeling for the hardships the settlers endured. Truckee and its surrounding area are a complete contrast to the glitz of South Lake Tahoe and have a more down-home feel.

ACCOMMODATION The Cottage Hotel has a $35 tariff for a double with share bathroom. It's on the main drag opposite Totally Board — Tel: 916-587 3108. Donner Lake, close to Sugar Bowl, also has good cabin rentals — Tel: 916-426 3622.

FOOD Tahoe Taps is open late and has a full menu. Downtown on Commercial Row, OB's has a cosy pub atmosphere with good food. El Toro Bravo across the street from Totally Board serves the best Mexican in town. Lake View Pizza in the Lucky Long Centre is the pick for pizzas, while Wong's has killer Chinese. If you're feeling flush, the Hill Top has a great menu to match the view.

NIGHTLIFE Tahoe Taps is the nightlife focus with food, live music and a huge selection of microbrews; it can rock even during the week. The Bar of America on Commercial Row has live music every Friday and Saturday with plenty of room for booty-shaking.

For South Lake Tahoe, see Heavenly review p.62.

Main picture — Burton rider Derek Heidt **Photo:** Jeff Curtes
Top inset — Lake Tahoe from Alpine Meadows **Photo:** Bruce Sutherland
Bottom inset — Reno **Photo:** Alex Badley

TAHOE CITY

Tahoe City sits on the bank of the Truckee River, at the intersection of Highway 28 and Highway 89. Restaurants, bars, a brew pub and a live band venue are interspersed on the main street by snowboard shops, the petrol station and the supermarket.

ACCOMMODATION The one-stop shop for all lodging information and details is Lake Tahoe Accommodations — Tel: 916-581 5210. There are a number of purpose-built sports resorts; the Granlibakken has its own lift on a bunny slope — Tel: 916-583 4242. The two star Tahoma Meadows complex has cottage-style cabins with kitchens and breakfast — Tel: 916-525 1553. Tahoe City Travelodge is more upmarket — Tel: 916-583 3766.

FOOD Hidden away on the waterfront, Lake House Pizza Parlour does great pizzas. The Hacienda has good Mexican food and a regular happy hour. Try the Naughty Dog for filling bar food. If you want to imbibe some fine microbrews as you devour heaped plates of good food, go to the Bluewater Brewing Co. or the Bridgetender. If you like Japanese food, the Yama Sushi has sushi and sake. Rosie Café has huge portions of great food and a convivial bar; be hungry when you go there.

NIGHTLIFE Nightlife generally revolves around Humpty's, a large venue where live music is the order of the evening. Before you go, warm up at the Bluewater with one of their six different home brews or play pool at the Bridgetender. If you've never drunk alcohol from a dog bowl, you'll get your chance at the Naughty Dog. They're famous for their Baywatch parties, cheap draughts and young fun crowd. The Pierce Street Annex has a huge dance area, three bars, two pool tables and more.

SNOWBOARD SHOPS
TRUCKEE: Totally Board
On the Donner Pass Road, this is the main shop and is run by the super cool and friendly Mickey family. B+B: $24, demo $29.
TAHOE CITY: Dave's Ski and Snowboard Rentals
Tel: 916-583 0400
The best snowboarders' stop for hard-core gear, tuning and repairs.
TAHOE CITY: Porters — Tel: 916-582 0900
Another chain store with an extensive rental fleet of cheap and cheerful boards. B+B: $15-$22.

GETTING THERE
By air: Reno, San Francisco, Sacramento and LA are the major gateways to the Lake Tahoe area. Delta flies to all four airports — Tel: 1-800-221 1212.
By bus: Greyhound services Truckee and Tahoe City from the major Cal cities — Tel: 1 800 231 2222. To get to Truckee and Tahoe City from Reno, TART (Tahoe Area Regional Transit) operate a daily service during the winter which connects with Greyhound and Amtrak — Tel: 1-800-736 6365. Budget Chauffeur Drive has a scheduled bus service from Reno to South Lake Tahoe and Truckee — Tel: 702-885 7550 or 1-800-426 5644.
By train: Amtrak has services running from Reno and San Fran to Truckee — Tel: 1-800-872 7245.
By car: Tahoe City is 14 miles (22 kilometres) from Truckee, head west out of Truckee on Interstate 80 and then south on Highway 89. San Francisco is 200 miles (320 kilometres) away. Drive west to Sacramento on Interstate 80 and then take Interstate 5 south to San Fran. Winter weather and road conditions can be changeable if you're driving from the high desert terrain of Reno to the Lake Tahoe mountains — Tel: 1-800-427 7623.

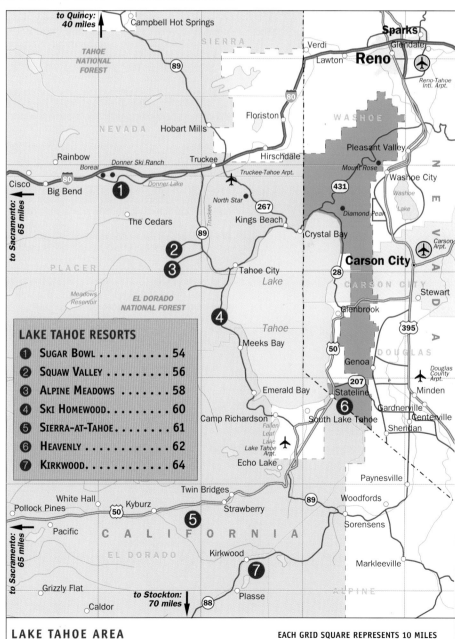

LAKE TAHOE AREA

EACH GRID SQUARE REPRESENTS 10 MILES

THE FACTS

ELEVATION

Summit:
8383ft, 2555m
Vertical drop:
1500ft, 457m
Base:
6883ft, 2098m

SNOWFALL

Average annual:
500 inches, 1270cm

Snow-making:
9%

AREA

Total area:
1500 acres, 606ha

Advanced: 40%
Intermediate: 43%
Beginner: 17%

SEASON
November — April

COMMUNICATIONS
Snow report: Tel: 916-426 1111
Web site: http://www.skisugarbowl.com
E-mail info@skisugarbowl.com
Mountain information:
Tel: 916-426 9000
Fax: 916-426 3723

LIFTS AND TICKETS
Number of lifts:
1 gondola, 2 high-speed quads, 7 chairlifts,
2 surface lifts
Lift pass prices:
1/2 day: $26
1 day: $41
Multi-day: $216 (6 days)
Season: $800
Other ticketing information:
Early departure credit gives you $15 off your next
day pass if you leave the mountain by 12.30pm.
There are frequent skier programmes, McDonald's
promotions, ski guarantees and corporate group
ticket discounts.

SNOWBOARD SHOPS
Sugar Bowl Ski and Sports — Tel: 916-587 1369
Rental gear can be picked up in their larger
Truckee shop next to Safeways and returned to the
mountain shop. B+B: $28

SNOWBOARD SCHOOL
Sugar Bowl Snowboard School
Tel: 916-426 6770
There's a bunch of good instructors who'll take you
wherever you want to go, be it the funpark,
freeriding or the good beginner slopes of Nob Hill,
Christmas Tree or Meadow.

GETTING THERE FROM TRUCKEE AND TAHOE CITY
By bus: The resort offers a bus service for groups
of 35 or more from any point in northern
California.
By car: Sugar Bowl is ten miles (16 km) west of
Truckee. Take the Norden Exit off Interstate 80.

Sugar Bowl

ON THE MOUNTAIN

Back in '38, a team of explorers including Walt Disney found a location near Donner Summit to build California's first chairlift. Almost 60 years later they are still building chairlifts and lodges on the closest main resort to the Bay Area. A three hour drive from San Fran gets you to a crescent of steep alpine peaks that reportedly receive more snow than just about anywhere in North America. This bold claim is coupled with some seriously bold terrain, providing extreme lines down the cliff bands of Mount Lincoln through to open bowls with tree clusters on Mount Disney. Add to this some back-country options when conditions are safe, and you have an all-round, boarder-friendly mountain still enjoying low crowd pressures and a laid-back atmosphere.

SNOW CONDITIONS Along with Kirkwood, Sugar Bowl enjoys some of the biggest and most consistent snowfalls in the Tahoe area, and its north-east to north-west aspect guarantees a good range of snow conditions throughout the day. The average snowfall is around 42 feet (12 metres).

FREERIDERS The West Palisades is cool for good intermediates, but the Middle and East Palisades are for experienced hard-core riders who like steep chutes and scary rocks. The '58 has some sick lines as do the Five Sisters which offer varying height cliff jumps for the brave, under the Silverbelt Chair. The Disney Chair will get you onto the east-facing runs for morning action and the powder usually ends up here if there are strong winds. Hike up Mount Judah and access a bunch of bowls and some tight trees, or head over the back and down towards Donner Lake where your unlucky mate can pick you up in the car.

FREESTYLERS Sugar Bowl will feel the dragon's breath when a pipe is built in the '97-'98 season. The funpark under the Mount Judah Express Quad is designed by Sims pro-boarder Noah Salasnek. Noah has you lining up the first big table tops (all at different degrees), then riding into diamond-shaped jumps, quarter hits and rhythm bumps (like motorcross Whoopy Doos). It's a good park with something for everyone including a reasonable possibility of rubbing edges with the stars. The resort has plans to double the size of Noah's park to include more terrain enhancements and more vertical.

CARVERS Hard-booters will enjoy the groomers off Crow's Nest and the Chute One trails. Only nine per cent of terrain is groomed and carvers may have to end up in the deep soft stuff for a bit of variety.

MOUNTAIN FOOD The Sugar Bowl Lodge cafeteria and the mid-mountain Day Lodge serve a selection of pizzas, soups, sandwiches and salads while the Lodge dining room provides on-mountain fine dining on weekends and holidays. The barbecue gets fired up for generous meaty lunches when it's good weather.

HAZARDS AND RULES Leashes are obligatory. If you cross the boundaries, you are fully responsible for your actions and any rescue efforts will certainly hurt you financially.

EVENTS AND COMPETITIONS Sugar Bowl is one of the stops for the North American Snowboard Series, offering a $10,000 Big Air purse and a huge party. It's usually held in the first week of April.

MOUNTAIN ACCOMMODATION The resort has limited slopeside accommodation in the original '39 lodge which offers package deals — Tel: 916-426 9000.

THANKS TO Greg Murtha, Trathen Heckman, Brian Bozack and Sean Ward.

For About Town, see Lake Tahoe Area review p.52.

Main picture — Omar Lundi **Photo:** Vianney Tisseau **Courtesy:** Burton
Inset — Trathen Heckman **Photo:** Bruce Sutherland

1

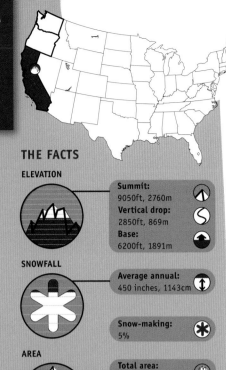

Squaw Valley

THE FACTS

ELEVATION

Summit:
9050ft, 2760m
Vertical drop:
2850ft, 869m
Base:
6200ft, 1891m

SNOWFALL

Average annual:
450 inches, 1143cm

Snow-making:
5%

AREA

Total area:
4000 acres, 1616ha

Advanced: 30%
Intermediate: 45%
Beginner: 25%

SEASON
November — July

COMMUNICATIONS
Snow report: Tel: 916-583 6955
Web site: http://www.squaw.com
E-mail: squaw@sierra.com
Mountain information:
Tel: 916-583 6985 or 1-800-545 4350

LIFTS AND TICKETS
Number of lifts:
1 cable car, 1 gondola, 4 high-speed quads, 20 chairlifts, 1 surface lift
Lift pass prices:
1/2 day: $31
1 day: $46
Multi-day: $228 (6 days)
Season: $1299
Other ticketing information:
The Ski Lake Tahoe ticket is transferable between the Big Six: Alpine Meadows, Heavenly, Kirkwood, Northstar, Sierra-at-Tahoe and Squaw Valley. The five day pass costs $220. Night-riding from 4.00pm to 9.00pm costs $12.

SNOWBOARD SHOPS
Snowave — Tel: 916-581 5705
Snowave at the turn-off to the resort has a large range of hard-core equipment and excellent tuning facilities. B+B: $25, demo $35.

SNOWBOARD SCHOOL
Squaw Snowboard School — Tel: 916-581 7263
Beginner packages with lift tickets, lessons and rentals cost $59 a day.

ON THE MOUNTAIN

Squaw is a big, brazen mountain consisting of a string of six peaks and ridges, with some of the most fearsome, in-bounds terrain anywhere in the US. From KT22's vert to Snow King's trees and gullies and over to Granite Chief's funky rollers and drops, Squaw's reputation is well-earned. You must also consider the acres of trails to tear apart between Squaw Peak, Emigrant and Broken Arrow, then throw into the pot one of California's best kept funparks and a razor sharp pipe and you've got a veritable boarding bonanza. The large lift system pumps out 49,000 bodies per hour so although you'll rarely wait to beat the next person up the hill, it's a scramble to track out the freshies. Squaw likes to bask in its former, '60s Olympic glory but they certainly have a forward-thinking approach in wholeheartedly embracing snowboarding and holding halfpipe and extreme comps.

SNOW CONDITIONS
Receiving an snowfall average of 38 feet (11 metres) plus 300 days of sunshine a season, good conditions are the rule not the exception. With a range of faces and aspects it's usually possible to escape the wind and find the powder, but if there's no new snow then man-eating moguls are the menu of the day.

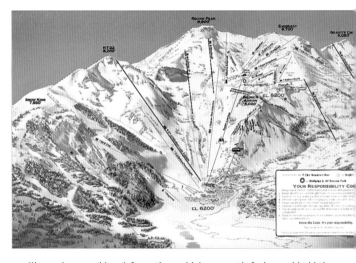

FREERIDERS
KT22's famous steeps are the place to head for after a good dump. Choose your path carefully as there are some nasty cliffs and chutes such as the Fingers. The Red Dog Chair accesses a diverse range of riding; the terrain is full of trees, gullies and some odd rock formations which are north-facing and hold the powder longer. Granite Chief has some nice trees and rocky outcrops which flatten out at the bottom near the lifts. Generally you can freeride all over this large resort especially after a good snowfall, otherwise brush up on your bump technique.

FREESTYLERS
Two of the best reasons for riding Squaw are the perfect pipe and park, serviced by the Riviera Chair and both open for 12 hours a day. The dedicated grooming crew cut the pipe with their Pipe Dragon every afternoon at about 3.00pm, re-opening for night sessions at 4.00pm. Watch out for the deceptive light just around dusk before the lights provide better definition, then check the killer sunsets. The pipe is patronised by a constant stream of good riders, meaning there are lots of queues to call "dropping". It's a rather daunting forum for inexperienced riders but it's certainly a good place to suss some moves and push your pipe riding to a new level. There are also plans to install a second pipe and funpark in the next few years.

The Terrain Park at Squaw is short on length but big on hits, comprising of a well laid-out, compact series of table tops. The hits on skier's right give beginners a go; the ones on the left are for intermediates and the two big muthas in the centre provide the main focus for the fly boys and girls. These two jumps sum up the entire Squaw philosophy that bigger and better is best. The grooming standard is excellent; two passes a day keep bumps, ruts and bomb-holed landings to a minimum.

CARVERS
Carvers can choose which levels of corduroy they want to wear thin: there's loose fit, hip-hugging or drain-pipe material. Consistent carveable trails are located from Shirley Lake to Solitude Chair, and from the Siberia Express towards Mainline. The leg-burning run from Gold Coast to the base has a varied pitch, with the option of doing the three mile (five kilometre) run under the lights when the crowds have bailed.

MOUNTAIN FOOD
The base station has a wide range of culinary choices from burgers to sushi, plus deli food at the Red Dog. Wallet drainers such as the resort at Squaw Creek and the full service restaurant at High Camp offer fine but expensive food. The Gold Coast offers the usual mountain meals and serves an expansive barbecue menu.

HAZARDS AND RULES
Leashes are obligatory and are always enforced at the base station lifts. If you transgress boundaries, flip inverted aerials or ride out of control, you will lose your pass.

ABOUT TOWN

Squaw is a sprawling mountain village, evolved as a direct consequence of hosting the '60 Olympics. It has gone from four double chairlifts and a rope tow to a modern 27 piece, state-of-the-art lift system. Lodgings and services have kept up with this growth, making it possible to stay in close proximity to the lifts and choose from 22 assorted cafés, restaurants, speciality food shops and bars, plus a cinema complex for evening entertainment. Alternatively you may choose to stay either at Tahoe City or Truckee which are both a short drive away on Highway 89.

ACCOMMODATION Considering there are 2400 beds within 400 yards of the lifts and another 15,000 in the immediate area, finding a bed should be easy. Squaw operates an efficient Central Reservations service which can hook you up with all sorts of accommodation from self-contained condos to plush hotels. They can also arrange airline tickets, car rentals, lift tickets and dining and entertainment options. Mountain pass packages start at $79 per night per person (based on double occupancy for three days or more) with lift tickets valid at Squaw, Alpine Meadows, Northstar and Sugar Bowl. Central Reservations — Tel: 916-583 6985 or 1-800-545 4350.

FOOD Along with some classy expensive restaurants like Plumpjacks, you can find reasonably priced meals such as Chinese from the Mandarin Villa. Sunnyside does a great fish taco on Wednesdays. At the cheaper end, the Squaw Valley General Store and Sandwich Company has super subs (bread rolls) and enough produce to sort out self-caterers. Coyote's Mexican Grill is heavy on portions but light on your wallet. If this selection leaves you still feeling hungry, there are more choices down the hill in Tahoe City.

NIGHTLIFE The hot aprés bar is the Red Dog which has a sun terrace. Later on there isn't too much going on in the valley for hard-core party types. Take in a movie or check out the bars in the hotels for lubrication after a night-riding session.

OTHER ACTIVITIES There's a bungy-jumping tower, an ice-skating rink, tennis courts, a swimming lagoon and spa, all located at the High Camp complex and accessed via the 150 person, lamped-up cable car. An indoor climbing wall is housed by the Cable Car Building Station for those who have any energy left over after a hard day of riding.

THANKS TO Brent MacLean, Mad Dog and the grooming team, plus the Burton boys and girls who shredded the pipe continuously.

For more About Town options, see Lake Tahoe Area review p.52.

GETTING THERE FROM TRUCKEE AND TAHOE CITY
By bus: An extensive shuttle service operates regularly from Reno and all round the lake to Squaw Valley.
By car: Squaw is on the north-west side of Lake Tahoe, conveniently located mid-way between Truckee and Tahoe City on Highway 89. The resort is 45 miles (70 kilometres) from Reno and 200 miles (320 kilometres) from San Francisco on Interstate 80.

Top — Jason McAlister **Photo:** Quinn Sheilds
Bottom — Squaw pipe **Photo:** Bruce Sutherland

THE FACTS

ELEVATION

Summit:
8637ft, 2634m
Vertical drop:
1802ft, 550m
Base:
6835ft, 2084m

SNOWFALL

Average annual:
425 inches, 1080cm

Snow-making:
9%

AREA

Total area:
2000 acres, 808ha

Advanced: 35%
Intermediate: 40%
Beginner: 25%

SEASON
Mid-November — end of May/July

COMMUNICATIONS
Web site: http://www.skialpine.com
Mountain information:
Tel: 916-583 4232 or 1-800-441 4423
Fax: 916-583 0963

③

LIFTS AND TICKETS
Number of lifts:
1 high-speed six person chairlift, 1 high-speed
quad, 9 chairlifts, 1 surface lift
Lift pass prices:
1/2 day: $32
1 day: $46
Multi-day: $205 (5 days)
Season: N/A
Other ticketing information:
Return your full day lift ticket before 12.30pm to
receive a credit coupon towards another day.
Choose from the many North Shore areas on the
Ski Tahoe North interchangeable ticket costing
$264 for six days. (See Squaw Valley review p.60
for the Ski Lake Tahoe transferable ticket.)

SNOWBOARD SHOPS
The Board Room — Tel: 916-581 8241
At the Alpine Meadows base, B+B: $40, demo $49.

SNOWBOARD SCHOOL
Alpine Meadows' Ski School — Tel: 916-583 4232
Beginner packages start at $49 (rental, lifts and
lesson). They also have intermediate and expert
classes from $32 for a two hour lesson.

Alpine Meadows

ON THE MOUNTAIN

Alpine Meadows sits on the ridge of mountains that merge into Squaw Valley and the two resorts have some terrain similarities. Meadows definitely has the more laid-back atmosphere however, along with the inauspicious title of being the last resort in the Tahoe area to allow snowboarders on their slopes. Since the gates have opened, riders have flooded into the area as it has some of the most boarder-friendly terrain and chilled boundary laws of the resorts around the lake. With Ward Peak and Scott Peak encircling the base area, it's impossible to see the wide expanses of the Back Bowls. These contain cornice drops and wooded areas sprinkled over a large open face of consistent steepness. Alpine Meadows' relaxed boundary policy allows riders access to some of the most beautiful back-country riding in the area.

SNOW CONDITIONS With an east to north-east orientation and a respectable 8637 foot (2634 metre) peak, Alpine gets its share of any snow about. The average snowfall is around 35 feet (ten metres).

FREERIDERS Alpine Meadows is a pure freeriding mountain with 12 lifts servicing a substantial powder playground. Most of the goods are way off the resort's beaten path although after a dump there are a ton of obvious lines in-bounds. The super smooth Summit Six will beam you up to the top of Ward Peak, where you can traverse out along the ridge with dozens of cornices and chutes leading into bowls and clumps of trees all the way back down to base. The run at the northern end of the ridge goes down to the carpark through wicked, rolling terrain. These trees, hits and open steeps on the resort boundary are the last slopes to be tracked out.

The Back Bowls and Sherwood Chair are a good morning venue for softer snow, or head towards the powder holding trees on the north side of Scott Peak and the Hidden Knolls area. If you're really into chasing the powder, then the hike past Big Bend Bowl opens up a wealth of possibilities. Between Counterweight Gully and Expert Short Cut, you'll find plenty of steep stuff in the trees around Sherwood Cliffs. Scott Chair and the Lake View Chair access consistent steeps so long as you stay off the groomers and head through the trees. The Back Bowls will provide some fine freeriding. This area is accessed from either the Sherwood Chair or by dropping over the back from Summit Six and the Alpine Bowl Lift. From Sun Bowl to Sherwood Face there are acres of shredable, wide open faces with a small traverse at the bottom to get back to Sherwood Chair. You'll probably find some freshies if you hike along the ridge into the chutes and tree runs past Big Bend Bowl, but be aware of your global positioning or you're in for a long hike out.

FREESTYLERS There is no funpark or halfpipe but if you can't catch any air in this resort, then you're not looking hard enough. To the right of the Weasel Chair is a long, winding gully-come-halfpipe with plenty of hits for the compulsive jibber. There are terrain park plans afoot for the '97-'98 season.

CARVERS Carvers will be happy riding Summit Six, then going down Alpine Bowl into the Rock Garden or taking a choice of good groomers back to base. Scott Peak has plenty of steep corduroy and Sherwood Run is the inside word for morning softeners.

MOUNTAIN FOOD The Base Lodge has all the regular mountain food at regular mountain prices. The tiny Ice Bar, a timber hut at the bottom of Sherwood Chair, does surprisingly good eats and has an afternoon happy hour. The Chalet is a good mid-mountain refuelling stop.

HAZARDS AND RULES Meadows gets the thumbs up for sensible open boundary rules, allowing you to use the lifts to access the back-country. This doesn't mean you can ignore signs, closed areas or the ski patrol.

EVENTS AND COMPETITIONS Alpine Meadows hosts King Carve, Boardercross and Lord of the Boards.

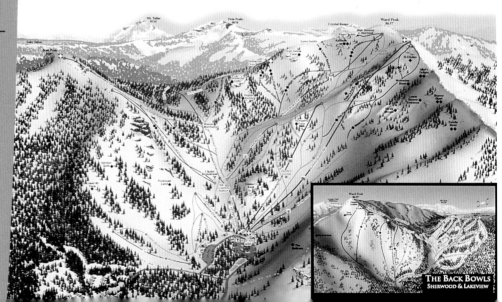

THE BACK BOWLS
SHERWOOD & LAKEVIEW

ABOUT TOWN

Alpine Meadows doesn't really qualify as a town although there are a lot of nice-looking residences tucked away in the trees. The focus of attention is the turn-off on Highway 89 where the impressive River Ranch Lodge clings to the banks of the tempestuous Truckee River. It has a 100 year-old history as a popular watering spot for passengers on the narrow gauge railway that used to run beside the river.

ACCOMMODATION Alpine Meadows has a Central Reservations service — Tel: 1-800-949 3296 for slopeside or Tahoe City pads. The River Ranch Lodge has rooms from $55-$125, all decorated with early American antiques — Tel: 916-585 4264 or 1-800-535 9900.

FOOD The River Ranch has great food served in a cosy environment. You can get seafood and steaks aplenty but their speciality is the selection of game meats. Experience elk for a tasty change.

NIGHTLIFE The River Ranch seems to be the only choice if you don't plan to go into Tahoe City. There's a good bar, beer, food and views — what more do you need?

OTHER ACTIVITIES Snowmobiling, ice-skating, food and alcohol.

THANKS TO Brinn Talbot, Justin Cox, Daryl Butterfield and Trathan Heckman.

For more About Town options, see Lake Tahoe Area review p.52.

Top — Justin Cox **Photo:** Bruce Sutherland
Bottom Left — Justin Cox **Photo:** Bruce Sutherland
Bottom Right — **Photo:** Gregory Beck **Courtesy:** Alpine Meadows Ski Resort

3

GETTING THERE FROM TRUCKEE AND TAHOE CITY

By bus: Local shuttle bus from Truckee or Tahoe City.
By car: It's a 13 mile (21 km) drive south on Highway 89 from Truckee, or six miles (ten km) north on Highway 89 from Tahoe City.

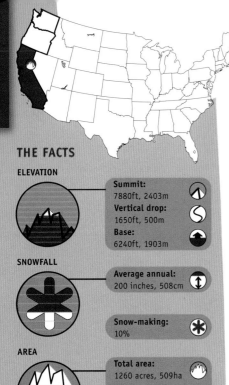

Ski Homewood

THE FACTS

ELEVATION

Summit:
7880ft, 2403m
Vertical drop:
1650ft, 500m
Base:
6240ft, 1903m

SNOWFALL

Average annual:
200 inches, 508cm

Snow-making:
10%

AREA

Total area:
1260 acres, 509ha

Advanced: 35%
Intermediate: 50%
Beginner: 15%

SEASON
Late November — late April

COMMUNICATIONS
Snow report: Tel: 916-525 2900
Web site: http://www.skihomewoodcom
E-mail: smile@skihomewood.com
Mountain information:
Tel: 916-525 2992

LIFTS AND TICKETS
Number of lifts:
4 chairlifts, 4 surface lifts
Lift pass prices
1/2 day: $25
1 day: $35
Multi-day: $93 (3 out of 4 days)
Season: $595
Other ticketing information:
Join the Frequent Flyer Programme for $15 and
save $5 on every day pass you buy, plus every fifth
ticket is free.

SNOWBOARD SHOPS
Ski Homewood Rental Shop — Tel: 916-525 2992
Offers top of the line Morrow snowboards and
Airwalk boots. B+B: $30.

SNOWBOARD SCHOOL
Ski Homewood Snowboard School
Tel: 916-525 2992
The beginner package includes rentals, lesson and
a beginner lift ticket; prices from $59. Caroline
Falkenburg runs Adventures in Snowboarding for
Women clinics six times throughout the season.

GETTING THERE FROM TRUCKEE AND TAHOE CITY
By car: Drive six miles (ten km) south from Tahoe
City on Highway 89, or drive 19 miles (30 km) north
from South Lake Tahoe on Highway 89.
By bus: Ride TART (Tahoe Area Regional Transit)
around north Lake Tahoe and Ski Homewood will
credit the bus fare towards the price of a lift pass.
By shuttle: The Tahoe Lake Lapper leaves South
Lake Tahoe at 8.00am and arrives at Homewood
one hour later, cost $5. The return trip leaves Ski
Homewood at 3.50pm.

Ski Homewood

ON THE MOUNTAIN

Ski Homewood is located just six miles (nine kilometres) south of Tahoe City on Lake Tahoe, and there are excellent lake views from every run. In laid-back Californian style, Homewood offers groomed boulevards and good tree riding in a small, friendly resort. What's more, the local resort employees are willing to divulge their favourite hidden powder stashes. The real gift that Ski Homewood has been blessed with is the small steep bowl on the southern boundary called Quail Face, which has truly sick tree riding in the right conditions. The main drawback is that all the steeps on the mountain are relatively short and it's easy to get caught in the long flat boundary runs back to the lift bases.

SNOW CONDITIONS Homewood's top elevation is protected by Ellis Peak at 8760 feet (2671 metres) which is an effective wind break for storms coming in predominantly from the west. The resort's abundant trees collect huge powder piles.

FREERIDERS Although much smaller than its neighbours, Homewood has some good options if you search the glades and fringes of this forested freeriding festival. There are two main areas for freeriders to explore. The first is the steep pitches of Quail Face on the southern boundary of the ski area. The tree riding on a powder day is the best on the mountain and rivals anything else in the Lake Tahoe region. The drawback is that the face is short, and you have to traverse the summit ridge from the top of the Ellis Chair to get there because the lift system channels riders towards the northern side of the ski area.

The second freeriding area on the northern side is more mellow, with trails cut into the trees on either side of the ridge. For a great warm-up with no crowds, head to Miner's Delight under the Quad Chair. On the other side of the Rainbow Ridge trail, Ivory Face offers face shots in pow and stays soft for days after a storm. Woody Fellers has almost guaranteed snow on account of its north-facing aspect and tight trees. After a dump head for the wide spaces of Glory Hole.

FREESTYLERS The park near the top of the Juniper-Nugget run was designed by pro-rider Terry Kidwell. It is open all season and the changing terrain features usually consist of four expert table tops, a spine and four smaller tables for intermediate riders. Nightly snowcat clean-ups keep it looking good.

CARVERS Speed demons will like the short sharp groomers but could get frustrated with the lack of vertical on the best runs. The Quad Chair is first pick for the open parallel trails which cut down to the northern boundary. Rainbow Ridge is a great warm-up; lay out a sharp left-hander onto any of the runs which dive off it for more of a challenge. Tailings has a good intermediate pitch and Jimmy's Run is a well-kept secret with corduroy that lingers till late afternoon. For a change of scene, the blue trails below Quail Face drop off nicely into a steep pitch at the base of the Quail Chair.

MOUNTAIN FOOD The Ridge Pub and Grill, at the north side Base Lodge, features a variety of meals including soups, salads, burgers, pizza and Mexican.

HAZARDS AND RULES Leashes are required but Homewood employees stick to explaining the rules rather than harassing people without them. Quail Face is a hazardous avalanche area, check with the ski patrol before attempting to ride it.

THANKS TO Collier Cook and the Ski Homewood crew.

For About Town in Tahoe City, see Lake Tahoe Area review p.52.

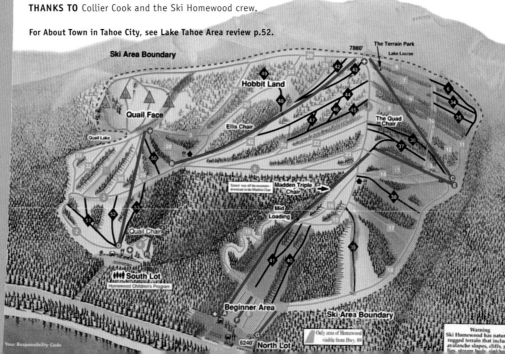

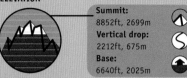

THE FACTS

ELEVATION

Summit:
8852ft, 2699m

Vertical drop:
2212ft, 675m

Base:
6640ft, 2025m

SNOWFALL

Average annual:
450 inches, 1143cm

Snow-making:
None

AREA

Total area:
2000 acres, 808ha

Advanced: 25%
Intermediate: 50%
Beginner: 25%

SEASON
Mid-November — mid-April

COMMUNICATIONS
Snow report: Tel: 916-659 7475
Web-site: http://www.sierratahoe.com
E-mail: sierra@sierra.net
Mountain information:
Tel: 916-659 7453
Fax: 916-659 7749

LIFTS AND TICKETS
Number of lifts:
3 high-speed quads, 6 chairlifts, 1 magic carpet
Lift pass prices:
1/2 day: $29, $22 (13-22yrs)
1 day: $42, $32 (13-22yrs)
Multi-day: $105 (3 out of 4 days), $81 (13-22yrs)
Season: N/A
Other ticketing information:
Parents can buy one transferable ticket and take turns with it. If you return a day pass by 12.30pm, you get a credit towards the next full day pass purchased. (See Squaw Valley review p.60 for the Ski Lake Tahoe transferable ticket.)

SNOWBOARD SHOPS
Boarding House — Tel: 916-542 5228
The place to rent, buy and get local tips on the best lines on the mountain.

SNOWBOARD SCHOOL
Sierra-at-Tahoe Ski and Snowboard School
Tel: 916-659 7453
A beginner package includes equipment, a full lift pass and 105 minute lesson for $52. They offer free Skill Improvement clinics for high intermediate and advanced riders on a limited availability basis.

GETTING THERE FROM SOUTH LAKE TAHOE
By car: Sierra-at-Tahoe is 12 miles (18 km) from South Lake Tahoe. Take Highway 50 over Echo Summit to the Sierra-at-Tahoe road on the left.
By shuttle: A free shuttle runs five times daily from South Lake Tahoe.

Sierra-at-Tahoe

ON THE MOUNTAIN

Sierra-at-Tahoe is the most densely forested resort in the Tahoe region. Ribbons of trails are cut into these magnificent trees, offering slope angles for everyone. Steeper terrain is found on the left side of the Base Lodge, intermediate runs on the right in the West Bowl area and gentle beginner slopes in front of the lodge. These three areas all have spanking new quad chairs installed next to the old dinosaurs which means more turns per session. Add a good halfpipe, multiple funparks and the fact that it's off the beaten track, and you'll find Sierra an essential Tahoe stop.

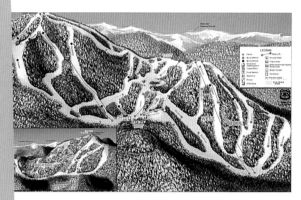

SNOW CONDITIONS With the bulk of the resort facing north-west and loads of Californian sun, soft afternoon conditions prevail. The trees act like a refrigerator however, storing the powder almost indefinitely. The resort is in the same storm path that brings huge average snowfall figures to Kirkwood, so lack of cover is rarely a problem.

FREERIDERS The maze of trails around the resort are either blighted by moguls if they're steep or by boredom if they're mellow. This is perfect because it keeps the freeriders in the trees and the pinheads on the trails. From the top of the Grand View Express, any number of lines can be taken through the timber from East About on the eastern boundary. The trunks are well-spaced with a steep pitch and the odd tight spot to negotiate. These off-trail areas are accessible when snow conditions permit and are not patrolled; enter at your own risk. Under the Nob Hill Chair you can ride the Ice Cliffs and some deceptively steep shots through the trees. More of the same can be found if you ride the trees around Horsetail in the West Bowl. Intermediates will dig all the runs on the right of the West Bowl Express Quad and the glades around Eldorado over on the Backside.

FREESTYLERS Named after the perfect Hawaiian wave, Pipeline is one of the longest halfpipes in North America. Situated on Upper Main, skier's right of Nob Hill Chair, this dragoned ditch provides excellent transitions and a razor sharp lip. There isn't one terrain park at Sierra — there are four, labelled as Fun Zones. The Zones are designed for both snowboarders and skiers and provide a consistent forum for maximising air time. Pyramid Park and the Gauntlet keep skiers out of your hair while you session Snowboard Alley and the boarder-only Pipeline. Banks, berms, quarterpipes, table tops, gaps, spines and boosting kickers abound, all with well-maintained landings. There are also some good wall hits on the way down Sugar N' Spice.

CARVERS Carving terrain is limited to the West Bowl where Clipper, Powder Horn and Dogwood provide some wide trails for arcing. All the steep stuff on the right of the resort gets bumped quickly, leaving you with the only sensible option; loosen up and hit the trees.

MOUNTAIN FOOD The Bake Shoppe Emporium does the coffee, muffin, smoothie, cookie thing in the Base Lodge. Here you'll also find the Aspen Café and the Sierra Pub where pizza and sandwiches slide down with the local microbrews. At the summit, the Grand View Grill and Lake View Barbecue provide a panoramic backdrop for recharging on pizza and great tortilla wraps. West Bowl Snacks is a tiny hut-come-caravan with picnic tables to keep you out there riding.

Swatch Boarder X course at Sierra
Photo: Bruce Sutherland

HAZARDS AND RULES Run-away equipment devices required. The off-trail terrain outside the Huckleberry Mountain boundary will get you to the goods but unless you know where to hit the road, you will be post-holing or worse.

EVENTS AND COMPETITIONS USASA series, Mountain Dew Snowboard Festival, Swatch/ISF World Boarder-X Tour, Boarding for Breast Cancer.

THANKS TO Ted Austin, Erin Entwistle, Bernie Bernthall and Suzanne.

For About Town in South Lake Tahoe, see Heavenly review p.62.

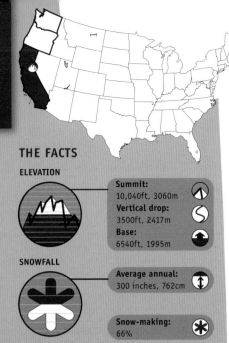

THE FACTS

ELEVATION

Summit:
10,040ft, 3060m
Vertical drop:
3500ft, 2417m
Base:
6540ft, 1995m

SNOWFALL

Average annual:
300 inches, 762cm

Snow-making:
66%

AREA

Total area:
4800 acres, 1943ha

Advanced: 35%
Intermediate: 45%
Beginner: 20%

SEASON
Mid-November — April

COMMUNICATIONS
Snow reports: Tel: 916-541 7544 or 702-586 7000
Web site: http://www.skiheavenly.com
E-mail: Via the web-site
Mountain information:
Tel: 702-586 7000

LIFTS AND TICKETS
Number of lifts:
1 aerial tram, 1 six-passenger high-speed chair,
3 high-speed quads, 15 chairlifts, 5 surface lifts,
1 magic carpet
Lift pass prices:
1/2 day: $33, $26 (13-15yrs)
1 day: $47, $34 (13-15yrs)
Multi-day: $246 (6 out of 8 days)
Season: N/A
Other ticketing information:
A ride in the Red Tram will cost you $12. (See
Squaw Valley review p.60 for the Ski Lake Tahoe
transferable ticket.)

SNOWBOARD SHOPS
The Village Mountain Surf Shop
Tel: 916-541 2726
This is the main boarders' shop — it has all the
gear along with rentals and repairs. B+B: $18,
performance $24, demo $27.
The Boardinghouse — Tel: 916-542 5228
Next to Long's Drugs on Highway 50.
Max Snowboard Rentals — Tel: 916-543 0779

SNOWBOARD SCHOOL
Heavenly Snowboard School
Tel: 702-586 7000
Caters for levels one to nine (pro). Beginner
deals start at $69, including equipment and a
limited lift pass.

LAKE TAHOE AREA
Heavenly

ON THE MOUNTAIN

Heavenly Mountain is situated on the south shore of Lake Tahoe, towering above the man-made casino towers that hug the slim swathe of flat land between the water and the peaks. Heavenly is an impressive bold-looking mountain with the unusual distinction of being bisected by the California-Nevada state line. The Californian side has a healthy covering of trees right to the top of the Sky Express Quad. The Nevada side has a more easterly aspect and more open terrain above the band of canyons which characterise the eastern boundary. The character of each state is reflected in the terrain; there are smooth groomed freeways among a maze of trees on the Californian side, and brash narrow chutes with fewer freeways and trees on the Nevada side. You can park in either state and access both sides providing you use the efficient lift system to avoid long traverses or walks. On powder days it lives up to its name and looking out over the lake, you'll think as Mark Twain did that this is where you 'obtain the air the angels breathe'.

SNOW CONDITIONS The sun hits the Nevada side in the morning and it's a good place to start if there's no fresh. Head for the Californian side late morning where the trees hold seemingly endless pockets of powder. Heavenly boasts an average annual snowfall of 21 feet (seven metres) and tops up with almost half that again of man-made snow.

FREERIDERS Freeriding for experienced riders is all contained in the Killebrew and Mott Canyon area where there are half a dozen chutes to choose from. Some are rad with cliffs and drop-offs while others build up walls of snow on the sides. Killebrew has some nice stuff on the eastern boundary but the traverse out will get your leg muscles screaming. Try out the lower front face runs from the top of the Aerial Tramway to the Californian Lodge. Intermediates will like the Ridge Run and Powderbowl Run as well as Big Dipper on the Nevada side. If it's tree runs you're after, head to the top of the Sky Express Quad. Take a minute to appreciate the incredible lake views, then choose any number of spots to drop into the well-forested slopes off the Skyline Trail.

FREESTYLERS The halfpipe is at the end of a spacious funpark under the Olympic Chair on the Nevada side. It's reasonably well-kept and definitely well-used; look out for the large catcher's mitt quarter hit at the end. Stylers can take-off, go flying and land at the funpark called the Airport. With the Olympic Chair as the viewing deck, you can watch riders wind their way down a selection of table tops, a few small berms and some nice little kickers to the halfpipe. Just after the pipe is a testy table top which launches you airborne into the Nevada desert vista.

CARVERS Carvers should head to Ellies and Orion near the Dipper Express Quad or to the front face runs if they're not too bumped out. There are plenty of trails about with sweet, smooth sections (such as Big Dipper and Galaxy) but beware of the flats, particularly around the Sky Deck Lodge.

MOUNTAIN FOOD The Top of the Tram restaurant serves excellent, reasonably priced food with the best eating view in Tahoe. East Peak Lodge has epicurean sandwiches. The Sky Deck has a barbecue scene where you can bring food and cook for yourself, although it's hard to beat their huge portions of ribs.

HAZARDS AND RULES Leashes are obligatory. Laws in both California and Nevada mean it's possible you'll be arrested for crossing the boundary or entering closed areas. At the very least you will lose your lift pass.

ACCOMMODATION Take a drive along South Lake Tahoe Boulevard and assess the multitude of hotels from the basic to the bourgeois. At the top end the Embassy Suites have fully serviced luxury rooms and an endless breakfast for $129 to $229 a double. At the budget end there are plenty of basic roadside motels from $29 and up. On the south-west shore lies Camp Richardson; the cool cabins are ideal for groups with fully kitted kitchens, tons of trees and a placid water front — Tel: 916-541 1801 or 1-800-544 1801. Central Reservations — Tel: 702-586 7000 or 1-800-243 2836.

FOOD At Harrah's casino-top restaurant, two people can dine superbly and will agree that the $100 was better spent upstairs than on the gambling table downstairs. If it's water views you're after, those at the Beacon at Camp Richardson will impress along with the reasonably priced menu and good seafood. Mulligan's serves decent food at decent prices, as does Chevy's tex-mex diner. La Familia is a tiny, authentic Mexican that's hard to find but well worth the effort, and Sato's is the cheapest sushi house in town. There's good coffee to be had at Hot Gossip and Alpen Sierra where coffee has become an art form. Try Red Hut, Ernie's and Chris's Café for breakfast, and Sprouts for a health food stop.

NIGHTLIFE Aside from spending fun-filled hours feeding the one-armed bandits or believing your luck will change on the Black Jack table, there are a few good night spots. On Thursday nights, Rojo's has good live bands such as Cosmic Freeway with the added bonus of $1 beers till 11.00pm. A typical, gregarious Irish bar with live music, Mulligan's always draws a crowd. McP's is another fine drinking venue up near the casinos, otherwise it's complimentaries at the casino which are only cheap when you win.

OTHER ACTIVITIES Cross-country skiing, snow-shoeing, climbing, tobogganing, mountain-biking, paragliding, bungy-jumping, wakeboarding, windsurfing and even surfing after a huge storm.

THANKS TO Monica Bandows and Bryan, Chris and Berto, Mike Weber and Tracey, Mark Cowley and Doug Atkinson.

6

ABOUT TOWN

The original inhabitants, the Washoe and Paiutes, thought of this place as the giver of life and called it 'Da ow a ga' which means 'edge of the big waters': Nowadays South Lake Tahoe is characterised by the obvious division of being split by the state line. The bulk of the population live on the Californian side while the Nevada side is instantly heralded by high rises and bright lights. A cluster of casinos cling to the border, channelling Californian cash into their coffers. Being a year-round destination resort, South Lake Tahoe has grown into a tourist metropolis with stunning views. Developments to the tune of $850 million are planned so there will be substantial changes to the region in the next few years.

Top left — **Photo:** John Kelly **Courtesy:** Heavenly Valley Ski Resort
Top right — Heavenly view to South Lake Tahoe **Photo:** Bruce Sutherland
Bottom — Heavenly pipe **Photo:** Bruce Sutherland

GETTING THERE

By air: Reno-Tahoe International Airport is serviced by nine airlines including Delta Airlines — Tel: 1-800-221 1212. The Tahoe Casino Express runs 18 times a day to South Lake Tahoe — Tel: 1-800-243 2836.
By bus: Greyhound — Tel: 1-800-231 2222.
By car: Straddling Highway 50, South Lake Tahoe is accessible from the west on Highway 50 (Sacramento in two hours and San Francisco in three and a half hours). From Reno, either take Highway 395 down to Carson City and hook up with Highway 50 around the south end of Lake Tahoe, or take Highway 80 onto the scenic route past Truckee and Tahoe City on Highway 89.
Getting around: A free shuttle bus runs every 20 minutes around South Lake Tahoe to the Heavenly base — Tel: 916-541 7548.

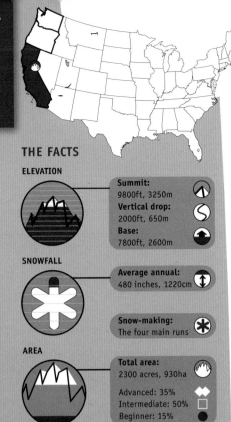

THE FACTS

ELEVATION

Summit:
9800ft, 3250m
Vertical drop:
2000ft, 650m
Base:
7800ft, 2600m

SNOWFALL

Average annual:
480 inches, 1220cm

Snow-making:
The four main runs

AREA

Total area:
2300 acres, 930ha

Advanced: 35%
Intermediate: 50%
Beginner: 15%

SEASON
Mid-November — May

COMMUNICATIONS
Snow reports: Tel: 510-939 SNOW or 916-448 SNOW
Web site: http://www.skikirkwood.com
Mountain information:
Tel: 209-258 6000
Fax: 209-258 8899

LIFTS AND TICKETS
Number of lifts:
10 chairlifts, 2 surface lifts
Lift pass prices:
1/2 day: $31, $23 (13-24yrs)
1 day: $42, $32 (13-24yrs)
Multi-day: $195 (5 days)
Season: $650
Other ticketing information:
Avid Skier Card purchasers earn one day free for
every four full day tickets purchased. Discounts are
available on Kirkwood's one day lift tickets, Learn
to Snowboard Programme and Mighty Mountain
Children's Centre at all northern California and
western Nevada Bass Ticket outlets. For special
group rates — Tel: 209-258 7284. (See Squaw
Valley review p.60 for the Ski Lake Tahoe
transferable ticket.)

SNOWBOARD SHOPS
Kirkwood Snowboard Centre — Tel: 209-258 6000
The centre has just spent half a million greenbacks
on a state-of-the-art facility full of new hardware.
B+B: $30.

SNOWBOARD SCHOOL
Kirkwood Snowboard — Tel: 209-258 6000
Beginner three-day packages are available for $55
per day (gear inclusive). Two and a half hour
snowboard clinics cost $25.

Kirkwood

ON THE MOUNTAIN

Speak to any snowboarder in the Tahoe region and they'll invariably say Kirkwood when asked for their favourite resort. The mountain is a special place that could easily be considered the largest natural snowboard park in the US. The high altitude, arcing ridge line contains steep chutes, wide open bowls, long gullies, crisp corduroy trails, hair-raising cliff drops and huge wind lips. Due to the high percentage of advanced terrain, Kirkwood hosts a round of the US Extremes. The mountain has a friendly atmosphere and everyone seems to be smiling all the time. This is mainly due to the superb riding and general lack of hustle and bustle in one of America's top five naturally snow-blessed resorts.

SNOW CONDITIONS Kirkwood has a predominantly northerly aspect and boasts an average snowfall of almost 40 feet (12 metres). It's one of the only resorts in California where you'll need a snorkel on huge powder days; Kirkwood can catch storms that the other resorts never get a sniff of. Steepness abounds, resulting in claims by the avalanche control that they use more dynamite than any other US resort.

FREERIDERS Powder days are what Kirkwood is all about. Get up early and head to Cornice Chair 6 because it always opens first. Sentinel Bowl (skier's left) and Wagon Wheel Bowl (skier's right) will get you warmed up for Wagon Wheel Chair 10. This takes you up to The Wall, from where you can head down to Eagle Bowl and the flats near Caples Crest Chair 2. This leads on to Sunrise Chair 4 and the whole east-facing, morning sun-catching side of the mountain. The chutes off Harry's Lip are steep and interspersed with some nice trees. Areas like The Sisters and Chamoix should only be attempted by pro-air junkies, and only when conditions are right. Apparently only two riders dropped Chamoix the whole '96-'97 season.

FREESTYLERS Kirkwood's funpark, located under Chair 2, maintains the high reputation of the resort with massive mounds designed by terrain park guru Darren McClaskey and pushed into shape by grooming svengali Rich Maile. It's easy to tell that Rich is an old surfer when faced with some of his waves of snow. The perfect quarterpipes, table tops, snake and large spine jump are nicely spread out. The lack of a halfpipe in the funpark isn't a disadvantage considering the plentiful natural gullies tucked away on the front face. These snaking, banked runs vary from wide and slow to narrow and fast with the odd kicker, lip and hit to give intermediates a more forgiving forum to practice in. Try The Drain, Snowsnake Gully and over underneath the Rabbit runs.

CARVERS The quality of the groomed slopes is excellent and the trails snake all over the mountain — it's all good. The Wagon Trail, off Wagon Wheel Chair 10, has the most consistent gradient for carving, plus there are some great rolling runs over by Sunrise Way.

MOUNTAIN FOOD Nachos from the main lodge are legendary and cheap, and can feed four hungry people at a sitting. Otherwise head for the Cornice Café (across the road from the bottom of Cornice Chair 6) where there's a full menu and tasty beers. The Warming Hut near the base of Sunrise Chair 4 is the on-mountain barbecue spot.

HAZARDS AND RULES Leashes are mandatory. A word of warning for all: this mountain can be extremely dangerous. It is not uncommon for avalanches to go all the way to the carpark. Respect closed areas; they are there for a reason. Boundaries are strictly enforced and although there is some nice looking back-country, it can't be accessed by using the lift system. Hiking to these areas is possible but not without an experienced local guide and all the safety kit.

EVENTS AND COMPETITIONS Kirkwood is the host site for the American Pro Snowboard Tour, US Extremes.

ABOUT TOWN

In 1860 Zachary Kirkwood crossed the Sierra Nevadas into a narrow valley. Surrounded by alpine lakes and towering cliffs, he staked his claim for land below a horseshoe-shaped mountain that now bears his name. Kirkwood is today a small town with most of the high standard services and amenities clustered along the access road (which doubles as the carpark) or in the resort's lodges.

The bulk of the houses, which are inhabited by locals and seasonal staff, are tucked away on side streets with only a small proportion of condos and units for holidaymakers. Most mountain users drive from South Lake Tahoe. Kirkwood is self-sufficient in terms of power, water and sewage which keeps another bunch of smiling powder-bums in work. Presently the town council are investing large sums in upgrading the lifts and in building further lodges and condos.

Isolated in the south-west ranges of Tahoe over Carson Pass, Kirkwood requires more time and effort to get to than most of the region's resorts. This helps cultivate the chilled-out atmosphere that characterises Kirkwood and keeps numbers down, especially in bad weather.

ACCOMMODATION Accommodation at Kirkwood is difficult to come by, especially during peak periods. The resort lets out 80 slopeside condos at average to high prices. The advantage is that if it snows hard and the road closes, you are in heaven with the privileged few and the prices become justified. One option is the cabins at Caples Lake Resort. They are cheap, particularly for groups, and have fine views across the lake to the resort — Tel: 209-258 8888. For information and bookings call Central Reservations — Tel: 209-258 7000 or 1-800-967 7500.

FOOD The Kirkwood Inn was built by Zachary in 1864, right on the county line. The establishment was famous for having had its bar on wheels so that it could be moved around depending on which sheriff showed up to enforce the prohibition laws. It is now famous for its large breakfasts, larger lunches and fine evening dining. The Caples Lake Resort has majestic views from its lakeside restaurant and food to match the rustic fireside atmosphere. If waiting till dinner is too much, the Cornice has a great menu for those with an afternoon appetite.

NIGHTLIFE Zac's bar in the Main Lodge is a favourite for local employees. Zac's closes early and most people head down to the Cornice. Due to its great selection of microbrews (including even Guinness) on tap, this is the town's favoured watering-hole. If things kick on from here, the Kirkwood Inn is the next stop, where upside-down shots and mustard races are local drinking rituals.

The good thing about Kirkwood's nightlife is that nothing tempts you out too late so you can still make the first lift with only a minimal hangover.

OTHER ACTIVITIES All the usual Lake Tahoe sports can be pursued here. In summer the mountain-biking scene is popular — catch a chair to the top and belt down all those runs you did in the winter.

THANKS TO Tania Magidson, Rich Maile and especially to Andrew Boucher who let us in on his considerable knowledge of the area.

7

Top — Andrew Boucher **Photo:** Bruce Sutherland

Middle left — Back-country lines **Photo:** Bruce Sutherland

Middle right — Kirkwood Inn back in the good ol' days **Photo:** Bruce Sutherland

GETTING THERE

By air: An airport shuttle runs regularly from Reno-Tahoe International Airport to South Lake Tahoe properties. If you're planning to stay in Kirkwood and fly into Reno, a rental car is recommended for ease.
By car: From South Lake Tahoe, the drive takes 35 minutes on Highway 89 south to Highway 88.
Getting around: Kirkwood offers a shuttle service from most of the Tahoe Lodging Properties for $3 (round trip). Reservations can be made upon arrival at your hotel — Tel: 209-258 6000.

June Mountain

THE FACTS

ELEVATION

Summit: 10,135ft, 3091m
Vertical drop: 2590ft, 790m
Base: 7545ft, 2301m

SNOWFALL

Average annual: 250 inches, 635cm

Snow-making: None

AREA

Total area: 500 acres, 202ha

Advanced: 20%
Intermediate: 45%
Beginner: 35%

SEASON

December — April

COMMUNICATIONS

Snow reports: Tel: 760-934 2224
Mountain information:
Tel: 619-648 7733 or 1-888-JUNE MTN
Fax: 619-648 7733

LIFTS AND TICKETS

Number of lifts:
2 high-speed quads, 5 chairlifts, 1 beginner tow
Lift pass prices:
1/2 day: $25, $20 (13-18 yrs)
1 day: $35, $25 (13-18 yrs)
Multi-day: $158 (5 out of 6 days)
Gold season pass: $1350 (includes Mammoth)
Other ticketing information:
$10 tickets are available on Wednesdays, excluding holidays.

SNOWBOARD SHOPS

Ernie's Tackle and Ski Shop — Tel: 619-648 7756
A small but well-stocked shop with essential spares. B+B: $27.

SNOWBOARD SCHOOL

June Mountain Snowboard School
Tel: 619-648 7733
Rentals and lesson packages are on offer from beginners' courses on gentle slopes to advanced halfpipe and funpark tricks. Beginners' day packages from $73 (equipment and lift pass inclusive).

ON THE MOUNTAIN

June Mountain is considered to be Mammoth's little sister, however with an altitude of 10,135 feet (3091 metres) it's no dwarf and is definitely larger in terms of snowboard facilities. June has without doubt one of the ruling snowboard funparks on the West Coast. A steep front face down to the carpark belies the varied terrain which you'll see once you head up to the June Meadows' Chalet. Beginners and intermediate riders are well-catered for, with lots of gentle, wide open swathes cut into the trees and an efficient, easy chair system. There are plenty of steep runs through the trees on the front face, and access to back-country is possible for experienced riders if the ski patrol deem it safe.

SNOW CONDITIONS June has a northerly aspect but still receives a good amount of sun on most of the trails. If there are any storms about, the wooded slopes offer protection from the howling wind that can close Mammoth's upper lift systems. There will always be fresh in the trees!

FREERIDERS Gull Canyon, The Face and Carson (between the June Meadows' Chalet and the carpark) are the main freeriding areas. The chutes under June Mountain summit are exceptional after a fresh dump, but go early as skiers bump them out quickly. Not only are the wooded areas great natural obstacle courses but they also tend to harbour the powder long after it has disappeared from the slopes.

FREESTYLERS June Mountain is a great destination for freestylers. The halfpipe is world-class and has been the site for the '94, '96 and '97 USSA Snowboard National Championships. Located in front of the June Meadows' Chalet on Surprise, the pipe is kept in good shape by a Pipe Dragon throughout the season. There is an observation tower at the bottom and pumping tunes to keep you amped up and hiking all day. The real attraction for freestylers is the outrageous Boarder Town snowboard park, lovingly piled up by designer Dan Rossier. It has a quarterpipe and intimidatingly steep jumps, table tops, log hits, weird hits and a smaller halfpipe at the bottom, placed just to make sure your legs have nothing else left to give. This is all located under the J4 Chair, giving riders the perfect view, a chance to analyse the hits and time to learn from others' moves and mistakes.

CARVERS Not too much here for dedicated carvers, however beginners and intermediates will appreciate the dozen or so groomed blue runs and general lack of crowds. Schatzl and Sunset are the steepest groomers for speed-freaks.

MOUNTAIN FOOD June has good food in its main chalet — sit, eat and savour the stunning views over the lakes. There are barbecues beneath the Main Lodge sundeck and at the Hutson Haus and Chair 7. Cool staff and a laid-back atmosphere make eating here easy and hassle free.

HAZARDS AND RULES The same rules apply here as in Mammoth — lose your board, lose your ticket, therefore use a leash. Boundary rules are flexible as long as you check with the ski patrol first and don't enter wilderness areas. The laws of the back-country apply — don't go out alone and carry your transceiver, shovels and probes.

EVENTS AND COMPETITIONS The halfpipe hosts many local and national competitions.

ABOUT TOWN

June Lake is a picturesque town nestled between lakes, deep in the Inyo national park. The town is spread out and its apparent smallness is due to it being split into two main areas. There are enough beds to accommodate 1700 people and the lodgings are varied; most tout spas, saunas or swimming pools. The town has little of the hustle and bustle of the bigger resorts and as such, the atmosphere is more conducive to maximising the great riding.

ACCOMMODATION Boulder Lodge — Tel: 760-648 7533 has rooms from $38. Gull Lake Lodge starts from $50 for two sharers mid-week — Tel: 1-800-631 9081. The Whispering Pines start from $49 per night based on one to four people sharing for five nights — Tel: 619-648 7762 or 1-800-648 7762. The Fern Creek Lodge starts from $45 per night for two people sharing — Tel: 1-800-621 9146. Reverse Creek Lodge starts from $55 for two people per night — Tel: 1-800-762 6440. For more info contact the mountain — Tel: 760-648 7733.

FOOD Good steaks are found at the Sierra Inn Restaurant, along with chicken, pizza and the town's best burgers. Due to its close proximity to Mammoth's plethora of restaurants, the options are a little limited — a drive is in order to expand the dining choices.

NIGHTLIFE The Sierra Inn Bar has a pool table, darts and is the general hang-out bar along with another snooker joint called the Tiger Bar. The vibrancy of the nightlife is in direct proportion to how many people are staying in June at the time. If you want to party hard, head to Mammoth.

OTHER ACTIVITIES Cross-county skiing, sledding, tobogganing, ice-skating and snowmobiling.

THANKS TO Paul McCahon at June, John Logue at Ernie's, Eric from the ski patrol, Aaron Bishop, Ted the Head and all the boys who charged the funpark and pipe for us.

Top right — Chris Carr in the pipe **Photo:** Bruce Sutherland
Middle — The funpark **Photo:** Bruce Sutherland
Bottom — June Lakes **Courtesy:** June Mountain

GETTING THERE
By air: See Mammoth review p.74.
By bus: There are no buses or shuttles direct to June, so if you don't have a car or a sexy, big thumb you won't be riding there. Greyhound does stop at the June Lake Junction on Highway 395, but that still leaves you about four miles (six kilometres) out of town.
By car: June is on loop road Highway 158, 20 miles (32 kilometres) north of Mammoth along Highway 395. The resort keeps the southern access open all winter but has to close the road near the loop's middle, so northern access by the loop road is impossible during winter.
Getting around: It's advisable to have a car to increase your choices.

⑧

Mammoth Mountain

ON THE MOUNTAIN

There is speculation that this active volcano was responsible for the last ice age when it blew its top and contemplating the enormity of the mountain, it seems plausible. This leviathan rises out of the Inyo national forest and has something for everyone, ranging from steeps, chutes and bowls to long stretches of perfectly groomed corduroy. Riding at Mammoth on a good powder day is something everyone should aspire to. Skiers tend to bump out a lot of areas but there are trees, cliffs and plenty of secluded routes left for searchers. An extensive network of confusingly numbered lifts gets you to where you want to go, so long as you know where it is you're going.

SNOW CONDITIONS The area boasts a 30 foot (nine metre) average snowfall which is one reason the season can last till July. Mammoth's northerly aspect and high elevation make it an epic powder dumping ground. One downer is the strong winds which regularly sweep across the high ridge, causing the top chairs and gondolas to close. Over 70 per cent of the season's days are blessed by sunshine, so riding at Mammoth is as reliable as it gets.

FREERIDERS All the runs reached by Gondola 2 and Chair 23 are steep, fast and long with dozens of different lines though chutes and bowls. Chair 9 and the Tail are the pick after a dump for great powder runs. For a king-kong hit, head off Chair 23 to the Cornice. From Chair 22 you'll find cliffs and trees with some good steep shots. Over the back towards Chair 14 are the wide open runs. A short hike skier's left will get you to a short, steep face called Hemlock. The back-country opportunities are many and varied but you'll need local hiking knowledge and a pick-up car.

FREESTYLERS The funpark has a selection of table tops, gap jumps, kickers and banked turns. There are no quarterpipes or halfpipes here during the winter so all the serious jibbers go to June, missing out on some fun natural gullies like Lower Dry Creek. When the summer camps are on, the resort constructs a pipe and borrows the Pipe Dragon from June Mountain. Next season Mammoth will have a halfpipe all year and its very own Pipe Dragon.

CARVERS Carvers will be in heaven as there are plenty of well-kept, immaculately groomed slopes ranging from mellow to steep (daily grooming reports are displayed at the base station). Early in the morning conditions are often perfect and the crowds are not there to make it a dodgem course. Check out Solitude, Sanctuary and the long Ricochet Run for some horizontal hula.

MOUNTAIN FOOD Mammoth has seven different on-mountain food services with Main Lodge and Canyon Lodge being the largest. They provide a range of hot and cold foods at reasonable mountain prices, including a roof terrace barbecue at Canyon Lodge serving large slabs of meat. Chair 15 has a killer stir-fry and an uncrowded, chilled-out atmosphere while Chair 14 has a sun terrace and is usually out of the wind. It has great views and does a very decent meal for under $10.

HAZARDS AND RULES Although leashes are not compulsory, if you lose your board you lose your ticket. Some trails can resemble LA freeways on the weekends so be prepared for traffic jams and the odd pile-up.

EVENTS AND COMPETITIONS In the '97-'98 season Mammoth is hoping to host the US Snowboarding Grand Prix in late January. They hold a season-long boardercross open to amateurs and pros, and a boardercross/motorcross event in December.

THE FACTS

ELEVATION
- **Summit:** 11,053ft, 3370m
- **Vertical drop:** 3100ft, 946m
- **Base:** 7953ft, 2424m

SNOWFALL
- **Average annual:** 353 inches, 897cm
- **Snow-making:** 20%

AREA
- **Total area:** 3500 acres, 1414ha
- Advanced: 30%
- Intermediate: 40%
- Beginner: 30%

SEASON
November — June/July

COMMUNICATIONS
Snow reports: Tel: 760-934 6166 or 213-935 8866
Web site: http://www.mammoth-mtn.com
E-mail: mammothmtn@aol.com
Mountain information:
Tel: 760-934 0645
Fax: 760-934 0603

LIFTS AND TICKETS
Number of lifts:
2 gondolas, 4 high-speed quads, 22 chairlifts, 1 surface lift
Lift pass prices:
1/2 day: $35
1 day: $45, $34 (13-18 yrs)
Multi-day: $191 (5 days)
Season: $1350, $900 (before September 30)
Other ticketing information:
Free lift access for first timers taking lessons.

SNOWBOARD SHOPS
Stormriders — Tel: 760-934 0679
Run by Ron McCoy and a bunch of dedicated boarders, the shop stocks the core stuff and has a uni-priced rental fleet ranging from step-ins to pro-models, plus all the tuning and repair toys. Ask here for details about skateboarding activities.
Wave Rave — Tel: 760-934 2471
Owned by extreme rider Steve Klassen, this mega-store stocks a wide range of everything and stays open late.

SNOWBOARD SCHOOL
Mammoth Snowboard School
Tel: 760-934 0685 or 760-934 2571
The school offers courses for kids (Big Kahuna Snowboard Club), adult learner camps and advanced courses such as the Afternoon Flight School. Group lessons start at $43 a day.

Mammoth Mountain ⑨

ABOUT TOWN

Mammoth Lakes is a four season resort town surrounded by mountains on three sides. It's a large mountain town servicing a large mountain, and can provide just about anything depending on how large your wallet is. The Lakes is a popular summer spot and as the season sometimes goes through till July, you can go rock-climbing, fishing, mountain-biking and boarding all in the same day. Due to the high number of weekend mountain users, food and accommodation outlets have the highest profiles as you drive up the main street. Beautifully wooded side streets contain most of the self-catering chalets and local residences. On clear days the views are spectacular from the township, and the sunrises over the lake are impressive.

GETTING THERE

By air: The nearest international airport is Reno-Tahoe, about three hours away. There is an airport just outside Mammoth, serviced by connections from Long Beach and Reno.
By bus: Bus services run from LA, San Francisco, Sacramento and Reno, but stop at indirect places.
By car: Situated in the eastern Sierra Nevada mountain range, Mammoth can be accessed from both the north and south on Highway 395.
Getting around: There is a free shuttle service between the town and the resort. The new People Mover rail-link gets you from Chair 2 to the Main Lodge.

ACCOMMODATION Mammoth Lakes has a bed capacity of 30,000, although many of these are allocated to wealthy condo owners who are rarely there. Cheap hotels are few and far between unless you are travelling in a group of three or more. Motel Six has a sliding scale starting at $36 for one adult, $42 for two adults and only $3-$6 more for each additional adult. Davison Street Guest House has hostel accommodation plus rooms starting from $17 — Tel: 760-544 9093. In the higher price bracket, there are condo apartments and hotels like the Travelodge which cost about $135 for two double beds and have all the amenities like pools, spas and saunas. The main hotel slopeside is the Mammoth Mountain Inn — Tel: 730-934 2581 or 1-800-228 4947. There are many accommodation services: North Village Properties — Tel: 760-934 3717, Mammoth Reservations — Tel: 1-888-GO MAMMOTH and Mammoth Sierra Reservations — Tel: 1-800-654 1143.

FOOD Besides having all the usual take-aways and American fast food institutions, Mammoth Lakes has some excellent dining. Cheap places include Tacos to Go, Angel's for burgers and beers, Matsu for Chinese, and Gringos for Mexican, telly and tequila. In the moderate to expensive range, Chart House is recommended. The Aspen Grill has an excellent and varied menu, good wine and service to match. It also has a well-stocked cigar humidor in the adjacent well-ventilated bar. Be certain to get to your restaurant early — a lot of places stop serving unusually early (especially mid-week) and you could find yourself going hungry! If you want to dine in style, savouring fine food prepared by a fine snowboarder, then Cervino's is the place. Rob Wilson prepares some of the tastiest north Italian dishes you will find anywhere outside Italy. Beware all the desserts!

NIGHTLIFE The main night-spot in town is the non-smoking Ocean Harvest Club which has a DJ till 2.00am. The Clocktower is also open till 2.00am for beers and pool. Both have restaurants upstairs. The Aspen Grill's Cigar Bar has a more convivial atmosphere, good whisky and, of course, a menu of cigars. The Goat Bar is a classic mountain-man hang-out for pool and is one of the only smoking bars in town. Gringos is another smoking bar and local favourite showing the latest videos while you decide which tequila to shoot.

OTHER ACTIVITIES Snowmobile tours, hot springs, summer lake activities and skateboarding.

THANKS TO Wendy Kelley, Tabby Mannetter, the Travelodge, all the boys at Stormriders, Chris, Rob, Teddy, Bishop and all the crew who helped out.

Opposite — Mammoth **Photo:** Bruce Sutherland
Top — **Courtesy:** Mammoth Mountain
Bottom — **Courtesy:** Mammoth Mountain

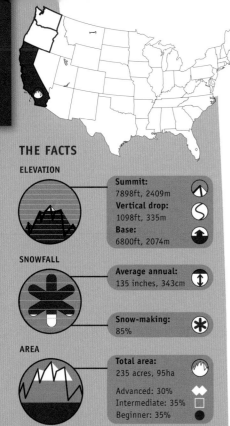

Snow Valley

THE FACTS

ELEVATION

Summit:
7898ft, 2409m
Vertical drop:
1098ft, 335m
Base:
6800ft, 2074m

SNOWFALL

Average annual:
135 inches, 343cm

Snow-making:
85%

AREA

Total area:
235 acres, 95ha

Advanced: 30%
Intermediate: 35%
Beginner: 35%

SEASON
Mid-November — late March

COMMUNICATIONS
Snow reports:
Tel: 909-867 5151 or 1-800-680 SNOW
Web site: http://www.snow-valley.com
E-mail: 102662.1536@compuserve.com
Mountain information:
Tel: 909-867 2751
Fax: 909-867 7687

LIFTS AND TICKETS
Number of lifts:
13 chairlifts, 1 handle tow
Lift pass prices:
1/2 day: $29
1 day: $34, $40 (holidays)
Multi-day: N/A
Season: N/A
Other ticketing information:
Swatch Access resort! Handy electronic watches
take the hassle out of pass checking. A ten run
minimum guarantee means that if you ride less
than ten runs you can use the balance on any
other day. For advance bookings call Ticket Master
— Tel: 213-480 3232.

swatch access

SNOWBOARD SHOPS
Snow Valley Rental Shop — Tel: 909-867 2751
A fully equipped rental and repair shop with Nitro
boards and Airwalk boots. B+B: $30.

SNOWBOARD SCHOOL
Snow Valley School — Tel: 909-867 2751
Beginner packages start at $39. Private lessons
cost $55.

GETTING THERE
By car: From LA: Take Interstate 10 east to
Highway 30 and onto Highway 330 north into
Running Springs. Snow Valley is five miles (eight
km) east of Running Springs on Highway 18. From
Big Bear Lake: Head west on Highway 18 for 45
minutes.
Getting around: Lake Arrowhead, 15 miles (24 km)
away, has accommodation, food and public
transportation to Snow Valley — Tel: 909-338 1113.

ON THE MOUNTAIN

Snow Valley is the largest ski area in Southern
Cal. It sits at the same base elevation as Bear
Mountain and Snow Summit but receives more
natural snow due to its location in the San
Bernadino Mountains. The steeps are decent
and the natural terrain throws up some nice
gullies and tree areas. There is a slamming one
and a half mile (two and a half kilometre)
terrain park, with 50 to 100 fat hits depending
on snow conditions. The goods at Snow Valley
are not visible from Highway 18 but the view
from the top of the lifts is more encouraging.

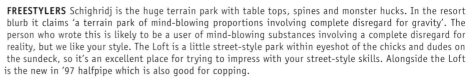

SNOW CONDITIONS Snow Valley gets as much natural
snow as you can hope for in Southern Cal, and like all
the other resorts in the area has invested heavily in
snow-making and grooming technology. It's sunny
four out of five days in winter.

FREERIDERS Freeriding will never be Southern Cal's
state sport but if there was ever a social extreme
freeride comp, Snow Valley would be odds on for the
host resort. It's no Jackson Hole, Verbier or Valdez
but in a state where a hill by a lake can be a credible
ski resort, Snow Valley feels like a mountain. Steeps can be tracked down at the top of Lift 10 on the East
Slide. The bowl at the bottom is skate material, so keep your speed up to rock into the natural gullies between
Snowbowl and Racepeak. Cut skier's left and it's all trees, trees, trees. On a Southern Cal scale of one to ten,
Snow Valley rates about a nine; on a national scale it's a four and a half. Exploring the mountain won't take
too long, but then there's the terrain park.

FREESTYLERS Schighridj is the huge terrain park with table tops, spines and monster hucks. In the resort
blurb it claims 'a terrain park of mind-blowing proportions involving complete disregard for gravity'. The
person who wrote this is likely to be a user of mind-blowing substances involving a complete disregard for
reality, but we like your style. The Loft is a little street-style park within eyeshot of the chicks and dudes on
the sundeck, so it's an excellent place for trying to impress with your street-style skills. Alongside the Loft
is the new in '97 halfpipe which is also good for copping.

When the lifts close, and just in case you haven't got lucky yet, you can nonchalantly swap your two bindings
for two trucks and display the depth and diversity of your character and skill in the Lot skate park. Not to be
confused with the Loft terrain park, as your wheels will jam in the snow. Here is your last chance to shine as
all the other unluckies head for their cars.

CARVERS There are not too many wide open, steep trails, and the few around get bumped out quick.

MOUNTAIN FOOD From burgers to
gourmet, it's all here. Fatty's Sports Bar
has live music and a full bar. The Chalet
has burgers and chilli, and the Deli
Express serves pastries and fresh coffee.
The loosest place is Margarita Beach with
beach chairs, body-bag races and
volleyball.

HAZARDS AND RULES Leash laws apply.

EVENTS AND COMPETITIONS State and
national comps in Schighridj Terrain Park.

OTHER ACTIVITIES Music festivals, the Lot
skate park, mountain-biking.

THANKS TO Jay Reid, Marc Hare.

Courtesy: Swatch

For About Town section, see Big Bear Lake
review opposite.

Big Bear Lake

THE FACTS

SNOWBOARD SHOPS

Goldsmith's Ski and Board Shop — Tel: 902-866 2728
Goldsmith's have a good attitude towards boarders and help out the USASA riders in town. Every second shop along Big Bear Boulevard sells or rents boards, so check them all for good deals and specials.
Bear Mountain Rental Shop — Tel: 909-585 2517
The resort has its own snowboard rental shop on site with a full array of equipment and sales.

GETTING THERE

By air: The closest international airport is LAX, hire a car and drive east on Interstate 10 to Big Bear Lake. Big Bear Shuttle has an on-call door-to-door service to LAX — Tel: 909-585 5514.
By car: Take Interstate 10 east from LA to the Running Springs exit in Redlands. Follow Highway 30 to Highway 330 to Highway 18 and turn right across the dam to Big Bear Lake. If roads are congested in the weekend, try the back route Highway 38 off Interstate 10 past the Redlands exit, or take Highway 18 from the San Fernando Valley.
Getting around: Mountain Area Rapid Transit Authority operates MARTA buses which make daily round trips to San Bernardino as well as local trolleys and door-to-door services — Tel: 909-584 1111. Call Bear Valley Transit for bus and taxi schedules — Tel: 909-866 4444.

ABOUT TOWN

The towns of Big Bear Lake and Big Bear City merge into each other on the shores of Big Bear Lake. The land was formerly christened Starvation Flats by disillusioned miners and later flooded by a scenic-minded engineer in 1884. **Bear Mountain** and **Snow Summit** are barely a couple of miles apart and are separated by Big Bear Boulevard which stretches along the lake perimeter for about 10 miles (16 kilometres). The two mountains are next-door neighbours on polite greeting terms; they have co-hosted big events but don't validate each other's tickets. Although both mountains are exceptionally snowboard orientated and attract

Bear Mountain deck scene **Photo:** Gina Dempster

streams of jibbers, there are surprisingly few cool venues to hang-out in at night, probably because most riders head back to the fiendish depths of LA. In three hours you can make Malibu beach or LAX international airport; waves, babes and haze.

ACCOMMODATION The Honey Bear Lodge has cute rooms in the heart of Big Bear Lake for $49 per night mid-week — Tel: 909-866 7825. The Wildwood Resort has cabins and studios; package deals cost $105 for weekend lift passes and lodging — Tel: 909-878 2178. Two minutes walk from the Snow Summit lifts are the Escape Condominiums, next to the Escape Ski and Racquet Club. The decor depends on the individual owner's taste; it can be anywhere from plastic '70s to fluffy Laura Ashley. For lodging referrals from the Big Bear Lake Resort Association — Tel: 909-866 7000 or 1-800-4BIG BEAR. Check the web page for info on their 1200 lodging units — http://www.bigbearinfo.com.

FOOD As you drive into Big Bear Lake sprawled along the lake, the road is decorated with numerous family restaurants interspersed with snowboard and ski shops for miles and miles. We ordered take-out from Giovanni's restaurant on Big Bear Boulevard without realising that the boulevard runs through the entire city and has shop numbers like 55,000 on it. Buying dinner requires more navigation skills than riding the mountains in Southern Cal. Also on the boulevard, Thelma's Restaurant has nightly prime rib specials and a bargain $2.75 breakfast, while Sizzlers all-you-can-eat salad bar includes pasta, enchiladas and chicken wings for people who don't get turned on by veggies. The alternative to cruising the boulevard is to park the car in Pine Knot Road and explore 'The Village' by foot. The Village is a touristy collection of shops, bars and restaurants ranging from Mongolian hotpot to pancakes and more Italian. It's also a good place to get a quick breakfast at the Pine Knot Coffee House and Bakery or outdoors at the Main Street Café.

NIGHTLIFE An amusing way to spend a couple of hours after the lifts close is to hang on the Bear Mountain deck and watch the cool shades parade, with their sponsored boards displayed next to pints of beer. At night the action is mostly private if private describes hundreds of boarders moshing to a live band while the house shakes. The sheriff doesn't look kindly on this sort of excess, and can be expected to arrive with power cutters and cans of mace just as the party peaks. Pub options are much tamer and tackier; the Chad has the best reputation in the village but plays uninspiring music to an uninspired crowd. They have several pool tables out the back.

OTHER ACTIVITIES The alpine slide at Magic Mountain, boat rentals, sea-doos, mountain-biking, four-wheeling, hang-gliding simulator.

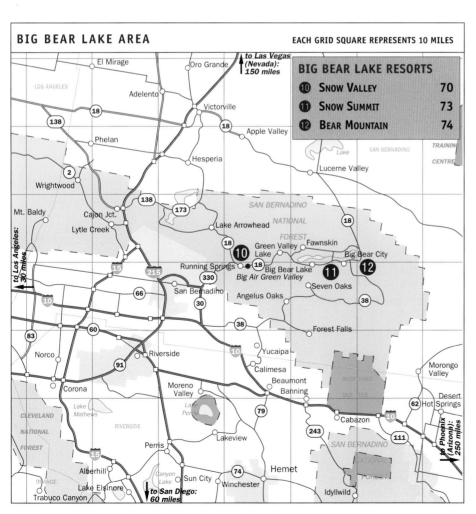

BIG BEAR LAKE AREA

EACH GRID SQUARE REPRESENTS 10 MILES

BIG BEAR LAKE RESORTS

10	SNOW VALLEY	70
11	SNOW SUMMIT	73
12	BEAR MOUNTAIN	74

Snow Summit

THE FACTS

ELEVATION

Summit:
8200ft, 2501m
Vertical drop:
1200ft, 366m
Base:
7000ft, 2135m

SNOWFALL

Average annual:
75 inches, 190cm

Snow-making:
100%

AREA

Total area:
230 acres, 93ha

Advanced: 25%
Intermediate: 40%
Beginner: 35%

SEASON
Mid-November — mid-April

COMMUNICATIONS
Snow reports:
Tel: 909-866 5766 or 310-390 1498 (LA)
Web site: http//www.snowsummit.com
E-mail: snow.summit@bigbear.com
Mountain information:
Tel: 909-866 5766
Fax: 909-866 3201
Big Bear Lake Chamber of Commerce:
Tel: 909-866 4607

LIFTS AND TICKETS
Number of lifts:
2 high-speed quads, 9 chairlifts,
1 surface lift at the halfpipe
Lift pass prices:
1/2 day: $28 (12.30pm-6.00pm)
1 day: $42, $35 (mid-week under 23yrs)
Multi-day: $76 (2 consecutive days)
Other ticketing information:
Night-riding tickets cost $24 (3.00pm to 9.30pm on
Fridays, Sundays and holidays), half night tickets
cost $17 (7.00pm to 9.30pm). Ski free on your
birthday with photo ID. Get a $17 credit against
your next ticket if you turn in your lift pass before
1.00pm. Reserve limited lift tickets by calling the
Snow Summit Telephone Credit Card Service —
Tel: 909-866 5841.

SNOWBOARD SHOPS
Snow Summit Snowboard Rental Centre
Tel: 909-866 5766
Rental boards include Joyride, World Industries
and Dryve and are equipped with Switch step-ins,
Concrete bindings and Vans boots.

SNOWBOARD SCHOOL
Snow Summit Snowboard School
Tel: 909-866 5766
The beginner package with a four hour lesson and
beginner lift pass costs $45 weekends and $35
mid-week. Snowboard rental adds $15 to the price.

GETTING THERE
By car: Snow Summit is on the borders of Big Bear
Lake. Drive though town on Highway 18 and take a
right at Summit Drive.

ON THE MOUNTAIN

Snow Summit is a fine example of how to take an average mountain with a less than average snowfall and create an excellent snowboarding environment. The natural terrain is in no way vast or much of a challenge, but the funpark literally covers half the mountain and will severely test and improve your riding skills. There are 6000 feet (1828 metres) of table tops, drops, gaps and spines plus two good halfpipes. Make no

mistake, this is jibber central with everything from beginner hits to huck monsters. The rest of the mountain however is not very steep and doesn't offer great freeriding possibilities. On busy days things get as hectic as Disneyland, so remember that every time you huck there are probably ten more huckers right behind you, and if you fall... MOVE. If being in the air is your concept of riding, then you should definitely make the effort to visit Snow Summit. For the '97-'98 season Snow Summit is adding more snowboarding terrain and will have more than two miles (three kilometres) of freestyle parks. Tickets are limited to the resort's 'comfort capacity' and the resort usually sells out for mid-winter weekends by Thursday or Friday.

SNOW CONDITIONS Santa Ana winds blow in from Utah and Nevada and gain heat only as they compress, passing over the mountains. On average the temperature is around 30 degrees cooler up the mountain than down in the Southern Cal valleys. Intensive snow-making ensures good snow coverage into March. The mountains are north to north-facing.

FREERIDERS Don't discount Summit even though there are no great hikes, all day expeditions or awesome natural terrain to blow you away. The east side of the mountain has a smattering of fun trees interspersed with cat-track drops which can be rad in good snow. The Westridge Freestyle Park has over one mile (1600 metres) of sick table tops, gaps, drops and launches in nice succession. A week of riding here will massively boost your air technique, skill and confidence.

FREESTYLERS You might expect Saint Peter in the ticket office, Jesus driving the Pipe Dragon and God as mountain manager at Snow Summit because this is as close to freestyle heaven as it gets. Did we mention the Westridge Freestyle Park already? There's another one called East Why of equally high quality, although it's much shorter. Both are accessible from the top of the All Mountain Express Chair with East Why ending at Chair 3 and Westridge running down to the base. There are also two halfpipes. The one on West Why is

Opposite — **Courtesy:** Snow Summit

Top — Todd Messick **Photo:** Sean Fredrick **Courtesy:** Snow Summit

Middle — ESPN X Games **Photo:** Nagel **Courtesy:** Snow Summit

Bottom — **Courtesy:** Snow Summit

11

scary and at its best early in the day as it gets rutted out later on when the crowds pick up. The ZZYZX is less scary, less perfect and less crowded. Next to the West Why halfpipe on the Westridge run are two huge hits: the first has a 15 foot drop over a 20 foot flat, then there's a long transition straight to the second jump, a 30 foot table top. It's all sick.

CARVERS Snow Summit does provide a few surprisingly good speed-freak runs on the eastern side of the mountain. Double black diamond trails Side Chute, Olympic and The Wall are extremely fast and avoided by the general masses. These three runs are surrounded by nice cruisy black and blue runs which tend to mellow off drastically at the base of the mountain.

MOUNTAIN FOOD The Lounge upstairs at the base of Chair 2 and Chair 11 is the place to go for cheap Mexican food, a full bar and music, skate, surf and snowboard videos. Downstairs at the Bear Bottom Bar there are more snowboard vids and a full service bar. The Summit Haus at the top of the All-Mountain Xpress is a great place to hang out, serving fast food on glass-shielded decks. Barbecue areas are located at the base area and on the decks of all the lodges.

HAZARDS AND RULES The number one unspoken rule at Snow Summit is not to lie around if you sketch out. Riders go off the jumps in twos and threes and there are no breaks for injury time, so get off the landing zone if you can still move. Book your tickets in advance for mid-winter weekends

and holidays to avoid a major bummer when you get there.

EVENTS AND COMPETITIONS The H2O Winter Classic is a two day surf and board classic held in February. Snow Summit Springfest features an annual slush comp. They also host USASA events including the National Championships, as well as the ESPN Winter-X Games and the American Snowboard Tour.

THANKS TO Genevieve Paquet.

For About Town, see Big Bear Lake review p.71.

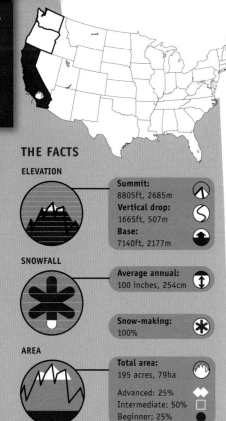

Bear Mountain

THE FACTS

ELEVATION

Summit:
8805ft, 2685m
Vertical drop:
1665ft, 507m
Base:
7140ft, 2177m

SNOWFALL

Average annual:
100 inches, 254cm

Snow-making:
100%

AREA

Total area:
195 acres, 79ha

Advanced: 25%
Intermediate: 50%
Beginner: 25%

SEASON
End November — early April

COMMUNICATIONS
Snow report:
Tel: 909-585 2519 or 213-683 8100 (LA)
Web site: http://www.bearmtn.com
E-mail: bearmtn@bigbear.com
Mountain information:
Tel: 909-585 2517
Fax: 909-585 6805
Big Bear Lake Chamber of Commerce:
Tel: 909-866 4607

LIFTS AND TICKETS
Lift pass prices:
1/2 day: N/A
1 day: $40, $34 (under 23)
Multi-day: $112 (3 days), $93 (under 23)
Season: N/A
Other ticketing information:
Buy a two day ticket on Saturday for $75 and board for free on Monday. The Vertical Plus Club costs $29 to join and entitles you to $7 off each lift pass, a free pass every seven days and chances to win.

SNOWBOARD SHOPS
See Big Bear Lake review p.71.

SNOWBOARD SCHOOL
Bear Mountain Snowboard School
Tel: 909-585 2517
Fax: 909-585 6805
The Vertical Improvement Programme offers FREE intermediate through advanced lessons for boarders; lessons last nearly two hours and begin hourly on week days between 10.00am and 1.00pm and half hourly at the weekends between 9.30am and 1.30pm, with a limit of eight students in a class. If there's a catch, we haven't found it. Introduction programmes cost $42 for a restricted lift pass, rentals and a two hour lesson.

GETTING THERE
By car: Drive through Big Bear Lake on Highway 18, turn right onto Moonridge Drive and follow it for two miles (three km) to the Bear Mountain base.

ON THE MOUNTAIN

Bear Mountain is as good as a day area gets. Having to cater for the colossal LA population has called for clever mountain management strategies in order to get this restricted area to service a wide range of mountain users. In the future as mountain sports become more accessible to the masses, many people's first snowsports experiences will be had on this type of small, meticulously managed ski area. Bear is a good torchbearer for this new direction in resort marketing because it's more about co-operation than corporation.

The Outlaw Funpark has featured in probably more magazines and videos than any other funpark in the world. Local shovel pushers include Jeff Brushie and the Guch who ensure the park is huck-worthy and the riding standard high. Bear Mountain gets over 300 sunshine days a year so the pictures and footage always look fantastic. The management, the marketing, the funpark and the climate are the main reasons why you've probably heard of Bear Mountain before, but the rest of the area has goods too.

SNOW CONDITIONS The bulk of the snow is man-made; luckily water is never in short supply with Big Bear Lake down the road so there's always adequate snow cover even into late spring.

FREERIDERS The resort is spread across three peaks: Bear Peak (the highest), Silver Mountain and Goldmine Mountain. Between these peaks are the tree-laden descents of Bow Canyon, Deer Canyon and Goldmine Canyon. If there is fresh snow then these are the places to head for. The trees on either side of Silver Mountain are open territory and avoided by most skiers. The base of Deer Canyon is the only flat spot worth avoiding. There are a few good natural features to launch off into the trees, but the funpark is hard to beat for air time.

FREESTYLERS Did we mention the Outlaw Funpark already? It's all that and a bowl of chips with salsa. It was a crazy, unfounded notion that snowboarders in charge of grooming equipment might be able to build facilities that were good for funpark users — a notion many resorts would laugh at today. But, strangely, it worked at Bear — go figure! As a result the park has hits for everyone, although some are so big you might question whether the earth really is round. The groomers never rest and some of their work doesn't even

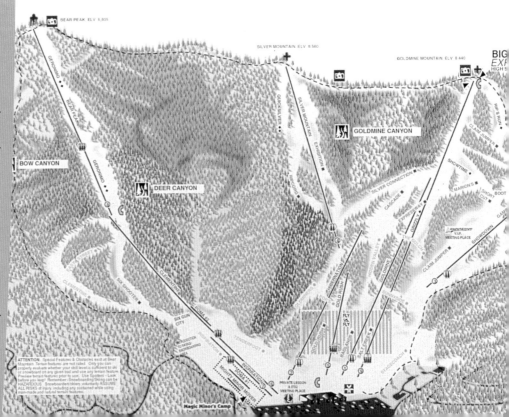

have names yet, but you'll find gaps table tops, pyramids and spines that will flashback at you in dreams for years to come. The Showdown Lift services the park. The halfpipe is also a state-of-the-art monster, born of a Pipe Dragon and located on the Cascade Trail below the Big Bear Express. It is 400 feet (122 metres) long with 10 foot (three metre) walls and it's constantly maintained. Stylers will also trip on the Reef Zone and Black Flys Fly vs Fly double barrel halfpipe in the Goldrush area.

CARVERS Not much to write home about. Geronimo from Bear Peak and Claim Jumper from Goldmine Mountain are the only two well-groomed, steep descents. Gold Rush is good and steep, but short and crowded. Silver Mountain is good but you can't ride it unless you ski.

MOUNTAIN FOOD The base of Bear Mountain is one of the coolest places to hang out in the American snowboarding world. They have a huge deck with an outside bar, live music and a view of their newest park and big air jump, where you can be entertained by 540s or live stretcher action. Beer is a higher priority for most than food but there are barbecue options and a java shack on deck. For something more substantial, the Silver Mountain Eatery downstairs has fresh baking and the Trapper's Restaurant upstairs has a more formal menu.

HAZARDS AND RULES Drinking all afternoon in bright sunshine on the infamous Bear deck can be a major hazard to your snowboarding health.

EVENTS AND COMPETITIONS Swatch/ISF World Boarder-X Tour, Bear Snowboard Series, Board Aid V, USASA events including the National Championships in '97, Killian's Downhill Madness — a $2000 prize goes to the fastest rider with combined ski and snowboard times on a rough and ready course. For event information — Tel: 909-585 2519.

THANKS TO Judi Bowers.

For About Town, see Big Bear Lake review p.71.

12

Opposite — Pond skimming at Bear **Photo:** Gina Dempster
Main picture — **Photo:** Richard Cheski

STEVE KLASSEN, photographed by Greg von Dorsten

STEVE KLASSEN
1973 1st time snowboarding
1994 became a Fire & Ice member
1995 1st time World Extreme Champion, Alaska
1996 2nd time World Extreme Champion, Alaska
     1st time World Extreme Champion, Verbier
1997 2nd time World Extreme Champion, Verbier

FIRE&ICE The way to Ⓑ BOGNER

MOUNTAIN WEST

Tina Basich, Wasatch Powder Birds **Photo:** Chris Murray

MONTANA

STATE INFORMATION

Population: 856,057
Time: Mountain West = GMT minus 6 hours
Capital city: Helena
Area of state: 147,138 sq miles (379,616 sqkm)

VISITOR INFORMATION SOURCES
Travel Montana:
Tel: 406-444 2654 or 1-800-847 4868
Web site: http://travel.mt.gov/

GETTING AROUND
Main airports: Helena — Tel: 406-265 4671, Billings —
Tel: 406-657 8495
By train: Amtrak — Tel: 215-628 1846 or
1-800-872 7245
By bus: Greyhound — Tel: 1-800-231 2222, Rimrock
Trailways — Tel: 1-800-255 7655
Road conditions: Tel: 406-444 6339 or 1-800-226-7623
Speed limits: Montana's daytime speed limit is
'reasonable and prudent'. Night limits are 65 mph (120
kmph) and 55 mph (104 kmph).

INTRODUCTION

Everything about Montana is big, hats and all.
Stretching for over 650 miles (1040 kilometres) from
east to west, the state covers an area larger than New
England and New York put together, and has a
population less than San Jose in California. Formerly
considered by many to be deepest, darkest nowhere,
Montana is a state fast attracting a new breed of
wealthy lifestylers escaping the inner city blues. Due
to its comparative isolation, Montana's resorts have
never been at the heart of the winter sports industry
but because of that, they offer a refreshingly casual
and unstressed riding experience with consistently
good, cool snowfalls. If there is a feature of Montana's climate that's notable, it's the misty,
foggy air affectionately known as 'the grey smoke'. Local people are almost universally
friendly; beer drinking is a central feature of Montana's social life and the saloons and bars
pump. The state's driving laws are unique; there is no daytime driving limit, but be aware of
wild game like deer and bison crossing the road at any time.

Main picture — Night signs **Photo:** Tim Rainger
Top and left — Montana road signs **Photos:** Tim Rainger

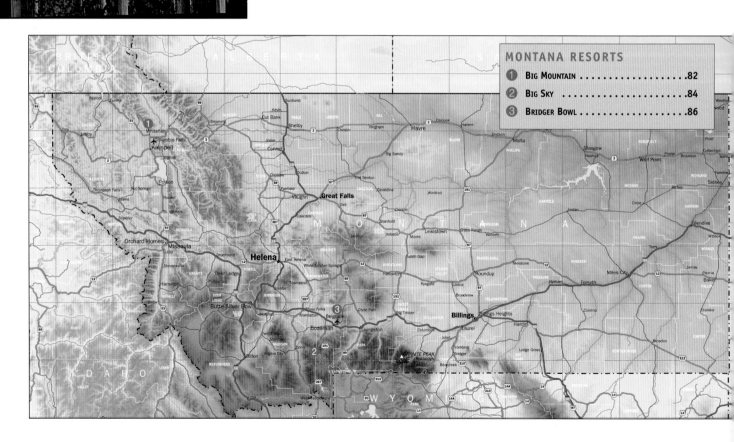

MONTANA RESORTS

1. BIG MOUNTAIN 82
2. BIG SKY 84
3. BRIDGER BOWL 86

Big Mountain

ON THE MOUNTAIN

'Great groomers', 'big fogs', 'long traverses' and 'beer' are a few of the phrases which pop up in a conversation about Big Mountain. Tucked away in the north-west corner of Montana near Glacier Park, Big Mountain covers over 3000 acres (1212 hectares), living up to its name. The in-bounds terrain is extensive although the density of the trees in the bottom two-thirds of the mountain makes this figure slightly deceptive. The Glacier Chaser Lift takes you to the summit from the base area in just seven minutes. From the summit you can appreciate the spectacular views of Glacier Park, but flat light and foggy days are a common occurrence and obscure the view. Visibility aside, the mountain is great fun with a combination of pleasures to suit all tastes.

SNOW CONDITIONS The mountain sits at a low altitude, and fogs rising up from the lake tends to lounge around the peaks. The snowfall is consistent with the occasional late, wet dump in the spring.

BACK-COUNTRY OPTIONS Snowcat riding is available for those with a taste for the great untracked; prices start at $40 for four hours with a guide and a minimum of four people — Tel: 406-862 2909. Neighbouring ridges off the back side can be hiked with some local knowledge.

FREERIDERS The Face is an open, sunny bowl just below the summit on the front side. It has some intermittent trees and an intermediate gradient leading down to the steepest stuff like Heap Steep, Powder Trap and Langley. The best snow can be tracked down on the North Face which has a big variety of drops, skier's left of Inspiration. It's consistently steep and tasty all the way to Russ's Street, but then you're stuck on one of the longest, slowest cat-tracks in North America. If you drop below Russ's Street cat-track, you will have to take the tiny Village Lift to get back to the Glacier Chaser Lift. Hellroaring was finally opened in '96-'97 after years of diligent poaching by the local community. The mountain has now made the gladed intermediate and advanced terrain lift accessible. Good Medicine is a challenging run below Hellroaring which scores as a locals' favourite after a good snowfall.

FREESTYLERS The funpark and pipe are both off Chair 2 on the Ranger trail. Named the Identity Snowboard Park, the funpark is lit at night till 9.00pm and has the usual collection of quarterpipes, hits, jumps, gaps and table tops. Weekly contests are held in both the pipe and park.

CARVERS The best trails are Toni Matt, Bench Run, Big Ravine and Inspiration. They provide top to bottom runs with a nice pitch and they're wide open so lay out your carves.

MOUNTAIN FOOD Moguls Bar and Grill does breakfast and lunch; go for the 'moguls', a hollowed loaf of sourdough bread with a casserole filling. For snacks and a quick munch, the Alpine Lodge is the pick. The Summit House Restaurant is a bit more expensive but has delicious food. The younger crowd hang out at the Zno Zone which serves great Mexican and has vids running all day till 9.00pm. Hellroaring Saloon is a big favourite for its great burgers, hot and cold sandwiches, salads and homemade soups.

HAZARDS AND RULES Everything is in-bounds.

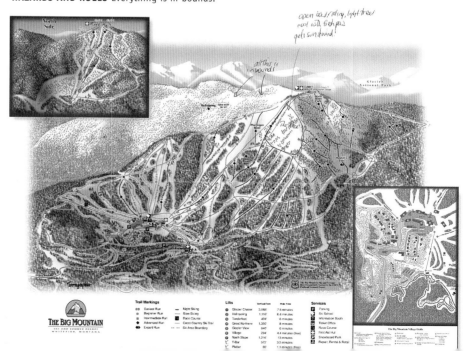

THE FACTS

ELEVATION

Summit:
7000ft, 2135m
Vertical drop:
2300ft, 701m
Base:
4700ft, 1433m

SNOWFALL

Average annual:
330 inches, 838cm

Snow-making:
3%

AREA

Total area:
3000 acres, 1212ha
Advanced: 25%
Intermediate: 50%
Beginner: 25%

SEASON
Late November — mid-April

COMMUNICATIONS
Web site: http://www.bigmtn.com/resort
E-mail: bigmtn@bigmtn.com
Mountain information:
Tel: 406-862 1952

LIFTS AND TICKETS
Number of lifts:
1 high-speed quad, 6 chairlifts, 1 platter lift, 1 T-bar
Lift pass prices:
1/2 day: $30
1 day: $40
Multi-days: $195 (5 of 6 days)
Season: $599
Other ticketing information:
The Platter Lift and Chair Six are free all the time — a great beginners' bargain. Night-riding from 4.00pm to 9.00pm costs $12.

SNOWBOARD SHOPS
Stumptown Snowboard Store — Tel: 406-862 0955
A full service shop located in downtown Whitefish, Stumptown has snowboard rentals, a skilled repair and tune-up department, and top companies for retail such as Burton, Salomon and Airwalk. In the summer, Stumptown becomes a skate shop and alternative clothing store.

SNOWBOARD SCHOOL
Big Sky Snowboard School — Tel: 406-862 2906
A private one hour lesson costs $52 for one person and $16 thereafter. Half day group lessons start from $23, and full day lessons cost $38.

Big Mountain

ABOUT TOWN

There is lodging around the small Big Mountain base area but be prepared to pay the premiums. Eight miles (12 kilometres) down the valley, the town of Whitefish is where most visitors choose to stay. The town has everything from cheap motel rooms to expensive condos with rooms overlooking Whitefish Lake. Whitefish is an old railroad and logging town which turned resort as the mountain became more of a tourist destination. It is still a small town with less than 5000 residents but provides boutiques, gift stores and a rocking nightlife with live bands in the season.

ACCOMMODATION Ptarmigan Village is the best place to stay. Two miles from Big Mountain and six miles (nine kilometres) from Whitefish, the Village is a cluster of condos starting from $70 a night for a one bedroom condo and $200 a night for a three bedroom unit — Tel: 406-862 3594 or 1-800-552 3952. Slopeside condos can be rented from Anapurna Properties — Tel: 406-862 3687 or 1-800-243 7547, Alpine Homes — Tel: 406-862 1982 or the Edelweiss — Tel: 406-5252. Central Reservations — Tel: 1-800-858 4157. For lodging options in Whitefish, call the Chamber of Commerce — Tel: 406-862 3501.

FOOD For breakfast, grab a bagel from the Whitefish Bagel Co. The Tupelo Grill serves a cajun-Montana blend that's pretty tasty. Jimmy Lee's serves Chinese in fat portions at reasonable prices; Jimmy cooks up the best sweet n' sour pork in the state. The Great Northern has good burgers, while the Dire Wolf dishes up pizzas, hot sandwiches and salads. There are many good places for lunch in town including the Trailhead Deli, Swift Creek Café, Mrs Spoonovers and the Bulldog. You can satisfy cravings for anything from juicy hamburgers to blackened chicken pita sandwiches and big salads with homemade dressings. Café Al Denté serves up a good Italian and the Whitefish Lake Restaurant has more formal dinner items such as steaks, seafood, pork and chicken dishes.

NIGHTLIFE Start at the Hellroaring Saloon, the on-mountain drinking hole with awesome nachos and pitchers of Montana's finest double-hopped. In Whitefish, the Black Star Brewery has beer-tasting on the premises during aprés-ski. The Palace and the Great Northern are the most popular bars in town. They both have live bands playing at the weekends and mid-week during peak season, alongside the pool tables, ping-pong tables and gambling machines.

OTHER ACTIVITIES Shopping in Whitefish, shooting pool in the saloons.

THANKS TO Dusty Hailey, Joe Tabor, Jenny Spiker.

Opposite — Trail sign **Photo:** Tim Rainger
Top — **Photo:** Tim Rainger
Middle left — Big Mountain from the Black Star Brewery **Photo:** Tim Rainger
Middle right — The dope **Photo:** Tim Rainger

GETTING THERE

By air: Glacier International Airport is serviced by several airlines including Delta Airlines — Tel: 1-800-221 1212. Shuttles to the mountain can be booked though Central Reservations and cost $22 a round trip.
By train: Amtrak runs east and west bound services every week to Whitefish.
By bus: Rimrock Trailways run a bus service to Whitefish — Tel: 406-862 1983.
By car: The resort is off Highway 93 and Highway 2, 60 miles (100 kilometres) from the Canadian border.
Getting around: Whitefish Area Rapid Transit offers ten daily shuttles from Whitefish to Big Mountain; shuttles run from 8.00am to 5.00pm — Tel: 406-862

THE FACTS

ELEVATION

Summit:
11,150ft, 3400m
Vertical drop:
4180ft, 1275m
Base:
6970ft, 2125m

SNOWFALL

Average annual:
400 inches, 1016cm

Snow-making:
10%

AREA

Total area:
3500 acres, 1414ha

Advanced: 43%
Intermediate: 47%
Beginner: 10%

SEASON
November — late April

COMMUNICATIONS
Snow report: Tel: 406-995 5900
Web site: http://www.bigskyresort.com
Mountain information:
Tel: 406-995 5894 or 1-800-548 5587

LIFTS AND TICKETS
Number of lifts:
1 tram, 1 gondola, 3 high-speed quads, 7
chairlifts, 3 surface tows
Lift pass prices:
1/2 day: $40
1 day: $47
Multi-day: $246 (6 days)
Season: $1000
Other ticketing information:
Children aged ten and under ski free all season (up
to two kids per adult).

SNOWBOARD SHOPS
World Boards — Tel: 406-995 3444
This classic, independent store is the nucleus of
the local riding scene and offers good stock,
superb repairs and tuning. Any queries about the
mountain, ask here.

SNOWBOARD SCHOOL
Big Sky Snowboard School — Tel: 406-995 5743
Two hour beginner lessons cost $27. The Never-Ever
package is a bargain which includes rentals, a
group lesson and a follow-up private lesson.

Big Sky

ON THE MOUNTAIN

Big Sky offers 3500 acres (1414 hectares) of incredibly diverse terrain spread over two mountains: Lone Mountain and Andesite Mountain. Lone Peak is the first thing you see as you drive up the road; it's an enduring icon and perennial challenge, even for strong riders. Before the Lone Peak Tram was built in '95, only crazies hiked the peak; Big Sky was then known to the paying public for its intermediate terrain and light queue lines. The tram has since escalated Big Sky's lift-serviced vertical into the league of top ranking US resorts, and opened up huge amounts of advanced and expert terrain. Both sides of the peak offer steep-as-you-like cliffs and chutes descending into the rugged bowl above the tree line and the main trails. There is truthfully no easy way down from the top and even the wide open South Face has a gradient of up to 50 degrees. Andesite is the 8800 foot (2684 metre) cone just south of the base area, featuring wide, groomed trails down both sides. It's named after the abundance of Andesite shale which has a voracious appetite for P-tex and steel edges.

SNOW CONDITIONS The resort receives dumps from storms coming from the west or south-west and the peak tends to pick up any snow in the area. Due to the predominantly southern and eastern aspects of the lower mountain, the slushies tend to come early.

FREERIDERS The most extreme freeride terrain is accessed from the Lone Peak Tram with most of it visible on the three minute ride up. For all you big Kahunas out there, check out the two couloirs: Little and Big. Both are almost straight in front of you on the way up and are

accessible when the back-country is open; ride with a partner and carry all the gear such as a transceiver and shovels. Depending on how brave you feel, you can either drop off Big Couloir which has a gradient of 48 degrees, or huck off the cornice at 30 degrees. Little Couloir is the steepest line on the mountain. Skier's left from the top of the tram, you'll see a bunch of chutes, and you can usually find a fresh line if they're open. The chutes are accessed by hiking straight up from the top of the triple chair where you have to sign out with the ski patrol. Another collection of runs called The Gullies face north above The Bowl and are accessible from the tram. Ride down Marx and drop in for a 38 degree slope.

The South Face has the steepest open terrain on the mountain. With fresh pow and bluebird conditions, there are a huge number of sweet lines down but its a freaky, slide-for-life nightmare when it's cooked. Highlights include staying skier's right down Thunder then plundering Liberty Bowl, or getting fresh lines down Dictator Chutes and Vertical Reality, both double as a black diamond gets. Little Tree is a short, intense freeride shot, skier's right off the top of the Challenger Chair. It starts out mellow and then gets steeper with little chutes, rocks and small trees.

FREESTYLERS Big Sky has no real park or pipe. Lobo laps are a popular jibbing favourite as the run has good hits and jumps either side. The Shedhorn side gets a bit of wind and some hefty snow drifts which can be good to bash. The attempt at a funpark is located under the Swift Current Quad. It was apparently pretty cool when it was first built but a bunch of skiers were hurt on it in '97, so they flattened the landings (actually making it more dangerous). There's also a small, natural halfpipe at the top of Lower Morning Star.

CARVERS Big Sky sure know how to groom their trails. The most fun runs are the groomers on Andesite Mountain, serviced by the two high-speed quads Ramcharger and Thunder Wolf. Check out Elk Park Ridge or Big Horn for a speed fix.

MOUNTAIN FOOD It's all in the Mountain Mall at the base. For snacks or a huge, hand-built sandwich, the Deli is the place. Another good, cheap lunch option is the pizza joint next to the Deli which sells fat slices to go for a couple of bucks. The Whiskey Jack sundeck is a fun place to sit down and chill.

HAZARDS AND RULES All ways down from Lone Peak are potentially hazardous to your health and intermediates are discouraged from riding there. Check conditions with the ski patrol before ascending.

ABOUT TOWN

Big Sky is a destination resort nearly an hour's drive from the nearest town, Bozeman. The resort has nearly twenty restaurants and bars, a snowboard store and a couple of lodges, so there's always something going on. It's unlikely you'll go stir-crazy within a few weeks but if you feel the symptoms coming on, get your ass to Bozeman to kick out the jams.

ACCOMMODATION Huntly Lodge is a great place to stay with rooms from $100 — Tel: 406-995 5002. The Golden Eagle is a basic motel in Meadow Village priced at $45 per night. The Corral is a roadhouse five miles (eight kilometres) from the resort turn-off, across from the Rainbow Ranch. The resort offers four person package deals costing $200 per person for four nights and three days. Contact Central Reservations — Tel: 406-995 5894.

FOOD If you're staying at Huntly Lodge, you'll wake up to the most awesome breakfast buffet imaginable. The Sun Dog Café is another good place to fuel up with expressos and fresh muffins. In the evening, the ribs at Mr Hummers are legendary. Scissorbills has the fattest burgers in town. For a more expensive meal, the Rainbow Ranch, First Place and Buck's T-4 are all excellent.

NIGHTLIFE Lolo's is a dance hall and saloon for hard-core drinking and occasional live music. Dante's Inferno and Chet's Bar are both bars with restaurants which whoop it up on a good night. Disco night at Dante's in particular sees frothing dance action.

OTHER ACTIVITIES Gambling is legal in Montana; indulge in a game at Chet's. A short drive south, Yellowstone National Park has great snowmobiling. The Bozeman hot springs, on Highway 191 between Big Sky and Bozeman, can be very therapeutic despite their dilapidated appearance.

THANKS TO Sarah Healy, Stephan and Mike, Junior, and all the crew at World Boards.

For more About Town, see Bridger Bowl review p.86.

Opposite — The summit **Photo:** Tim Rainger
Top — Big Sky panorama **Photo:** Tim Rainger
Middle — Big Sky, big kids **Photo:** Tim Rainger
Bottom — Big Sky, big air **Photo:** Tim Rainger

GETTING THERE
By air: Delta and several other airlines have daily services to Gallatin Fields Airport at Bozeman — Tel: 1-800-221 1212. The resort is an hour's drive from Bozeman. 4X4 Stagelines offer a return shuttle for around $40 per person — Tel: 406-388 6404 or 1-800-517 8243.
By car: The mountain is three miles (five kilometres) off Highway 191 which runs between West Yellowstone and Bozeman up the side of the Gallatin River. If you're commuting from Bozeman, get on the road early as the drive can be slow and treacherous with new snow.

2

Bridger Bowl

THE FACTS

ELEVATION

Summit:
8100ft, 2470m
Vertical drop:
2000ft, 610m
Base:
6100ft, 1860m

SNOWFALL

Average annual:
350 inches, 890cm

Snow-making:
10%

AREA

Total area:
1200 acres, 484ha

Advanced: 40%
Intermediate: 35%
Beginner: 25%

SEASON
December — April

COMMUNICATIONS
Snow report: Tel: 406-586 2389
Web site: http://www.bridgerbowl.com
E-mail: skitrip@bridgerbowl.com
Mountain information:
Tel: 406-587 2111 or 1-800-223 9609

LIFTS AND TICKETS
Number of lifts:
6 chairlifts
Lift pass prices:
1/2 day: $25
1 day: $29
Multi-day: N/A
Season: $410-$440
Other ticketing information:
Tickets cost $12 for children 12 and under.

SNOWBOARD SHOPS
World Boards — Tel: 406-587 1707
This shop is a purists' store with everything you
could imagine, and service and know-how to
match. The coffee's always brewing.

SNOWBOARD SCHOOL
Bridger Bowl Ski School
Tel: 406-587 2111 or 1-800-223 9609
Snowboard lessons lasting 90 minutes are available
from $20.

ON THE MOUNTAIN

Bridger is a wild frontier, home to skiers and snowboarders with a crazed look in their eye.
There's no big talking scene and no posers, just earthy people grabbing freshies away from the

spotlight. The Bridger Range runs north to south
for 70 miles (112 kilometres). Bridger Bowl Ski
Resort in the Gallatin National Forest is a
private, non-profit corporation associated with
Montana State University, designed to offer
affordable skiing and riding to local citizens. For
that reason it has a welcoming atmosphere and it
won't be long before you'll know everyone on
the mountain. Bridger Bowl should in fact read
Bridger Bowls as the resort occupies two bowls
and two ridges, The Nose and The Ridge. It is divided into Upper and Lower Mountain by the
lift system. The Lower Mountain is very flat up to the Deer Park Chalet but it turns into black
diamond terrain by the time you get to the Bridger Chair. From the top of the chair, you can
traverse either way or hike the last 500 vertical feet (150 metres) to the top of the ridge.

SNOW CONDITIONS The seasonal snowfall average is normally 30 feet (nine metres) although the '97-'98
season saw more than 35 feet (ten metres) by March. Unfortunately the whole resort faces east so when the
'grey smoke' clears in late March to early April, the sun bakes the snow fairly uniformly.

FREERIDERS The Ridge is the single main reason to come to Bridger and, despite the hike, the area can get
800 to 1000 visits on a big day. The Ridge is an in-bounds/out of bounds area, 500 feet (150 metres) above
the Bridger Lift. It's only a 15 minute hike but it's straight up. Once at the top, you have two choices: walk
north (skier's left) or south (skier's right). There are an infinite number of lines down either way, so it's
usually possible to find some freshies. The run is not hugely long and the locals lap it up to ten times a day.
Lower Mountain primo areas include the North and South Bowls which are awesome on a powder day. From
the top of the Bridger Lift, take either High Traverse or North Bowl Road. Directly below the High Traverse,
the Whirlpool harbours some choice terrain: cliffs, chutes, trees and double black diamonds like The Zits,
Avalanche Gulch, and Sluice Box. Above South Bowl and Pierre's Knob is an area known as The Fingers which
has good steeps and chutes running back into South Bowl. The nearby South Boundary often has fresh pow.

FREESTYLERS There are loads of natural obstacles on Bridger Bowl but nothing man-made. Lower Avalanche
is a big natural halfpipe. Jibbers hang out on the run below the Alpine Lift where a boardercross was held
in the '96-'97 season. There are also some fairly large road gaps in-bounds.

CARVERS There's good carving from top to bottom on Pierre's Knob and Deer Park. When they groom the
North and South Bowls, be ready for some steep corduroy. Long mellow runs abound off the Alpine Chair.

MOUNTAIN FOOD The cafeteria at Jim Bridger Lodge has your standard burgers and friendly staff. The
Expresso Café is a cool place to hang on the terrace; it's the locals' choice for coffee during the day and
afternoon beers. Another full service cafeteria is located at the mid-mountain Deer Park Chalet and sells
soups, baked goods and hot chillies.

HAZARDS AND RULES If you're riding The Ridge and The Fingers you must take a partner, a shovel and a
transceiver. Sign out with the patrol box at the base of the walk.

ABOUT TOWN

Bozeman is a college town of about 30,000 inhabitants and despite the relative isolation, it has a lot going on. The many bars and restaurants are busy every night of the week, in part due to the lively student population. During the day, you'll find a big choice of facilities not available at many other resort towns. Bozeman shares the overall flavour of Bridger Bowl with a lightly beat-up but super fun feel.

ACCOMMODATION The cheapest on-mountain accommodation is the Bangtail Bungalow where three nights cost $400 for up to six people. The Silver Forest Inn is a more personal B&B with double rooms from $78 to $120 a night. Set in the woods, the Mountain Cabin is a cool place sleeping up to six per cabin and costing $800 for four nights. In Bozeman, the Imperial Inn is a motel on Main Street costing $38 per person per night. The resort offers package deals, such as three days' riding and three nights' lodging for $120. Central Reservations — Tel: 406-586 1518 or 1-800-223 9609.

FOOD La Parilla has huge burritos for less than $5 on West Babcock Street. Another place for cheap, killer burritos is Sobie's on the corner of Main and Rouse Street. The Bistro on Main Street is legendary for good food but can be expensive. MacKenzie River Pizza is the place for crusty pizzas dripping with tasty toppings. The Bozeman Inn is a good breakfast stop located on East Main Street. For homecooked food, the Stockyard Café off Story Mill Road does breakfast and lunch from Friday till Monday. Finding the restaurant is part of the trip; the card reads: 'Fine it. A find dining experience'.

NIGHTLIFE The Zebra is the hot spot. Molly Brown's is a big pool hall and bar on Babcock Street. The Hoffbrau, home to local band Tex Tucker and Tetones, has big carousing nights. The crowd is an odd cross between hippy bikers and uni students. Owing to the cold weather, the local crew hook up at the bars and then go on to house parties. They're quick to invite out-of-towners along who seem cool and can hack the pace.

OTHER ACTIVITIES Mountain biking, hiking, behaving like a student.

THANKS TO Doug Wales, Margaret, Jeremy at World Boards, Bernie Bernthal.

Opposite — Bridger Bowl **Photo:** Tim Rainger
Top — Walking the ridge **Photo:** Tim Rainger
Middle — Margaret **Photo:** Tim Rainger
Bottom — The terrain off the ridge **Photo:** Tim Rainger

GETTING THERE

By air: Gallatin Field Airport, serviced by Delta Airlines, is only a ten minute drive from Bozeman — Tel: 1-800-221 1212.
By bus: Greyhound stops at Bozeman — Tel: 1-800-231 2222.
By car: Bridger Bowl is 16 miles (25 kilometres) from Bozeman on Highway 86. Bozeman is easily accessed on Interstate 90 between Billings and Butte.
Getting around: Two mountain shuttles leave from Bozeman. They pick up from all the lodgings in town for $7 return. Shuttles leave at 8.00am, 9.30am and 11.30am, returning at 1.15pm and 4.30pm.

3

IDAHO

STATE INFORMATION

Population: 1,200,000
Time: Pacific Standard Time = GMT minus 8 hours
(north of the Salmon River) Mountain Standard Time
(south of the Salmon River) = GMT minus 7 hours
Capital city: Boise
Area: 83,557 sq miles (215,577 sqkm)

COMMUNICATIONS

Idaho Tourist Board:
Tel: 208-334 2470 or 1-800-VISITID
Fax: 208-334 2631
E-mail: tourism@idoc.state.id.org
Web site: http://visitid.org

GETTING AROUND

Main airports: Sun Valley — Tel: 208-733 5215,
Idaho Falls — Tel: 208-529 1221
By bus: Greyhound — Tel: 1-800-231 2222
By train: Amtrak — Tel: 1-800-872 7245
Road conditions: Tel: 208-336 6600
Speed limits: Varies between 55 and 75 mph
(88 and 120 kmph).

OTHER VITALS

Avalanche advisory service: Tel: 208-788 1200

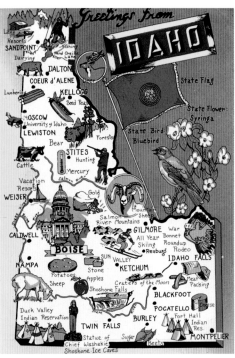

INTRODUCTION

The northern two-thirds of Idaho sit on the western slopes of the Rockies, whose highest peaks reach over 10,000 feet (3,000 metres). It's a glorious, pristine state with 40 per cent of its area covered by coniferous forest. Idaho's population of 1,200,000 are thinly spread across the large area and they enjoy the space and the outdoors. Although there are comparatively few mountain resorts in Idaho, Sun Valley is universally known for both its celeb appeal and the fact that in '39 it was the first resort in the world to design and construct a chairlift to be used by skiers. More generally, it's a hunting, fishing and belching sort of state known mainly for its potatoes. You'll find no cities of major importance; it's a lifestyle place where people are friendly, and have time to spare.

Main picture — Keith enjoying the goods courtesy of Sun Valley Heliski **Photo:** Tim Rainger
Left — Ketchum **Photo:** Tim Rainger

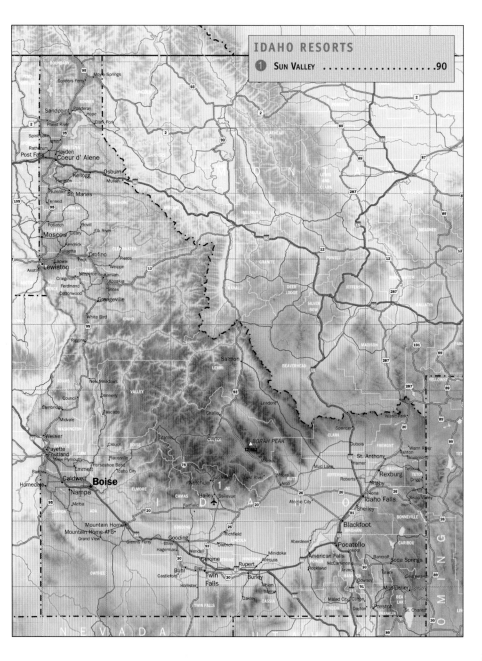

IDAHO RESORTS

1 SUN VALLEY .90

ELEVATION

Summit: 9150ft, 2790m	
Vertical drop: 3400ft, 1037m	
Base: 5750ft, 1753m	

SNOWFALL

Average annual: 250 inches, 635cm	
Snow-making: 78%	

AREA

Total area: 2067 acres, 832ha	
Advanced: 17%	
Intermediate: 45%	
Beginner: 38%	

SEASON
Late November — May

COMMUNICATIONS
Snow report: Tel: 208-622 2093 or 1-800-635 4150
Web site: http://www.sunvalley.com
E-mail: sunval@micron.net
Mountain information:
Tel: 208-622 2248 or 1-800-634 3347

LIFTS AND TICKETS
Number of lifts:
7 high-speed quads, 10 chairlifts
Lift pass prices:
1/2 day: $36.50
1 day: $50
Multi-day: $282 (6 days)
Season: N/A
Other ticketing information:
Children under 15 stay and ski free for as many days as their parents during low season periods in January and after mid-March.

SNOWBOARD SHOPS
The Board Bin — Tel: 208-726 1222
The Board Bin has been selling fine snowboarding equipment for nine years. Girl Street inside has equipment and clothing for women. Stop by for demos, Keith's legendary tune-ups and good prices on boards.

SNOWBOARD SCHOOL
Sun Valley Ski School — Tel: 208-622 2248
Lessons for all abilities cost $40 for two hours.

Sun Valley

ON THE MOUNTAIN

Averell Harriman, owner of the Union Pacific Railroad, put Count Felix Schaffgotsch (whoever the hell he was) on a train and told him to find the best place in the US for a ski resort. Sun Valley was his choice. The world's first chairlift was subsequently designed and constructed here in '39 using techniques for loading bananas onto boats. More recently, it's been no accident that both US downhill ski queen Picabo Street and current snowboard world champion Sandra Van Ert grew up racing on this mountain. Bald Mountain (affectionately known as Baldy) has a steep, nearly perfect gradient from peak to base. Sun Valley may not get as much snow as its neighbours, but you get quality turns from top to bottom, with no flats to get stuck on and bowls that beg you to go full throttle.

SNOW CONDITIONS Although 20 feet (seven metres) of natural snow a year doesn't exactly make Sun Valley a powder Mecca, the cold climate and mainly northern exposures preserve what snow it does get. Add the world's largest automated snow-making system and you get consistently good snow. There are also a multitude of south-facing slopes which turn to corn in late March for great spring conditions.

BACK-COUNTRY OPTIONS Sun Valley Helis operate a friendly heli-guide service. Prices are based on how many vertical feet are clocked up. They fly in the ranges behind Baldy and can always access the goods — Tel: 208-622 7936 or 1-800-872 3108. About 20 miles (32 kilometres) north of Ketchum, Galena Summit has great back-country terrain which is pretty hairy in places. Avalanche hotline — Tel: 208-788 1200.

FREERIDERS If you hit Sun Valley on a powder day, head straight to the bowls accessed from the top of the Lookout or Challenger Chair. Go early for freshies as locals devour the soft stuff like piranhas. Some good tree powder stashes lie between Limelight and Picabo Street, and between Picabo Street and Flying Squirrel. The trees off Fire Trail are also worth a look. The Board Ranch side, outside the boundary to the left of International, is loaded with acres of tree shots. The Frenchman's area has narrow tree-lined runs with a good pitch and is a good place to loiter in bad light conditions. To avoid getting lost and having to hitch-hike home, keep traversing to the right. Better yet, go with someone who knows the area and the hazards.

FREESTYLERS The freestyle scene in Sun Valley is pretty much the silent majority. Silent because most of the good freestyle stuff lies off the major runs. There are some radical cat-track hits for large air if you look for them at the top of Canyon, along Warm Springs and at the top of Olympic. I-80 is a steep cat-track that has about a mile of hits on the uphill wall. Every snowgun on the groomed runs builds into a hit; these can be great for learning technical tricks.

CARVERS Sun Valley is an unreal mountain for carving due to the endless, perfectly groomed black diamonds. Warm Springs and Mid River Run offer big banked gullies that are groomed way up the walls. They ride like a rollercoaster. Take care as many groomed runs are speed control areas. For an unrestricted autobahn, hit Limelight when it's groomed or Upper Ward Springs to Flying Squirrel for a top to bottom streak down the hill.

MOUNTAIN FOOD Seattle Ridge, Warm Springs and River Run Lodges all offer great food in ridiculously ritzy lodges. If you can stomach hot dogs, Irving's Red Hots at the base of Warm Springs makes a mean one with the works and chips for $2. The Apples' Bar and Grill pumps out the best French fries in town.

HAZARDS AND RULES Be mindful of the slow skiing areas as the patrol will pull your pass for speeding or catching air. Skiing out of bounds is permitted since it is all US Forest Service land, but be forewarned that a patrol service is not provided. If you get hurt in the back-country, you will be liable for rescue costs that can run to the thousands.

Sun Valley

ABOUT TOWN

Confusing as it may seem, Sun Valley Ski Resort is actually in Ketchum, an old town founded by miners in the 1880s. Sun Valley was created as a resort in the late '20s for wealthy socialites and film stars, but Ketchum is the real heart and soul of Sun Valley. The core of K-town is Main Street which looks like the main street from any Western spaghetti movie. Bruce Willis, Demi Moore, Jamie Lee Curtis and Arnold Schwartzenegger drink coffee and hang out here, and Ernest Hemingway played, gambled and finally shot himself in the town. His granddaughter Muriel rides daily, hangs out and takes yoga classes for snowboarders.

ACCOMMODATION There are three different areas to stay in: Sun Valley (near the lifts), Ketchum or Elkhorn. If you're a literature fan, the Ketchum Korral across from the Lift Tower was an old Hemingway and Ezra Pound haunt. Rooms start at $58 per night — Tel: 208-726 3510. The Ski View Lodge is in the $40-$60 range and is close to everything — Tel: 208-726 3441. Packages start from $233 for three nights' lodging and a two day lift pass, or from $55 for seven nights' lodging and a six day lift pass. Call Central Reservations — Tel: 208-726 5163 or 1-800-462 8646.

FOOD Desperados, across from the Board Bin, serves cheap Mexican food and bottomless soft drinks. Try the fish burrito special or the vegetarian zucchini burrito. Authentic Mexican by the kilo at Mama Inez's will appeal to the budget minded. Globus Noodle and China Pepper both serve good Asian dishes but are a tad pricey. The Panda has tasty Chinese food at reasonable prices, including a mean hot and sour soup that could cure cancer — well, at least a cold. Java on 4th Street has coffee and muffins, and is open till midnight. The best sushi you'll ever eat is at Sushi on Second. The only food available after 10.00pm is from the Hot Dog Adventure Company and you don't want to know what the adventure is.

NIGHTLIFE Ketchum wails. After an aprés-ski drink at Apples, the crowd heads to Grumpy's, a serious locals' pub with a sign that reads 'Sorry — we're open'. Beers come in a 34 ounce schooner resembling a fish bowl. Music plays at Whiskey Jacques and the Roosevelt Tavern, directly across from each other on Main Street. Whiskey Jacques claim that Ernest Hemingway drank here, but then old Hem drank everywhere. Still, this is the pub where Hemingway sank his last wee dram at 11.00am before pasting his brains on the wall with his Dad's shotgun. All roads lead eventually to the Casino where you can score big, cheap drinks from the town's busiest, friendliest bartenders. Trash Disco on Thursdays at Bruce Willis' club, the Mint in Hailey, is a notorious meat market. For an insider's guide to Sun Valley, check out the Sun Valley Underground Magazine on the web: http://www.svund.com/.

OTHER ACTIVITIES If you're around in the spring, don't be surprised to see sensible-looking people carrying what look like very high tech mortars. They're not militia, just practitioners of Idaho's state sport, potato shooting.

THANKS TO Jim and Karin, Dana, Dave, Keith and all the Board Bin Crew, Jack Sivvach, Mark and Kim, Doug Ellsley, JET.

Top — Keith, Sun Valley back side **Photo:** Tim Rainger
Bottom — Sun Valley sign **Photo:** Tim Rainger

GETTING THERE

By air: Sun Valley has its own airport, serviced by Delta Airlines — Tel: 1-800-221 2121. If the weather is snowy, flights are diverted to Twin Falls, 90 minutes away by bus. The airlines have stopped paying for the bus from Twin Falls so fly at your own risk. Bald Mountain Cabs and A1 Taxis can pick you up at the airport and take you to town for $10.

By bus: Sun Valley Stages drive to the resort from Boise, Idaho Falls, Twin Falls, Idaho and from Salt Lake City, Utah — Tel: 208-383 3085 or 1-800-821 9064.

By car: From Boise: Take Interstate 84 east to Mountain Home. Head east on US 20 and then north on Highway 75 to Ketchum. Drive time is two to three hours. From Salt Lake City: Take Interstate 15 north and Interstate 84 west to Twin Falls. Follow Highway 93 north to Shoshone and then Highway 75 north to Ketchum. Drive time is four to five hours.

Getting around: A free bus service is provided by Ketchum Area Rapid Transit (KART) with stops all over town — Tel: 208-726 7140.

Island Lake Lodge

Palmer, Wallace

Signature Boot Series

TEAM Vans ™

WYOMING

STATE INFORMATION

Population: 453,588
Time: Mountain Standard Time = GMT minus 7 hours
Capital city: Cheyenne
Area: 97,914 sq miles (252,678 sqkm)

VISITOR INFORMATION SOURCES

Wyoming Tourism:
Tel: 307-777-7777 or 1-800-225 5996
Fax: 307-777 6904
E-mail: polson@missc.state.wy.us
Web site: www.state.wy.us/state/welcome.html

GETTING AROUND

Main airports: Jackson Hole — Tel: 307-733 7695,
Cheyenne — Tel: 307-634 7071
By bus: Powder River — Tel: 307-682 0960
Greyhound — Tel: 307-634 7744
Road conditions: Tel: 307-635 9966
Speed limits: Up to 75mph (120 kmph) on some
interstates, otherwise it's 65mph (104 sqkm).

INTRODUCTION

Wyoming is the least populated of the 50 states, but nearby Yellowstone National Park is a magnet for five million tourists each year, turning summer in the parks into the great outdoors' answer to Disneyland. It's also total wild west and almost impossible to escape the iconography. Not everyone wears a stetson and Wranglers, but nearabouts. Famous place names from wilder days (like Fort Laramie, the Big Horn Mountains, the Badlands, The Black Hills, Cheyenne, Cody and more) pepper the map. The Oregon trail and the Union Pacific stamped a path through here, and after the Shoshone and Arapahoe Indians were wiped out, cattle barons settled the surrounding plains. Owing to the primal landscape and low population density, there are moments when you feel little has changed.

Wyoming's two prime snowboard resorts lie amidst some of the most spectacular mountains in the US. The peaks of the Grand Teton Range are younger and less flattened by time and the elements than many of the Southern Rockies, with a steepness and character which appeals to mountain purists. The snowboard, ski and climbing scene at both Jackson Hole and Grand Targhee are very integrated and the social vibe is mighty hospitable.

Opposite — Bryan Iguchi **Photo:** Wade McKoy
Top — **Photo:** Tim Rainger
Middle — The Tetons and Snake River **Photo:** Tim Rainger

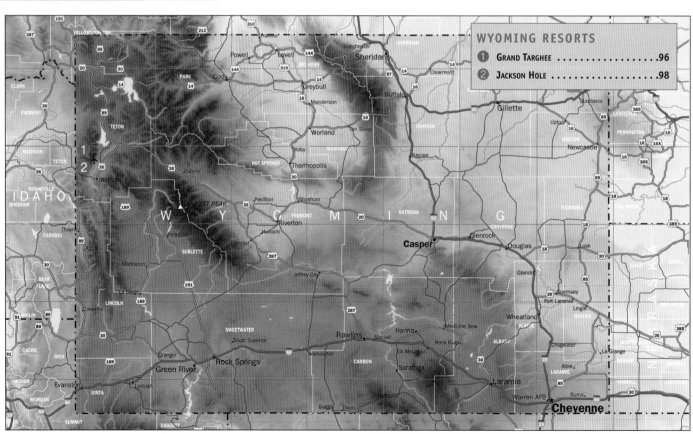

THE FACTS

ELEVATION

Summit:
10,250ft, 3126m
Vertical drop:
2200ft, 840m
Base:
8000ft, 2440m

SNOWFALL

Average annual:
504 inches, 1270cm

Snow-making:
From heaven

AREA

Total area:
3000 acres, 1212ha

Advanced: 20%
Intermediate: 70%
Beginner: 10%

SEASON

Mid-November — mid-April

COMMUNICATIONS

Snow report: Tel: 1-800-TARGHEE
Web site: idahonews.com/targhee/powder.htm
E-mail: targhee@pdt.net
Mountain information:
Tel: 307-353 2300 or 1-800-TARGHEE

LIFTS AND TICKETS

Number of lifts:
3 chairlifts, 1 handle tow
Lift pass prices:
1/2 day: $28
1 day: $38
Multi-day: $170 (5 days)
Season: $800
Other ticketing information:
If you purchase a Value Plus Card for only $49 you
will receive $15 off a full day ticket. If you
purchase more than ten tickets during the season
you'll receive one free day. See Jackson Hole
review, p.100 for more options.

SNOWBOARD SHOPS

Phat Freds — Tel: 307-353 2300 ext. 1385
The core store for sales and rentals located in the
Base Lodge. They also have Joyride and Burton
boards, and Switch bindings available for demo.
B+B: $25.

Grand Targhee

ON THE MOUNTAIN

Spectacularly stashed on the west side of the Tetons in the Targhee National Forest, Grand Targhee undoubtedly houses the goods. The name itself is an abridged reference to both Grand Teton Mountain, which soars above the resort to almost 14,000 feet (4260 metres), and to a local Indian hero. Chief Targhee kept the peace between the white settlers and his tribe, despite federal double dealings and a litany of broken promises that saw his land unceremoniously stolen in the second half of the 1800s. His painted likeness watches over the base complex and Dreamcatcher Quad.

Targhee is a wide intermediate area dotted with trees and punctuated by a few short steeps. There are actually two peaks: Fred's Mountain where the lifts are located, and Peaked Mountain where the cats operate. Mary's Nipple pokes up between them and though it appears to be back-country, it's actually in-bounds and patrolled by the resort, though it's often closed due to avalanche risk. The only lift-accessible back-country is called 'Steve-Ba Bowl' and it's strictly for the advanced as it's unpatrolled on national forest land. The ski patrol can provide an emergency rescue service at stiff cost.

SNOW CONDITIONS Targhee gets hellish amounts of snow. The mountain is west-facing and so any kind of precipitation from the west or south just tends to hang in the valley, hence it's local nickname, 'Grand Foggy'. Grand Targhee often has fresh snow when Jackson is scraped out.

BACK-COUNTRY OPTIONS A day of cat-boarding on Peaked Mountain costs $210; the price includes lunch, snacks and beverages — Tel: 1-800-827 4433.

FREERIDERS There are plenty of good lines. For most of us this place is heaven; there's only minor grooming, a consistent (though not extreme) pitch and uncrowded acres of wide open pow fields. From the top of the new Dreamcatcher Chair, go skier's left down the Teton Vista Traverse and drop any line you like. The run starts off open and flattish at the top and gets steeper as you drop into the open trees before the cat-track. If you follow the line skier's left to the base of the Peaked Cliffs, it runs out down a high-walled natural halfpipe called Waterfall.

The Headwall and Chutes are where you'll find most of the short steep shots available like Good Medicine, Bad Medicine and the Ugly. From the top of Dreamcatcher Chair, head skier's right from the top along the ridge line. You can drop six to 20 feet (two to seven metres) off the cornice at any point along the ridge.

When the in-bounds hiking is open, you can do a couple of cool hikes like Mary's Nipple, visible from the Teton Vista Traverse. You hike the ridge, pick a line, ride it, then hike the 700 steps back up. It's not too bad if it's been boot-packed which is usually the case. You can also walk the cat-territory on Peaked Mountain. Once at the drop-in point, take a line among the lightly-spaced trees and ride out the cat-track back to the base. Don't drop below it or you're in for a hike out. It's possible to ride the ridge and then huck the cliffs and chutes, but you have to be an animal as it's insanely steep.

FREESTYLERS You can't realistically call a drainage ditch under the lift a halfpipe, but in the resort's defence who wants to ride a pipe when there's so much fresh on the ground?

CARVERS It's a not steep or long enough to be renown as a hard-boot hill. There's too much pow; who needs hard edges?

MOUNTAIN FOOD All the eateries are located at the base. Snorkel's does fat sandwiches.

HAZARDS AND RULES Leash controls are enforced. They are pretty cautious about opening up the back-country, which can be a downer.

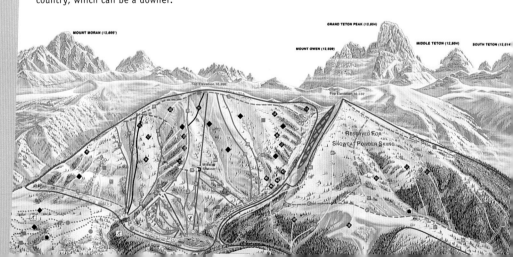

Grand Targhee

ABOUT TOWN

Grand Targhee is located in the town of Alta, Wyoming, but Alta is little more than an idea and a dot on the map. There are no towns nearby (other than Driggs or Jackson). The amenities at Grand Targhee are comprised of an eclectic collection of buildings including lodges, restaurants, an outdoor pool complex and administration offices. A very European looking clock tower guards a currently small, sleepy resort which has just changed ownership, finalised in the dying weeks of the '96-'97 season. For many years, Targhee has been privately owned but now George Gillette (owner of Northstar, Sierra Tahoe, Bear Mountain and other resorts) has added it to his portfolio. The good news is that he's very pro-snowboarding and has been a part of its progression. Expect no changes right away, but a lot in the future. Presently it's not the kind of place to come to for either shopping or nightlife as there isn't the population or the impetus. It's for people who want to ride, eat, sleep, wake up and ride fresh pow.

Top — Photo: Tim Rainger
Middle left — The Base Lodge Photo: Tim Rainger
Middle right — Grand Targhee, aka Grand Foggy Photo: Tim Rainger

ACCOMMODATION Targhee is a small resort and its bed space is in three main buildings: two hotel type lodges and a 32 unit multi-storey condo building. All are within walking distance of the lifts. For more information contact Central Reservations — Tel: 1-800-827 4433. You can also stay at Driggs or there are a couple of B&Bs on road to the mountain.

FOOD There are four places to eat in Targhee. During the day, Wild Bill's Café has a good selection. Snorkel's is a hot-pastry lunch stop with a coffee bar by the Dreamcatcher Quad. The Wizard of Za has pizza and Mexican food with cheaper dinner options. For family dining, Skadis has good food and relaxed service, but it's not cheap. The General Store at the Base Lodge sells an assortment of foods though its by no means a supermarket. If you're wisely staying in a condo, stock up on curiosity foods before you arrive. If you're coming over from Jackson for the day, the Breakfast Shoppe, just before the mountain turn-off at Driggs, provides a filling start to the day.

NIGHTLIFE There isn't any really, except for the Trap Bar in which sometimes has live music. In Driggs, the British Rail is a traditionally styled English pub of little fame and less repute.

OTHER ACTIVITIES Hot-tubs, cross-country skiing, dog-sledding, fitness workouts or sitting in the condo eating and watching TV.

THANKS TO Chief Targhee, Susie Barnett-Bushong, Paul and his wife.

GETTING THERE

By air: Targhee is served by airports in Jackson, Wyoming and Idaho Falls, Idaho. Airport shuttles run from Jackson Hole, Idaho Falls and Teton Peaks Airports — Tel: 1-800-TARGHEE. Delta Airlines flies to Jackson — Tel: 1-800-221 1212 for more information.

By bus: The Targhee Express travels over the Teton Pass from Jackson and Teton Village once daily; prices from $15 return.

By car: From Jackson it's a 42 mile (67 kilometre) drive via Driggs and Wilson. The road over the pass from Jackson normally closes two to three days a year but during the '96-'97 season it was closed for nearly three weeks. One avalanche that buried the road was 30 feet (ten metres) thick and took nearly eight days to clear away over the Christmas period. It's worth considering these risks if you're planning on driving this road.

Getting around: There is no need for a car if you are planning on staying at the resort. Daily hitching from Driggs is possible.

Jackson Hole

2

THE FACTS

ELEVATION

Summit: 11,102ft, 3385m	
Vertical drop: 4139ft, 1261m	
Base: 6314ft, 1925m	

SNOWFALL

Average annual: 402 inches, 975cm	
Snow-making: 5%	

AREA

Total area: 2500 acres, 1010ha	
Advanced: 50% Intermediate: 40% Beginner: 10%	

SEASON
Early December — mid-April

COMMUNICATIONS
Snow reports: Tel: 307-733 2291
Web site: http://www.jacksonhole.com/ski
E-mail: info@jacksonhole.com
Mountain information:
Tel: 307-733 2292 or 1-800-443 6931
Fax: 307-733 2660
Jackson Hole Chamber of Commerce:
Tel: 307-733 3316

LIFTS AND TICKETS
Number of lifts:
1 aerial tram, 1 gondola, 1 high-speed quad,
6 chairlifts, 2 surface lifts
Lift pass prices:
1/2 day: $36
1 day: $48
Multi-day: $258 (6 days)
Season: $1000
Other ticketing information:
Jackson Hole, Grand Targhee and Snow King sell a
Jackson Hole Ski Three voucher-book which
contains five lift vouchers valid at any of the three
resorts. All vouchers must be redeemed within a
week of the first one being used; price: $220.

SNOWBOARD SHOPS
Hole in the Wall — Tel: 307-739 2687
This is the specialist on-mountain store. B+B: $25.
Boardroom of Jackson Hole — Tel: 307-733 5228
The only independent store in town staffed by
riders that know their stuff and can pass on back-
country tips. B+B: $15.
Teton Mountaineering — Tel: 307-733 3595
A hard-core mountaineering shop on the northern
edge of town.

SNOWBOARD SCHOOL
Jackson Hole Ride School — Tel: 307-739 2663
Group lessons start at $55 for a full day. They have
a Steep Snowboard Camp held in March which
includes steep couloir, powder riding and climbing
instruction. The school also runs a three day Wild
Women's Snowboard Camp.

ON THE MOUNTAIN

The Jackson Hole Ski Area sits astride some of the most epic mountains in North America,
ascending 4139 feet (1261 metres) from the flats of Jackson and the Snake River to the peaks
of Rendezvous Mountain. Jackson Hole lays claim to having
the largest continuous vertical drop in the US. The resort
consists of two peaks, both accessed from Teton Village:
Aprés Vous, or Lower Mountain, is neatly separated from the
mega double diamonds of Rendezvous Mountain. While Aprés
Vous, or Lower Mountain won't enthral those seeking steeps,
it's an excellent learner and intermediate playground with
uncrowded lifts and some steep but legal out of bounds in

Saratoga Bowl. Rendezvous Mountain is split; the top half is an extreme snowboarders' Mecca
but becomes more manageable lower down. For the '97-'98 season, the Bridger Gondola
development will run from the base of the Rendezvous Mountain to the Headwall, and opens
up good intermediate and expert terrain which you currently have to hike to.

SNOW CONDITIONS Jackson Hole's season is shorter than some areas because of the low base elevation, but
it still gets around 32 feet (ten metres) of good fluffy snow each season. Most of the slopes are north-facing
and there are plenty of woods to find late powder stashes.

BACK-COUNTRY OPTIONS High Mountain Helis are found in Teton Village Sports at the base of the
mountain. Owned and operated by Junie Fuchs, they cover some of the most incredible terrain in North
America. A day of six runs costs $495 per person with extra runs for $60 — Tel: 307-733 3274. If you don't
have the budget but want to clock some quality back-country vertical, ride the Teton Pass, west of Jackson,
on the road to Grand Targhee. There's a huge amount of terrain accessed by hikes of varying length.
Jackson Hole Mountain Guides offer guided tours for intermediate to advanced riders in this area. A full day
for one person costs $200, each extra person is $35. A half day is $100, plus $35 per extra person — Tel:
307-733 4979. Avalanche hotline — Tel: 307-733 2664.

FREERIDERS Almost half of Jackson's terrain is known as expert and to get to most of it, you take The Tram.
The Tram is consistently stuffed with 50 or so of North America's, and the world's, best skiers and
snowboarders who are attracted by the myriad dizzying black and double black diamond runs. To stay in-
bounds you have to go skier's right from the top, either into the notorious Corbet's Couloir or across to the
East Ridge Traverse. Either option is steep and not for the faint-hearted. Head into Tensleep Bowl from the
East Ridge Traverse to access the soon to be out-dated hike to the Headwall. Extreme riders have been
known to sneak right from the top of The Tram which commits you to traversing the top of a cliff band,
shooting a vertical chute and breaking the boundary rules — so we're not recommending it.

On the lower half of Aprés Vous first timers will enjoy the Teewinot Chairlift (Teewinot is the Shoshone Indian
name for the Tetons meaning 'many peaks' or 'high pinnacles') and the Eagle's Rest. From Teewinot, keep
going up the Aprés Vous Chair. Once you're at the top, there are two broad choices; you can either cruise the
blues to the base or mash up the Teewinot face. If you're looking for steeps, there is an open boundary into
the Saratoga Bowl, weather and snow conditions permitting. Be wary of missing the Saint John traverse cat-
track back to Teewinot. The Saratoga Bowl is definitely not for beginners.

The Crystal Spring Chairlift leads to the Casper Bowl Chair which drops you above some cool intermediate to
advanced stuff. If you traverse skier's left from the top, you can either drop into the mellow terrain of
Sleeping Indian, or keep traversing and drop into Moran Woods, a great tree area. This can be a good place
to ride on flat light days and also when The Tram is closed due to winds (quite a frequent occurrence). Follow
the fall-line and you'll end up back at Teton Village.

FREESTYLERS There is an OK-ish halfpipe located beneath the Teewinot Chair, but funpark freaks will have
to go to Snow King Ski Area. Gros Venture is a good freestyle track which has a bunch of natural hits on an
average gradient. There are also a couple of natural halfpipes, Sundance Gully and Dick's Ditch.

CARVERS Obviously a big, steep mountain like Jackson is going to be a fun place to carve it up. The Easy-
Does-It side, skier's right from the top of the Casper Bowl Chairlift, is one of the prime-cut carving areas —
it's always kept well-manicured. It can be a smooth carpet all the way through to Sundance Gully.

MOUNTAIN FOOD There is a good café at Corbet's Cabin which does snack-food at the top of The Tram.
Casper's, located mid-mountain, has reasonable cafeteria-type food. If you could eat a horse, Nick Wilson's
Cowboy Café in the Clocktower provides reasonably priced, filling food. The Mangey Moose has a buffet salad
bar where the health conscious can stuff their faces with all they can eat for $7.

HAZARDS AND RULES The flexible boundary means the back-country is accessible when conditions allow.
There is information on the signs at the base. The ski patrol at Jackson are pretty hard-core so don't think you
can out ride them easily.

ABOUT TOWN

Jackson used to be a valuable summer hunting ground for the Arapaho, Sioux, Ute, Cheyenne and Shoshone Indians. The US acquired the area from France in 1803 and now the town sprawls along Broadway, then turns north up Highway 26. It's graced with more millionaires than any other back-country zip code in the US. Ironically it's most popular in summer when the trailer-home hoards go on bumper-to-bumper summer migration to Yellowstone and Grand Teton National Parks. Winter is the off season and it's an easy time to find accommodation and services. The town is a 15 minute drive from the mountain. At the base of the mountain is Teton Village, a small purpose-built complex. If you're here to ride hard, stay here.

ACCOMMODATION In Jackson town there's a number of options starting with The Lodge at Jackson, a comfortable, mid-priced hotel with a pool, and big whirlpool baths in your room — Tel: 307-739 9703. The Alpine House is run by former Olympians and climbers and has a great atmosphere; rooms cost $75-$95 — Tel: 307-739 1570. The Teton View B&B starts from $60-$80 — Tel: 307-733 7954. The Jackson Hole Racquet Club Resort has condos and excellent rooms for rent — Tel: 307-733 2992. The Bunkhouse is a hostel with dorm beds priced from $18 per night — Tel: 307-733 3668 or 1-800-234 4507.

If you want to stay by the mountain base at Teton Village, The Hostel offers slopeside rooms from $44 per night, an unbeatable deal if you consider the convenience — Tel: 307-733 3415. For luxurious surroundings with hot-tubs and saunas, the Soujourner Inn has twin rooms from $85-$200 — Tel: 307-734 0037. Central Reservations — Tel: 307-733 7182 or 1-800-443 6931.

FOOD Starting with a big breakfast, go to Bubba's Bar-B-Que, also a local evening favourite for grill dinners. The Calico and Mountain High Pizza Pie have mid-priced pizzas. The Bunnery has healthy food, including sandwiches, stews and grills. Café Amano has good Mexican and is also cheap. For Chinese, try out the Lame Duck. Antony's is a mid-priced lunch and dinner restaurant serving Italian food. Gourmet meals are served at both the The Blue Lion and the Snake River Grill. Jackson has over 80 restaurants, so call up the tourist office for a copy of their dining out guide.

NIGHTLIFE The Mangey Moose and the Pub at the Sojourner are the places to go for a cold beer after riding. The Moose could almost be classed as an early evening nightclub. The place goes wild with aprés-skiers, particularly at the weekends when there is live music. The pub at the Sojourner is a better place for a beer if you don't want to riot but don't miss the jägermeister shots.

One of Jackson's best known landmarks is the Million Dollar Cowboy Bar. It's like a traditional pool hall and bar, good and grungy. The Snake River Brew Pub is a clean, comfortable but expensive watering hole with regular live music. The Shady Lady at the Snow King also has live music on a Wednesday. The Log Cabin, five blocks down on Cash Street, is a popular locals' bar. The Rancher has pool tables and is pretty cool in a wild-west style — wear your cowboy hat.

OTHER ACTIVITIES Entry to the recreation centre costs $5; it has an excellent pool room. There's an indoor climbing wall just past McDonald's.

THANKS TO Chris Welbrecht, Peter Grant and Mikey.

Opposite — Jackson Hole resort **Photo:** Tim Rainger
Top — Jackson street view **Photo:** Tim Rainger

GETTING THERE

By air: The Jackson Hole Airport is located nine miles (15 kilometres) north of Jackson and 19 miles (30 kilometres) from the resort. Delta offer three daily Boeing 737 flights through Salt Lake City —Tel: 1-800-221 1212. For shuttles from the airport, call Gray Line of Jackson Hole — Tel: 307-733 4325, Jackson Hole Express — Tel: 307-733 1719 or Jackson Hole Transportation — Tel: 307-733 3135. The bus prices cost around $12 one-way.
By bus: Greyhound stops at Jackson.
By car: From Salt Lake City, head north on Interstate 15 to Highway 26. Cross the Teton Pass on Highway 31 and follow the signs for Jackson Hole or Teton Village.
Getting around: START run buses between the town of Jackson and Teton Village from 6.30am to 10.30pm during the winter season. A ride costs $2 each way — Tel: 307-733 4521.

RENDEZVOUS MOUNTAIN 10,450' (3185 METERS)
Greatest Continuous Vertical Rise in the United States 4,139' (1261 Meters)

UTAH

STATE INFORMATION

Population: 1,900,000
Time: Mountain West = GMT minus 7 hours
Capital city: Salt Lake City
Area: 84,000 sq miles (216,720 sqkm)

VISITOR INFORMATION SOURCES

Utah Tourism Board:
Tel: 801-538 1030
Fax: 801-538 1399
E-mail: kkraus@e-mail.state.ut.us
Web site: http://www.utah.com

GETTING AROUND

Main airports: Salt Lake International Airport —
Tel: 801-575 2400
By train: Amtrak — Tel: 801-364 8562
By bus: Greyhound — Tel: 1-800-724 8000
Road conditions: Tel: 801-964 6000
Speed limits: On major highways the speed limit is
75mph (120 kmph).

OTHER VITALS

Utah Avalanche Forecast Centre — Tel: 801-364 1581
Utah Snow Conditions — Tel: 801-521 8102

Main picture — Tanner Irion at Brighton **Photo:** Richard Cheski
Top right — Revisionist state plates **Photo:** Tim Rainger
Bottom left — Utah road sign **Photo:** Tim Rainger

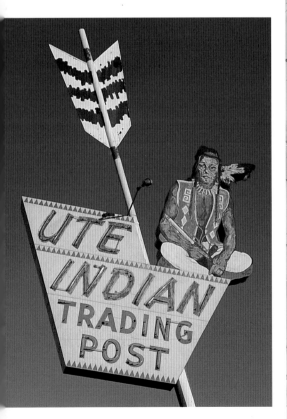

INTRODUCTION

Utah has to be one of the wierdest states in the US, with some of the strictest rules in the Christian world, and the lowest tolerance towards snowboarders on the planet. But Utah has always been a magnet for US riders and a few clued-in foreign visitors. The attraction is pure and simple: long winters with regular deliveries of light dry powder. Despite a ban on snowboarding by Park City, Solitude and Alta for at least a decade, a whole counter-culture has grown up amidst the Utah mainstream, emerging en-masse when the riders come out to play on bluebird days at resorts like Brighton and Snowbird. Park City and Solitude have finally relented in the face

of a groundswell of change in the winter sports' market. Salt Lake City is hosting the 2002 winter Olympics, which is generating a flood of new development, and should see widespread modernisation and facelifts at all the surrounding mountain resorts.

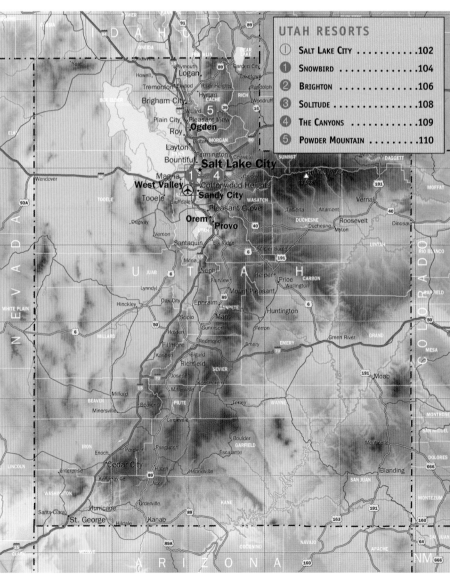

Salt Lake City

ABOUT TOWN

Salt Lake City was founded on July 2, 1847 by a group of Mormons led by Brigham Young, and consisting of 143 men, three women and two children. Mormons now make up 70 per cent of Utah's population and Salt Lake City is the commercial capital of the state. Temple Square was the centre of the old city and from there blocks radiated in a 10 acre (four hectare) grid, separated by 132 foot wide (40 metre) streets which were originally designed to allow a team of four oxen and a covered wagon to turn around. Despite the anomaly that Utah has more microbreweries than in other state in America, liquor laws are stringent and grocery stores only sell 3.2 per cent alcohol.

Most importantly, Salt Lake City sits at the base of the Wasatch Range, less than a 20 minute drive to the nearest airport. The city will host the 2002 Winter Olympics. For more information on what's going on, pick up a copy of Salt Lake This Week or check out: http://www.citysearch.com.

ACCOMMODATION The Wasatch Front Ski Accommodations has awesome condos at the base of the canyons on Wasatch Boulevard. It's an ideal place to stay on the outskirts of town, close to all the Cottonwood resorts. The apartments have it all with jacuzzis on the balconies, drive-in parking, huge beds and kitchens — Tel: 801-486 4296 or 1-800-762 7606. For more options, contact the Salt Lake City Visitors' Bureau — Tel: 801-364 8562.

FOOD The Fong Ling serves fat portions of good Chinese food at the Benches by the 7-11 store at the bottom of the canyons. The Cotton Bottom has burgers and pool tables; it's a cool place to hang out. For delicious vegetarian food, try the Park Ivy Garden Café. Over the Counter Café offers a hearty, cooked breakfast for around $5.

NIGHTLIFE Bars as you know them don't exist in Utah. To drink at a licensed establishment, you have to be a member of a club. The most frequently used method of getting around the legislature is 'sponsorship' by a local (possibly the barperson themselves) — don't be shy about asking. Proper clubs can charge short-term memberships for a group but local residents will have annual memberships allowing them to take guests. Restaurants can serve alcohol but won't display the list so again, don't be shy about asking. There are a lot of good brew pubs; Squatters is one of the microbreweries that's especially cool. The Pie has pizzas and beer. Other clubs worth a look include the Manhattan Club, Bricks Club, the Holy Cow, Spankies, Club DV8 and Zephyr.

THANKS TO Richard Cheski.

Opposite — Tina Basich flying with Wasatch Powderbirds **Photo:** Chris Murray
Inset — Salt Lake City from the freeway **Photo:** Tim Rainger
Top — Little Cottonwood Canyon **Photo:** Tim Rainger

GETTING THERE
By air: Salt Lake International Airport is serviced by a number of international carriers including Delta Airlines — Tel: 1-800-221 1212. The airport is a 20 minute drive from the city.
By bus: UTA (Utah Transit Authority) run a cheap, efficient bus system which services Little Cottonwood and Big Cottonwood Canyons — Tel: 801-287 4636 or Tel: 1-800-BUS-INFO. UTA also operate a fare-free zone in Salt Lake City.

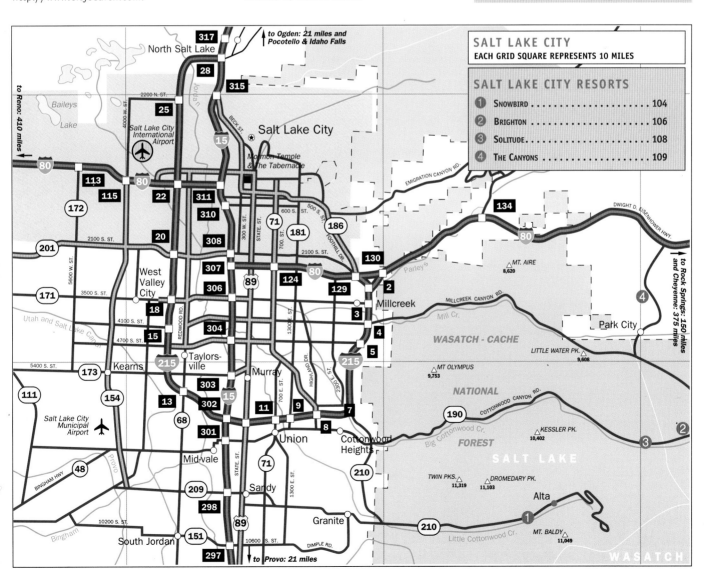

SALT LAKE CITY
EACH GRID SQUARE REPRESENTS 10 MILES

SALT LAKE CITY RESORTS

Snowbird

THE FACTS

ELEVATION

Summit:
11,000ft, 3355m
Vertical drop:
3240ft, 988m
Base:
7760ft, 2366m

SNOWFALL

Average annual:
500 inches, 1270cm

Snow-making:
2%

AREA

Total area:
2500 acres, 1010ha

Advanced: 45%
Intermediate: 35%
Beginner: 20%

SEASON

Mid-November — late May

COMMUNICATIONS

Snow reports: Tel: 801-742 2222 ext: 4285
Web site: http//:www.snowbird.com
E-mail: lccbird@aol.com
Mountain information:
Tel: 801-742 2222 ext. 4130
Fax: 801-742 3344

LIFTS AND TICKETS

Number of lifts:
1 tram, 1 high-speed quad, 7 chairlifts
Lift pass prices*:
1/2 day: $39, $32 (chairs only)
1 day: $47, $39 (chairs only)
Multi-day: $126 (3 out of 4 days)
Season: $1600
Other ticketing information:
* Full price tickets include the Tram and all
chairlifts. Smiths, the grocery chain-store, sells
discounted tickets for $38. Try the one just off
Wasatch Boulevard.

SNOWBOARD SHOPS

Powder Tools — Tel: 801-742 3449
It's a small, clued-in snowboard store facing onto
the plaza deck near the Tram entry.

SNOWBOARD SCHOOL

Snowbird Ski and Snowboard School
Tel: 801-742 2222 ext. 5170
Full day lessons start at $62. The school offers three
day Women's Camps in January costing $310 (lifts
not included), and a summer halfpipe camp in June.

GETTING THERE FROM SALT LAKE CITY

By air: Snowbird is 29 miles (40 kilometres) from Salt
Lake City International Airport.
By bus: Canyon Transportation have a 4WD shuttle to
Little Cottonwood resorts from the airport ($36 round
trip) — Tel: 1-800 255 1841. See Salt Lake City p.102.
By car: Take Interstate 80 east from Salt Lake City
and then Interstate 215 south to Highway 620 south.
Follow the ski area signs which lead up Highway 210.

ON THE MOUNTAIN

Snowbird is the boss: it's a mythically huge, double black diamond behemoth. The mountain has
become something of a benchmark for aspiring freeriders who migrate here from far and wide for
long winters of abundant, light powder and steep terrain. The meeting of like minds contributes
to a well-cooked scene. Dimitrije Milovich developed the first Winterstick swallow-tail powder
gun here, many of which now grace the walls of Milo Sport in Salt Lake City. Unfortunately the
lift system doesn't match the Bird's fast growing international reputation although the new
high-speed quad could alleviate some of the long lift queues. The most persistent queues are
for The Tram which takes 125 die-hard powder heads to 11,000 feet (3355 metres) in eight
minutes. Once there, it's a desperate scramble to clip in quick and score freshies.

SNOW CONDITIONS Snow depth averages over 40 feet (12 metres) from Thanksgiving Day until May. The
westerly snow pattern is boosted by the local precipitation contributions of the Great Salt Lake which lies
conveniently in the main storm path.

BACK-COUNTY OPTIONS For the ultimate Utah riding experience, telephone the Wasatch Powderbird Guides.
They run a champagne-style operation which can be group booked to take you almost anywhere in the Wasatch
Range — Tel: 801-742 2800. Snowcat boarding accesses over 400 acres (161 hectares) in the Mineral Basin Bowl,
at the top of Hidden Peak — Tel: 801-742 2222.

FREERIDERS The whole mountain is sick; just look at the trail map. At least half the available terrain is black
or double black diamond and encompasses everything from open bowls to steep chutes, cliffs and gladed
trees. For the best trees, ride the Gad Valley lifts: Gad 2 Chair or the new high-speed quad Gadzoom. Riding
The Tram gives you a complete visual of the best part of the mountain. The cliffs off the Cirque Traverse will
launch you as small or as big as you want to go. The Cirque is a long ridge separating the two sections of
the mountain. On one side, the Regulator Johnson trail leads to all the Gad Valley lifts and the hidden
stashes of powder. The more popular side of the mountain is referred to as The Chips. The Chips offers the
best top to bottom rides with natural halfpipes, trees, chutes and powder runs.

FREESTYLERS The halfpipe in Little Cloud Bowl opened in spring of '97 and will hopefully evolve over
subsequent seasons.

CARVERS There aren't too many hard boots on the mountain but there are a ton of steeps. If you want to
rip, this a good place to do it.

HAZARDS AND RULES Leashes are supposed to be worn but the rule is minimally enforced.

MOUNTAIN FOOD The Keyhole in the Cliff Lodge serves south-western food. For less expensive food, the
Rendezvous Café under the plaza deck serves burgers and the usual sandwiches and fries. The Fork Lift at the
plaza deck also has standard fare at reasonable prices. Filling $4 sandwiches are served at Gritts on the first
level of the Cliff Lodge.

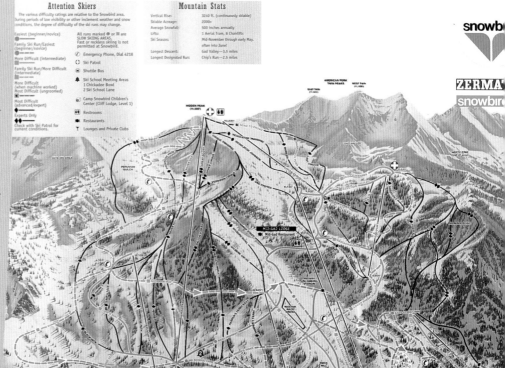

Snowbird

ABOUT TOWN

Snowbird is located in Little Cottonwood Canyon, about 25 miles (40 kilometres) from the middle of Salt Lake City. A mile up the road is the small ski town of Alta. Snowbird's main focus is the 12 storey Cliff Lodge, a complete on-mountain experience with a full service spa. The resort has a big, clean, corporate feel and it's not cheap. If you overlook its countenance, the village provides decent lodgings and food. Besides, some of the best powder in Utah is here to ride.

ACCOMMODATION The Cliff Lodge has good facilities but the atmosphere is quite family orientated. At night you are stranded up the canyon unless you take on the drive to Salt Lake City or use Canyon Transportation. Slopeside dorm beds cost $45-$59 per person in a four bedroom room. A standard room costs $135-$209 with early and late season packages for Amex holders. Condo units cost $105-$195 and sleep four. Other options are the Lodge at Snowbird and the Iron Blossom Lodge; prices for both start from $297 per night for a one bedroom condo. Central Reservations — Tel: 801-742 3344.

FOOD For a small town, there are a number of good places to eat. Try the coconut-battered prawns covered with jalepeno jelly at the Lodge Club. The Aerie restaurant at the top of the Cliff Lodge has a delicious sushi bar. The Steak Pit lives up to its name with great steak and seafood. For north Italian, the Wildflower Ristorante has enormous pastas, pizza and great food.

NIGHTLIFE The Tram Club in the Snowbird Centre sometimes has live music. The Keyhole serves pain-killing margaritas and the Lodge Club is also open till 1.00am. The Alta Peruvian Lodge at Alta is cool (for a skier's lodge) and is only two miles from Snowbird. The Wildflower Lounge is where the local working staff hang out.

OTHER ACTIVITIES The 115 foot (35 metre) climbing wall on the west face of the Cliff Lodge is one of the tallest in the world.

THANKS TO Kim Peterson, Misty Clark, Ox, Brenner Adams, Orion Burnham, Richard Cheski.

Main picture — Dan Ray **Photo:** Richard Cheski
Inset — The Tram **Photo:** Richard Cheski

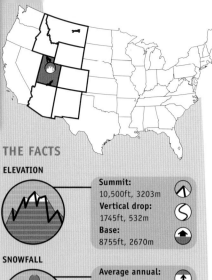

THE FACTS

ELEVATION

Summit:
10,500ft, 3203m
Vertical drop:
1745ft, 532m
Base:
8755ft, 2670m

SNOWFALL

Average annual:
500 inches, 1270cm

Snow-making:
24%

AREA

Total area:
850 acres, 344ha

Advanced: 39%
Intermediate: 40%
Beginner: 21%

SEASON

Mid-November — late April

COMMUNICATIONS

Snow report: Tel: 801-532 4731
Web site: http://www.skibrighton.com
E-mail: info@skibrighton.com
Mountain information:
Tel: 801-532 4731 or 1-800-873 5512

LIFTS AND TICKETS

Number of lifts:
7 chairlifts
Lift pass prices:
1/2 day: N/A
1 day: $29
Multi-day: N/A
Season: $725
Other ticketing information:
A day ticket is valid from 9.00am to 4.00pm or
12.30pm to 9.00pm. A superticket from 9.00am to
9.00pm costs $35 and night-riding from 4.00pm to
9.00pm costs $20. A single ride ticket costs $6 and
gets you up the mountain if you want to hike the
rest of the day. A full car in weekends and holidays
entitles all occupants to $1 off day lift passes.

SNOWBOARD SHOPS

There is no real snowboard store, though Brighton
Mountain Sports sell ski clothing and some
universal accessories. B+B: $28. The service centre
in the main building does waxes, edge grinds and
base repairs.

SNOWBOARD SCHOOL

Brighton Ski and Snowboard School
Tel: 801-532 4731
The Intro Package costs $50 and includes a
learner's lift ticket, equipment rental and a half
day lesson.

Brighton

ON THE MOUNTAIN

Salt Lake locals have been skiing here since '36, and Brighton also has one of the oldest
snowboard scenes in Utah and the US. The mountain is well-known and consistently patronised
for historic, pragmatic and financial reasons. When no-one in Utah welcomed snowboarding
(Alta still doesn't), Brighton opened their lifts to riders. On a practical level, the terrain
includes a satisfying mix of steeps, trees, hits, rocks and access to a heap of good back-
country. And to the relief of your wallet, the lift pass is the cheapest in the area.

SNOW CONDITIONS Like all the Cottonwood
mountains, Brighton has an impressive
snowfall record. Salt Lake contributes
serious amounts of moisture to the storms
which hit the canyons and dump up to three
inches of snow in an hour.

FREERIDERS Mount Millicent is one of the
main reasons snowboarders started coming
here — it's sublime. The Great Western has
the most difficult terrain in Brighton as
most of the runs are very advanced with only
a couple suitable for intermediates. From
the top of Clayton Peak, you have access to
some great back-country and hidden canyons. Ride around and down into the canyon through the trees and
keep left. You'll eventually pop out at the bottom of the Great Western Chair. If you miss the chair, you'll
end up on the road. To the right of Milly is the Wolverine Cirque; all the terrain is awesome with steeps,
chutes and other gnarly stuff. Tuscarora is the big run to the right of the Crest. Hike for an hour from the
top of Milly towards skier's left. There are a couple of thousand vertical metre (3000 foot) drops through
the chutes and the bowl. Ride out near the Crest Chair.

FREESTYLERS The halfpipe is left at the top of Majestic. It's a couple of hundred yards long and generally
well-maintained. A new funpark planned for the '97-'98 season will include a table top, a quarterpipe
leading into a transition, hips, elbows and some little ramps. The park should be pretty cool.

CARVERS The Great Western Elk Park Ridge, Aspen Glow (on a 35 degree slope) and Golden Ridge are places
to lay back and drive an edge.

MOUNTAIN FOOD For café-style food, try the Alpine Rose. Molly Green's is a private club/bar serving good
food and alcohol — the private part means that they have a full liquor license. The burrito bar at the bottom
of Milly is a relaxed place to hang out and scope the kids.

HAZARDS AND RULES Brighton has an open boundary policy which means no prosecution for riding out of
bounds — it's like Europe!

Brighton

ABOUT TOWN

Out of the Big Cottonwood Canyon mountains, Solitude's name is the one that sums up the night scene. Brighton has even fewer non-riding options than Solitude, with only one lodge at the base of the mountain. If you have ideas of doing anything more than crashing out and getting up very early, stay in Salt Lake City. It's an easy 35 minute commute with shuttle buses running from the city and the carpark at the mouth of the canyon. A good titbit to keep in mind after a heavy snowfall is that the Big Cottonwood Road is usually opened faster than the Little Cottonwood Road, and face shots beat traffic jams any day.

ACCOMMODATION Brighton Lodge is the only accommodation up at the resort and has basic cell-type rooms with differing classes and costs — first class costs $88 and hostel beds start from $57. The price includes a continental breakfast, outdoor hot tub (open till 10.00pm), a heated pool and a common area with fireplace and microwave. Be warned: there's is very little to do when staying up here, and the lodge is very family oriented and books out fast due to its small size. The advantage is that you don't have to pack the car to ride — Tel: 801-532 4731 or 1-800-873 5512.

FOOD For more options About Town, see Salt Lake City, p.102.

NIGHTLIFE Next to none. Molly Green's stays open till 11.00pm; it's a good place to meet the locals over a game of pool.

OTHER ACTIVITIES Waiting for daylight.

THANKS TO Dave Downing, Mike and Tina Basich, Shannon Dunn, Shannon Smith, Brad Schoffrel, Chris Jorgenson, J.P. Walker, Jeremy Jones.

Opposite — Brighton back-country **Photo:** Tim Rainger
Top — Scott Sullivan **Photo:** Richard Cheski
Panorama — **Photo:** Tim Rainger

GETTING THERE FROM SALT LAKE CITY
By air: The airport is a 45 minute drive from Brighton.
By bus: UTA bus shuttles service Brighton from Salt Lake and the carpark at the bottom of Big Cottonwood Canyon.
By car: Brighton is 35 minutes south-east of downtown Salt Lake City. Take Interstate 215 to Exit 6.
Getting around: A car is useful but not essential.

Solitude

THE FACTS

ELEVATION

Summit:
10,035ft, 3059m
Vertical drop:
2047ft, 624m
Base:
7988ft, 2432m

SNOWFALL

Average annual:
450 inches, 1143cm

Snow-making:
8%

AREA

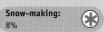

Total area:
1600 acres, 648ha

Advanced: 30%
Intermediate: 50%
Beginner: 20%

SEASON

Early November — late April

COMMUNICATIONS

Snow report: Tel: 801-536 5777
Web site: http://www.skisolitude.com
E-mail: solitude@mail.xmission.com
Mountain information:
Tel: 801-534 1400
Fax: 801-649 5276

LIFTS AND TICKETS

Number of lifts:
1 high-speed quad, 6 chairlifts
Lift pass prices:
1/2 day: $30
1 day: $36
Multi-day: $170 (5 days)
Season: N/A
Other ticketing information:
Pay for your rides with the Swatch Access System by purchasing a $4 Access Card or special Swatch watch. The access gates automatically click off one ride each time you pass through — you don't even need to get your pass out. Rides are purchased in groups of ten. Once you clock up ten rides in a day, the rest are free. Two kids under ten can board free with each adult pass purchased.

swatch+ access

SNOWBOARD SHOPS

See Salt Lake City review p.102.

SNOWBOARD SCHOOL

Solitude Snowboard School — Tel: 801-536 5730
All day lessons cost $50 and half day lessons cost $40. A learner package includes a two hour lesson, beginner lift ticket and rental for $55.

GETTING THERE FROM SALT LAKE CITY

By bus: See Salt Lake City p.102.
By car: Take Interstate 80 east from Salt Lake City and head south to Interstate 215. Get off at Exit 6 and follow the signs to Solitude.

ON THE MOUNTAIN

Solitude opened to boarders in the '95-'96 season, and the first souls venturing into the territory were greeted with a ten foot sign reading 'Snowboarders Welcome'. The tiny letters below added 'Tuesday, Wednesday and Thursday'. Things have moved on since then; the mountain is now open to boarders all week and there is some excellent terrain on the top half of the mountain to explore. Much of the bottom half is flattish learner terrain with groomed trails, but the deep canyons on either side of the lift summit are packed with big cliffs and trees. The 400 acres (162 hectares) of Honeycomb Canyon, skier's left of the summit, has hell glades, and the V-shaped gully collects the snow which stays in primo condition. Boarders who visit Big Cottonwood Canyon tend to head straight to Brighton and regard Solitude as a staunch skiers' mountain, but the secret is getting out that there is some wild riding to be had here too.

SNOW CONDITIONS As part of the Utah front range mountains, Solitude is gifted with big storms which pass straight from the sea over the desert and drop their load on Utah. The snow at Solitude is as light and dry as the alcohol situation in Salt Lake City. Conditions can get slick in the spring when the big dumps keep coming but soften and freeze solid at night.

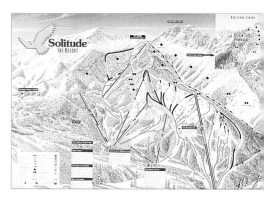

FREERIDERS Solitude has mega freeriding potential in the ridges and canyons on each side of the Summit Chairlift. Honeycomb Canyon is a massive V-shaped gully which you drop into from the top of the Summit Chairlift. If you choose to traverse, you can get to the other side of the gully which has some very intense steeps high up. The whole canyon is a legend of steep trees and cliffs, and it's a long run down to the Wood Lawn trail which exits at the Eagle Express Quad. Honeycomb Canyon has the same vertical drop as the whole Solitude resort. It's accessed from the highest lift-serviced point and drops down to the lowest lift base, but unfortunately the lift system isn't set up to take advantage of this and it's a tedious three lift ride back to the top.

More vintage Utah freeriding can be found in the glades on the smaller gully to skier's right of the Summit Chairlift. Both sides of the lift are steep tree riding zones which follow the lift line down to the gully bed. The double diamond runs Middle Slope, Parachute and Milk Run are deceptively steep and have some major roped-off cliffs tucked away in the trees. Check out this zone well before you go blasting into it as mistakes can be fatal when the conditions are sketchy. Lucky people have spent hours clinging to trees and waiting to be roped out by the ski patrol and unlucky people have died. On a big powder day, you could get air here like you wouldn't believe. Although the trails on this mountain are fairly gentle, the freeriding is challenging and there isn't much competition (as yet) for first boarder tracks.

FREESTYLERS Solitude doesn't provide anything used solely by boarders as yet, so you won't find a pipe or funpark. There are mega cliffs to huck.

CARVERS Solitude has similar trails to Brighton with good wide carvers and a decent pitch. If you're looking to stay purely on trail, the mountain qualifies as great intermediate terrain with mostly blue runs. Most challenging are the undulating Dynamite and Liberty from the top of the Summit Chairlift, which merge into Deer Trail and follow the gully bed down to the bottom of the Powder Horn Chairlift. To wake your thighs up first thing, take the Eagle Ridge run and crank some turns on the steeply pitched Challenger.

MOUNTAIN FOOD Choices for lunch are either the Sunshine Grill mid-mountain or the Last Chance Mining Camp at the base area. Both are decent cafés which serve sandwiches and hot grills. New evening restaurants are springing up at the base. For adventurous eating, ski or snowshoe to the Yurt, a Mongolian restaurant in the woods, or take the open sleigh to the Roundhouse for a five course stomach stuffer.

HAZARDS AND RULES The bottom half of the mountain is flat and it's essential to keep up your speed while keeping your sixth sense open for unpredictable learners. Watch the cliffs in the trees; they are roped but on icy days it can be too late by the time you see the thin piece of plastic which is supposed to hold you back.

MOUNTAIN ACCOMMODATION It is now possible to sleep at Solitude, either in the Euro-style Inn at Solitude or in the Creekside condos. Double rooms in the hotel start at $180 and one bedroom condos cost $295 per night — Tel: 801-534 1400 or 1-800-748 4754. See Salt Lake City review p.102 for more options.

THANKS TO Logan Curtis, Caroline Shaw, Gina Dempster.

The Canyons

THE FACTS

ELEVATION

Summit:
9380ft, 2859m
Vertical drop:
2580ft, 786m
Base:
6800ft, 2073m

SNOWFALL

Average annual:
300 inches, 762cm

Snow-making:
20%

AREA

Total area:
2000 acres, 808 ha

Advanced: 46%
Intermediate: 38%
Beginner: 16%

SEASON
November — April

COMMUNICATIONS
Snow report: Tel: 801-649 5400
Web site: http://www.thecanyons.com
E-mail: snowtalkinfo@thecanyons.com
Mountain information:
Tel: 801-649 5400

LIFTS AND TICKETS
Number of lifts:
9 chairlifts
Lift pass prices:
1/2 day: $24
1 day: $32
Multi-day: $140 (5 day coupon book)
Season: $455-$850

SNOWBOARD SHOPS
Ride On! — Tel: 801-649 4950
Located at the base area, the shop carries a range of rentals, equipment, accessories and clothing. If you want more choice, head for Salt Lake City.

SNOWBOARD SCHOOL
The Canyons' School — Tel: 801-649 5400
The Canyons claims to be the number one PSI rated school in the area and many of the teachers are among the best riders on the mountain. Instruction is available in all disciplines.

GETTING THERE
By air: The Canyons resort is located 25 minutes from Salt Lake International Airport, serviced by Delta Airlines — Tel: 1-800-221 1212.
By bus: There is a free shuttle service to and from Park City every 30 minutes.
By car: Head east on Interstate 80 up Parley's Canyon and turn off at the Park City Exit. Follow the road for about three miles and look for the signposts to the right.

ON THE MOUNTAIN

The Canyons (formerly known as both Wolf Mountain and Park West) has been welcoming snowboarders for at least ten years in stark contrast to Park City, Solitude and Alta. Consequently it has a thriving snowboard scene with riders making up 30 per cent of mountain users, including a fair mix of freeriders and freestylers as befits the varied terrain. It used to be smallish, low key resort, but was added to the American Skiing Company's portfolio at the end of the '96-'97 season. They are overhauling the area to the tune of $18.2 million; a mission which includes installing a gondola and three high-speed quads. When the expansion is finished around the time of the 2002 Olympics (in adjacent Park City), the resort is aiming to have the second largest amount of skiable acres in North America.

SNOW CONDITIONS With an average of around 25 feet (eight metres) between Thanksgiving and May, The Canyons get less than the Cottonwood resorts, but the figure is still good.

The funpark and halfpipe **Photo:** Tim Rainger

FREERIDERS The in-bounds terrain spreads over three spines which run roughly east-west. The north-facing parts are all steep, hold the snow well and add up to some of the most challenging freeride terrain in the area. Canis Lupus and the surrounding trees are a great first shot for the day, draining out into one of the mountain's natural halfpipes. Gecko Glade has some well-spaced tree runs. There are some insane turns if you hike from Condor Peak and drop down into Bald Eagle Bowl before rejoining Upper Boa. The south side chutes off the Condor Chair are among the steepest terrain on the mountain. With the advent of so many new lifts and runs over new terrain in the coming few years, this may well prove an inadequate description of the best lines available.

FREESTYLERS The '96-'97 funpark and pipes were located by the Humpback Whale Lift. A Pipe Dragon is used at least once a week to keep the pipe sharp. The Snowboard Park, one of the few in Utah, is directly next to the pipe and has the usual collection of table tops, spines, steps, rails, log-slides and fun boxes.

CARVERS The Canyons hosted a USSA slalom event in the '96-'97 season and are planning another event for the '97-'98 season. The resort has well-maintained trails and a high percentage of groomed steeps which make for a good carving mountain. They recently purchased six new Bombardier Stealth groomers, including a winch cat for steep stuff.

MOUNTAIN FOOD The Rockin' Mount Grill at the top of the Golden Eagle Chair features music, grilled foods and good views of the Wasatch Range. The new owners are planning a mid-mountain restaurant with a big sundeck. Watch this space.

MOUNTAIN ACCOMMODATION The resort property management have condos from $120 per night for a one bedroom slopeside condo — Tel: 801-649 6606. R&R Properties charge $150 for a two bedroom condo — Tel: 801-649 9372. For a low cost option, try Chateaux Apres — Tel: 801-649 9372 or the Alpen Haus — Tel: 801-649 3551. Chamber of Commerce — Tel: 801-649 6200.

THANKS TO Allen Titensor and Beth Moon.

Powder Mountain

THE FACTS

ELEVATION

Summit:
8900ft, 2714m
Vertical drop:
1300ft, 396m
Base:
7600ft, 2318m

SNOWFALL

Average annual:
500 inches, 1270cm

Snow-making:
No need.

AREA

Total area:
1600 acres, 646ha

Advanced: 30%
Intermediate: 60%
Beginner: 10%

SEASON
October/November — mid-April

COMMUNICATIONS
Snow report: Tel: 801-745 3771
Mountain information:
Tel: 801-745 3772 or 801-745 3619

LIFTS AND TICKETS
Number of lifts:
3 chairlifts, 1 rope tow
Lift pass prices:
1/2 day: $20
1 day: $25
Multi-day: $110 (5 of 6 days)
Season: N/A
Other ticketing information:
Night-riding tickets cost $12.50 and a day-night combo pass costs $30.

SNOWBOARD SHOPS
There are two ski stores, one at Powder Mountain Lodge and one at Sundown Lodge. Both do snowboard rentals and some accessories. See Salt Lake City review p.102 for more board shops.

ON THE MOUNTAIN

Powder Mountain is a small, low elevation, family-owned mountain with fairly average trails and some unreal, ungroomed freeriding. The mountain has a soulful attitude and despite getting the most snow in Utah, it is lift queue free. Due to the slightly longer drive from Salt Lake City, Powder Mountain has remained a secret spot enjoyed by a small handful of appreciative riders, and like the brochure says, 'you're only a stranger once, then you're part of the family.' While this area is gaining in popularity, it is unlikely to match the pace of places like The Canyons and Park City.

SNOW CONDITIONS The average snowfall is over 42 feet (12 metres) of primo Utah pow-pow. The terrain is mainly north-facing so it doesn't take a genius to work out why it's called Powder Mountain.

BACK-COUNTRY OPTIONS Snowcats operate on Friday, Saturday, Sunday and Monday, weather permitting. They open up big, ungroomed terrain by adding 1200 acres (485 hectares) in the Cobabe Canyon to what appears to be a smallish resort. A transferable 12 punch pass, good for more than one season, costs $90. The resort also includes 1200 extra acres (485 hectares) of 'back Powder Country' which gives the green light for some hell hiking.

FREERIDERS Powder Mountain is divided into three areas. The first area has mellow, patrolled trails. The second area is The Drain, a fun area with some great trees and a few drops but nothing too severe. The cat operation picks riders out of The Drain and takes them back to the Base Lodge. The third area is the lift-accessed, ungroomed terrain on both sides of the road. Skier's left of the top of the Timberline Chair, you drop into an area known as the Back Side. Either traverse around the ridge skier's left and drop into the steepest stuff, or follow the fall-line, cross the cat-track and ride out the big natural pipe to the road where a free shuttle takes you back up the hill. The driver Woody is a popular local figure and the service opens up superb, intermediate freeride terrain. After their runs, everyone jams into a small school bus and the shared buzz is super infectious. The bus does a continual loop with a maximum wait of 30 minutes. If you don't feel like waiting, you can hitch back pretty easily. Powder Mountain is set amongst some unreal, open hiking terrain and a pair of snowshoes would reap rich rewards.

FREESTYLERS The halfpipe is in the Hidden Lake area. There is no funpark but there is tons of the natural stuff.

CARVERS If you come to Powder Mountain to carve the groomers, you need your head examined.

MOUNTAIN FOOD There are three lodges grouped quite near to each other: one at the Sundown Lift, one at the resort base adjacent to the carpark and a third between them. Expect great homemade food including superb soups, scones and biscuits. As with everything else at Powder Mountain, prices are generally cheaper than other Utah resorts. A burger costs around $4.50.

HAZARDS AND RULES Retention devices and metal edged boards are required. Poaching the cat terrain is not officially sanctioned, particularly on days when the cats aren't operating and it's totally unpatrolled. Some do ride it and hike out up the cat-track.

Powder Mountain

Top — Jennifer dropping into The Drain **Photo:** Tim Rainger

Bottom — The bus **Photo:** Tim Rainger

ABOUT TOWN

Powder Mountain has no real resident population or facilities of substance. The nearest urban area is Ogden, 20 miles (32 kilometres) from the hill. While it's not the most exciting town in the US, it does have a wide range of services and shops, including one or two licensed liquor stores.

ACCOMMODATION The Columbine Inn features slopeside suites and rooms — Tel: 801-745 3772. The Snowberry Inn is a family-run B&B about five miles (eight kilometres) from the mountain. Hosts Roger and Kimare are mountain guides and excellent hosts; what they don't know about the area, you don't want to know. Prices start from $75 per night for a double — Tel: 801-745 2634. Central Reservations — Tel: 801-745 3772.

THANKS TO Lavar Lowther, Jen, Jez and Jumongie.

For About Town, see Salt Lake City review p.102.

GETTING THERE FROM SALT LAKE CITY

By air: Powder Mountain is 55 miles (88 kilometres) north of Salt Lake City Airport, serviced by Delta Airlines — Tel: 1-800-221 1212.

By car: Take Exit 347 off Interstate 15 at Ogden, then drive east on Route 39 through Ogden Canyon to Eden and on to Pow Mountain. It generally takes between 60 and 90 minutes from Salt Lake City depending on the traffic. The drive through the canyon is spectacular, though the last few miles are steep and require a 4WD and chains after a heavy snowfall.

5

Sedway
JAMIE LYNN
SESSIONS
CREATORS OF QUALITY OUTERWEAR, SNOWEAR, WARMWEAR, KEEP YOU ON THE MOU

AARON VINCENT

KEVIN SANSALONE

Sedway

15 Janis Way, Scotts Valley CA 95066
Fax: 408.461.4680   www.sessions.com

COLORADO

STATE INFORMATION

Population: 3,294,394
Time: Mountain west = GMT minus 7 hours
Capital city: Denver
Area: 104, 091 sq miles (268,555 sqkm)

VISITOR INFORMATION SOURCES

Tel: 1-800-COLORADO
E-mail: thinksnow@skicolorado.org
Web site: http: //www.skicolorado.org

GETTING AROUND

Main airports: Denver International Airport —
Tel: 303-342 2000
By train: Amtrak — Tel: 1-800-872 7245
By bus: Greyhound — Tel: 1-800-231 2222
Road conditions: Tel: 303-639 1111
Avalanche information: Tel: 970-668 0600

Opposite — Loveland Pass **Photo:** Tim Rainger

Top — **Photo:** Gina Dempster

INTRODUCTION

Once you hit the interstate out of Denver, don't look back. Denver is a city of sprawling warehouses and graffitted overbridges which give it a grim, doomed feel. But the mountains are a world unto themselves. There are so many and the boarding is so consistently good that you could get lost in the labyrinth for a couple of years and emerge at the other end, wondering where your head has been. In terms of riding, Colorado offers pure, open freeriding with sick trees and some massive terrain to cover, and unlimited

manicured groomers for the hard boot fraternity. Freestyling is also a big theme with world-class pipes and big parks scattered around. With the exception of Crested Butte, the steeps aren't the most extreme that you'll find but it's made up for by the consistent, light snow and varied riding. For parties and sheer acreage, go to Vail or Aspen, but if you're after a more low key reality, Telluride is full of dedicated snow fanatics. Some of the best hiking is centred around A-Basin; it's strictly no frills for those that can take the drop.

COLORADO CONTENTS

THE FACTS

ELEVATION

Summit:
10,568ft, 3223m
Vertical drop:
3668ft, 1118m
Base:
6900ft, 2104m

SNOWFALL

Average annual:
335 inches, 850cm

Snow-making:
20%

AREA

Total area:
2939 acres, 1087ha

Advanced: 30%
Intermediate: 56%
Beginner: 14%

SEASON
Late November — mid-April

COMMUNICATIONS
Snow report: Tel: 970-879 7300
Web site: http://www.steamboat.com
E-mail: information@steamboat-ski.com
Mountain information:
Tel: 970-879 6111
Fax: 970-879 7844

LIFTS AND TICKETS
Number of lifts:
1 gondola, 2 high-speed quads, 15 chairlifts
Lift pass prices:
1/2 day: $39
1 day: $48
Multi-day: $258 (6 out of 8 days)
Season: N/A
Other ticketing information:
Children 12 years and under ride free when a parent purchases a five day plus multi-day pass. For each parent buying a season pass, one child 12 years or under in the same family receives a free season pass. Groups of over 25 receive one complimentary ticket.

SNOWBOARD SHOPS
Powder Pursuit — Tel: 970-879 9086
All the goods. Go there.

Powder Tools — Tel: 970-879 1645
Good stock, good rentals, good tune-ups and a good attitude. Go there too.

SNOWBOARD SCHOOL
Steamboat Snowboard School
Tel: 970-879 6111 ext.351
The school is extensive and offers a guarantee that they'll teach you how to ride or the next lesson is free. A half day lesson costs $40, one day (with lunch) costs $59 and five days (with lunch) cost $266. Learn to Snowboard weekends include a two hour lesson, a special Lower Mountain lift ticket and rental equipment for — get this — $15 a day.

Steamboat

ON THE MOUNTAIN

The resort of Steamboat covers four peaks: Thunderhead, Storm Peak, Sunshine Peak and Mount Werner. Mount Werner is the highest at 10,600 feet (3233 metres) and is also the main exit to Steamboat's various back-country stashes. Originally named Storm Mountain, it was renamed in honour of Buddy Werner, a great Olympic ski racer who died in an avalanche in '64. Each peak has its own variety of freeriding and air-able terrain while all the north-facing slopes share good high-speed aspen tree riding. You can put your money on a good snowfall here, especially in the cold months of December and January. In the '96-'97 season, Steamboat saw 37 feet (13 metres) of powder fall from early November though till late April.

SNOW CONDITIONS As the first barrier in northern Colorado to storms arriving from the Pacific, Steamboat catches big volumes of snow. The snow is formed in light 'rimed crystals' unique to northern Colorado; the term 'champagne powder' was coined here in the '50s as attribute to its quality.

BACK-COUNTRY OPTIONS The best back-country for the price of a lift ticket is in the Fish Creek drainage area — go with a local. Start at the top of the Morningside Chairlift, head right to Gate D and follow the access road back to the ski area. Halfway down the road in the flat section is an exit gate; walk for ten minutes and face the canyon. The terrain consists of north-facing slopes with steep, surprisingly open pines, classic rock jumps and boulder fields. Another good way to experience the back-country is to take a trip with Steamboat Snowcats of Buffalo Pass, run by Jupiter and Barbara Jones — Tel: 970-879 5188 or 1-800-288 0543.

FREERIDERS You will probably spend most of your time searching for fresh in the trees and accessing the east and north-facing sides of Mount Werner. Take the Morningside Chairlift to the Morningside Bowl. The top section has a line on the far left that leads to a good seasonal rock jump, below which locals sometimes build a decent rodeo kicker. For the most extreme lines on Mount Werner, try the chutes to skier's right of the Stormpeak Express Quad. Chute One has moguls except on powder days when it's good, Chute Two is tighter, shorter and has the more mellow line. The next option is the north-facing cirque which has five access gates. Christmas Tree Bowl and Gates A and B are good but can trap you in a flat forest at the

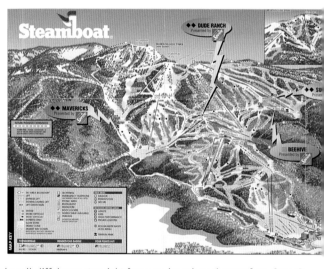

bottom. Gate C is strewn with rocks and small cliff drops; stay right for an easier exit to the east face. Gates D and E at Microwave Towers provide the exit point for the out of bounds Fish Creek Canyon area (Touts). The first two pitches beyond these gates are still in-bounds, and are loaded with snow drifts and rock jumps with names like Million Dollar Rock, Diving Board and Wind Lip (a rock shaped like a wind lip).

FREESTYLERS Sunshine Reef is Steamboat's premier snowboard park and the Sunshine run lead-up is dedicated to the cause of catching air. The park boasts at least six table tops in a row with spines in the middle section. Watch out for Tony Sabatellis' masterpiece, a table top at the bottom which requires serious speed to get the goods. There is also a halfpipe at the top of the BC and Elk Head Chairs called the Dude Ranch, shaped by Pipe Dragon a few times a season.

CARVERS The Women's World Cup downhill run, Heavenly Daze, is one of the baddest runs for carvers. The morning hours are the best time because it's less crowded; you point it and descend nearly a thousand feet (300 metres) of vertical in five or six big turns. The face of Storm Peak offers good carving as well as an incredible view. While sometimes crowded, Buddy's run has good learning conditions.

MOUNTAIN FOOD Start the day with an all-you-can-eat buffet breakfast from BK Express Breakfast Buffet. There are numerous places to eat lunch, from the basic burgerville of BK Café to the gourmet lunches of Ragnar's. With happy hour bargains in mind, head to the Heavenly Daze Brewery and Grill at the day's end. The Inferno in the base area has pizza and other bar food. For good food and fiestas, try the famous Tugboat Saloon and Eatery.

HAZARDS AND RULES BC Skiway is flat and to be avoided.

Steamboat

ABOUT TOWN

Steamboat Springs is an eclectic mix of Victorian and cowboy architecture, a five minute drive from the lifts. It was named by three French fur trappers who were travelling down the Yampa River. They heard a noise they thought was a steamboat but which turned out to be a gurgling mineral spring. The most isolated of all the Colorado resorts, Steamboat is miles from the Denver front range and avoids the day traffic of other Colorado resorts. Most people take advantage of packages and stay at the mountain base.

ACCOMMODATION The cheapest option is to book a package for a week — the resort has specials such as the White Sale Snowsaver, running for four weeks from January to February. It offers six nights' lodging and a five day lift ticket for $419 per person. Weekend Breakaway Packages start from $147, including two nights' lodging and two days' riding with one child free per adult. Central Reservations — Tel: 970-879 0740 or 1-800-922 2722.

FOOD There are a heap of places to eat, and you can peruse all the venues and their menus by getting hold of Steamboat's Dining Guide — Tel: 970-879 2800. We recommend starting at Johnny B. Goods Diner near 8th Lincoln Ave. The food is classic American with meatloaf, shakes and malts in true '50s style. Yama Chan's is Steamboat's sushi headquarters; you'll not want to miss out on the sushi and sashimi. For Mexican and pain-killing margaritas, head to either Dos Amigos or La Montana. Gnarly Charlie's Pizza has steaming door-to-door deliveries — Tel: 970-879 7846.

NIGHTLIFE Steamboat boasts over 60 bars and restaurants and most of them are downtown so you're bound to find something to do. An added bonus is that if you feel you've had too much to drink and can't drive, you can turn your keys over to the bartender and they will call the Tipsi Taxi for a free ride home. Some of the best nightlife at Steamboat rocks at the Heavenly Daze Brewery and Grill at the base area. The menu covers it all, the place has bands every weekend and the proprietors have an endless supply of their own brews. Another spot at the base area is the Inferno. During happy hour prices are dictated by the shot wheel; shots of tequila, whisky and kamikazes can cost as little as 35 cents. The music ranges from hip-hop to disco. The Tugboat Saloon and Eatery has an older crowd listening to good-time, acoustic rock.

OTHER ACTIVITIES Ballooning, snowmobiling, golf.

THANKS TO Barbara Jennings, Dave Pinkerman, Tony Sabatelli.

GETTING THERE

By air: Yampa Valley Regional Airport is located near Hayden, 22 miles (35 kilometres) from Steamboat, and is serviced by TWA and United Airlines. The Steamboat Express runs from Yampa Valley Airport and costs $36 for a round trip — Tel: 1-800-545 6050.
By car: Steamboat is a 157 mile (253 kilometre) drive north-west of Denver. From Denver take Interstate 70 west through the Eisenhower Tunnel to the Silverthorne Exit 203. Follow Colorado Highway 9 north to the town of Kremmling, then head west on Highway 40 to Steamboat.
Getting around: Steamboat offers free off-site parking. Free shuttle buses run continuously all day between the slopes and the town — Tel: 970-879 5585.

Top — Photo: Tim Rainger
Bottom — Tony Sabatelli, Steamboat's snowboard director, testing the product **Photo:** Tim Rainger

Winter Park

THE FACTS

ELEVATION

Summit:
12,060ft, 3678m
Vertical drop:
3060ft, 933m
Base:
9000ft, 2745m

SNOWFALL

Average annual:
355 inches, 900cm

Snow-making:
11%

AREA

Total area:
2581 acres, 1044ha

Advanced: 12%
Intermediate: 30%
Beginner: 58%

SEASON
Mid-November — mid-April

COMMUNICATIONS
Snow report: Tel: 303-572 7669
Web site: http://www.skiwinterpark.com/wpmj
E-mail: hansonkj@csn.net
Mountain information:
Tel: 970-726 5514 or 303-892 0961 in Denver
Fax: 303-892 5823 in Denver
Winter Park Chamber of Commerce:
Tel: 970-726 4118 or 1-800-903 7275

LIFTS AND TICKETS
Number of lifts:
7 high-speed quads, 15 chairlifts, 2 magic carpets
Lift pass prices:
1/2 day: $28
1 day: $45
Multi-day: $216 (6 days)
Season: N/A
Other ticketing information:
One day lift tickets in November and mid-April
cost $26.

SNOWBOARD SHOPS
Powder Tools
Tel: 970-726 1151 or 1-800-525 5520
Powder Tools has three locations: one at Cooper
Creek Square, one next to Gasthaus Eichler in
downtown Winter Park and one at the Vintage
Hotel near the base. Score the second-hand two
metre Libtech Doughboy or something more
modest from a full range of rentals, boards and
clothes.

SNOWBOARD SCHOOL
Rider Improvement Centre — Tel: 970-726 1551
Beginners can take advantage of the Learn for Free
programme offered in January. Buying a lift pass
during that month entitles you to a First Timer
lesson for free.

ON THE MOUNTAIN

The resort is made up of two mountains: Winter Park and Mary Jane. Winter Park is a sedate, mellow area cut into a forested north-facing ridge. Mary Jane has a wilder feel with a narrow front bowl, steep back side and exposed above-tree line bowl. The peak was named after a prostitute in the rough and tumble days, who earned title to the land through her rough-and-tumbling in a shack at the top of the Continental Divide. The word that is inextricably linked with Mary Jane is bumps. Skiers get excited over them but unless you're a boarder with a mogul fetish, there are probably few things that you'd less like to look at. This leaves you

with the short runs on Parsenn Bowl, the mellow trails on Winter Park Peak, some good tree runs and a hit-and-run chance at Mary Jane on a deep powder day. The '97-'98 season should see some changes as Winter Park is planning to open the Vasquez Cirque, a 1000 acre (404 hectare) back-country playground with 45 degree alpine chutes and gladed riding.

SNOW CONDITIONS Over the past ten years, Winter Park has had one of the most consistent snowfalls in Colorado. The snow is light with an average water content of six per cent, rivalling Utah's infamous feathery fluff. Most of the resort faces north and west, keeping the snow in good condition for the heavy snowfall months of March and April.

FREERIDERS You couldn't call Winter Park a freeriders' paradise; everything except the groomed trails and trees gets mogulled out fast. If you hate moguls, avoid the front bowl of Mary Jane after a dry spell especially Outhouse and Drunken Frenchmen. However the ski area does get consistent snow and on a powder day, the short chutes on Mary Jane are the first place to head. The most hard-core chute is Hole-in-the-Wall, easing off down through Baldy's Chute and Awe Chute to Runaway. Parsenn Bowl gets left alone by the skiers; it's a small, alpine bowl which runs down into loosely spaced trees. The novelty of the bowl wears off fast because the run is so short, but the trees around Kinnikinnic can give you a few extra minutes of tight riding down to the Sunnyside Chairlift.

The trees on both mountains are reasonably dense so it's good to follow a local into them to work the lines. The tree runs on the front bowl of Mary Jane are good and steep but get tracked out fast, and moguls even rear their ugly heads in the trees between Drunken Frenchmen and Outhouse. The trees off Jaberwocky remain relatively undiscovered and still hold powder four or five days after a dump. They're tight and unpredictable but open up in places. There isn't much hiking to be done from the field itself, but just down the road is Berthoud Pass which is pure back-country.

FREESTYLERS There are three terrain parks on the mountain which split would-be jibbers into ability groups. The Knuckledragon taunts beginners with their first taste of air and the Mad Hatter's Terrain Park has big jumps lacking in run-up speed. For the '97-'98 season there are plans to expand this park to twice its present size. The Stone Grove is a wooded park on Mary Jane which uses natural features for advanced hits. There's also a good Pipe Dragoned halfpipe called Gentle Smiling Jaws on Lower Jabberwocky. Lower Arrowhead Loop is a local favourite because of the many kickers along the sides.

CARVERS The groomed trails are mostly found on Winter Park Peak, although Forget-me-not in Parsenn Bowl is a lovely fast track to warm up on with plenty of elbow room. Although most trails don't qualify as steep, the excellent corduroy grooming guarantees fast, sweet lines. This would be a perfect place to learn to carve and speed-freaks will enjoy it. From the top of Winter Park Peak, take Cranmer onto Larry Sale for a thigh-stinging run back to base, where the fast Zephyr Express Quad will take you back up to the peak for more.

MOUNTAIN FOOD The Coffee and Tea Market at the base of the mountain has fresh cakes and hot drinks. If a $10 burger won't make you gag in public, then the Lodge at Sunspot is a good mid-mountain meeting spot. Call Mama Mia's Pizza Parlour from the summit Sunspot kiosk and pizzas will be ready to pick up when you get to the Snoasis mid-mountain café.

HAZARDS AND RULES Big moguls, huge moguls and monster moguls.

EVENTS AND COMPETITIONS Cross the Boarder, Rocky Mountain Summer Camps held in May and June.

Winter Park

ABOUT TOWN

The town is two miles (three kilometres) down Highway 40 from the Winter Park base. There are a couple of pubs around the mountain carpark which get busy on happy-hour nights, but otherwise most of the action (such as it is) can be found in town or in Fraser two miles (three kilometres) further down the road. There are plans to develop a 'pedestrian village' at the base but tomorrow's glorious vision of concrete is churned mud in the carpark today. As for the town itself, let's just say that if you had an unlimited budget for a '99 New Year's Eve party, there's approximately no chance at all that you'd choose Winter Park over, say, Jamaica. On the other hand, getting totally trashed at locals' night has a certain grunge glamour.

ACCOMMODATION Winter Park Central Reservations makes bookings from a choice of over 100 places ranging from condos to B&Bs. Prices for a double room start from $60 for a motel, and from $100 for a lodge with breakfast and dinner — Tel: 970-726 558 or 1-800-729 5813. The Snow Mountain Ranch (YMCA of the Rockies) runs a lodge out of town and specialises in groups and families — Tel: 970-887 2152 or 303-443 4743 in Denver.

FOOD Winter Park has the full range of cheapie take-aways and multiple pizza places. Jimmy's Pizzas live up to their self-styled 'best pizza in the area' reputation with fresh basil and garlic in the crust. If you can't face another slice of pizza, Fontenot's Cajun Café has the most enticing menu in town with herb-blackened catfish to try. For a moderately priced breakfast or lunch, the Moffat Bagel Station downtown has the world of bagel sandwiches from the New Yorker to the Parthenon. The Last Waltz is the locals' favourite and there is some fine grilling and frying going down here. Eating after 10.00pm is a problem; only the Lord Gore Arms still serves steaks and salads at this indecent hour.

NIGHTLIFE As primarily a drive-in, drive-out mountain for Denver front rangers, there isn't a great demand for night entertainment and

consequently there isn't much of it. The Pub is the only place in downtown Winter Park to go, so that's why it comes recommended. The Slope near the mountain has a locals' night on Tuesday. Adolph's was riotous on Mardis Gras night but apparently it's a once a year occurrence. The best place to swig on an afternoon beer is the deck of the Derailer Bar at the Base Lodge.

OTHER ACTIVITIES Snowmobiling, snowshoeing and pizza eating.

THANKS TO Claude and his family for their hospitality, Joan Christensen, Mary Nichols.

GETTING THERE

By air: Denver International Airport is serviced by international carriers including Delta Airlines — Tel: 1-800-221 1212. The drive from Denver is 85 miles (136 kilometres), making Winter Park the closest major resort to Denver.
By bus: The Colorado Department of Transportation runs a sponsored 7NEWS SkiXpress bus every weekend to five Colorado resorts — Vail, Winter Park, Keystone, Copper Mountain and Loveland. The bus departs from Boulder and Denver, and returns after the lifts close. The round trip costs $15 and discounted lift passes are sold on the bus — Tel: 303-937 7287. Home James Transportation Services drive door-to-door several times daily from Denver airport for $34. Call Winter Park Central Reservations — Tel: 970-726 5587 or 1-800-729 5813.
By train: Amtrak serves Winter Park daily from Chicago and the West Coast. The Ski Train makes the return trip from Denver on winter weekends; the two hour trip winds through wild scenery and costs $35 — Tel: 303-296-4754.
By car: Take Interstate 70 west out of Denver and turn off at the Winter Park Exit 232. Highway 40 winds up and down Berthoud Pass. Beware of bad markings and hairpin corners which can play havoc with your head, especially at night. For Grand County road conditions — Tel: 970-725 3334.
Getting around: The Lift is a free shuttle which runs around the base area and the valley. The Smart Shuttle is also free and runs along the Highway 40 corridor from 10.30pm to 2.00am on Fridays and Saturdays; the idea is to flag it down as you stumble home.

2

Top right – **Photo:** Byron Hetzeler **Courtesy:** Winter Park
Middle – **Photo:** Byron Hetzeler **Courtesy:** Winter Park
Bottom right — One of the pipes at Winter Park base area **Photo:** Gina Dempster

Arapahoe Basin

Arapahoe Basin

THE FACTS

ELEVATION

Summit:
13,050ft, 3978m
Vertical drop:
2250ft, 686m
Base:
10,800ft, 3292m

SNOWFALL

Average annual:
367 inches, 932cm

Snow-making:
None

AREA

Total area:
490 acres, 197ha

Advanced: 40%
Intermediate: 50%
Beginner: 10%

SEASON
Mid-November — mid-June

COMMUNICATIONS
Snow report: 970-468 4111
Web site: http://www.ski-ralston.com/resorts
Mountain information:
Tel: 970-468 0718 or 1-800 222 0188
Fax: 970-468 4106

LIFTS AND TICKETS
Number of lifts:
5 chairlifts
Lift pass prices:
1/2 day: N/A
1 day: $45
Multi-day: $180 (5 out of 6 days)
Season: N/A

SNOWBOARD SHOPS
Arapahoe Basin Rental Shop — Tel: 970-496 7012
A small, efficient rental shop with K2 boards. B+B:
$28, B+B with step-ins: $32.

SNOWBOARD SCHOOL
Arapahoe Basin Snowboard School
Tel: 970-468 4170 or 1-800-255 3715
A two hour lesson with restricted lift pass and
rentals costs $59.

GETTING THERE
By car: At Silverthorne, take Exit 205 off
Interstate 70 and drive 13 miles (21 km) on
Highway 6 to Arapahoe Basin.
Getting around: A free shuttle runs every 20
minutes to Arapahoe Basin from the Keystone
Mountain West Shuttle Stop — Tel: 1-888-ARAPAHOE.

ON THE MOUNTAIN

Arapahoe Basin is the highest lift-serviced resort in North America and remains somewhat of an enigma due to the total lack of commercialisation and the awesome, high altitude terrain. Known as 'The Legend', its reputation for dubious weather and steep faces have kept the clientele in the 'die-hard locals' category. There are some good slopes for beginners and intermediates in the middle slice of the ski area, but the essence of A-Basin is the hiking on the east and west arms of the basin. The resort is strictly no frills, and for anything except snow you have to bail to Keystone, Silverthorne or Dillon.

SNOW CONDITIONS Because of its mega altitude and north-facing aspect, A-Basin receives a more than respectable amount of snow which remains rideable until August in a good year. A-Basin has a separate weather pattern to the rest of Summit County, and tends to get late, heavy snowfalls with March being the biggest month.

BACK-COUNTRY OPTIONS Drive up Highway 6 from A-Basin and join the rest of Summit County for a Loveland Pass full moon party or a powder fest. Hike up the hill facing A-Basin and head west to the Professor or drop the cornice to the Widow-Maker. From the A-Basin lifts, you can see Black Mountain on your left with some classic chutes. These imaginatively named chutes (Shit for Brains, Dog Shit and Dog Leg) can also be hiked from Highway 6, just past A-Basin. Locals can be protective of their special stashes and may give you a hard time if you try to tag along — take some bribes.

FREERIDERS Killer freeriding and no crowds; the only limit is your lungs and imagination. If you like to hike, it doesn't get much better than A-Basin on a powder day. The Beavers is a 40 minute run among the sweetest trees around; walk a couple of minutes to the USFS access gate from the Norway Lift and head west down the ridge before dropping in. Champagne powder, spread out trees and some big airs will greet you. Follow the tracks out and boot-track five minutes back to Highway 6, then it's a one mile hitch back up to the Base Lodge. An alternative route from the USFS gate is to drop straight into the out of bounds Montezuma Bowl. The huge 25 to 40 foot (eight to 12 metre) cornice here always has a super soft landing, but check for avalanche danger as it's not blasted and sometimes slides. The Montezuma Bowl is flat at the bottom and comes out near the ghost town of Montezuma, six miles (ten kilometres) from A-Basin. It's a tedious hitch back, so a good option is to climb back up the ridge from the flat part and do the west side of the Beavers out to Highway 6.

From the Norway Lift, you can follow the boundary line and drop the 50 degree chutes which all funnel out into the Beavers Valley. The first, second and fourth chutes are the most mellow but all six chutes are avalanche paths and can be totally unstable and life-threatening. The East Wall is in-bounds hiking terrain; the upper section above the tree line needs heaps of snow before it opens and is best in spring. A giant rock face with chutes and launching pads, it opens out onto the alpine lower East Wall and glades. This is just a taste of the A-Basin magic; it's a core playground.

FREESTYLERS No pipe, no funpark. If you can't find any hits or rocks to launch off, then trade your board in for a set of knitting needles.

CARVERS You wouldn't use the term manicured to describe A-Basin and few hard-booters show their edges around here. A couple of trails do get groomed, mainly the mellow runs which funnel back under the East Wall to the Base Lodge. A good warm-up run is Grizzly Road from the top of Pali Chair to the top of Exhibition Chair.

MOUNTAIN FOOD There can only be one: the A-frame. It's nothing fancy but you can get beers and burgers and keep warm. A local tip is that enough sugar will solve the coffee flavour problem.

HAZARDS AND RULES Leash laws apply. The East Wall is in-bounds but is serious hiking terrain and should only be attempted by experienced hikers and riders. There are frequent slides at A-Basin due to the steep pitch, but the ski patrol blast the in-bounds terrain to pieces and keep it relatively safe. Back-country, use your judgement.

EVENTS AND COMPETITIONS Beachin' at the Basin is an impromptu March festival which involves keg parties and portable hot tubs in the carpark. Other fun events are the spring festival and the A-Basin endurance race.

THANKS TO Ron Simenhoise, Ryan Runke, Jawn Ross, Gina Dempster.

For About Town, see Keystone review opposite.

Keystone

THE FACTS

ELEVATION

Summit:
12,200ft, 3721m
Vertical drop:
2900ft, 885m
Base:
9300ft, 2837m

SNOWFALL

Average annual:
230 inches, 584cm

Snow-making:
9%

AREA

Total area:
1749 acres, 708ha

Advanced: 51%
Intermediate: 37%
Beginner: 12%

SEASON
Late October — mid-April

COMMUNICATIONS
Snow report: Tel: 970-468 4111
Web site: http://www.snow.com
E-mail: kenp@ski-ralston.com
Mountain information:
Tel: 970-496 2316 or 1-800-239 1622
Fax: 970-453 3202

LIFTS AND TICKETS
Number of lifts:
2 gondolas, 4 high-speed quads, 10 chairlifts,
5 surface lifts
Lift pass prices:
1/2 day: N/A
1 day: $45
Multi-day: $180 (5 out of 6 days)
Season: N/A
Other ticketing information:
Tickets are valid for Arapahoe Basin and
Breckenridge. A Keystone pass can be used at Vail
with an upgrade cost of $5.

SNOWBOARD SHOPS
Keystone Rental Shop — Tel: 970-496 4170
The staff are clued in but they only have rental
boards. B+B: $25.

SNOWBOARD SCHOOL
Keystone Snowboard School
Tel: 970-468 4170 or 1-800-255 3715
Halfpipe, freeride and 'quick carve' instruction for
skiers converting to boarding. A morning lesson,
full lift pass and rental costs $76.

GETTING THERE
By air: Denver International Airport is serviced by
Delta Airlines — Tel: 1-800-221 1212.
By bus: From Denver take the Resort Express —
Tel: 970-468 7600 or 1-800-334 7433. See Winter
Park p.118 for the 7NEWS SkiXpress bus from
Denver.
By car: Follow Interstate 70 west from Denver and
take Exit 205 to Highway 6.
Getting around: The free Ski KAB Express runs
from Keystone to Breckenridge all day and evening.
From Breckenridge the free Summit Stage services
all Summit County towns.

ON THE MOUNTAIN

Keystone opened its lifts to boarders in the '96-'97 season and they were queuing at 2.00am on opening day to be the first. The ski area is vintage Colorado with curving trails cut into a series of forested ridges. The north face of Keystone Mountain is mostly an interconnecting web of intermediate trails but the terrain in behind has the goods, with some easy hikes opening up a vista of sick trees and big cliff drops for hucksters. Despite a late awakening, Keystone is definitely the low-down with boarders and has the best halfpipe in Summit County.

SNOW CONDITIONS Keystone prides itself on opening early in the season, outweighing the lowest average snowfall in Summit County with extensive snow-making to build up the base. Northern exposures help to keep the snow in good condition.

FREERIDERS Freeriders should head straight to the Outback Bowls on the furthermost ridge from the Base Lodge. The Outback Express Quad drops you off at the beginning of the ridge, and it's a basic hike to find a good drop-in spot. The upper alpine slopes of the South Bowl are good and steep but the run-out through the trees is tediously flat. The North Bowl trees are the business on a powder day. If it has been a few days since the last dump, the trees just outside the boundary by the Outpost Gondola hide secret stashes and freshies can be had on almost any day of the season if you're prepared to hike for half an hour. There's a wicked cliff band to launch off too.

FREESTYLERS Keystone has a styling halfpipe and the purchase of a Pipe Dragon in the '97-'98 season will keep the vert even sweeter. They've done well to set up the Terrain Garden in their first snowboarding year but it isn't spaced out right; the jumps are OK but the run-ups aren't aligned for maximum air time. Paymaster off the Montezuma Express Quad is 'styler kingdom. Rollers, fat carved-out hits and drops into the trees give this trail the Jibmaster nickname.

CARVERS Speed addicts will enjoy the uncrowded steep pitch of Go Devil on the western boundary of Keystone Mountain. Wild Irishman is also a rush but watch out for wild intermediate skiers.

MOUNTAIN FOOD The Mountain House Café has cheapish mountain food.

HAZARDS AND RULES The ski patrol are low-key and it takes a lot to annoy them. They don't put up too many ropes and leash laws aren't heavily enforced.

Javier **Photo:** Tim Rainger

ABOUT TOWN

Keystone Village is mainly condo territory with a couple of bars and restaurants. Most locals live in Silverthorne or Dillon, but Breckenridge is the best option if you want to party hard for a few days.

ACCOMMODATION Slopeside double hotel rooms cost $185 per night at the Inn, and a two person studio is priced from $145. A condo for four people costs $200. Keystone Central Reservations — Tel: 970-468 4242 or 1-800-239 1622 or 0-800-89 8727 (Europe toll-free). For budget options, check out Dillon or Silverthorne.

FOOD Most of the food in Keystone is pricey; at the cheaper end of the scale, try Ida Belle's for Mexican or Gassy's for a barbecue fest. The Mint in Silverthorne has $3 all-you-can-eat nights for locals on Mondays. The Dam Brewery, also in Silverthorne, has good grills and burgers with fresh brews and music.

NIGHTLIFE First bar to hit off the mountain is the Free Water Saloon where the après scene rages. The only late night option in Keystone Village is Kickapoos which goes off with live music and heavy drinking until 2.00am. Alice's in Dillon is the bar where local kids go to party; the atmosphere is chilled and low-key. For a blow-out, the Underground in Breckenridge gets packed out.

OTHER ACTIVITIES Ice-skating, sleigh rides, snowmobiling, snowshoeing.

THANKS TO Ryan Runke, Vahid, Gina Dempster.

Vail

THE FACTS

ELEVATION

Summit:
11,450ft, 3490m
Vertical drop:
3330ft, 1015m
Base:
8120ft, 2475m

SNOWFALL

Average annual:
335 inches, 867cm

Snow-making:
7%

AREA

Front Side/Back Bowls

Total area:
4677 acres, 1873ha

Front Side		Back Bowls
32%	Advanced	64%
36%	Intermediate	36%
32%	Beginner	0%

SEASON
Early November — late April

COMMUNICATIONS
Snow report: Tel: 970-476 4888
Tune into 'Good Morning Vail' every morning from 7.00am to 10.00am on KVBA-TV8.
E-mail: vailbcr@vail.net
Web site: http://vail.net
Mountain information:
Tel: 970-476 9090
Fax: 970-845 2609
Vail Valley Chamber of Commerce:
Tel: 970-949 5189

LIFTS AND TICKETS
Number of lifts:
1 gondola, 11 high-speed quads, 11 chairlifts, 5 surface lifts
Lift pass prices:
1/2 day: $44
1 day: $52
Multi-day: $336 (7 days)
Season: N/A
Other ticketing information:
Vail's pass is interchangeable with Beaver Creek's. Discount coupons ($10 off lift price) can be bought at REI and Garp Bros in Denver. The Vail Valley Club Card costs $15 and saves $5 on every day pass for Vail and Beaver Creek. With a Vail/Beaver Creek multi-day pass (over four days), you can ride Breckenridge, Keystone or Arapahoe Basin for $5 and vice-versa. Ticket office — Tel: 970-479 4232.

SNOWBOARD SHOPS
One Track Mind — Tel: 970-476 3839
With branches in Lionshead and Vail Village, this shop has all the name gear and a slouch couch to watch videos from.

SNOWBOARD SCHOOL
Vail and Beaver Creek Snowboard School
Tel: 970-476 3239 or 1-800-354 5630
Fax: 970-479 4377
The school runs introductory lessons, freestyle and alpine classes and signature programmes.

ON THE MOUNTAIN

The wild thing about Vail is it's so huge that the snow lasts and lasts and lasts. The resort is hard to write about purely because it's all good: trees, bowls, chutes and trails — Vail and sister mountain Beaver Creek have it all. The longer you spend here, the more you'll love it. The ridges of Vail run east to west, and the steepest front side terrain is found towards the eastern boundary.

Over the back of the ridge line are the infamous Back Bowls, a set of five dishes exposed to sun and snow. The bowls were deforested by fire a century ago. Legend has it that Ute Indians set them alight as a revenge against gold miners who pissed them off. And a big favour they did for the rest of us. The Back Bowls are scarcely touched by the groomers and are

prey to weather fluctuations in ways which give American resort owners night-sweats. They can be crusty, they can be porridge or they can be the sweetest thing since Ben and Jerry's.

SNOW CONDITIONS The front side of Vail faces north which keeps the 29 feet (eight and a half metres) of annual snow in good nick. The Back Bowls are south-facing and crust up quickly once warmer February temperatures arrive, especially as the lack of trees contribute to the sun exposure.

FREERIDERS The Back Bowls are awesome after a dump. The area is a five mile (eight kilometre) wide, wet dream of ungroomed bowls, chutes, cliffs and a few trees. Head for the High Noon Lift early in the day then move on to the Orient Express Lift when the crowds arrive. Tree-hounds will enjoy the North-East Bowl with sweet-smelling spruce trees; they can get tighter than a gnat's arse in places. Christmas Trees and Sheer Terror Glades on the other side of Northwood's Express Lift have more of the same. Lower areas around Vail Village feature aspen trees with clean trunks which tree novices can weave around without fear of decapitation. There are plenty of hiking opportunities out of the open gates close to East Vail. Ask advice from the ski patrol before you venture out. The snowboard gullies (marked on the Ride Guide) are excellent fun and will improve your skills with log slides, luges and obstacles. Vail is currently planning a 2000 acre (806 hectare) expansion to be completed by 2000. The expansion is currently under review by the US Forest Service and will add two north-facing gladed bowls with a 2000 foot (610 metre) vertical drop.

FREESTYLERS The TAG Heuer Snowboard Park at Adventure Ridge has two halfpipes; one measures 400 feet (122 metres) by 12 feet (nearly four metres), and the other is 300 feet (90 metres) by nine feet (nearly three metres). The Pipe Dragon keeps the transition sweet and the park is set up with night lights and a surface lift. The Peanut Peak Comp Pipe is the straighter of the two. A third 300 foot (90 metre) 'technical' pipe and chairlift were unveiled in February '97 in the Unvailed Park next door. Vail has had the forethought and acreage to develop hits in natural terrain, which takes jibbing out of the parks and back onto the mountain. Below the parks, Cheetah Gully is a gladed run swinging through a natural gully with huge log slides and a big air. Jib Line, skier's right of the Avanti Express Lift, stars a big table top and metal handrail to slide.

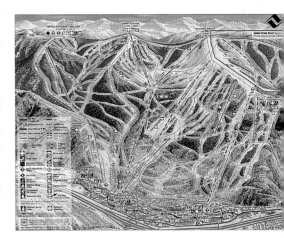

CARVERS The lower trails into Lionshead are wide, steep and well-groomed but plenty of skiers converge around the bottom — go slowly or get kebabed. Bwana, Safari and Simba runs around the Born Free Lift are all good. The blue cruisers off the Mountaintop Express Lift are solid but shortish: check Whistlepig, Expresso, Cappuccino and Swingsville.

MOUNTAIN FOOD To eat fast and cheap (as cheap as it gets) on the mountain, either try one of the traditional ski cafés at the top of most major lifts or look for the express stands like the Wok'n'Roll, offering barbecue, fried rice or burgers.

HAZARDS AND RULES Leashes are compulsory.

ABOUT TOWN

Vail is one of the names which define American skiing and boarding and the mystique has permeated into the non-snow culture. Evolving from its incarnation as a chilled ski-bum scene in the Telluride mode, Vail has moved up-market into romantic glitz with red wreaths and fairy-lights wrapped around every tree, shop and telephone pole. It's a surreal landscape where road-rage and cult suicides seem like a vague bad dream in someone else's life.

The town snakes along the borders of Interstate 70 but East Vail and West Vail are mostly deserted at night as it's luxury condo terrain. Don't bother venturing in unless you have a key to one of them. The happening places are around Vail Village and Lionshead off Exit 176. Wild parties resound every night and excellent bands play live; it's a city vibe in a small town so you soon recognise the community of loose-heads once you hit the party circuit. Locals are a collection of snow junkies from all over the country; most work two jobs to survive, party big and some of them even find time to ride.

ACCOMMODATION A double hotel room mid-season will cost upwards of $150 in Minturn or $200 in Vail itself. Vail/Beaver Creek Reservations — Tel: 970-845 5745 or 1-800-525 2257. Condos in Vail cost from $115 per night for a one bedroom condo up to $300 for a three bedroom condo.

FOOD Finding budget food in Vail takes some perseverance but it can be done. Cleaver's Deli in Vail Village and Lionshead has creative sandwich fillings and 'scramblers' (fried breakfast food in a pita pocket) to cure any hangover. Other coffee shops serving fresh fruit scones and pastries are the Daily Grind in Vail Village and Fresh Tracks in Lionshead. Blu's, near the covered bridge in Vail Village, has an eclectic menu at reasonable prices — from $10 to $15 for a main. At busy times there can be a queue for tables but there's a bar to relax in with a happening buzz. Vendetta's make mean pizza slices into the early hours and is a good place to sit, take stock of the night's wanderings and plan the next move.

NIGHTLIFE Heart's desires can be satisfied in Vail or minds blown, depending on what you're after. Vail rocks, discos, trances, skanks a bit and occasionally digs some funk. There's live music every night and a choice of clubs to groove in.

Garton's is the biggest venue with the staunchest bouncers and so attracts the best-known bands and fattest beats. The Daily Grind has less in-your-face music to suit a coffee and wine crowd. The best night to visit is Thursday for wine-tasting; get there for 6.30pm to be part of a mad $10 frenzy of wine guzzling. The George is an English-run English pub where all the local Americans hang out. They play pool sort of European style but there are no 'two shots' and winner stays on. Dartswise, teach the locals '501' and 'around the clock'. Two other rocking venues are the Red Lion in the centre of Vail Village and Garfinkle's in Lionshead. Vendetta's has a chat-up bar upstairs which goes off early in the evening. Once you're fully tanked and need to shake booty, go to Nick's.

OTHER ACTIVITIES Eagle's Nest at the top of Vail Mountain has snowmobiling, skating, tubing, bobsledding and a halfpipe.

THANKS TO Paul Witt, Robert Perlman, Sage and Scott for room and board, Jim and Jack of Room and Board Productions, Arn Menconi — President of Snowboard Outreach Society. Oh! ...and the elusive Josh Hemminger.

Top left — Aerial view of Vail Mountain **Photo:** Jack Affleck **Courtesy:** Vail
Top right — Vail pipe **Photo:** Gina Dempster
Bottom — Vail Village **Photo:** Gina Dempster

GETTING THERE
By air: Vail-Eagle County Airport is 35 miles (56 kilometres) from Vail Village. Connections can be made with most US cities, including daily flights from Atlanta on Delta Airlines — Tel: 1-800-221 1212. Rental cars or shuttles from the airport can be booked by calling Vail/Beaver Creek Reservations. Colorado Mountain Express charge $54 for their Denver to Vail shuttle — Tel: 970-949 4227 ext. 6202 or 1-800-525 6363.
By bus: See Winter Park review p.118 for details of the 7NEWS SkiXpress bus from Denver.
By car: Vail is 100 miles (160 kilometres) west of Denver on Interstate 70. Exit 176 gets you to the main part of Vail Village and Lionshead; Exits 173 and 180 are for East Vail and West Vail. Parking can be a hassle and the best bet is the main carpark building near tourist information (the first 90 minutes are free).
Getting around: Free buses run frequently from the eastern end of Vail Village to the western end of Lionshead, and scheduled buses run to East and West Vail. Buses also run to Beaver Creek and Avon via Interstate 70, prices from $2. For more information and bus timetable details — Tel: 970-949 6121.

⑤

Beaver Creek

THE FACTS

ELEVATION

Summit:
11,440ft, 3488m
Vertical drop:
4040ft, 1233m
Base:
7400ft, 2255m

SNOWFALL

Average annual:
330 inches, 838cm

Snow-making:
45%

AREA

Total area:
1625 acres, 655ha
Advanced: 38%
Intermediate: 43%
Beginner: 19%

SEASON
Late November — mid-April

COMMUNICATIONS
Snow report: Tel: 970-476 4888
Tune into 'Good Morning Vail' every morning from
7.00am to 10.00am on KVBA-TV8.
E-mail: vailbcr@vail.net
Web site: http://vail.net
Mountain information:
Tel: 970-476 9090
Fax: 970-845 2609

Vail Valley Chamber of Commerce:
Tel: 970-949 5189
Fax: 970-949 4385

LIFTS AND TICKETS
Number of lifts:
5 high-speed quads, 8 chairlifts
Lift pass prices:
1/2 day: $44
1 day: $52
Multi day: $336 (7 days)
Season: N/A
Other ticketing information:
Beaver Creek's ticket includes Bachelor Gulch and
Arrowhead resorts which are connected to Beaver
Creek by trails and express lifts. A Beaver Creek lift
pass is also valid for Vail Mountain. See Vail review
p.122 for discounts.

SNOWBOARD SHOPS
The Other Side — Tel: 970-845 8969
The staff are a diverse collection of grungers,
Aussies, hippies and college boys but what they
have in common is technical expertise and a passion
for spreading the snowboard word. They take more
effort setting up a one day rental board than most
shops take with a new board. Open till 8.00pm.

SNOWBOARD SCHOOL
Vail and Beaver Creek Snowboard School
Tel: 970-476 3239 or 1-800-354 5630
See Vail review p.122 for lesson details.

ON THE MOUNTAIN

Beaver Creek resort is less flashy than Vail but for hard-core tree riding it rules. Combine the trees with a hot halfpipe and thick corduroy trails and Beaver Creek is no poor cousin. Three or four days after a big dump, pockets of thigh-deep snow are still waiting for the kiss of a board. And despite the two million skier days recorded at Vail and Beaver Creek each season, once you're in the trees you might as well be stranded in the Antarctic circle for all the crowds you'll be fighting — except there's no penguins.

Beaver Creek Mountain stands beside Grouse Mountain with a steep, forested gully bisecting the two. The top of Beaver Creek Mountain is mellow and flattish; Grouse Mountain is much more challenging. West of Grouse Mountain is Arrowhead Mountain. Two express lifts link Bachelor Gulch Village and Arrowhead Village with the main Beaver Creek resort, Euro-style. There are intermediate and beginner trails on Arrowhead Mountain but no steeps. Locals boast that lift queues don't happen at Beaver Creek except for a few days over Christmas.

SNOW CONDITIONS A base elevation of 7400 feet (2255 metres) and a northerly orientation make for light dry snow. The mountain can be sketchy early in the season but is consistently good from January through to closing. Wall-to-wall trees keep the snow pristine until it's searched out by some onto-it tree freak.

FREERIDERS Steeps and trees are the key to Beaver Creek with locals claiming they have 'the sickest trees in the state, if not the country'. The gladed runs off Grouse Mountain are legendary for proficient riders. Thresher Glade has aspen trees to use as slalom gates, but they are more like concrete poles if you head-butt one so wear eye-ball protectors. The Bald Spot off the Stump Park Lift is the spot to pick up wind-blown powder and has graduated cliff jumps ranging from ten to 30 feet (three to nine metres). Trees on the mountain follow the fall-line perfectly and if you're not afraid to explore or bust through tight gaps, you'll find the goods. Short hikes access endless back-country and offer fresh tracks at any time in the season. Avalanche information is updated daily — Tel: 970-827 5687 and 970-668 0600.

FREESTYLERS Stickline is a tree-bound park off Centennial Lift which has radical log slides and hits in a huge gully. The halfpipe on Moonshine trail is steep and deep with a monster table top at the end. The Other Side staff provide day-to-day maintenance on the pipe. A totally supportive atmosphere rules in the pipe with riders egging each other on to go big and land it.

CARVERS Beaver Creek has steep trails and is known for its meticulous grooming, making for excellent carving conditions. Centennial is a fast, long pitch below the Centennial Express Lift and is excellent for a warm-up run. Look for the double blacks on the Westfall Lift between Beaver Creek Mountain summit and Grouse Mountain summit.

MOUNTAIN FOOD The burritos at McCoys at the base of the mountain are good and so is the pizza sold by the slice at the Blue Moose, a three minute walk away. Alternatively grab a $5 take-away sandwich at the Dancing Bear in West Vail before you head up the mountain. Tater's is the only express, cheap option on the mountain. They serve baked potatoes and chilli at the top of the Strawberry Park Express Lift.

HAZARDS AND RULES Launching off the Gold Dust cat-track hits is a temptation but the rules say no jumping. Leashes are compulsory.

Beaver Creek

ABOUT TOWN

The riding scene in Beaver Creek Village is extra low key. Most of the riders who hang out in the trees during the day scamper back to their nests in Avon or Minturn at night. The reason that there are no live-in locals is that accommodation in Beaver Creek and the linked villages of Bachelor Gulch and Arrowhead is mighty expensive and limited to condos. The people who stay there tend to be executive families who can afford the $8 parking fees. There are lots of exclusive restaurants and one or two bars with a good buzz when the lifts close. The most fun things to do in the village are visiting the Other Side snowboard shop to play on their roller-boards, and going to Vail.

ACCOMMODATION A double room in Beaver Creek will cost upwards of $250 peak-season; a room in Minturn starts from $150. Vail/Beaver Creek Reservations can arrange accommodation and transport — Tel: 970-845 2612. It is possible to book through their web site: http://vail.net or E-mail: vailres@vail.net.

FOOD Beaver Creek is wealthy territory and food prices suck. If armageddon seems a likely bet in the next week, splash out on a six-course gourmet meal at Beano's Cabin. Originally the home of an optimistic lettuce farmer, the 'cabin' (more the size of a shearing shed) blazes forth light onto Beaver Creek Mountain and is reached by a cat-drawn sleigh. The Blue Moose is the only pizza restaurant in Beaver Creek and is packed with kids and their mothers in the weekends. Coyote's has a relaxed pub feel and styling burgers.

Sushi loyalties in the valley are divided between Masato's in Avon and Nozawa's in West Vail; both must be good to get people so worked up. If you're heading down Interstate 70 to Vail Village for the night, the Dancing Bear at West Vail has a huge choice of large meals in basic diner decor. You pay less for the lack of pretentions and it's also good for filling breakfasts or sandwiches to take up the mountain. DJ's Diner in Lionshead is open 24 hours.

NIGHTLIFE Beaver Creek caters to families and so nightlife is minimal compared to the party scene in Vail. Coyote's gets the nod as the venue for beers and yummy veggie burgers but for a big night out Vail is the call.

OTHER ACTIVITIES Beaver Creek Centre for the Arts is under construction and will offer music, drama, comedy and visual arts for the culturally aware in the '97-'98 season. An ice-skating rink is also scheduled to open in December '97.

THANKS TO Paul Witt, Robert Perlman Jimmy Delong and the staff at the Other Side for their technical assistance.

For more About Town, see Vail review p.122.

Top — Beaver Creek pipe **Photo:** Gina Dempster
Bottom — Stefan Gimpl **Photo:** Gina Dempster

GETTING THERE
By air: Beaver Creek is 25 miles (40 kilometres) from the Vail-Eagle County Airport . See Vail review p.122 for European connections and shuttles.
By bus: See Winter Park review p. 118 for details of the 7NEWS SkiXpress bus from Denver.
By car: Beaver Creek is 10 miles (16 kilometres) west of Vail. Take Interstate 70 to Exit 167 for Avon. Park at the bottom of Beaver Creek Mountain and catch the free shuttle to the Beaver Creek base. The ride takes five minutes and will save you $8 in parking fees.
Getting around: The Bus runs regularly between Vail and Beaver Creek via Interstate 70 and costs $2. The same company also runs a cheap bus between Vail, Avon and Minturn — Tel: 970-949 6121.

THE FACTS

ELEVATION

Summit:
12,313ft, 3754m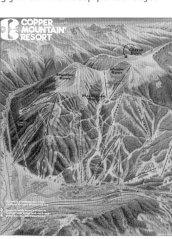

Vertical drop:
2601ft, 794m

Base:
9712ft, 2961m

SNOWFALL

Average annual:
280 inches, 711cm

Snow-making:
11%

AREA

Total area:
2400 acres, 969ha

Advanced: 54%
Intermediate: 25%
Beginner: 21%

SEASON
Mid-November — early May

COMMUNICATIONS
Snow reports: Tel: 970-968 2100
E-mail: cmr-co@ix.netcom.com
Web site: http://www.ski-copper.com
Mountain information:
Tel: 970-968 2882
Fax: 970-968 6142

LIFTS AND TICKETS
Number of lifts:
3 high-speed quads, 14 chairlifts, 4 surface lifts
Lift pass prices:
1/2 day: $33
1 day: $45
Multi-day: $222 (6 out of 14 days)
Season: $925
Other ticketing information:
Pre-purchase passes are available for $33 per day (minimum of three days, only available by mail and before mid-February) — Tel: 1-800-458 8386 ext. 7885 in the US or 0-800-458 8386 ext. 7885 from the UK. A Copper Club Card entitles you to cheap lift passes for you and up to three friends each day, as well as discounts for shopping and lodging in Copper Village. Adult lift passes are reduced to $30 in peak season and down to $22 in early and late season. The card costs $10 from all King Sooper's front range locations after December 15. Copper runs the K and L Board Free programme on selected days in January and April, offering free access to beginner terrain accessed by the K and L Lifts. Complimentary tickets can be picked up at the Union Creek sales office — Tel: 970-968 2882.

SNOWBOARD SHOPS
Max Snowboard Rentals — Tel: 970-968 2323
The shop has super-friendly staff and a large range of styling boards for hire. Ask Eric or the boys for some local tips on the best runs around.

SNOWBOARD SCHOOL
Copper Mountain Snowboard School
Tel: 970-968 2318 ext. 6330
Group lessons start at $41.

Copper Mountain

ON THE MOUNTAIN

Copper Mountain was first exploited for its heavy minerals in the 1800s. Miner Doug Deep named the mountain after his faithful chihauhau who died bringing help to Doug as he lay inebriated in a freak July snowstorm. Today the mountain lives up to Deep's name with an average snowfall of over 24 feet (seven metres) and corporate-recreation owners, Intrawest, mine the mountain for cash. Copper is part of the Summit County group but has never quite achieved the high profile of Keystone, A-Basin and Breckenridge. This could change as money is being pumped in to expand the mountain in all directions; developments include a new snowboard park and the 900 acre (363 hectare) Copper Bowl expansion which will give Copper the largest acreage in Summit County.

The mountain is naturally segregated into a hierarchy of beginners in the west, intermediates in the centre and experts in the east. Most of the expert runs are above tree line and off the front and back sides of Copper Peak and Union Peak. There are wide open bowls and trees on the front side. The only drawback is the lack of serious steeps which can bog you down on deep powder days.

SNOW CONDITIONS Copper Mountain has a reputation for consistent snow and in true Colorado style, it's light enough to float on. It also has a reputation for sunshine but most of the slopes are north-facing so the snow hangs around.

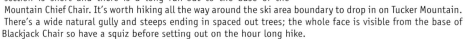

BACK-COUNTRY OPTIONS Look across Interstate 70 from Copper Village and up towards the sky and you can see it written before your eyes — SKY. These are the impressive SKY chutes which can be dropped (at the risk of loosing lift passes) from Breckenridge or hiked (if you're into extreme body fatigue) from the base of Copper. The chutes are a serious day mission and all back-country sense applies. For back-country and avalanche information, call the Summit County Search and Rescue Group — Tel: 970-668 0600.

FREERIDERS On a powder day the prime spot to hit first is Copper Bowl, riding the Mountain Chief and Blackjack Chairs. From the top of the Mountain Chief Chair, hike skier's right along the ridge until you can't resist the lure of the sweet snow below. Decent runs can be reached with a quarter to half hour hike, although the steepish section is short and there is a long run-out to the base of the Mountain Chief Chair. It's worth hiking all the way around the ski area boundary to drop in on Tucker Mountain. There's a wide natural gully and steeps ending in spaced out trees; the whole face is visible from the base of Blackjack Chair so have a squiz before setting out on the hour long hike.

Once the novelty of Copper Bowl has worn off, Spaulding Bowl and Resolution Bowl are next on the list. Spaulding Bowl has short, sharp chutes merging into heavy glades. Resolution Bowl is rewarding when the snow is fresh but can be disappointing in a dry spell. Good places to check for late stashes are Far West in Union Meadows and the open glades of West Encore.

FREESTYLERS The brand-new park was designed by local Matt Castell who also designed Vail's snowboard park. He did well. The opportunity is there to go big but there's nothing too gnarly to freak out casual jibbers. The ten hits and quarterpipe can all be hit from at least two different approaches and the flow of the park is designed to change with the snow levels. Hits are rated from green to black and all the landings are nice and steep. It's a perfect park to try out some new tricks or launch that extra foot.

CARVERS Copper has big wide trails suited for carving which reflect the mountain's traditional East Coast connection; many instructors hail from the eastern carving mountains. The American Flyer and trails further to skier's left are fast and smooth, and the Timberline Express Quad gets you back up without wasting vertical time. The Main Vein is the GS course and follows the line of the American Eagle Chair straight back to base.

MOUNTAIN FOOD Copper Commons has a huge inside area resembling a football stadium and an outside patio which is the most happening place on the mountain. They have cheapish food like chilli and soup for $3-$4. If clapping along to a guitar-playing country singer appeals, try the Copper Commons Bar populated by an older ski crowd. Beneath the American Flyer, Flyers has snacks and drinks and is a great place to hang out and watch the world go by.

EVENTS AND COMPETITIONS The Copper Mountain Snowboard Series features USASA events. They also host an annual Supercross Snowboard Challenge, a boardercross competition for pro-riders. For more information about what's up this season, contact Dan Smith — Tel: 970-729 1473.

Copper Mountain

ABOUT TOWN

The resort at Copper Mountain is a custom-built nest of comfortable condos and restaurants at the base of the lifts. Copper Village is alive during the day and early evening but fades fast once the sun goes down. Unless it's a huge holiday weekend, no-one hangs around the resort at night and all the easy-going local boarders live in Frisco.

Commuting is made easy by the free Summit Stage; head to Breckenridge for a big, flashy night out or drive the five miles (nine kilometres) to Frisco if you're looking for a real local town. If you're interested in exploring Summit County beyond Copper Mountain, Frisco or neighbouring Dillon make a good budget base-camp for all four mountains.

ACCOMMODATION Copper Village has a full range of non-budget accommodation at the foot of the mountain. All guests receive free use of the Racquet and Athletic club which has steam-baths, saunas and pool. A double hotel room peak-season will cost $180 to $205 per night. Call Central Reservations for rooms, lift passes and internal airline flight bookings — Tel: 1-800-458 8386 in the US or 0-800-89 4964 in the UK.

If cosy condos don't appeal, a good option is finding a B&B or motel in Frisco, Silverthorne or Dillon. Call Summit County Central Reservations — Tel: 970-468 6222 or 1-800-356 6365.

FOOD Lizzie's Bagelry and Coffee-house is hidden around the back of Copper Village, beside the Chinese restaurant in Village Square West. Ask locals for directions as they are the main consumers of the fresh-baked fruit bagels and cappuccinos. On a bad weather day, there are interesting books to peruse on the history of Beat and Indian culture. O'Shea's has good pub food at the base of the American Eagle Chairlift and the added benefit of being a mere staggering distance from bed. For a selection of salads and healthy food, Racket's at the Racquet and Athletic Club is where all the health-freaks go.

Once you've exhausted the range of steak, burgers and pasta which the resort offers, you might be tempted to roam further down to Frisco. The Moosejaw offers cheap, soft and easily digestible food in a dingy, plaid-jacket atmosphere. It's

adorned with drunk punters, volleyball trophies and memorabilia reflecting the evolution of a pub's personality. Barkley's Margaritagrille adds a Mexican tangent to the steak and burgers. That's as radical as Friso gets in the food department.

NIGHTLIFE Although Copper Village dies with the light, Frisco parties on. Even if there are only a couple of locals to be found in a bar, you can bet freshies they will be inebriated. The first place to fly-by is the Moosejaw, a seedy pub which has seen a few flowers wilted in its time. You get the choice of participating in slurred conversation or watching from the sidelines. El Rio, a Mexican sports-bar, has the best selection of tequilas in Summit County and a cocktail pint glass of margarita will set you back $3.50-$5.50.

OTHER ACTIVITIES Cross-country skiing, ice-skating and sleigh rides.

THANKS TO Eric, Kyle and Brian at Max.

Top left — Aerial view of Copper Mountain **Photo:** Ben Blankenburg
Courtesy: Copper Mountain Resort
Top right —Dropping in on Tucker Mountain **Photo:** Gina Demspter
Bottom left — USASA slopestyle comp **Photo:** Gina Dempster

GETTING THERE
By air: Denver Airport has connections to all major American terminals and you can fly directly to Europe on Delta Airlines — Tel: 1-800-221 1212. Denver is a 90 minute drive from Copper Mountain. The Resort Express from Denver to Copper, Frisco, Keystone and Breckenridge runs hourly till 12.00pm. Check in at the counter near the rental car desks in the main terminal, prices from $78 return.
By bus: See Winter Park review p.118 for details of the 7NEWS SkiXpress bus from Denver.
By car: Head west on Interstate 70 for 60 miles (90 kilometres) until you hit Copper Mountain; it's within spitting distance of the highway.
Getting around: The free Summit Stage provides transport within Summit County. Ask at any hotel for the schedule — Tel: 970-668 0999. Copper has a free local shuttle within the resort — Tel: 970-968 2882.

Aspen Snowmass

THE FACTS

ELEVATION

Summit:
11,835ft, 3610m
Vertical drop:
3723ft, 1136m
Base:
8112ft, 2474m

SNOWFALL

Average annual:
300 inches, 762cm

Snow-making:
5%

AREA

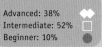

Total area:
2575 acres, 1043ha

Advanced: 38%
Intermediate: 52%
Beginner: 10%

SEASON
End November — mid-April

COMMUNICATIONS
Snow report:
Tel: 970-925 1221 or 1-800-525 6200 ext. 2400
Web site: http://www.com/skiaspen
E-mail: aspenint@rof.net
Mountain information:
Tel: 970-925 1220 or 1-800-525 6000
Fax: 970-920 0771
Snowmass Resort Association:
Tel: 970-923 2000 or 1-800-598 2006
Fax: 970-923 5466

LIFTS AND TICKETS
Number of lifts:
7 high-speed quads, 8 chairlifts, 2 surface lifts
Lift pass prices:
1/2 day: $42
1 day: $56
Multi-day: $296 (6 days)
Season: N/A
Other ticketing information:
Lift passes are valid for Buttermilk and Aspen Highlands as well. Early season tickets (before mid-December) go for $39.

SNOWBOARD SHOPS
Aspen Velo — Tel: 970-923 5507
The shop is located at 88 Snowmass Village Mall, and there you'll find super-helpful staff with rentals, repairs and full technical back-up.

SNOWBOARD SCHOOL
Aspen Snowboard Programme
Tel: 970-923 1227 or 1-800-525 6200
For $149 you get three days of lifts and lessons, and a guarantee that you will be able to board Snowmass and Buttermilk top to bottom. The reward for being a failure is that you get an extra day free.

ON THE MOUNTAIN

From the base station it is hard to imagine why Snowmass is so named but once you pass over the first ridge on either the Fanny Hill Chair or the Wood Run Chair, the massiveness of the area becomes apparent. Snowmass has 2575 acres (1043 hectares) of rideable terrain which is more than Buttermilk, Highlands and Aspen Mountain put together. The resort has three main areas of interest: Big Burn, the Cirque and High Alpine. The highest point on the mountain is the Cirque, an open alpine bowl with steep chutes leading down into scattered trees. There are no lifts in the bowl but the hiking commitment pays off big-time on a powder day. If you're a wilderness kind of person and you dig kicking back, warming huts and nature in general, then the Elk Camp area is the place for you. It's worth having a map in your head to avoid the frustrations of traverses and cat-tracks; spend some time sussing each area well before you move on. It's also worth making back-up meeting plans if you can't handle boarding without your buddies, as once you lose people there's damn small chance of stumbling across them again.

SNOW CONDITIONS Snowmass gets less snow than some of its Colorado counterparts but the snow stays in good condition due to the high altitude and predominantly north-facing slopes. The big snowfall months are February and March.

BACK-COUNTRY OPTIONS Aspen Mountain Powder Tours access 1500 acres (606 hectares) of untracked back-country terrain by snowcat. If by any remote chance you like the sound of deep freshies in trees with drops and steeps — Tel: 970-925 1220. A day of serious riding with lunch will set you back $225 per person.

FREERIDERS Do yourself a favour and check out the whole place. Hiking to the top of the Cirque takes you to the very highest boundary point of the mountain and presents you with a smorgasbord of chutes, drops, free-range powder and open glades further down. Snowcats offer free rides to the top of the Cirque ten times daily weather permitting — or so the brochure claims but we didn't see any begging us to jump on. The best place to check the cat status is the Up 4 Pizza hut at the top of the Big Burn Chairlift. Before riding this area, check that all runs are officially open as you will lose your pass if caught in a closed area — and we can guarantee that this isn't just an empty threat. You can ride from the top of Big Burn across to the base of Alpine Springs and scarcely touch a groomed trail. The Hanging Valley Glades are a ten minute hike from the top of the High Alpine Chair. Hanging Valley is laced with steeps, cliffs, trees and the occasional powder meadow. All the well-known freeride areas tend to get tracked out fairly quickly but with a little common sense and some exploratory gusto, it will take a long time to get bored at Snowmass.

FREESTYLERS The snowboard park is located at the base of the Alpine Springs Lift and has all the usual stuff in fairly well-maintained conditions. Immediately after the park is a wide halfpipe with good vertical sections. You can hike the park or take the Funnel Lift back up. If you're an absolute park fiend, check out the park at Buttermilk. It's a little more intense.

CARVERS Plenty here for you freaks. All the lower groomed areas are long, wide and fast. Unfortunately speed restrictions are enforced by the ski patrol on busy days at Snowmass, but you'll be so burned by the time you reach them that you'll be glad of the excuse to take it easy. Check out the runs on Big Burn, Campground and Sam's Knob for varying levels of carving highway.

MOUNTAIN FOOD There are six restaurants on the mountain including a pizza joint called Up 4 Pizza on Big Burn. The Timbermill at the base of the Fanny Hill Chair has the busiest sundeck and is a good meeting place. Snowmass Village is packed with sandwich, coffee and pizza bars.

HAZARDS AND RULES Watch out for closed signs: no excuses and no mercy shown.

SNOWMASS SKI AREA

ABOUT TOWN

Snowmass Village has been developed specifically to service the impressive mountain area — it's 12 miles (18 kilometres) west of Aspen town where it all really happens. Many Aspenites actually live in Snowmass Village but use the facilities of the town. At the end of a hard day, you'll be glad to fall into a room just off the slopes but once you've had a soak, some food and some beer, you'll be on the bus headed to Aspen for further kicks.

ACCOMMODATION Snowmass works out to be considerably more expensive than Aspen. The trade-off is slopeside for partyside. One week's 'economy' lodging and six days' boarding will cost $440 per person in Aspen (during the regular season of February and March) and $800 in Snowmass. The Wildwood Lodge has outdoor hot-tubs to bask in — Tel: 970-923 3550. Snowmass Central Reservations — Tel: 1-800-215 7669.

FOOD At the village entrance-way to the slopes, Timbermill has a grill menu and gets raucous from when the lifts shut till it closes at 7.00pm. The Caboose on the upper level of Snowmass Village is a good place for homemade tacos, pizzas, sandwiches and chilli-dogs for under $5. Also on the upper level, Café Ink serves bagels, coffee, smoothies and veggie stuff. Everything else is restaurant-style but you can choose from Chinese, Mexican, lobster or Colorado bistro cuisine. Krabloonik serves wild game in a cabin and the Mountain Dragon dishes up MSG-free stir-fries and fortune cookies which advise you to 'be aggressive and you will win'. Aspen has a huge choice of gourmet restaurants; head there if Snowmass is a little restrictive for your tastes.

NIGHTLIFE Get the bus to Aspen! It costs $3 each way; you need the right change or a token from the bus station. Most places in town close at 2.00am and the last bus back to Snowmass is at about 2.15am — throw yourself in front of it if it doesn't slow down. Cowboys and the Tower are bars in Snowmass Village Mall. May the force be with you.

OTHER ACTIVITIES Fresh-Tracks Nature Tours provide a free guided nature tour for each of Aspen's four mountains. For a Snowmass tour, go to the Wildlife Interpretative Centre at the top of the Elk Camp Lift at 11.00am or 1.00pm on Monday, Wednesday or Friday.

THANKS TO Adam Longnecker for showing us round the mountain, Aspen Velo for the wax and Switch insert, Claudia Jacobsen, Lisa Bruening and William Burwell. And no thanks to the bus driver who didn't stop for us when it was snowing at 2.15am.

For more About Town, see Buttermilk and Aspen Highlands review p.130.

For more About Town, see Buttermilk and Aspen Highlands review p.130.

8

Opposite — Hiking Hanging Valley **Photo:** Gina Dempster

Top — **Photo:** Gina Dempster

Middle — **Photo:** Gina Dempster

Bottom — Low Pressure journalists fall foul of the 'Nazski' Patrol whilst engaged in serious boundary law research **Photo:** Gina Dempster

GETTING THERE

By car: Snowmass Village is 12 miles (19 kilometres) up the road from Aspen. Parking at the base of Snowmass costs $8 per day, so it's best to get the free shuttle from town or park free at the rodeo lot.

Getting around: The Roaring Fork Transit Authority (RFTA) bus from Snowmass to Aspen runs regularly until 2.30am. It costs $3 (you need the right change) and takes about 20 minutes — Tel: 970-925 8484.

Buttermilk & Aspen Highlands

THE FACTS

ELEVATION

	Buttermilk	Highlands
Summit		
	9900ft, 3018m	11,675ft, 3559m
Vertical drop		
	2030ft, 619m	3635ft, 1108m
Base		
	7870ft, 2399m	8040ft, 2451m

SNOWFALL

	Buttermilk	Highlands
Average Annual		
	200 inch, 508cm	300 inch, 762cm
Snow-making		
	26%	18%

AREA

	Buttermilk	Highlands
Total area		
	410 acres, 166ha	619 acres, 251ha
26%	Advanced	47%
29%	Intermediate	33%
35%	Beginner	20%

SEASON
Mid-December — mid-April

COMMUNICATIONS
Snow report:
Tel: 970-925 1221 or 1-800-525 6200 ext. 2400
Web site: http://www.aspen.com/skiaspen
E-mail: aspenint@rof.net
Mountain information:
Tel: 970-920 0771 or 1-800-525 6000
Aspen Chamber Resort Association:
Tel: 970-920 7145 or 1-800-262 7736

LIFTS AND TICKETS
Number of lifts:
Buttermilk: 1 high-speed quad, 5 chairlifts,
1 surface lift
Highlands: 2 high-speed quads, 5 chairlifts,
1 surface lift
Lift pass prices:
1/2 day: $42
1 day: $56
Multi-day: $296 (6 days)
Season: N/A
Other ticketing information:
Lift passes are valid for all three riding mountains:
Snowmass, Highlands and Buttermilk.

SNOWBOARD SHOPS
The Alternative Edge — Tel: 970-925 8272
The Alternative Edge is the one-stop shop with
extensive product lines, superior service and
funny-ass staff in purple fluffy hats.
Aspen Velo — Tel: 970-925 1495
Their second location in downtown Aspen has a
similar vibe to the Snowmass shop.

SNOWBOARD SCHOOL
Aspen Snowboard Programme
Buttermilk — Tel: 970-920 0788
Highlands — Tel: 970-544 3022
Buttermilk is centred around beginners so it's the
one to head for if you've never been on a board
before. For more challenging lessons, Highlands or
Snowmass are better suited.

ON THE MOUNTAIN

Aspen Mountain still doesn't allow snowboarding but both Buttermilk and Aspen Highlands are snowboard friendly. Highlands has only 619 acres (251 hectares) of terrain but is the locals' favourite and on powder days, it's an assured bet for fresh. It's the mountain to freeride if you get bored at Snowmass. Buttermilk is the least challenging

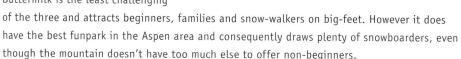

of the three and attracts beginners, families and snow-walkers on big-feet. However it does have the best funpark in the Aspen area and consequently draws plenty of snowboarders, even though the mountain doesn't have too much else to offer non-beginners.

SNOW CONDITIONS Buttermilk doesn't get the same big dumps as the other mountains around Aspen, but then it doesn't have the same natural obstacles to cover either. As with Snowmass, both Buttermilk and Aspen Highlands have a high altitude and northerly aspect and that says it all. Substantial snow-making facilities make up for any shortfall.

FREERIDERS Confident freeriders will enjoy spending more time at Highlands as it has more challenging terrain than Buttermilk. Two particularly good areas are the Steeplechase to the left of the Loge Peak Chairlift, and the Olympic Bowl at the top of the Olympic Chairlift. Both feature steep powder chutes with burly drops and tasty smatterings of trees. The whole mountain is steep, so aggressive riders will be grinning. Buttermilk doesn't have so much adrenaline to offer but the Tiehack side has powder stashes if you have a free day. Stay well clear of the slow, slow Buttermilk West Chairlift and the surrounding flat trails.

CARVERS Both areas have extremely well-groomed trails. Buttermilk's are wide and uncluttered while Highlands' are steeper and more amped.

FREESTYLERS The Buttermilk funpark wins hands down. It was designed by Adam Longnecker and the Aspen Snowboard Club, and skillfully shaped by groomer extraordinaire known only as 'Bruce the cat-driver'. There are some big things to throw yourself off and there are some huge things to throw yourself off; there is even a G-shaped bowl at the bottom. From the park you look down over Pitkin County Airport at planes taking off. It's unproven but the theory is that this keeps the standard of riding high.

MOUNTAIN FOOD Mid-mountain on Aspen Highlands is the Merry-Go-Round which has soups, veggie specials and apple strudel to munch on the sundeck. The Highlands Café at the Base Lodge specialises in tacos. Café West at the base of West Buttermilk has French café food like crêpes, and the Cliffhouse has American café food like pizza and fries.

HAZARDS AND RULES Closed areas on Highland are enforced by pass confiscation so take notice of the signs.

EVENTS AND COMPETITIONS The Buttermilk BoarderFest in mid-December closes the mountain to non-boarders for two days while cheap $29 lift passes, equipment demos, big air comps and live music blast forth. Buttermilk loves snowboarders, Peter King the mountain manager loves snowboarders and so does Bruce the cat-driver. Call 'Team Buttermilk' to know more — Tel: 1-800-525 6200.

Buttermilk&Highlands ⑨

ABOUT TOWN

Aspen is the core town for all four mountains and has everything you could want. Aspenites are proud of the Hollywood image of their town and they're even more proud to have Hunter S. Thompson living in Woody Creek. His random pot-shots at wannabe interviewers add grunge depth to Aspen's glitzy image. The Aspen concept was the brainchild of a man named Walter Paepcke, whose original Aspen Company set out in '45 to build a community 'where (people) can earn a living and profit by healthy physical recreation, with facilities at hand for the enjoyment of art, music and education'. Is snowboarding not an art form? Nowadays Aspen has become a bastion of Bogner outfits, but look beyond the hype because there's more than gold in them thar hills.

The town is easy to work out with a grid layout centred around Hyman Ave. Glossy shops and expensive restaurants are the norm; it takes a bit of work to track down cheap eating spots. Despite Aspen's reputation as a star-infested resort, all sorts roam the streets.

ACCOMMODATION The advantages of staying in Aspen instead of Snowmass Village are firstly that it's cheaper and secondly that it's close to the night action. Budget-wise, the second consideration will probably cancel the first but at least you'll have some party yarns to spin. One week's 'economy' lodging and six days' boarding will cost from $440 per person in Aspen (during the regular season of February and March). Aspen Central Reservations — Tel: 1-800-290 1325.

FOOD Aspen town has over 100 restaurants and eateries ranging from pizza, crêpes and sandwiches to caviar and champagne. New York Pizza is open till 2.00am with free delivery and is a good locals' hang-out. Other recommended places are Su Casa or the Cantina for Mexican and margaritas, and Maxfield's Sports Bar and Grill on Dean Street. If you're self-catering, Aspen has a couple of well-stocked supermarkets but the prices are cheaper at in Glenwood Springs, El Jebel and Basalt. The Aspen Wine and Spirit Co. does free deliveries of wine, spirits and beer and takes Amex, Master Card and Visa — Tel: 970-925 6600 for a keg party.

NIGHTLIFE Aspen has a vast and treacherous nightlife and all within walking distance. Start at Maxfield's Sport's Bar and Grill with the locals. You can play pool, table football and air hockey or just drink and watch videos. Eric's Bar behind Su Casa is a more flashy haunt which sits adjacent to a nice pool hall and a swish cigar room with armchairs.

Booty-shaking happens mainly in four places after midnight. The Tippler has a loud dance floor playing disco and LCD (lowest common denominator) house. Club Soda in Hyman Mall sets out a classier agenda but with the same music: we

asked for Wu Tang and got Mariah Carey and Ol' Dirty Bastard. If you get frustrated, head downstairs as the pool room is pure luxury. The locals prefer Club Freedom, also on Hyman Mall. The music, the atmosphere and the lights were all darker and dingier, so therefore better by our standards. For live music six nights a week, Double Diamond is the spot. If you want to do the beat thing and get the Hunter S. vibe, head to the Woody Creek Tavern at Woody Creek Plaza. It's wieerrd man!

OTHER ACTIVITIES Greenbacks buy anything here. You want it, you pay for it, you got it. Look out for the Ultimate Taxi. It's the only recording studio, theatre, nightclub, planetarium, toy store, internet-connected taxi-cab in the world.

THANKS TO See Aspen Snowmass.

All Photos: Gina Dempster

GETTING THERE

By air: Aspen has its own Aspen-Pitkin County Airport — Tel: 970-920 5380. Delta Airlines fly direct to Aspen regularly during the winter season — Tel: 1-800-221 1212. The airport is located next to Buttermilk (you can see it from the funpark). Shuttles are available from Denver International Airport and cost around $80 one-way. The trip takes four to five hours, contact: High Mountain Taxi — Tel: 970-925 8294 or 1-800-528 8294 or Airport Shuttle of Colorado — Tel: 970-925 1234 or 1-800-222 2112 or Colorado Mountain Express — Tel: 970-949 4227 or 1-800-525 6353.
By train: Amtrak runs to Glenwood Springs, 40 miles (64 kilometres) from Aspen — Tel: 1-800-USA RAIL. Airport Shuttle Colorado and High Mountain Taxi provide transport to and from Glenwood Springs.
By bus: Greyhound also goes as far as Glenwood Springs and you can take a RFTA bus from there — Tel: 970-945 8501 or 1-800-231 2222.
By car: Take Interstate 70 from Denver and turn onto Highway 82 at Glenwood Springs. The drive from Denver is 220 miles (354 kilometres), most of it on the interstate — Tel: 970-920 5454 for road conditions.
Getting around: RFTA provides a free service within Aspen and to the airport between 6.30am and 2.30am, and to all four mountains during lift hours. For more information — Tel: 970-925 8484.

Crested Butte

THE FACTS

ELEVATION

Summit:
12,162ft, 3709m
Vertical drop:
3062ft, 934m
Base:
9100ft, 2775m

SNOWFALL

Average annual:
298 inches, 757cm

Snow-making:
20%

AREA

Total area:
1160 acres, 470ha

Advanced: 58%
Intermediate: 29%
Beginner: 13%

SEASON
Mid-November — mid-April

COMMUNICATIONS
Snow report: Tel: 970-349 2323
Web site: http://www.colorado.com/crestedbutte
E-mail: cbinfo@rmi.net
Mountain information:
Tel: 970-349 2390 or 0-800-89 4085 (toll-free UK)
Fax: 970-349 2250
Crested Butte Chamber of Commerce:
Tel: 970-349 6438

LIFTS AND TICKETS
Number of lifts:
2 high-speed quads, 7 chairlifts, 4 surface lifts
Lift pass prices:
1/2 day: $35
1 day: $47
Multi-day: $278 (6 out of 7 days)
Season: N/A
Other ticketing information:
One day of a five day plus multi-day pass can be
swapped for snowmobiling, Nordic skiing, horse riding
or a reduction on massage or hot-air ballooning. Take
advantage of Butte's free lift pass offer for the first
three weeks and last two weeks of the season. Ring
the mountain to confirm dates for the coming season
(usually early December and mid-April).

SNOWBOARD SHOPS
Colorado Boarder — Tel: 970-349 9828
This is a serious slopeside shop where helmets are
the number one accessory due to the extreme
terrain. They also stock a good choice of sale and
rental boards, and the staff will entertain you with
their dry wit.

SNOWBOARD SCHOOL
Crested Butte Snowboard School
Tel: 970-349 2252
Call at the Gothic Building ski school desk. A First
Timer package with rental, lift pass and a four
hour lesson costs $55.

ON THE MOUNTAIN

Crested Butte kicks butt. It's steep, it's ungroomed, it's packed tight with cliff jumps and radical tree runs and it's steep. The Butte (or 'Beaut' as it's pronounced) is the site of the US Extremes for both skiing and boarding, and is unreal after a dump. The local riders are hot and don't give a damn what you ride on so long as you go big. Dominating the base area is the Banana Funnel, a striking pyramid peak. Looking up the mountain you can see the steep tree runs below the alpine slopes of the funnel; to the left are the cruisier groomed trails of the mid-mountain area. On the eastern side of the ski area is the notorious North Face terrain. The bowls, glades and avalanche run-outs on this side are just a shade off vertical and boost Crested Butte into the elite stratosphere.

SNOW CONDITIONS Crested Butte attracts storms from differing directions and stores snow by virtue of having such a high altitude. The most challenging areas (North Face, Headwall and Banana Funnel) face north-east and stay ungroomed due to 40 degree plus gradients.

FREERIDERS The whole point of going to Crested Butte is to freeride and the best place for an adrenaline fix is the North Face where the US ski and board extremes are held. As you enter the area from the North Face Poma, the sign reads: 'This terrain is the steepest lift-served terrain in North America'. Immediately below the poma are the heavily wooded glades of Powder Rock and Pinball. The North Face has some huge stepped cliff jumps which suit skiers as they can arrest on the snow pillows halfway down the rocks. Boarders have to go really big and take their chances on a soft landing at the bottom. The open front face can suffer from mogul invasions but there are rad steep chutes in the trees at the top.

Follow the hiking tracks from the top of the poma and you get to the stashes in the three sweet powder bowls: Spellbound, Phoenix and Third. The one thing which can jolt you out of this freeride mirage is the lifts; it's a tedious traverse and three lift ride back up. Banana Funnel glitters temptingly on a clear day; the lower slopes and glades can be accessed from the Silver Queen Quad via a traverse to skier's left. If you want to go higher, the peak was opened to unguided riding between 10.00am and 2.00pm for the first time in the '96-'97 season. The base is rocky so it's only worth it when the snow is abundant.

FREESTYLERS The Snowboarding Terrain Park on the Smith Hill run is about as exciting as the name suggests. The funpark has log slides and quarterpipes but most Crested Butte jibbers are essentially freeriders pulling 540s off moguls.

CARVERS The slicing section of the mountain is between the Silver Queen Quad and the Paradise Lift. Runs are fast and rolling; it's a great place to get an impromptu Chinese Downhill happening. The mountain doesn't groom every run daily so small moguls crop up, but generally the standard of grooming is high. Ruby Road onto International is a speed festival back to base.

MOUNTAIN FOOD The Paradise Warming House is the place to hang out if you're on the North Face. At the base, Rafters in the Gothic building has a sun-baked balcony and underneath is the Gothic Cafeteria.

HAZARDS AND RULES The hike to Third Bowl closes at 2.30pm and if you go in after this time, your pass will be yanked.

EVENTS AND COMPETITIONS Crested Butte offers the biggest discount we've come across: ski for free in the first three weeks and last two weeks of the season, with degrees of nudity involved during the last day's riding. Crested Butte also hosts a round of the US Extreme Skiing and Snowboarding Championships.

substantial meal, The Avalanche have a full grill and serve enormous piles of nachos. They also cook great pancakes first thing in the morning.

NIGHTLIFE Mount Crested Butte rocks for a couple of hours as soon as the lifts close. The Rafters and the Saloon compete for the beer-drinking crowd with happy hours and live bands. All the late night gigs are on Elk Street in downtown Crested Butte

and no big decisions have to made about where to go because they're all staggering distance apart. The Talk of the Town is the rowdy pool and football venue with the highest rating for trouble potential, which translates into your highest chance of waking up on a cold cell floor. The main music venue The Idle Spur features woolly DJ Harry playing disco on Friday nights. If you're looking for a groovier scene with live bands, try the Eldorado. Kochevar's has a dodgy, 'forty year-old, pissed and grumpy' reputation amongst locals who aren't, but it's still on the local pub route.

OTHER ACTIVITIES Fly tandem with the Pterodactyl Paragliding School — Tel: 970-349 2836. The No Limits Centre run mountaineering, ice-climbing and avalanche courses — Tel: 1-800-349 5219.

THANKS TO Janet Antram, Ryan's friend Dev, Gina Kroft and Gordon Reeves.

10

ABOUT TOWN

Butch Cassidy and the Sundance Kid hid out in downtown Crested Butte in 1902 and not much has changed since then except the colour scheme — think of a black and white Western in psychedelic pastel. Pubs go crazy at nights with hard-hitting drinking sessions to match a hard day's riding. The base area is a cluster of condos, up-market hotels, bars and eating places called Mount Crested Butte. It's functional but hasn't got the history and vibe of the downtown area three miles (five kilometres) away. For the total non-tourist option, Gunnison is a college town 28 miles (45 kilometres) from Crested Butte. This is where you'll find cheap basic accommodation and food, and you'll be slumming it beside the many students who've managed to convince their parents that they're working hard towards a future career in marketing. Crested Butte will soon be the best marketed mountain on the planet.

ACCOMMODATION Lodge accommodation in Mount Crested Butte starts at $50 per person per night; amongst the cheapest are the Crested Butte Lodge — Tel: 970-349 4747 and the Manor Lodge — Tel: 970-349 5365. All of the condos are located in Mount Crested Butte near the lifts and start at $95 for the cheapest two bedroom units: Castle Point Condos, Castle Ridge Condos and Paradise Condos — Tel: 0-800-89 4085. The Grande Butte Hotel opens onto the slopes with rooms from $100 per night — Tel: 970-349 4000 or 1-888-879 7315. For lodging reservations, call Crested Butte Mountain Resort — Tel: 1-888-879 7315 or Crested Butte Vacations — Tel: 970-349 2390 or 1-800-544 8448. Cheaper beds can be found in Gunnison. The Cattleman's Inn next to Safeways on Highway 50 has rooms from $25 — Tel: 970-641 1061. Otherwise find a doss-pad on a student couch.

FOOD The Bakery Café in downtown Crested Butte has good deli food and baking. Donita's specialises in Mexican food. For some carbo-loading before a big powder day, Bacchanale's is the pasta option. Lil's Land and Sea, a fresh seafood and sushi bar, will amp your taste-buds and libido at the expense of your wallet. Mount Crested Butte doesn't have the same range of restaurants but it does have good breakfasts and lunches. The Mount Crested Butte Bakery, located through the bank near the main bus-stop, is the cheapest option with fresh cinnamon rolls, muffins and sammies to take-away. The best coffee fix and local rumour hot-spot is Tom's Cart, right beside the main bus-stop. For a

Top left — Jason Troth at the '97 US Extreme Snowboard Championships
Photo: Tom Stillo **Courtesy:** Crested Butte
Top right — **Photo:** Gina Dempster
Inset — Banana Funnel **Photo:** Gina Dempster

GETTING THERE

By air: Gunnison-Crested Butte airport has direct flights on four airlines including Delta — Tel: 1-800-221 1212. The mountain is a 30 minute drive from the airport and Alpine Express shuttles meet every plane — Tel: 970-641 5074.
By bus: Greyhound provides a daily service to Gunnison from Grand Junction.
By car: Take Highway 285 from Denver to Poncha Springs, then Highway 50 west into Gunnison. Turn onto Highway 135 north to Crested Butte. The 230 mile (368 kilometre) drive should take four to five hours.
Getting around: A free shuttle runs regularly from Mount Crested Butte to downtown Crested Butte. The Alpine Express costs $1.50 each way from Gunnison to Mount Crested Butte; buy a ticket at local stores or bus-stops.

Telluride

THE FACTS

ELEVATION

Summit:
11,890ft, 3626m
Vertical drop:
3165ft, 965m
Base:
8725ft, 2661m

SNOWFALL

Average annual:
300 inches, 770cm

Snow-making:
12%

AREA

Total area:
1050 acres, 448ha

Advanced: 32%
Intermediate: 47%
Beginner: 21%

SEASON
Late November — mid-April

COMMUNICATIONS
Snow report: Tel: 970-728 7425
Web site: http://www.telski.com
E-mail: telluride_information@infozone.org
Mountain information:
Tel: 970-728 4431 or 1-800-525 3455
Fax: 970-728 6475
Telluride Visitor Information Centre:
Tel: 970-728 4431 or 1-800-525 3455

LIFTS AND TICKETS
Number of lifts:
1 gondola, 2 high-speed quads, 7 chairlifts,
2 surface lifts
Lift pass prices:
1/2 day: $39
1 day: $49
Multi-day: $258 per day (6 out of 7 days)
Season: $800-$1050
Other ticketing information:
Lift passes cost $2 extra for the two weeks over
Christmas and New Year. Pre-Christmas tickets cost
$32 for a full day and $26 for a half day.

SNOWBOARD SHOPS
Free Wheelin' Snowboard
Tel: 970-728 4734 or 1-800-433 9733
Telluride's one and only purist boarding shop on
East Colorado Ave.

SNOWBOARD SCHOOL
Telluride Snowboard School — Tel: 970-728 7533
An all day beginners' clinic with rental and lift
pass costs $85. For intermediates and above, All
Day Adventures cost $60 and focus on carving and
race technique, trees and park, and extreme on
different days of the week. Take all three in a row
for $150. Telluride's four day ($400) or five day
($460) Triple Treat Snowboard Camps are designed
for intermediate to advanced riders and cover all
disciplines.

ON THE MOUNTAIN

Telluride is unsurpassable for terrain, attitude and atmosphere. Dizzy Gillespie said: "If Telluride ain't paradise then heaven can wait." He must have just hiked Gold Hill and cut down to Lift 6 through the trees. Telluride has always been famous for its freeriders. History has it that Butch Cassidy robbed his first bank here in 1889, about the same time the Swedes and Finns first introduced telemark skiing to the area. The tradition of free-heel skiing has lived on and the high numbers of wild-bearded, pinheaded types is an omen that the freeriding will be good.

The terrain is naturally segregated with challenging stuff on the east side around Lift 8 and Lift 9 and the faces of Gold Hill. The chutes, trees and meadows on Gold Hill are quintessential freeriding. Blue cruising runs converge in the centre of the resort heading down towards Mountain Village. Beginners have their own territory around the Sunshine Express Chair on the western boundary. Telluride is considered a Class A, high risk avalanche area in the same league as Jackson Hole, Wyoming and Snowbird, Utah due to a relatively shallow snowpack and drastically changing temperatures. It's therefore important to respect all warnings or ride with people who know the place.

SNOW CONDITIONS A lot of the resort is north to west facing, and with Gold Hill's 12,247 foot (3735 metre) altitude, snow settles once it falls. Fresh powder is still found in the wooded areas weeks after a dump.

FREERIDERS To avoid lift queues in the morning, head up Lift 8 and onto Lift 9 instead of taking the Gondola to find gold. From the top of Lift 9, hike up Gold Hill for between three and 30 minutes and drop into the chutes, glades and open meadows. Traverse skier's right to get back to Lift 6, otherwise it's a five minute hike out or a 45 minute lift ride back up from the bottom of the learners' pitch. The East and West Drains are natural gullies running through heavenly tree areas back to the base of Lift 9. From Lift 9, keep going down the log-filled canyon called the Plunge and you'll come out at the base of the Gondola and Lift 8. All the runs around Lift 6 are kicking. If you get bored with these routes (or more likely with the ride up, since Lifts 6, 8 and 9 are also the slowest), check out the rest of the mountain or hook up with the telemarkers. Follow the simple rule of the thumb that the riding will be good where the snow is shaded.

Telluride is planning a 700 acre (282 hectare) expansion which will include trails in three killer new bowls and five new lifts. When completed, Telluride will have the highest lift-served terrain in North America and a vertical drop of 4010 feet (1624 metres). Think about moving there.

FREESTYLERS If you must stay in one place all day and jump off the same dozen hits, then there's also a place for you in Telluride. The funpark is located mid-mountain below the Gorrono Ranch. It's advisable to take it easy on your first run as this park is designed to be hit all the way round. The builder of the park Tom 'Sniglet' Paffel advises: "It's easy to get too much air. You've got to ride through it to get the hang of it." The park is stylish and smooth, and is a perfect place to progress. If you feel the need to express yourself on a larger canvas, read the freeride section.

CARVERS It's all good. There are steep groomed runs and mellow to bloody hard bumps on the face. Mountain Village has wide open trails but the gradient is not very testing. Once tracks have been laid, Gold Hill has fast chutes: Electra, Dynamo and Little Rose are heralded by locals. There are plans to run a lift into the Palmyra Bowl which will be a great day for carverhood.

MOUNTAIN FOOD Giuseppe's is a cosy mid-mountain hut with Italian dishes for under $10. The Gorrono Ranch near the Ride Park has a huge sundeck. For the best early morning Columbian caffeine fix, head to the Java Shack in the Mountain Village.

HAZARDS AND RULES Hiking up Gold Hill you pass an untouched, bottomless chute in Bear Creek Canyon, aptly nicknamed Temptation Chute. In the '80s an open gate policy ruled in Bear Creek Canyon but the policy was reversed in '92 after a string of deaths and a land access dispute. Seven people have been flushed down the 2000 foot toilet and dropping in there now could get you arrested or killed.

EVENTS AND COMPETITIONS USASA events.

Telluride

Garfinkels. Almost all the bars in town have pool tables and there are full billiard tables at the Sheridan Bar and the Swede-Finn Hall. Check Koto 91.7 FM, the cool community radio station with no ads, for details on what's going down.

ABOUT TOWN

The town is as near to an old western town as you're ever likely to come across. Time-warp aside, Telluride sits at an altitude of 8750 feet (2600 metres) which may account for why everyone seems so high. The cowboys of the gold rush days have been replaced by wild, bearded hippies with dreadlocks in Patagonia gear. Apparently Remmington shaver megalomaniac Victor Kiam has been trying to open a store here for years. Yet beards are practical; not only do you save on sunblock but you probably won't get asked for ID at every bar you go to.

The way to get orientated is to walk down Colorado Ave a couple of times. Bars and chow-downs are scattered along the main street and the mountains dwarf the wooden buildings. The new Gondola is a two-in-one; it accesses the mountain for snow-riders and the Mountain Village (on the other side of Coonskin Ridge) for condo-dwellers. The Mountain Village offers slopeside beds and not much else in the way of food or entertainment, but the 11 minute free gondola ride down to Telluride town is the most scenic way you'll ever go to the pub.

ACCOMMODATION Prices start between $131-$180 for B&Bs and $111-$260 for hotels. Bargain season runs from November to early February (excluding Christmas and New Year), and prices drop again in early April. Condos start at $136 for a one bedroom unit with kitchenette and $498 for a four bedroom unit. Accommodation at Mountain Village is mainly modern condos with a couple of hotels; prices are slightly higher than town. Central Reservations — Tel: 970-728 4431 or 1-800-525 3455.

FOOD Almost all the eating houses are on Colorado Ave with the odd hideaway on the cross streets. For snacks and cheap food go to Baked in Telluride on South Fir Street. They serve tasty pizza, bagels and sandwiches and brew their own beer. The Steaming Bean Coffee Co. is a coffee shrine which serves wholesome hippie food. The Fat Alley Barbecue specialises in hickory smoked meats with a choice of side orders for about $8. For something different, Honga's Lotus Petal flex their skills on the sushi deck and make mean Thai food. They also serve Moroccan mint tea with free refills. It's not the cheapest place in town but is possibly the best. The only place to eat late is The House on North Fir Street where you can scoff bar snacks until 1.00am. It doubles up as a peanut bar so participate in non-violent shelling of the place and leave the debris on the floor.

NIGHTLIFE Telluride is not the most rocking town in Colorado but it does have its occasional high points. If there's a party on in town everyone is dedicated to the cause; witness the Bluegrass Festival or Indie Film Festival which have spread Telluride's fame across the planet. Live bluegrass gigs at the Sheridan Opera House are unique, with much whoopin' and hollerin' and banter with Sam and John (from the Bluegrass Revival Band). For late night bars, live music and disco nights with DJ Harry, try Fly Me to the Moon Saloon and

OTHER ACTIVITIES Gliding, fly-fishing, hut to hut cross-country skiing and snowmobiling, historic walking tours, climbing, mountaineering, paragliding, a climbing wall, sled-dog tours, hot springs in Ouray. Telski organises free naturalist tours — Tel: 970-728 7525.

THANKS TO Nick Guidabaldi aka Brother Layback for inspiration and guidance, Mike Shimkonis and Virginia Verney.

GETTING THERE

By air: The closest international airport is Denver which Delta Airlines fly to regularly — Tel: 1-800-41 4141. Domestic flights land at Montrose Airport, 65 miles (105 kilometres) north, and at Telluride Airport, six miles (nine kilometres) west of town. Call one of the local shuttle companies for a $7 ride from Telluride Airport or a $25 ride from Montrose: Skip's Taxi — Tel: 970-728 6667, Telluride Transit — Tel: 970-728 6000, or Western Express — Tel: 970-728 9606.
By bus: Greyhound can get you to Ridgway, 30 miles (45 kilometres) away. From there try calling one of the transit companies above. If they need to make a special trip, it will cost you around $75.
By car: Telluride is 335 miles (539 kilometres) from Denver. Take Interstate 70 west to Highway 50 south and onto Highway 550. Turn west onto Highway 62 at Ridgway and follow Highway 145 south to Telluride. Road conditions — Tel: 970-249 9363.
Getting around: Telluride is walking territory although a free Tell-U-Ride shuttle runs around town for the lazy. The only transport challenge is how to get from Mountain Village to Telluride town, and the answer is a free ride on the Gondola. It takes a mellow 11 minutes (compared to an icy eight mile, 20 minute drive) and runs from 7.00am to 11.00pm.

11

Opposite — Temptation Chute, the 2000 foot toilet **Photo:** Gina Dempster
Top — Telluride town **Photo:** Gina Dempster
Panorama — Looking out from Gold Hill **Photo:** Gina Dempster

Purgatory

THE FACTS

ELEVATION

Summit:
10,822ft, 3300m
Vertical drop:
2029ft, 619m
Base:
8793ft, 2682m

SNOWFALL

Average annual:
240 inches, 610cm

Snow-making:
28%

AREA

Total area:
1200 acres, 486ha

Advanced: 26%
Intermediate: 51%
Beginner: 23%

SEASON
Late November — early April

COMMUNICATIONS
Snow report: Tel: 970-247 9000
Web site: http://www.ski-purg.com
E-mail: information@ski-purg.com
Mountain information:
Tel: 970-247 9000
Fax: 970-385 2107
Durango Area Chamber of Commerce:
Tel: 970-247 0312

LIFTS AND TICKETS
Number of lifts:
1 high-speed quad, 8 chairlifts, 1 surface lift
Lift pass prices:
1/2 day: $30
1 day: $40
Multi-day: $160 (4 days)
Season: $625-$725
Other ticketing information:
A four day plus multi-day pass allows one day pass
to be swopped for an off-slope activity like
snowmobiling, a train ride or a massage. Ask at the
Village Centre ticket office or Durango Central
Reservations.

SNOWBOARD SHOPS
Bubba's Boards — Tel: 970-259 7377
Located on Highway 550 between Purgatory
mountain and Durango, Bubba's has great service
and a wide selection of boards.
Shred Shed — Tel: 970-259 0913
The Shed is a skate derived board shop off the
main drag in Durango.
Pandemonium — Tel: 970-385 2118
Pandemonium at Purgatory Village is the nearest
shop to the slopes and is best for rentals.

SNOWBOARD SCHOOL
Purgatory Ski School — Tel: 970-385 2149
First time adult lessons are half price at $19 for a
two and a half hour lesson. The resort also hosts a
free Learn to Snowboard week mid-December and a
free carving clinic in January.

ON THE MOUNTAIN

Purgatory is not the most challenging mountain in the Colorado area but with the college town of Durango just down the road, the snowboarding scene remains healthy. The resort owes its name to the Animas River which took the life of a 16th century Spanish explorer. His grieving friends named the river 'Rio de las Animas Peridada' or the 'River of Lost Souls'. In the 19th century a witty cartographer named a tributary that flows into the river Purgatory Creek. The puns have proliferated on the mountain: there are Dante's Restaurant, Catharsis, No Mercy, the Lower Hades and no doubt more will ensue.

As far as snowboarding goes, you're somewhere between heaven and hell depending on your skills (and how good you've been). If you are a beginner to intermediate snowboarder, you'll have a great time here and have room to push yourself. Black runs make up 26 per cent of the resort but most of these are short and mogul-covered so serious freeriders may get frustrated.

SNOW CONDITIONS Purgatory is a cornerstone as it sits at the meeting place of four states and three unique landscapes: mesa, mountains and desert. It gets enough serious storms to dump 20 feet (six metres) each year, but the rest of the time the weather is sunny and relatively warm with predictable consequences for the snowpack.

FREERIDERS There are some good areas for freeriding. These are found mainly around Lift 1 and Lift 8. Both these areas have good tree runs and are steeper than the rest of the resort. From the top of the Hermosa Park Express Quad, you can traverse down to the Lift 8 base without too many problems. The locals surreptitiously say that the best riding at Purgatory is past the Lift 8 boundary, however getting caught in that area would result in losing your pass.

The B, D and M Express across the top of the mountain is flatter in some parts than the road to Durango, making cross-mountain traversing quite tedious. The initials are attributed to the founders of the resort but are rumoured to stand for Boring, Dull and Monotonous. Flat spots seem to be the biggest problem in Purgatory; stick to the rule of the thumb that if you don't know where you're going, go fast.

FREESTYLERS There is a funpark but it's not well looked after and is used by skiers as a short cut, resulting in moguls on all the run-ups. There are plenty of hits and things to jump off all over the mountain. Watch for the small cliff drops visible from Lift 5 and Lift 8. The resort is planning a new park and halfpipe for the '97-'98 season.

CARVERS There doesn't seem to be a resort in the world where carvers can't have a good time; even in Purgatory with its limited terrain there are still plenty of rolling trails for carving hard and fast. The black runs around Lift 1 and Lift 6 are fast, wide and probably the most groomed on the mountain. Legends is worth a burn from the top of the Hermosa Express Quad.

MOUNTAIN FOOD The Powderhouse serves only pizza, pasta and salad in the belief that it's better to do one thing well, if not with imagination. The Double Diamond Grill has good burgers in a cafeteria setting. The Heaven Eleven Deli at the base area has bargain sammies and lasagna. It's also good for breakfast.

HAZARDS AND RULES Watch out for tedious traverses and flat spots.

EVENTS AND COMPETITIONS An all-comers downhill race will be held every Thursday in February; sign the liability release and the first rider, skier or telemarker down the hill wins the prize. In March the resort hosts a halfpipe and boardercross event.

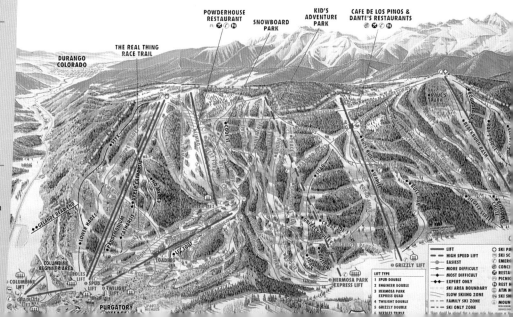

Purgatory

ABOUT TOWN

Durango might still be on the Colorado side of the border but there is a south-western tang in the air. Cowboys, hippies and retirees mix it up to reggae, jazz or country and western as fashions and music converge. Durango is a college town, but due to US drinking laws students don't have the same party impact that they do in other countries. Town is quiet during the week. The big plus for Durango is that it is cheap; winter is off-season and motels compete along the highway strip with $25 room specials. Purgatory Village, 25 miles (40 kilometres) north at the base of the mountain, has resort accommodation and a few restaurants and bars for the basics.

ACCOMMODATION Motels are plentiful in Durango and start at $25 a room; look out for bargains on Highway 550 as you drive into town. There is a ski-dorm on Second Ave which is central but keeps inconvenient hours. Call them before you turn up on the doorstep — Tel: 970-247 9905. The Hampton Inn is in the mid-price range with hot-tubs and a ski shuttle for $65-$135 a double room, including buffet breakfast — Tel: 1-800-HAMPTON.

Econo Lodge has rooms from $29 — Tel: 970-247 4242. Condos at the Purgatory base area are mostly in the $130-$300 range. A four day lift pass with five nights' lodging at the base of Purgatory will cost upwards of $440 mid-season. The same package with five nights in Durango starts at $298. Durango Central Reservations — Tel: 970-247 8900 or 1-800-962 4077.

FOOD Durango residents boast that it's a meat and potatoes type of town. Prime ribs and steaks are rife but there is choice beyond red meat. Mama's Boy on 36th and Main serves ample portions of Italian — try the angel-hair pasta with barbecue-sized shrimps. The chocolate and walnut pie with chocolate ice-cream is too much. Gazpachos makes no apologies for cooking hot, hot Mexican. A waitress gave us her key to the menu: red chilli is made with red chillies and green chilli with green chillies. The Ore House on East College Drive has steaks and trout in an old-timer saloon.

Up at Purgatory Village the food is standard American fare: burgers, grilled sandwiches, pizza and Mexican. The Columbine Kitchen at the Purgatory turn-off is a laid-back place to eat with cheap soup and chillies in a wood cabin. Café Cascade at Cascade Village has a twist on the red meat tangent, serving exotic wild game at $15-$20 for a main meal. Think of it as a bargain compared with Vail or Aspen prices.

NIGHTLIFE The Olde Schoolhouse Café is an aprés bar with bar food — no salad but lots of good pizza and cold beer. It's across from the petrol station on Highway 550 as you leave the mountain and is worth a visit to pump the locals on what's happening in town.

Durango has a weird collection of English, Irish, jazz, country and western pool bars. Colorado Pongos is a billiard parlour with a relaxed drinking atmosphere. They have comfortable tables to watch the action from and cheap shish 'ka-bobs' to munch on. Farquarhts has a more committed party feel with serious alcohol consumption and jazz bands from New Orleans. The reggae night at the 6th Street Loft is the most happening event on a Wednesday. English nostalgia rules in the Victorian settings of the Old Muldoon and the Diamond Belle, and in the modern Chelsea London Pub — all on Main Ave.

OTHER ACTIVITIES Snowmobile Adventures at Purgatory Mountain have kilometres of guided trails and a huge meadow for a blast. Wander around the cliff homes of the Anasazi civilisation, abandoned hundreds of years ago in the Mesa Verde National Park. Trimble Hot Springs, Narrow Gauge Railroad, 24 hour Sky Ute Casino with free shuttle.

THANKS TO Shamus at the Laughing Leprechaun Tattoo Studio and Mike Smedley.

GETTING THERE

By air: The Durango-La Plata County Airport is the gateway to Purgatory resort, 12 miles (20 kilometres) south-east of Durango with connections to every major US city. Durango Transportation run the airport shuttle — Tel: 970- 247 4161.
By bus: Greyhound have a daily service to Durango.
By car: Durango sits at the intersection of Highway 160 and Highway 550. From Denver take Interstate 70 south to connect with Highway 550, a distance of 333 miles (536 kilometres).
Getting around: A free trolley runs along Main Ave and Highway 550 every 30 minutes until 7.00pm. Durango Lift buses will also get you from one end of town to the other for $0.75. The Express Ski Shuttle costs $12 for the round trip to Purgatory base. Reservations are essential — Tel: 970-247 4161. Although some of the pricier motels offer free shuttles to the mountain, not having a car could be a hassle as many of the motels are stretched along Highway 550 and the mountain is 25 miles (40 kilometres) north. New for the '97-'98 season is a bus service between the town and the resort.

12

Top left — Purgatory trails **Photo:** Gina Dempster
Top right — Mesa Verde **Photo:** Gina Dempster
Bottom — Durango streets **Photo:** Gina Dempster

LOW PRESSURE

THE LOW PRESSURE GROUP Unit 21, Pall Mall Deposit, 124-128 Barlby Road, London W10 6BL
Tel/Fax: +44 (0)181 960 1916 **Email:** mail@lowpressure.demon.co.uk **Web:** www.lowpressure.demon.co.uk

ARIZONA

STATE INFORMATION

Population: 4,500,000
Time: Mountain West = GMT minus 7 hours
Capital city: Phoenix
Area: 118,000sq miles (305,502 sqkm)

VISITOR INFORMATION SOURCES

Arizona Tourism Department:
Tel: 602-255 4600 or 1-888-520 3434
Fax: 602-240 5475
Web site: http://www.arizonaguide.com

GETTING AROUND

Main airports: Tuscon International Airport — Tel: 520-573 8825, Sky Harbor International Airport (Phoenix) — Tel: 602-273 3300
By train: N/A
By bus: Greyhound — Tel: 1-800-231 2222
Road conditions: Statewide — Tel: 520-651 2400
Speed limits: The speed limit is 65-75mph (104kmph-120kmph).

INTRODUCTION

Arizona is the life-stylers' state. Retiree 'snowbirds' migrate south for the winter in their RVs which cost the same as a large house and are about as mobile. Phoenix is a desert oasis for corporate drop-outs who can't handle the violence in LA or the winters in Denver. The whole state is full of people with a snow phobia, except for the two skiing and snowboarding outposts of Arizona Snowbowl and Sunrise Park. Snowbowl is to freeriders what Guy Burgess was to the British — the double bluff, old chap. To find a big Arizona mountain with open steeps, cornices and hikes off the peak down to the access road seems as trippy as Lucy finding diamonds in the sky, but we swear it's the honest-to-God truth. Despite a short season and unpredictable snowfall, Snowbowl after a dump will rock your preconceptions about American snowboarding stalling at the Colorado state line.

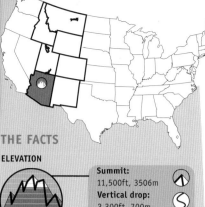

Arizona Snowbowl

THE FACTS

ELEVATION

Summit:
11,500ft, 3506m
Vertical drop:
2,300ft, 700m
Base:
9,200ft, 2806m

SNOWFALL

Average annual:
250 inches, 635cm

Snow-making:
None

AREA

Total area:
777 acres, 315ha

Advanced: 21%
Intermediate: 42%
Beginner: 37%

SEASON
Mid-December — early April

COMMUNICATIONS
Snow report: Tel: 520-779 4577
Web site: http://www.azsnowbowl.com
E-mail: azsnowbowl.com
Mountain information:
Tel: 520-779 1951
Flagstaff Visitor Centre:
Tel: 520-774 9541 or 1-800-842 7293
Fax: 520-556 1308

LIFTS AND TICKETS
Number of lifts:
4 chairlifts, 1 surface lift
Lift pass prices:
1/2 day: $25
1 day: $31
Multi-day: $60 (2 out of 3 days)
Season: N/A
Other ticketing information:
Get a $6 credit towards your next lift pass if you return your full day pass before noon. Ski free on your birthday with ID. Pick up a Frequent Skier Card at the ticket window and get a stamp for each day pass you buy, every sixth lift ticket is free.

SNOWBOARD SHOPS
AZP — Tel: 520-774 3020
Located on Route 66 downtown, the crew at AZP are the summer halfpipe diggers at Mount Hood and can set you up with whatever you want or need. They can also give an insider's run-down on snow conditions.

SNOWBOARD SCHOOL
Snowbowl Snowboard School — Tel: 520-779 1951
Call at Hart Prairie Lodge, the first lodge on the mountain road. The snowboard package includes rental, lift pass and a two hour lesson for $60.

ON THE MOUNTAIN

Arizona Snowbowl is possibly the best all-round boarding mountain in the south-west. Located in the San Francisco Peaks, Mount Agassiz is the lift-serviced peak which is hikeable to 12,356 feet (3769 metres). Neighbouring Mount Humphreys is the tallest peak in Arizona, rising to 12,633 feet (3853 metres). The San Francisco Peaks are the eroded rim of an ancient volcanic crater, shaped like a horseshoe with the mouth to the east. From the top you can see across the tribal lands of the Hopi and Navajo to the Grand Canyon 70 miles (113 kilometres) away.

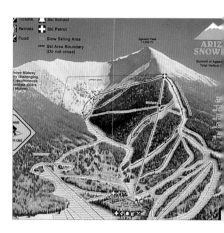

Once you stop tripping off the view you'll find countless ways down the mountain. The in-bounds terrain coincides with the wooded slopes of Mount Agassiz, but the vast hikeable area includes the high alpine bowl which sits between Agassiz Peak and Humphreys Peak, and the snow-filled crater on the back side of Upper Bowl Ridge. Arizona Snowbowl has 'soft closures', meaning that you can go out of bounds at your own risk but cannot cut back into the in-bounds terrain. It is crucial that you check with someone who knows these areas first, as they are not patrolled and this is a proper mountain with proper hazards and proper hike-outs. The relaxed back-country attitude opens up huge tracts across Upper Bowl towards the slopes of Humphreys Peak, and off the back of Upper Bowl Ridge into the crater. Inside the boundary, the ski area offers good steeps, nice trees, a funpark, natural gullies and graduated cliffs.

SNOW CONDITIONS Snowbowl receives an average annual snowfall of 21 feet (six metres). The prime months are January and February as spring comes early and hots up quickly in this part of the world. Seasons are variable; some years the snow can rival the best in America and some years it just doesn't happen. When it does dump, the extensive terrain and small hiking population means that the snow stays primo for days.

FREERIDERS It's all good. Jeff Jewitt is in charge of snowboarding activities at Snowbowl; his team know the mountain well and are the people to bribe to increase your thrills. The Agassiz Chairlift stops at 11,500 feet (3508 metres) and from there you can hike up Agassiz Peak and across the ridge to drop into Upper Bowl at any point. After a snowfall you are guaranteed fresh tracks every run, as long as you're prepared to hike a little bit further round the ridge than the guys cutting tracks below. One option is to traverse the bowl as high as you can from the top of the chair, and then boot-track the vertical to the middle of the ridge.

Dropping the other side of the ridge opens up 4000 feet (1120 metres) of vertical. South Side to 2.5 is the moniker for the second gully which has a good run-out onto the road at Mile 2.5. If you mess up the traverse then you'll be stuck post-holing your long way home. It's a good idea to check out the whole of the South Side as you drive up the mountain early in the day, because there is a high chance of losing your gully bearings in the excitement of the moment and getting bushed in the flats. Best advice, as always, is to communicate with a local rider and the ski patrol.

There are other excellent options without the sweat of a hike. The steep, spread out trees to skier's right of the chairlift are killer on a powder day, but unfortunately this isn't classified information and everyone else is in there too. Look out for the wide gully and the Wild Turkey natural halfpipe where the trees thin out. Upper Sundance is a graveyard of gnarly mangled wood and consistent wind drift gaps. There are some sizeable rocks around; to drop the ten to 35 foot (three to 11 metre) Shiprocks, keep traversing skier's right past Upper Sundance. Arizona Snowbowl won't disappoint your freeride needs if you explore a bit, consult a bit, hike a bit and huck.

FREESTYLERS Snowbowl has a styling funpark with huge hits and nice transitions. It's called the North Star Snowboard Park and is at the top of the Sunset Chairlift. A fun jibber line is ducking through the trees off the Spur Catwalk and launching off the Midway Catwalk, the big kicker on Tiger and all the back side hits (for regulars) down to the park.

CARVERS Carvers get it sweet too. The groomed trails are steep and fast, especially Upper Ridge to skier's right of the Agassiz Chairlift. The Upper Bowl has endless, wide open runs. Most of the black trails get moguled in a dry patch but are awesome on a powder day.

MOUNTAIN FOOD There are two main spots at the base. The Hart Prairie Lodge, known as the Lower Lodge, is the biggest and has a more extensive menu. The Agassiz Food Court is more basic but has a patio with a mountain view where the locals hang out.

Arizona Snowbowl

ABOUT TOWN

Flagstaff is one of the highest cities in the US and a former stop-off on the legendary Route 66. The population of 50,000 includes a large student contingent. It lies south of the Grand Canyon and north of the mystical red rocks of Sedona. The downtown area at the intersection of Interstate 40 and Interstate 17 is the grooviest part of town with hang-outs, snowboard shops, bars and young folk. Flagstaff is a cool place with a happening nightlife scene, a good choice of food and some huge camping shops.

ACCOMMODATION Flagstaff is the jump-off town for the Grand Canyon which makes winter low-season and motels cut-throat competitive. The Weatherford Hotel — Tel: 520-774 2731 runs an up-market hostel upstairs from Charly's Pub, and there is also the Dubeau Hotel — Tel: 520-774 6731 on the south side of the railway. Motel rooms can be just as cheap as hostels at this time of year; check out the ones on Beaver Road as you exit off Interstate 40 into town. The mountain can arrange lift and lodging packages from $46 a day including breakfast — Tel: 1-800-828-7285. Little America is a huge hotel with a 24 hour restaurant. Their Ski Spree programme costs $135 and includes a double room, lift tickets and breakfast for two — Tel: 1-800-352 4386. Flagstaff Central Reservations — Tel: 520-527 8333 or 1-800-527 8388.

FOOD Route 66 and the railway cut the town in half and in good 'ol American tradition, south of the tracks is the grungier side of town with some great cheap eats. Macey's is a coffee house and mainly vegetarian café on Beaver Road; they get the local vote for best value food. Sitting at their picnic tables on the pavement is a quick way to suss who's in town. The Black Bean Burrito Bar has cheap filling burritos for under $5; you might be able to smuggle one into the Flag Brewery to eat with a beer on a quiet night. If you're happy to spend a bit more, Charly's Pub on North Leroux Street has excellent food for between $8 and $15 a main. Pasto's on East Aspen Ave has a more sedate atmosphere and great Italian food for similar prices.

NIGHTLIFE Flagstaff boasts live bands every night of the week and has plenty of good bars. The cocktail lounge in the basement of the Monte Vista Hotel is the sleaziest, with booths, pool tables, live guitar music, veneer tables and Guinness on tap. We loved it. Monsoon's is the other established music venue with an upbeat, hippie crowd packing the place out. The Flag Brewing Co. and Beaver Street Brewery serve their own beers and the Mad I (for Italian) is another good place to start the night off with a few quiets. There's currently an outbreak of new bars in Flagstaff; check with the boys at AZP to see which ones have the stamina to make it through to next winter.

OTHER ACTIVITIES The Grand Canyon is 70 miles (113 kilometres) north on Highway 180, Sedona is 20 miles (32 kilometres) south, Vertical Relief Rock Gym, Lowell Observatory, mountain-biking, hiking.

THANKS TO Jeff Jewitt, Jeff Fox, Lynda Fleisher and Priscilla Whitaker.

Top — Agassiz and Fremont Peaks as seen from the city of Flagstaff
Photo: Tom Brownold
Bottom — Ridge line of Inner Basin, the San Francisco Peaks
Photo: Tom Brownold

GETTING THERE

By air: Phoenix is the closest major airport and it's an easy 142 mile (229 kilometre) drive north to Flagstaff on Interstate 17. Navi-Hopi Tours offer scheduled transfers — Tel: 520-774-5003 or 1-800-892-8687. Delta fly there regularly — Tel: 1-800-221 1212. Daily connections are also available from Phoenix to Pulliam Airport, four miles (six kilometres) south of Flagstaff.
By train: Amtrak arrives and departs daily — Tel: 520-774 8679.
By bus: Greyhound has a service to Flagstaff — Tel: 520-774 4573.
By car: Flagstaff is located at the intersection of Interstate 40 and Interstate 17. From Flagstaff follow Highway 180 north for seven miles (11 kilometres), then take the Snowbowl Road for the final seven miles (11 kilometres) to the base. Cross-winds can get strong and the drive takes 30 minutes in good conditions.
Getting around: In high season, or if the ski road requires chains, a $4 return shuttle bus runs up the mountain from Highway 180. Locals say it's super-easy to hitch from town.

1

Sunrise Park

ON THE MOUNTAIN

Sunrise Park is located in the White Mountains of Arizona and is the largest ski area in the state. The resort is spread over three peaks: Sunrise, Apache and Cyclone Circle. Apache Peak has a couple of very nice cornices which the ski patrol informed us are totally do-able in good snow — 21 feet (six and a half metres) of fresh snow a season translates to do-able. The lifts are elderly but there is a new high-speed quad on Sunrise Peak which will halve the time of the present main lift ride.

Now get this: *You cannot ride any trees on the entire resort!* Sunrise Park resort insurance is not extensive enough to cover accidents in the wooded areas, therefore you are prohibited from entering them on pain of instant pass confiscation. This doesn't leave much of the 800 acres (324 hectares) to ride, and up to 40 per cent of what's left is too flat. There are plenty of other activities in the White Mountain area like golf, fishing, gambling and hiking.

SNOW CONDITIONS Sunrise gets plenty of snow in a season and the area is underpatronised by users above intermediate level, so large areas of the resort remain untouched. Sounds good, but Arizona is the hottest state in America and the sunny weather doesn't allow powder to sit around in its glorious state for more than two days. The powder in the tree areas is untracked and deep all season long but as you know you can't ride there.

FREERIDERS AND CARVERS The very essence of freeriding is undermined at Sunrise because you are not free to ride the trees. So for the purposes of this section, we will call it 'freetrailriding' to avoid confusion. Free the trees! Sunrise Peak is the peak immediately in front of the base station and is therefore the most crowded. The goods for freetrailriding are on the other two peaks. Cyclone Circle is the locals' favourite and has the trails with the best gradients. Tempest, Lower Tempest and Hurricane Ridge follow the fall-line and are worth riding. Peak to peak riding is difficult due to the many flat spots between the areas. Apache Peak has two steep runs called Geronimo and Lupe's Rainbow. There is also a sick cliff drop on Geronimo which you can see from every lift; it overshadows everything else on the mountain.

FREESTYLERS Sunrise does have three snowboard specific areas, two on Sunrise Peak and one on Apache Peak. The standard is fledgling to high intermediate with no scary stuff or huge transitions. If you haven't ridden a funpark before then it's a good place to start. It would be helpful if the resort could enforce a 'no skiers' policy in these areas, as some of the largest moguls on the entire mountain are to be found on the run-ups to hits.

MOUNTAIN FOOD Main eats are in the big, wooden A-frame at the base of Sunrise Peak, although there are also cafés at the bottom of Cyclone Circle and the top of Apache Peak. Food is standard but at least it's food and there are no other options for 20 miles (32 kilometres).

HAZARDS AND RULES Chairlift VI up to Cyclone Circle is especially frustrating but all the lifts are slow. Incredible as it may sound, you will lose your pass if you depart from the trails into the trees. "This is Arizona, not Colorado," we were told. You'd better believe it.

THE FACTS

ELEVATION

Summit: 11,000ft, 3355m
Vertical drop: 1800ft, 549m
Base: 9200ft, 2806m

SNOWFALL

Average annual: 250 inches, 635cm
Snow-making: 10%

AREA
Total area: 800 acres, 324ha
Advanced: 20%
Intermediate: 40%
Beginner: 40%

SEASON
Mid-December — late March

COMMUNICATIONS
Snow report: Tel: 1-888-804 2779
Mountain information: Tel: 520-735 7600
Eagar and Springerville Chamber of Commerce: Tel: 520-333 2123
White Mountain Apache Office of Tourism: Tel: 520-338 1230

LIFTS AND TICKETS
Number of lifts:
8 chairlifts, 4 surface lifts
Lift pass prices:
1/2 day: $26
1 day: $32
Season: $625
Other ticketing information:
Night-riding runs from 4.30pm to 9.00pm on Fridays and Saturdays in January and February, tickets cost $15. A half day with night-riding costs $28.

SNOWBOARD SHOPS
Action Ski Rental and Sport — Tel: 502-735 7240
A large shop on the mountain with a good stock of rental boards and staff who know what's up. The only snowboard action near Sunrise Park.

SNOWBOARD SCHOOL
Sunrise Park Snowboard School
Tel: 520-735 7518
The beginner package offers lessons, rentals and a full day limited-use lift pass for $40.

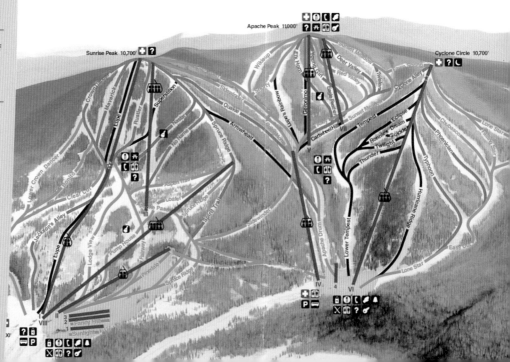

ABOUT TOWN

Sunrise Park is owned and operated by the White Mountain Apache tribe, but it doesn't have the same 'whatever goes' attitude as the Mescalero Apache-owned Ski Apache resort in New Mexico. Development of infrastructure around the mountain has been blocked by the tribe which has the benefit of preserving the natural beauty. The flip side of the coin is a 20 mile (32 kilometre) drive to food and beds, unless you pay the premium to stay in the Apache-owned Sunrise Resort Hotel by the mountain turn-off. Other than the hotel, the closest settlement is Greer which has a backwoods feel and advertises solitude and isolation as its main drawcards. Eagar and Springerville are mall towns with lots of concrete and tex-mex restaurants. After a couple of days out in the woods, a mall may be a welcome taste of civilisation.

ACCOMMODATION There's only one hotel close to the mountain. The Sunrise Resort Hotel is nothing fancy and charges between $94 and $138 per person per night, depending on whether you stay at peak times or mid-week. The room price includes a lift pass and free night-riding in the weekends — Tel: 1-800-554-6835. If something cheaper and less isolated appeals, the best bets are the towns of Eagar and Springerville which are an easy 30 minute drive from the mountain — Tel: 520-333 2123 for an accommodation run-down.

FOOD Food can be a problem if your stomach isn't coordinated with the pre-set Sunrise Park timetable. The only edible substances close to the mountain are found in the Base Lodge or at the Tempest restaurant in the Sunrise Resort Hotel. The Tempest is reasonably priced for a regional monopoly but has unreasonable hours. That means it's closed whenever you want to eat between meals, and the only option for miles is the hotel's chocolate dispenser — Mmmmm — M&Ms. Greer is a wipe-out on the food front: Eagar and Springerville offer neck rouge, tex-mex or pizza.

NIGHTLIFE There's a bar in the Sunrise Resort Hotel; it smells of stale smoke and stale beer and will only go off if you hit the liquor cabinet with a bomb. Greer has one pub which looks like a meeting place for underground, subversive, automatic weapon-carrying, nice red-neck folk. Eagar and Springerville have some slick mall pubs and the Hon-Dah Casino in Hon-Dah (bet you didn't know that in Apache hon-dah means 'welcome' all you suckers) may dispense gold and then you'll never have to drive a Japanese car of the same name (Honda) again. Besides these treasures, the scenery is inspirational.

OTHER ACTIVITIES Hon-Dah Casino, ice-fishing, golf, trekking, food hunting, freeing the trees!

THANKS TO Tracy Ott and the White Mountain Apache tribe for their sense of humour.

Top — **Photo:** Gina Dempster
Middle — Sunset at sunrise **Photo:** Gina Dempster
Bottom — Free the trees **Photo:** Gina Dempster

GETTING THERE
By air: The closest international airport is Phoenix. For a Great Lakes flight schedule — Tel: 1-800-274 0662.
By bus: Bus service schedule — Tel: 520-537 4539.
By car: Drive east from Phoenix on Highway 60 to Show Low and onto Eagar and Springerville. Sunrise Park is between Show Low and Springerville on Highway 260, 30 minutes from Springerville and 45 minutes from Show Low.
Getting around: There are no shuttles and chances are you'll be staying in Eagar or Springerville. Take a car and call to check on road and weather information — Tel: 520-537-ROAD.

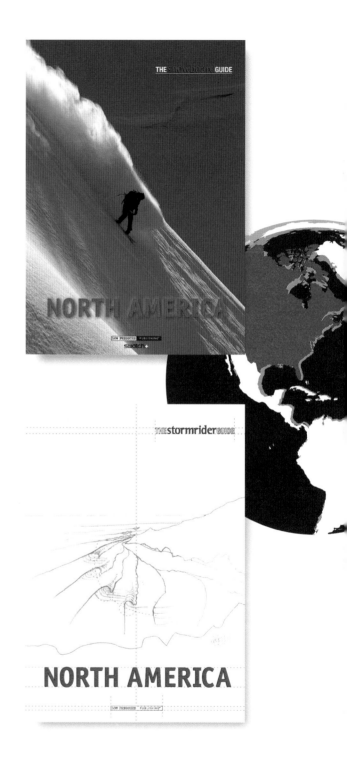

NEW MEXICO

STATE INFORMATION
Population: 1,616,000
Time: Mountain West: GMT minus 7 hours
Capital city: Santa Fe
Area: 121,666sq miles (313,898 sqkm)

VISITOR INFORMATION SOURCES
New Mexico Tourism Department:
Tel: 505-827 7400 or 1-800-SEE-NEW-MEX
or 1-800-733 6396
Web site: http://www.newmexico.org/.
E-mail: enchantment@newmexico.org

GETTING AROUND
Main airport: Albuquerque International Airport —
Tel: 1-800-851 6655
By train: Amtrak — Tel: 1-800-872 7245
By bus: Greyhound — Tel: 505-471 0008
Road conditions: Tel: 1-800-432 4269
Speed limits: Up to 65 mph (104 kmph) maximum.

INTRODUCTION
The highway in New Mexico stretches before
you to the horizon and behind you to the
horizon. The land is all geometric angles:
flat, flat earth and a straight yellow line
bisecting the dust. Jagged gorges slash the
plains and make you question the reality of
snow in this place of dust and sun, but it
just takes some searching out. You won't
find any heart-stopping freeriding but locals
make their own fun with snowcats, shovels
and a good crew. Thing is, once you hang
out with them for a few days, fly off the
giant kickers, hike up to the rocks at full
moon and get a couple of job offers to
design a new funpark, you start thinking
that New Mexico wouldn't be such a bad
option for a mellow season.

NEW MEXICO CONTENTS

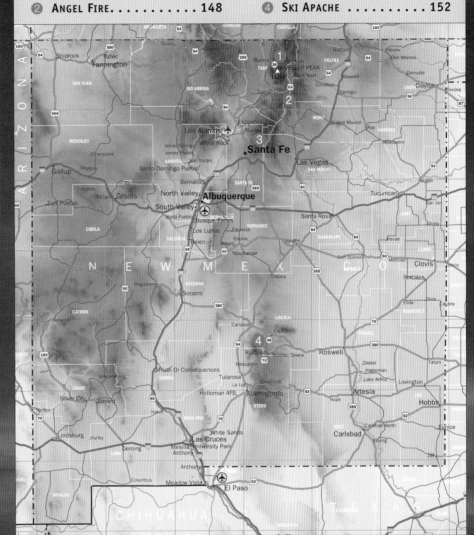

Red River

THE FACTS

ELEVATION

Summit:
10,350ft, 3157m
Vertical drop:
1600ft, 488m
Base:
8750ft, 2669m

SNOWFALL

Average annual:
214 inches, 544cm

Snow-making:
75% of trails

AREA

Total area:
242 acres, 98ha

Advanced: 30%
Intermediate: 38%
Beginner: 32%

SEASON

Late November — late March

COMMUNICATIONS

Snow report: Tel: 505-754 2220
Web-site: http://taoswebb.com/nmusa/redriver
Mountain information:
Tel: 505-754 2223
Fax: 505-754 6184
Red River Chamber of Commerce:
Tel: 505-754 2366 or 1-800-348 6444

LIFTS AND TICKETS

Number of lifts:
6 chairlifts, 1 surface lift
Lift pass prices:
1/2 day: $26
1 day: $36
Multi-day: $165 (5 days)
Season: N/A
Other ticketing information:
For the first two weekends in December, lift
passes, lodging and rentals are all half price.
During January, three day passes cost $75.

SNOWBOARD SHOPS

Sitzmark Sports
Tel: 505-754 2456 or 1-800-843 7547
Red River don't have no ski-board specific shop to
speak of, but board hire, repairs and info about
the mountain can be found at Sitzmark Sports.
Anything else should be attended to before arrival.

SNOWBOARD SCHOOL

Red River Snowboard School — Tel: 505-754 2223
"Hell, boy! I didn't pay five hunnered bucks for you
ta use one edge. You need ta turn more!"* Go take
some lessons. First time packages including rental,
lifts and three hours of lessons cost $69. More
advanced carving and freestyle lessons cost $28.
Meet at the Red River Ski Lodge.

ON THE MOUNTAIN

If you ride Red River, remember that it's a miracle there's even a resort in such a sunny geographical location and nothing else will disappoint you. Beginner to intermediate snowboarders will have a great time here but if you're after gnarly hikes, big drops and powder meadows, you either need to turn up immediately after a dump or go somewhere else.

Red River has some steep areas, some nice natural gullies and some surprisingly good tree runs. The problem is that once the hot sun melts the snowpack, everything untracked becomes akin to wet cement. If you fall over you'll be diggin' but if you stay upright, then you're surfin' New Mexico dude. If you do get fresh snow you're guaranteed plenty of new tracks, 'cause going off the trails is somethin' nice Red River folk don't do.

There is a ten year plan for developments which could eventually quadruple the acreage at Red River, but money is tight and no-one would commit to a date as to when the plan will be implemented. Any rich Texans looking for a good tax write-off should call Wally Dodds DA, Head of Red River Marketing, immediately on Tel: 1-800-CASH.

SNOW CONDITIONS Conditions are lovely within three days of a snowfall and pleasant to concrete thereafter. Snow-making facilities, covering 75 per cent of the trails, make up the shortfall where needed. Much of the field is shaded in the afternoon so the snow crisps back up early.

FREERIDERS All the black runs are steep enough to enjoy and the trees and gullies are inviting, but if the snow isn't fresh you could end up having to stick to the main trails a lot of the time. There are no traverses as the terrain is just up and down. If you only have a couple of hours to enjoy Red River, head up Copper Chair or Red Chair and ride all the areas under the two lifts.

FREESTYLERS Like the man says: *"You crazy ski-boarders could have a good time in a fish bowl, flippin' all the way round an' upper-side down like y'all do."** Red River is a fish bowl, where flipper-types can find plenty of hits. There is nothing particularly huge or treacherous but enough to make each run worth it. Red River has a funpark; it's hand-built by local riders with Red River provided shovels. Generous, but if the boys at Red River had some cat-time to sort the park out properly, there might be something to get psyched about. Again, contact Wally Dodds DA on Tel: 1-800-PARK.

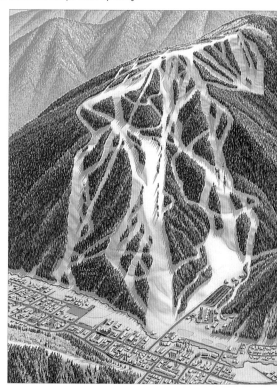

CARVERS *"OOOEE! Boy! Y'all be in Little Texas right now, ya unnerstan!"** Texans and Oklahomans 'll be whoopin' it up all over as you speed-freak past them on every groomed run on the mountain, and there's plenty in these parts.

MOUNTAIN FOOD There are four choices: the Ski Lodge cafeteria with grilled meat, the Ski Tip with beer, wine and stuff with meat, Jalapeno Pete's with meat, soup and sandwiches or nothin'.

HAZARDS AND RULES Steer clear of Texas-tuck skiers (that's all skiers on the mountain).

EVENTS AND COMPETITIONS Mardi Gras, Western Winter Carnival, Cardboard Box Derby.

ABOUT TOWN

Some statistics about Red River: there are 290 acres, 380 people and ten bars. That's one bar for every 38 people that live here. They call Red River 'Little Texas', and if you ain't from Texas then you's probably from Oklahoma. Action involves walking up and down the main drag with your buddies, sporting a jacket with a map of Texas on the back.

ACCOMMODATION As Wally Dobbs says: *"We got sixty-one hunnered beds within five hunnered feet of a lift. A lotta people don't realise that."** Red River does have a surprising amount of condos and lodges. The Riverside at the base of the Copper Chair has balconies onto Main Street which are excellent for Tex-spotting — Tel: 505-754 2252 or 1-800-432 9999. Rooms cost $52-$72 and apartments are also available. Accommodation in Red River is relatively cheap with many lodge rooms starting at $35-$40; try the Deer Lodge —Tel: 505-754 2961 or the Golden Eagle Lodge — Tel: 505-754 2227. A couple of RV parks stay open during the winter for $15-$25

per night — Tel: 505-754 2293. The helpful Red River Chamber of Commerce can tell you more — Tel: 1-800 348 6444. For package information, call Red River Ski Area — Tel: 1-800-331 SNOW.

FOOD *"You couldn't chew this if ya had a chain-saw in ya mouth! I know mah meat. Who supplies to y'all? I'd appreciate it if y'all could go back there and find out what's up now!"** Texans take red meat seriously and Texas Red's Steakhouse was packed cheek to double chin. Veggie options are limited to the extras of the steak meal: side salad and baked potato. For good pasta with friendly service, check out Capos Corner near the Red Chairlift. Brett's is a stomach-filling little stop in town with a good varied menu at average prices. Shotgun Willies is a no-nonsense diner at the base of the mountain on Main Street but beware the chicken fried steak. It's a steak cooked in breadcrumbs and spices like chicken but not actually containing any chicken. Most restaurants shut at 9.00pm so note there are no city hours here.

Black Crow Coffee House is the nicest place in Red River to chill and eat freshly baked banana cake with cappuccino, and it's Texan-free (no red meat). Morning Mesa Coffee outside Der Markt has bagels and coffee to take-away.

NIGHTLIFE They've got both kinds of music in Red River: country and western. They've also got both kinds of beers: Bud and cold Bud. If this sounds like a hoe-down, then you must be a Redneck and should either move to Texas or Red River. The Bull o' the Woods is where you can wear your Wranglers tight-as-you-like and your stetson better be too big to come in the door or it ain't welcome. Else-wise you can rodeo-on over to the Mother Lode across the street. If a wider selection of beers and microbrews and less foot-stompin' appeals, go to the bar behind the liquor store downtown. It closes at 8.00pm and they also serve bar food and Guinness.

OTHER ACTIVITIES There's a torch-light parade down the mountain every Saturday at 7.00pm. Snowmobiling, yahooin' and straight drinkin'.

THANKS TO Wally Dodds, Lauren and Drew Judycki for the wine and kebobs, Mark for showing us all the runs — good luck, Trevor from Ski Rio, Justin and his babe.

* All Texan interjections are directly quoted from our stay in Red River and are in no way slanderous bitchin's.

Opposite — Snow plough Red River style **Photo:** Gina Dempster
Top — Slopestyle competition **Photo:** Gina Dempster
Bottom — **Photo:** Gina Dempster

GETTING THERE

By air: Albuquerque International Sunport is 165 miles (264 kilometres) south of Red River. The Enchanted Circle Taxi and Shuttle service runs to Red River — Tel: 505-754 3154.
By car: From Denver: Take Interstate 25 south to Highway 160 west. Highway 522 south will get you to Questa. Follow Highway 38 through the gorge to Red River. The drive takes about four hours.
From Albuquerque: Take Interstate 25 north to Santa Fe and keep heading north to Taos on Highway 285. Highway 522 north will take you to the Highway 38 turn-off in Questa. The drive takes about three hours.
Getting around: A free trolley runs through Red River town and past the ski lifts. Chances are that you will be in Red River as part of a road trip so you'll have a car.

THE FACTS

ELEVATION

Summit:
10,650ft, 3248m
Vertical drop:
2050ft, 625m
Base:
8600ft, 2623m

SNOWFALL

Average annual:
220 inches, 559cm

Snow-making:
50%

AREA

Total area:
391 acres, 157ha
Advanced: 8%
Intermediate: 59%
Beginner: 33%

SEASON
Late November — early April

COMMUNICATIONS
Snow report: Tel: 1-800-633 7463 ext. 4222
Web site: http://www.angelfireresort.com
Mountain information:
Tel: 505-377 6401 or 1-800-633 7463
Angel Fire Chamber of Commerce:
Tel: 505-377 6353 or 1-800-446 8117

LIFTS AND TICKETS
Number of lifts:
1 high-speed quad, 4 chairlifts, 1 surface lift
Lift pass prices:
1/2 day: $26
1 day: $35
Multi day: $160 (5 days)
Season: $475, $250 (student 13-18yrs)
Other ticketing information:
The Angel Fire Club Card costs $25 and saves $5 on every daily lift ticket. Card holders ski free on the first day of purchase and every seventh day for the rest of the season. Season passes bought before November cost $425 for adults and $200 for students. A Ski 3 Card costs $25 and saves $5 on every day pass for Angel Fire, Red River and (the anti-boarder police state of) Taos.

SNOWBOARD SHOPS
Experience Snowboards — Tel/Fax: 505-377 8012
Experience Snowboards at the Village Centre are the home of the Free Taos campaign and the only proper snowboard store in Taos County. Repairs, rentals, lessons, skateboards and gear.

SNOWBOARD SCHOOL
Angel Fire Snowboard School
Tel: 1-800-633-7463
Go to the Ski School ticket office or meet at the Ski School Yard at the base of the Chile Express Quad. A full day lesson costs $36, a half day $24. Rent B+B from the mountain shop for $25.

Angel Fire

ON THE MOUNTAIN

As you drive up the long, flat valley towards Angel Fire, the front side of the mountain doesn't look too terrifying. Most of the trails on the front side are intermediate cruisers or cross-mountain traverses which funnel down to the only high-speed quad in New Mexico (known in the local vernacular as the high-speed quad to nowhere).

The back side of the mountain has a more rider friendly fall-line with fat cruisers and bumps erupting on the steeper trails around Lift 6. Much of the mountain remains untracked after a snowfall due to the fact that the terrain is intermediate and so are most of the riders. The only problem is that the hot weather doesn't allow soft powder stashes to stay dormant for too long. There are some trees to explore but in the spring the snow congeals to a molasses consistency and you won't be going far fast.

The mountain has had recent investment in the form of a high-speed quad and the next step is an expansion of the skiable terrain on the back side which will essentially offer more of the same. Four new runs for intermediate to advanced riders should be accessible by snowcat for the '97-'98 season and could add some spark to an otherwise gentle day's riding.

SNOW CONDITIONS On average there are 300 days of sunshine per year so the snow is at its best when the months are coldest: December, January and February. Spring tends to bring very icy mornings and slushy afternoons; any pockets of untracked snow end up heavily water-logged.

FREERIDERS The first local we met said that he'd "boarded with poles yesterday and it worked pretty good." It's mindful advice for most of the front side, however the area around Lift 6 has some steepish blue and black runs and is a little more challenging. There are good tree runs, moguls and a few small ledges to drop off. Maxwell's Grant and Silverchute are the two chutes at the top of the Chile Express Lift which are as close as Angel Fire comes to hard-core.

FREESTYLERS The '96-'97 season saw the funpark properly maintained and used for the first time, so there have been a few teething problems which will hopefully get sorted in time. All the lips are perfect and launch you into orbit, however the landing transitions are non-existent and you land on the flats. There are plenty of other hits around the legendary Lift 6.

CARVERS Like we said in 'Freeriders' it all happens round Lift 6 if you want steeps, but you could get enough speed coming down the main front side runs like Jasper's and Bodacious to get back to the base station.

MOUNTAIN FOOD The Village Haus at the base and the Mountain Haus at Lift 6 serve greasy-spoon breakfasts. The bar at the Village Haus is open till 9.00pm in the weekends. The Sugar Shack at the top of the mountain has hot drinks and sugary snacks. The best cappuccinos and cream-soaked hot chocolates are found at the Espresso Bar at the base of Lift 2.

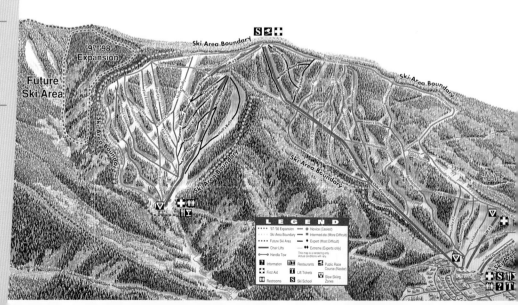

ABOUT TOWN

Angel Fire is a retirement centre for Texan Exxon oil execs looking for unspoilt countryside. There ain't no oil wells here and not many places to quench a thirst neither but it sure is a beautiful part of the planet. The town is scattered around the base of the mountain access road and along Highway 434. A car is essential unless you want to be cloistered in the bars and restaurants of Legends Hotel at the base of the lifts. You'll find most of the bars and restaurants in town are linked to accommodation and there's not much to do at night except eat and sleep. The video store is beside the Liquor Mart.

Top left — **Photo:** Gina Dempster
Top right — Not the high-speed quad to nowhere **Photo:** Gina Dempster
Bottom — **Photo:** Ben Blankenburg **Courtesy:** Angel Fire Resort

ACCOMMODATION A double room slopeside at Legends Hotel starts at $105 and an economy studio starts at $130 peak season — Tel: 1-800-633-7463. Wildwood Lodging has one bedroom condos from $150 peak season can sleep four people in two bedroom condos for $210 or in two bedroom houses for $260 — Tel: 505-377 0676 or 1-888-377 0676. Rooms at the Inn at Angel Fire start at $60 — Tel: 505-377 2504 and rooms at Angel Nest Apartments start at $65 — Tel: 505-377 6157. Central Reservations — Tel: 505-377 3072 or 1-800-323 5793.

FOOD First choice for the locals is hangin' out at Pizza Stop for beers 'n' pizza. Try the Breckenridge Ale to bring on nostalgia for Summit County and the garlic bread balls for a twist on pizza dough. Near the gas station, the Coyote Café has candles and a standard grill and Mexican menu for around $8.95. Legends Hotel at the base of the mountain has two restaurants: Senor T-Bone's steak restaurant and Moreno's pasta buffet. There's also a couple of places serving steak and Mexican on Highway 434. The Elkhorn Lodge Restaurant is your best bet for vegetarian and Zebediah's Lounge and Restaurant has a big screen TV.

NIGHTLIFE Angel Fire is seriously lacking in country and western bars, or in any bars for that matter. If you're in dire need of a drink, Jasper's Bar at the Legends Hotel or the Village Haus bar will serve you one. Best to take some good friends to party with.

OTHER ACTIVITIES Tubing park, DAV Vietnam veterans' national monument.

THANKS TO Greg Morton.

GETTING THERE

By air: Fly to Albuquerque International Airport and drive 112 miles (180 kilometres) north. There is a small airport at Santa Fe with connecting flights to Denver.
By car: From Albuquerque: Drive north on Interstate 25 to Santa Fe. Keep heading north on Highway 285 to Taos, then turn onto Highway 64 towards Eagle's Nest. Follow signs at the Highway 434 turn-off to Angel Fire. From Denver: Take Interstate 25 south to Highway 64 south towards Taos. Turn off Highway 434 to Angel Fire.
Getting around: The Angel Fire Magic bus goes from the mountain base to Highway 434 for $0.50 and ten miles (16 kilometres) down the road to Eagle Nest for $2.

Sante Fe

ON THE MOUNTAIN

Many resorts in New Mexico look and feel like freak snow-covered hills with limited possibilities, but Santa Fe Ski Area in the Sangre de Cristo range just north of Santa Fe city is definitely a mountain. The resort is spread across a huge bowl with good steep descents. The main areas of interest are accessed from Tesuque Peak via Lift 3 and Lift 6, with steep groomed runs, trees and a couple of rocks to choose from. Skier's left of the peak, the Big Tesuque Bowl is a wide open, natural powder bowl with spaced out trees. This run is currently outside the official boundary and ends at the entrance road three miles (five kilometres) downstream; from there you can hitch back to the lift base. The traverse along the Sunset trail is a bit of a calf-number but all the drops off the trail are worth it. The area below the mid-station is very flat and gets congested with weekend warriors and never-evers, so the real riding acreage is restricted.

THE FACTS

ELEVATION

Summit:
12,000ft, 3660m
Vertical drop:
1650ft, 503m
Base:
10,350ft, 3157m

SNOWFALL

Average annual:
225 inches, 572cm

Snow-making:
30%

AREA

Total area:
550 acres, 223ha

Advanced: 40%
Intermediate: 40%
Beginner: 20%

SEASON
Late November — early April

COMMUNICATIONS
Snow report: Tel: 505-983 9155 or 505-857 8977
Web site: http://www.santafe.org
E-mail: 102234.1070@compuserve.com
Mountain information:
Tel: 505-982 4429
Fax: 505-986 0645
Santa Fe Chamber of Commerce:
Tel: 505-983 7317
Sante Fe Convention and Visitors' Bureau:
Tel: 505-984 6760

LIFTS AND TICKETS
Number of lifts:
4 chairlifts, 3 surface lifts
Lift pass prices:
1/2 day: $26
1 day: $39
Multi-day: $142 (4 days)
Season: N/A
Other ticketing information:
A $5 lift ticket discount is offered to drivers with three passengers to reduce traffic and pollution. A Skier Plus Card costs $25 and entitles you to a $7 reduction on each lift pass.

SNOWBOARD SHOPS
Beyond Waves — Tel: 505-988 2240
A fairly standard collection of 'surf gear for the soul'.

SNOWBOARD SCHOOL
Santa Fe Snowboard School — Tel: 505-982 4429
The Never-Ever Snowboard Package includes an all day lesson, a lift pass and rentals for $69.

SNOW CONDITIONS Santa Fe resort receives an average snowfall of 19 feet (nearly six metres) but with over 300 sunshine days a year, the snow generally doesn't stay in good condition for too long. That said, the groomed trails are well-looked after and keep a solid cover until late in the spring.

FREERIDERS Although the acreage isn't huge, there is enough variation in the terrain to test all manner of freeriding skills, from tight, steep trees to cliff drops and cornices. Skier's right of the Tesuque Chairlift is the obvious first destination, as the gradient here is generally the steepest and it has the most interesting terrain. Runs to look out for are Tequila Sunrise, Wizard and Columbine, all dropping off the Sunset trail. The thickets between

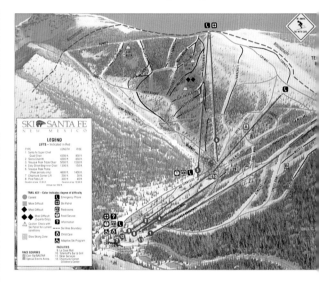

each of these runs vary in tree density but are all good. Big Rocks, between Wizard and Columbine, is the best place to find natural things to jump off. Skier's left of the Tesuque Chairlift is wide open and steep. On powder days this area is a heavenly meadow of loveliness and leads to the out of bounds Big Tesuque Bowl. This is real back-country which isn't patrolled by Ski Santa Fe so if you feel the need for adventure, take someone who knows the way.

FREESTYLERS Santa Fe has two designated styling areas. Both the parks are off the Gayway trail, accessed by the Tesuque Chairlift. The main attraction is a full-on funpark with table tops, gaps and spines. Nothing particularly scary but the place is well-maintained with a good variety of hits and an enthusiastic local crew who session the area regularly. The park also has a small halfpipe which is shovel-maintained to a moderate condition and is welcoming to any wannabe Terjes. The Alternative Terrain Park is more like a tame boardercross track for kids. No huge airs to be had as not one of the landings has any kind of transition.

CARVERS Not heaps to carve up but there are a couple of highlights you won't forget. The Gayway trail from the Tesuque Chairlift leads to the steepest groomed runs. Take the right fork 300 feet (100 metres) into the descent onto the Parachute trail. It looks as if you will be launched miles into the desert, then the gradient intensifies and it almost feels like you are freefalling to the base. Take care as this run crosses the Santa Fe trail which is the easy way down for nervous people, and it's a blind crossing until you are right on top of it. Most of the trails referred to in the Freeriders section, skier's right of the Tesuque Chairlift, are unmogulled with good steep tilts. The lower blue runs are cruisy, rolling trails.

MOUNTAIN FOOD La Casa Café and Outdoor Grill is the main lunch spot at the base of the mountain. Totemoff's Grill mid-mountain has a barbecue and a full bar. The bar is better supplied than the barbecue.

HAZARDS AND RULES Slow zones at the base of the Tesuque Chairlift and the Tesuque Poma are vigilantly enforced in the weekends. The Tesuque Poma is faster than the triple chair and is the way to go after lunch.

EVENTS AND COMPETITIONS Southwest Snowboard Championships.

ABOUT TOWN

Founded in 1607, Santa Fe is the oldest state capital in the US. Gold prospectors poured into the region via the Santa Fe trail which crossed America and ended in the Santa Fe plaza. Settlers and miners took the land as theirs to remould, and the US government furthered the desecration in the '40s by exploding the world's first atomic bomb in the deserts of southern New Mexico. The bomb was invented at Los Alamos, down the road from Santa Fe.

Santa Fe is a Mecca for art and historical buildings. The plaza is the central shopping centre and buildings from the 1600s are still in use. Most of the city's 175 art galleries are located on Canyon Road and rich tourists weighed down with Indian jewellery congregate there. For more standard purchases, the malls on Cerrillos Road are the place to shop and go to the movies. The city is only 16 miles (26 kilometres) from Santa Fe Ski Area but the road is gnarly with ice and sharp bends. It's best not to drive it in a stressed-out or vacant state of mind.

ACCOMMODATION Santa Fe Central Reservations can arrange four nights' lodging and three day lift packages from $217 — Tel: 505-983 8200 or 1-800-776 7669. Plenty of cheap motels can be found on busy Cerrillos Road; try the Budget Inn of Santa Fe — Tel: 505-982 5952 or the Cactus Lodge — Tel: 505-471 7699 or check out the specials as you drive by. The Santa Fe International Hostel is at 1412 Cerrillos Road — Tel: 505-988 1153 or 505-983 9896. Rancho Encantado is set in wild desert seven miles (11 kilometres) north of Santa Fe. It's fantastic but so are the rates; the Dalai Lama and Joan Collins stay here when they're in town.

FOOD Santa Fe is proud of the uniqueness of their cuisine which is based around chilli. Chilli sauce is used more liberally than salt and comes in three formats: red made from dried chillies, green made from fresh chillies and Christmas — you guessed it, the dual sauce. If you throw yourself into the experience, chances are you'll never want to see chilli ever again and will spend the next few years eating soft, white bread sandwiches.

For cheap, delicious breakfasts (with chilli), try Tia Sophia's on West San Francisco near the plaza. It closes at 3.00pm so there are no late lunches. The Blue Corn Café at 133 Water Street is a cheapish option with substantial meals, but don't have the flan unless you fancy eggs for dessert as well as breakfast. Nouveau New Mexican cooking was invented at the Coyote Café, a legend in Santa Fe. It's a bit more pricey but the place has a good buzz and freebie desserts if you show them your Santa Fe lift pass.

The Atalya restaurant on South Guadalupe serves healthy, home-baked food and unhealthy, thick peanut butter and chocolate shakes. One of the locals' favourites for burgers and grilled sandwiches is Harry's Roadhouse on the Old Las Vegas Highway. If you can be bothered driving out of town, the Tesuque Village Market shares space with the Tesuque Deli; it's a relaxed café with delicious food for around $8 a meal.

NIGHTLIFE At night, Santa Feans are more turned on by food than pubs and clubs. The wildest clubs belong to the gay scene: pubs are scattered through the city and you have to know where you're heading for before you set out. El Farrol is hidden amongst the art galleries on Canyon Road; low ceilings and murals by famous artists set the scene for loose flamenco parties. La Fonda is the other main hang-out in San Francisco Street, just off the plaza. Clubs to check include Club Alegria on Lower Agua Fria and Club Doctor No on Canyon Road for funk and reggae. For the best run-down on what's on, read the Santa Fe Reporter.

OTHER ACTIVITIES Sante Fe has an excessive choice of art galleries, museums and performing arts — it's the cultural headquarters of New Mexico. The desert landscape and sunsets are superb, especially if you can get out of the city to relish the vastness and quiet. A tempting pull-over four miles (six kilometres) up the Santa Fe ski road is the Ten Thousand Waves Japanese Health Spa with mountainside hot tubs and kimonos.

THANKS TO Salange, Steve Lewis, Debbie Owen and Don Strel.

Opposite — Photo: Gina Dempster
Top — Photo: Gina Dempster
Middle — Adobe building at Santa Fe Photo: Gina Dempster
Bottom — Ryan Runke heading for a sketchy landing Photo: Gina Dempster

GETTING THERE

By air: Santa Fe city is 65 miles (105 kilometres) from Albuquerque International Airport and the drive takes about one hour. Transfers can be arranged with Shuttlejack — Tel: 505-982 4311 or Santa Fe Transportation Company — Tel: 505-982 3504. Both run a ski shuttle from Santa Fe to the mountain.
By train: The closest train station is Lamy, 16 miles (26 kilometres) south, serviced daily by Amtrak. Call the Lamy shuttle for transportation to the city — Tel: 505-982 8829.
By bus: Greyhound, TNM&O and Shuttlejack Bus Lines all have daily bus services to the Santa Fe bus station — Tel: 505-471 0008.
By car: Take Interstate 25 north from Albuquerque or south from Denver to the city of Santa Fe. To find the mountain, head north-east from the city on Highway 475. The road is demanding and takes a good half an hour to drive.
Getting around: Santa Fe is a big, spread out city and the mountain is 16 miles (26 kilometres) away. Unless you stay at a reasonably up-market and central motel which has a shuttle deal to the mountain, a car is essential and is definitely the best way to explore the city itself.

THE FACTS

ELEVATION

Summit:
11,500ft, 3507m
Vertical drop:
1900ft, 579m
Base:
9600ft, 2928m

SNOWFALL

Average annual:
180 inches, 450cm

Snow-making:
30%

AREA

Total area:
750 acres, 303ha

Advanced: 45%
Intermediate: 35%
Beginner: 20%

SEASON

Late November — late March

COMMUNICATIONS

Snow report: Tel: 505-257-9001
Web site: http://www.skiapache.com
Mountain information:
Tel: 505-336 4356
Fax: 505-336 8327
Ruidoso Valley Chamber of Commerce:
Tel: 505-257 7395 or 1-800-253 2255
Fax: 505-257 4693

LIFTS AND TICKETS

Number of lifts:
1 gondola, 8 chairlifts, 2 surface lifts
Lift pass prices:
1/2 day: $27
1 day: $39, $42 (holidays)
Multi-day: $111 (3 days)
Season: $750
Other ticketing information:
Season prices start at $325 for non-holiday week days only.

SNOWBOARD SHOPS

The Ski Apache Snowboard Shop
Tel: 505-336 4356
The shop, tucked away at the top of the base area near the Kiddie Korral, has good quality rental boards, clothing and accessories. Burton is the featured brand for boards and boots.

SNOWBOARD SCHOOL

Ski Apache Snowboard School
Tel: 505-336 4356
Go to the Ski School Desk in the Base Lodge. If you're a first-time snow-boarder, you get a free lesson with the purchase of a lift pass. More experienced riders get a half day lesson for $30 or a full day for $45.

Ski Apache

ON THE MOUNTAIN

Ski Apache is an alpine oasis in the barren deserts of southern New Mexico. The resort is owned and operated by the Mescalero Apache Indian tribe and has a uniquely mellow feel. A sunshine yellow gondola dating from the '60s creaks up to 11,500 feet (3509 metres) and the variety of descents makes Ski Apache seem like a much larger mountain than it is. Almost all the in-boundary area is rideable and most of it is really good fun. The natural terrain throws up all kinds of good hits and gullies; local boarders and staff have free reign to go big as most paying punters are families who think air is to be breathed.

Ski Apache breaks down into two main areas: the front side with good steeps and trees, and the wide open Apache Bowl which has a series of interconnecting natural halfpipes to launch out of. The locals are Mescalero Apaches who either work for the mountain or just ride on their free tribe pass. They all huck and they're all cool, so make friends early and enjoy yourself.

SNOW CONDITIONS The mountain gets an average snowfall of 15 feet (four and a half metres) and has good snow-making facilities. Boarding is best in January and February as spring conditions come early in New Mexico.

FREERIDERS Ski Apache is nicely spread out so each run feels like you're covering a good distance — you won't get bored freeriding here. From the top of the gondola you can drop any part of the front side through steep trees or groomed runs with all kinds of rollers, cat-tracks and lips to hit. Otherwise head into Apache Bowl which has plenty of natural spines, gullies, trees and in late spring, grass patches to fly over. Below the bowl are walled runs which you can hit all the way down. There is some hiking to be done on Buck Mountain (if your trip happens to coincide with the biggest fall of the season), but it's definitely not to be explored without the guidance of locals or you could get stuck in the woods at the bottom for a very long time. The peak looks tempting but is sacred to the local tribe so it's not cool to be running around up there.

FREESTYLERS The mountain has some great natural hits which are preserved and enhanced by local boarders who ride hard. The Apache Bowl has a unique interlocking system of natural halfpipes and in the dead of winter you can get killer air from one halfpipe to the next. If they can't be hit in late spring, there's plenty of other stuff to spin and jump off: cat-tracks, grass patches, quarterpipes and walls. Even the green runs back to the lifts on the front side have walls and cat-tracks to pop off. The best thing is that no-one's too worried about what you do, as long as you don't take out any of the family skiers.

CARVERS A lot of the groomed runs get mogulled out but the bumps are fairly mellow due to the high percentage of novice skiers on the mountain. The front side runs are the steepest but also the shortest. The bowl area is wide open and cruisy with enough space to get plenty of turns in.

MOUNTAIN FOOD The Base Lodge is retro '70s. Grease is the major food group on offer and the outdoor barbecues are possibly the tastiest way to digest it. The pub behind the café is a must when the lifts close; business picks up from early lunchtime when locals settle in for a demanding afternoon on the mountain.

HAZARDS AND RULES The mountain is run in a more relaxed way than most and the staff are a wild and tangential bunch. It's not unusual to see lifties building kickers beside their chairlift or running around in devil costumes. There's no staunch enforcement of rules or anal whistle-blowing to be wary of.

Ski Apache

ABOUT TOWN

On a first drive through Ruidoso, the town has the sinister air of the opening scene in a horror movie — dark, forested streets waiting for an axe-crazed psycho to mow down the population. But don't be phased, it does grow on you. The town is spread out in the trees and even a quick visit to the corner shop requires a car. The best way to get to know the town is to drive through it and then keep going because there are hidden pockets of shops and restaurants for the next few miles. Ruidoso is 18 miles (29 kilometres) from Ski Apache and the narrow road winds up the mountain to give an incredible 200 mile (320 kilometre) view of lava fields and white sands. There's not much to do in town except drink a few beers, hang out with the locals and eat Mexican food but you're guaranteed a few laughs while you do it.

ACCOMMODATION Located near the turn-off to the resort, the Best Western Swiss Chalet Inn has indoor pools, hot-tubs, saunas, video rental and large rooms for $60 — Tel: 505-258 3333 or 1-800-47 SWISS. The cheapest places in town start around $30 a night and these include the Innsbruck Lodge — Tel: 1-800-680 4447, the Bestway Inn — Tel: 505-378 8000 and the romantic Sierra Mesa Lodge — Tel: 505-336 4515. Campers can head to the Little Creek RV Park — Tel: 505-336 4044 where prices start from $19. A two bedroom condo at the West Winds starts at $600 a week — Tel: 1-800-421 0691. The Inn of the Mountain Gods is owned by the Mescalero Apache tribe and offers B&B with a free margarita and your chance to gamble in the Casino Apache for $88 per night. For winter package deals — Tel: 505-336 4589 or 1-800-545 9011. Central Reservations — Tel: 1-800-253 2255.

FOOD The choice of food is limited to Mexican, Italian or steak. If you're keen on a drinking night at Farley's pub, you can balance the alcohol diet with substantial portions of good food; the fajitas come recommended. Casa Blanca also has a Mexican menu and a relaxed scene. It's packed out every night which is a local vote for the best eats in town. Other places to try include Michelena's Italian Restaurant, Coyote's Pub (for more Mexican) and the Cattle Baron Steak and Seafood, all on Sudderth Drive. No prizes for innovative chefing here. The best deli in town is Schlotsky's with fresh baking and excellent sammies.

NIGHTLIFE The only guaranteed way to have a big night in Ruidoso is to hook up with some locals at the bar in the Base Lodge as soon as the lifts close. The next port of call is Farley's in town; some psyching out goes on at the pool tables but the atmosphere loosens up as the night progresses. Most of the town congregates here in the weekend. The sedate bar downstairs at the Casa Blanca is a good place to relax in front of the fire. Music and late night options are zilch unless you drive to Mescalero and risk the hip-hop to country smorgasbord at the Mescalero Nightclub in Carrizo Canyon Road. If you've got a heavy wallet, gambling at the slot machines or blackjack tables at the Mescalero Inn is a popular diversion.

OTHER ACTIVITIES Giant sand dunes of White Sands National Monument, fishing, movies, skate ramp behind the golf-course, full moon hiking.

THANKS TO Steve Henry, Jane, Ewell, Becka, Earl and Fuji, Riker Davis.

4

Opposite — View of the peak **Photo:** Gina Dempster
Top left — The boys chillin' **Photo:** Gina Dempster
Top right — **Photo:** Gina Dempster
Bottom — Ewell styling a New Mexican grass hit **Photo:** Gina Dempster

GETTING THERE

By air: The closest international airport is El Paso in Texas. Rent a car and drive north 124 miles (198 kilometres) on Highway 54 to Ruidoso.
By bus: Several buses arrive each day from Albuquerque and El Paso.
By car: Ski Apache is 200 miles (320 kilometres) south of Albuquerque. Take Interstate 25 south and then follow Highway 380 to Ruidoso. From Ruidoso, drive six miles (nine kilometres) on Highway 48 and then 12 miles (19 kilometres) west on Ski Run Road to the Ski Apache base.
Getting around: The Ski Shuttle picks up passengers from Sudderth Drive and Mechem Drive before 7.30am — Tel: 505-2570203.

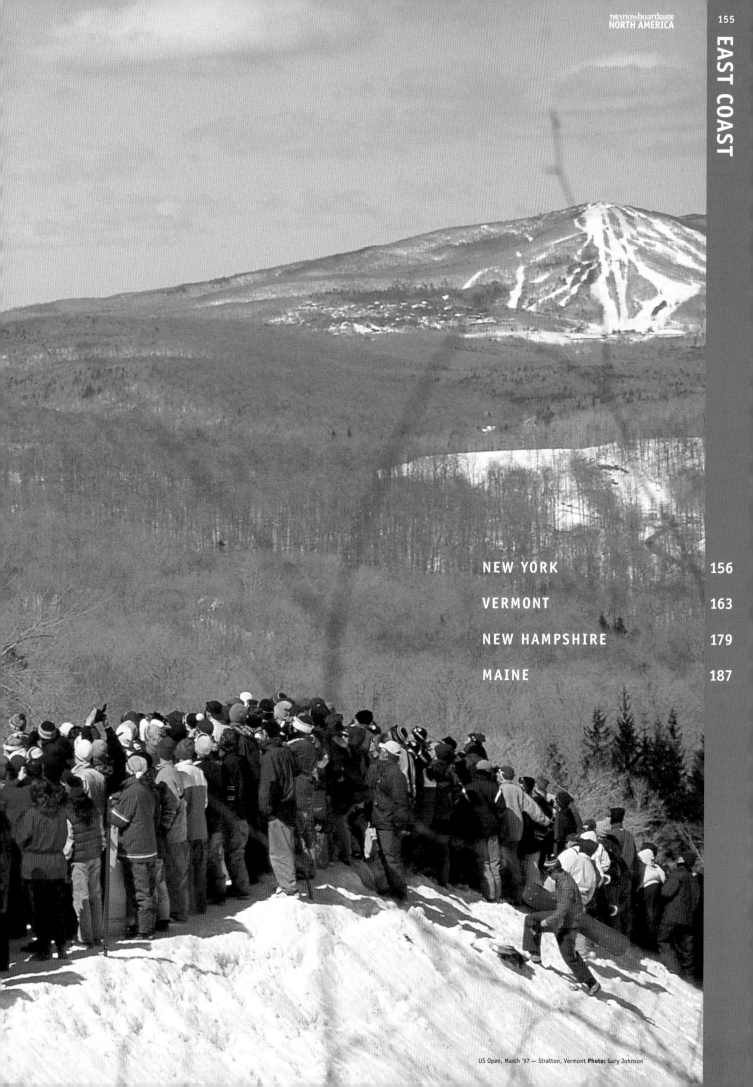

US Open, March '97 — Stratton, Vermont **Photo:** Gary Johnson

NEW YORK

STATE INFORMATION

Population: 18,477,400
Time: Eastern Standard Time = GMT minus 5 hours
Capital city: Albany
Area: 49,576 sq miles (128,352 sq km)

VISITOR INFORMATION SOURCES
New York Chamber of Commerce:
Tel: 518-474 4116 o 1-800-CALL-NYS
Fax: 518-484 6416
Web site: http://iloveny.state.ny.us
E-mail: iloveny@empire.state.ny.us

GETTING AROUND
Main airports: John F Kennedy International —
Tel: 1-800-247 7431
Train: Amtrak — Tel: 1-800-USA-RAIL
Bus: Greyhound — Tel: 972-789 7532
Road conditions — Tel: 1-800-847 8929
Speed limits: Up to 65 mph (104 kilometres) on the interstates.

Opposite — Photo: Gary Johnson
Right — Times Square in the heart of the Theatre District, New York City

INTRODUCTION

"You can't, you won't and you don't stop," say the Beastie Boys and we say the same about riding in New York. Either up-state in the Adirondacks or closer to New York City in the Catskills, the same mantra can be chanted. In the north part of New York state, the close-knit, gritty crews hide off-trail and refine their already accomplished tree skills. They seem a world apart from their southern buddies, the hip-hop disciples who escape across the Hudson River from the Big Apple at weekends, trading skateboards for snowboards. They benefit from sophisticated snow-making systems that allow all-mountain riding all season long. The northerners have a less high tech set-up but they've got the vertical; Whiteface is the highest peak at 3149 feet (960 metres). Big city, big attitude riding — would you have it any other way?

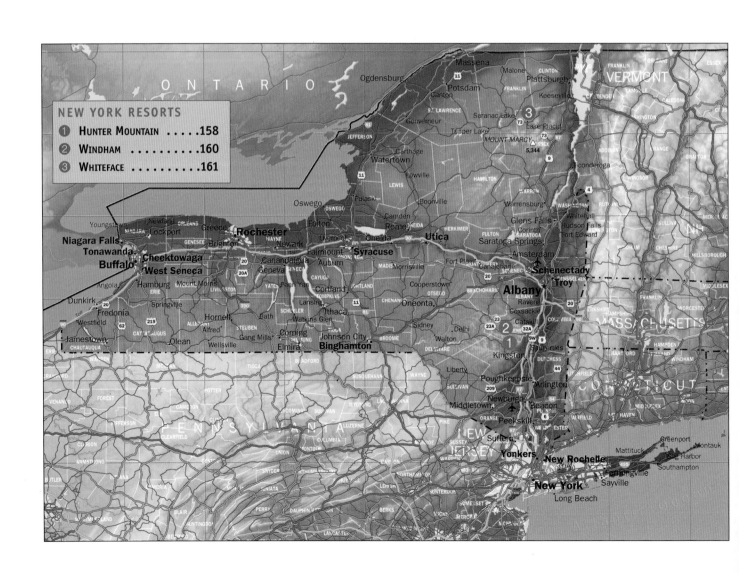

NEW YORK RESORTS

Hunter Mountain

THE FACTS

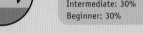

ELEVATION

Summit:
3200ft, 976m
Vertical drop:
1600ft, 488m
Base:
1600ft, 488m

SNOWFALL

Average annual:
125 inches, 317 cm

Snow-making:
100%

AREA

Total area:
230 acres, 92ha

Advanced: 40%
Intermediate: 30%
Beginner: 30%

SEASON

Late November — May

COMMUNICATIONS

Web site: http://www.huntermtn.com
E-mail: hunter@albany.net
Mountain information:
Tel: 518-263 4223 or 1-800-FOR SNOW
Hunter Chamber of Commerce:
Tel: 518-943 3223
Tourist directory:
Tel: 518-263 4286 or 1-800-524 2655

LIFTS AND TICKETS

Number of lifts:
1 high-speed quad, 8 chairlifts, 3 surface lifts
Lift pass prices:
1/2 day: $27, $32 (weekends and holidays)
1 day: $34, $42 (weekends and holidays)
Multi-day: $90 (3 days)
Season: $890
Other ticketing information:
The Frequent Skier Card costs $119 and gives you
25 per cent off weekends and holidays and 50 per
cent off week days. The mid-week Frequent Skier
Card costing $49.95 gives you a 50 per cent
reduction on non-holiday week days.

SNOWBOARD SHOPS

Board Room — Tel: 518-263 4666
The on-mountain shop does all the basics.
Snowbird Snowboard Shop — Tel: 518-263 4433
Rentals, service and repairs in town.

SNOWBOARD SCHOOL

Hunter Snowboard School — Tel: 518 263 4223
Beginner and intermediate programmes guarantee
the next lesson free if you don't have it sorted
after the first one.

ON THE MOUNTAIN

Hunter is a rugged little number that gives a misleading impression from the highway; it looks slightly more than a lump (even by eastern resort standards) and it's not until you're up and riding that the potential becomes apparent. There are a couple of reasons for the initial misapprehension; the first is that from the highway you can't see the Hunter West back side where most of the challenging terrain lies. The second reason is that until you're up close, you can't witness the extensive power of Hunter's snow-making system. There is lots of hype about pushy New Yorkers but compared to European lift queues, these guys are grannies.

SNOW CONDITIONS Because of its low altitude, Hunter's snowfall is sometimes random and the resort relies heavily on snow-making.

FREERIDERS Hits are generated all over the mountain as the artificial snow is accumulated in large pyramid piles. The main run on the front face is Hellgate which always has snow coverage. K27 is steep and sometimes gets moguled out but that should not dissuade riders from a great run — it's a true test to avoid being pitched tip over tail. Over on Hunter West, the Way Out trail contracts and expands in width with banks forming on the sides. Roll-overs and drops abound.

FREESTYLERS Hunter learned a valuable lesson in the '96-'97 season and in '97-'98 will be building their halfpipe entirely out of snow instead of relying on an earth base. It will also be moved further up the hill to take advantage of a 15 per cent gradient, an improvement on the 10 per cent angle it sat at this year. Riders can find a few hits on the Park Avenue approach to the pipe.

CARVERS Carvers spend their days on the Heuga Express which bends around the wide run-outs of Broadway and Kennedy Drive.

MOUNTAIN FOOD The Base Lodge is spread over two floors and has a number of eateries and drink stops. The cafeteria stews a soup second-to-none and their burgers and sandwiches are also tasty. You can get lunch in most of the Lodge's eat and run stops for under $5.

HAZARDS AND RULES Hunter is relaxed on leash laws.

Hunter Mountain
Hunter One
Hunter West

ABOUT TOWN

New Yorkers get their way in Hunter; even after a good two and a half hour drive into the heart of the Catskills, you can still hear the nightly thump of a bass beat at select spots around town. As the closest resort to New York City, the townsfolk are almost obliged to provide some city home comforts. While the aesthetic appeal may not match that of the surrounding hamlets, the range of facilities include everything you'll need to have a good time.

ACCOMMODATION The Villa Vosilla is unmissable. Sitting on Route 23A between Tannersville and Hunter, motel rooms and country cottages flank the grandiose Main Lodge. The rooms are large, clean and comfortable though the decor is strictly retro; prices from $60 — Tel: 518-589 5060. Also on Route 23A is the Scribner Hollow Motor Lodge where prices start at $85 — Tel: 518-263 4211 and the Hunter Village Inn; prices from $80 — Tel: 518-263 4788. Hunter Area Condo Rentals can provide information on condos and houses for rent — Tel: 518-263 4723. Hunter Mountain Lodging have details of the B&B network and other options — Tel: 1-800-775 4641.

FOOD Hunter, Windham and Tannersville between them provide a comprehensive selection of restaurants, bars and fast food outlets. In Hunter, Tequila's is a good stop; it's funky, rustic and fun-filled. The margaritas can bite so soak them up with large portions of tex-mex food. The Cheese Shop is rated highly, especially the hot reuben sandwich washed down with hot apple cider or one of their extensive range of beers. Momma's has the best pizza in town with a good sauce and solid dough cooked in true New York style. PJ Larkin in Tannersville has mean tortellinis, entrees for around $12 and nightly specials such as 'Two-Fers' (two dinners for $19.95). For self-caterers and lunch-makers, there's a Grand Union supermarket on Route 23A between Hunter and Tannersville.

NIGHTLIFE A good first stop is the happy hour with free snacks at the Barrister's Bar in the Hunter Inn. Situated on Route 23A to Tannersville, Slope's is the New Yorkers' venue. There's no cover charge for live bands and their wild DJs spin everything from alternative to house. The place also has decent pizza, a large selection of beers and heaps of promo prizes. Club Chapter Eleven, a bar-come-club off Route 23A, is a little more low key. It's a laid-back joint hosting bands like the Conehead Buddhas' — a reggae, ska and jazz combo. They have a complete menu and full bar with $1 shots and drafts. On the main street of Tannersville, Tanner's continues to use the lure of the 'ladies drink free' happy hour which says it all.

OTHER ACTIVITIES Battling your way out of snowdrifts back to New York City.

THANKS TO Marie Basil and Terry Duffield.

Opposite — **Courtesy:** Hunter Mountain
Top — **Courtesy:** Hunter Mountain
Middle left — **Photo:** Gary Johnson

GETTING THERE

By air: The nearest airport is Newburgh although Albany provides a more frequent service. There are no transfers but both airports have car rentals.
By bus: Pick-ups are available from New York City, New Jersey and Long Island on Monday, Wednesday, Friday and Saturday — Tel: 1-800-552 6262.
By car: From New York City, take Interstate 87 north to Exit 20 at Saugerties and onto Route 32A to 23A to Hunter.

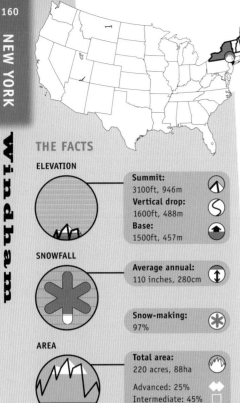

THE FACTS

ELEVATION

Summit:
3100ft, 946m
Vertical drop:
1600ft, 488m
Base:
1500ft, 457m

SNOWFALL

Average annual:
110 inches, 280cm

Snow-making:
97%

AREA

Total area:
220 acres, 88ha

Advanced: 25%
Intermediate: 45%
Beginner: 30%

SEASON
Mid-November — April

COMMUNICATIONS
Snow report: Tel: 1-800-729 4766
Web site: http://skiwindham.com
E-mail: skiwindm@aol.com
Mountain information:
Tel: 518-734 4300
Windham Chamber of Commerce:
Tel: 518-734 3852

LIFTS AND TICKETS
Number of lifts:
1 high-speed quad, 5 chairlifts, 1 surface lift
Lift pass prices:
1/2 day: $26 (mid-week only)
1 day: $31, $40 (weekends and holidays)
Multi-day: $89 (3 days)
Season: $840
Other ticketing information:
The Frequent Skier Card costs $119 and gives you
25 per cent off in weekends and holidays and 50
per cent off on week days. The Mid-Week Frequent
Skier Card costs $49.95 and gives you a 50 per
cent reduction on non-holiday week days.

SNOWBOARD SHOPS
Snowbird Snowboard Shop — Tel: 518-734 3747
All the goodies.

SNOWBOARD SCHOOL
Windham Snowboard School — Tel: 518-734 4300

GETTING THERE
By air: Albany Airport is a one hour drive away,
Newark is a two hour drive away.
By bus: The Ski Windham Shuttle leaves from Long
Island, Queens, Manhattan and Northern New
Jersey — Tel: 516-360 0369 or 718-343 4444.
By car: From New York: Take the New York State
thruway to Exit 21, then follow Route 23 west
directly to Windham.
From Boston: Take Interstate 90 west to Albany
and exit onto Route 32 south, then head west on
Route 23 to Windham.

Windham

ON THE MOUNTAIN

Windham resort sits amid the Catskill range, ten miles (16 kilometres) north-west of Hunter Mountain and a couple of hours north of New York City. The resort spans two peaks; the western face is the most developed with a flamboyant, shiny-new Base Lodge. The eastern face is served by a solitary lift, the Why Not Chair. There's also a moderately sized terrain park that will be enlarged next season. If you're wondering why all the lifts and trails begin with W, it's W for Windham, wish of the w-esort's policy makers.

SNOW CONDITIONS The snow-making is not quite up to Hunter's standard but it covers the mountain.

FREERIDERS Upper Wraparound offers hits and rolls the length of the tree line and man-made hits to complement the natural stuff. On the eastern side of the resort, check the legal tree runs to the side of Why Not and Wonderfully Wicked. There's also secluded tree riding in the sections under the main Whirlwind Quad. A word of caution to those who venture into the trees off Wipe Out: don't drop too low or you'll end up in the town of Jewett and have to hitch-hike back. On powder days, the trees below Wide Connection are the place to hit. Another lift that should be utilised is the Wheelchair Chairlift. It loads at the mid-station and is the one to ride when you are exploring the lines off Wide Connection.

FREESTYLERS The Wanna Be Wild funpark, located at the lower section of the Whiteway Triple Chair, contains half-a-dozen elements which change shape day to day. Customarily you will find a table top, a spine, a gap and a couple of quarterpipes. For the '97-'98 season, the mountain is promising to extend the park to the top of the Whiteway Triple Chair — a move that shows commitment.

CARVERS Key runs for the carving clan are Whistler and Wolverine, with Wonderama as the pick of the bunch.

MOUNTAIN FOOD The Lodge at Ski Windham covers the food options.

HAZARDS AND RULES The rule is no snowboards in the Lodge. The hazard is the battle-axe bouncer at the front door who enforces the rule.

ABOUT TOWN

Windham is a bundle of restaurants and stores gathered along a stretch of Route 23; it's a quaint place and functional with it. The village moves at a rural pace leaving 'city life' responsibilities (like providing nightclubs) to Hunter. There is a hardware store, a post office, two video outlets and a smattering of white-washed houses lining the street. Windham Mountain provides an awesome backdrop.

ACCOMMODATION The Windham Arms has rooms from $55 — Tel: 518-734 3000. Albergo Allegria is on Route 296 heading toward Windham; you can get a quality B&B for $90 — Tel: 518-734 5560. Ski Windham Reservations — Tel: 518-754 9463. The hamlets of Cannan, Greenville, Tannersville and Hunter are close to the resort and offer comprehensive lodging alternatives. Call the Hunter Tourist Directory for more options — Tel: 518-263 4286 or 1-800-524 2655.

FOOD On Route 23, the Brooklyn Bridge Restaurant and Pub is a convivial establishment serving gourmet burgers. The Mill Rock and Brandywine both specialise in Italian cuisine. Further afield, look for Cheer's Pub and Restaurant on Route 23A in Tannersville; their all-you-can-eat buffet for $7.95 on Wednesdays keeps you going for days. The China Pavilion on Tannersville's main street delivers take-outs — Tel: 518-589 6666.

NIGHTLIFE Late nightlife is not found in Windham itself so a party urge necessitates a venture to Tannersville. Check out the Chapter Eleven Bar or Slope's on the main street for a quiet beverage.

OTHER ACTIVITIES Mountain-biking, golf.

THANKS TO Sally Johnstone, Ingrid Emerton and AJ Savasta.

For more About Town, see Hunter review p.160.

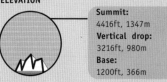

Whiteface

THE FACTS

ELEVATION

Summit:
4416ft, 1347m
Vertical drop:
3216ft, 980m
Base:
1200ft, 366m

SNOWFALL

Average annual:
168 inches, 427cm

Snow making:
95%

AREA

Total area:
170 acres, 68ha

Advanced: 28%
Intermediate: 37%
Beginner: 35%

SEASON
Mid-November — mid-April

COMMUNICATIONS
Web site: http://www.lakeplacid.com
E-mail: info@orda.org
Mountain information:
Tel: 518-946 2223 or 1-800-462 6236
Lake Placid Essex Country Visitors' Bureau:
Tel: 518-523 2445 or 1-800-447 5224

LIFTS AND TICKETS
Number of lifts:
9 chairlifts, 1 surface lift
Lift pass prices:
1/2 day: N/A
1 day: $39, $34 (weekends)
Multi-day: $114 (3 days)
Season: N/A

SNOWBOARD SHOPS
High Peaks Adventure Centre — Tel: 518-523 3764
It's all here.

SNOWBOARD SCHOOL
Whiteface Snowboard School
Tel: 518-946 2223 or 1-800-447 5224
Beginner packages cost $50 per day. B+B: $30.

GETTING THERE
By air: Adirondack Airport is 16 miles (26km) from Lake Placid on Route 86.
By bus: Adirondack Trailways operate a bus service from Albany and New York City to Lake Placid — Tel: 1-800-225 6815.
By car: From New York: Take Interstate 87 north to Exit 30. Follow Route 9 north to Route 73 and onto Lake Placid. The drive takes five hours.
From Boston: Take Interstate 90 west to Albany, then drive north on Interstate 787 to Cohoes. Take Route 7 west to Interstate 87 north. Get off at Exit 30 and follow the directions above.

ON THE MOUNTAIN

'Spectacular' is not strong enough to describe the view from the top of Whiteface Mountain. The mountain has the biggest vertical drop of any eastern resort. The trail system is stamped into the hillside in the shape of a boomerang; the upper half is steep enough to keep Olympic downhillers happy and the lower half is tamer and better suited to novices. Whiteface is

owned and run by the state and an all-in-the-family atmosphere prevails. As a bastion for national and international skiers training for World Cup and Olympic events, snowboarding has played second fiddle at Whiteface. The new funpark and staging of big air events signal recent winds of change.

SNOW CONDITIONS Wind gusts on the upper mountain can create icy slopes, so if this is the case, head for the trees where the snow stashes hide out.

FREERIDERS The Excelsior trail is a winding, snow-banked favourite of freeriders. Head left onto Lower Northway trail and across the top of Upper Valley to hit a nice drop off the Broadway Headwall. Upper Cloudspin is a wide trail with steep sections. Use the whole trail as there are hits on both sides. Confined trails have developed in the woods off Upper Skyward, and Upper and Lower Switchback. Excelsior and Upper MacKenzie are notorious tree runs. Those wanting to climb the 450 feet (137 metres) to the Whiteface Summit and access the out of bounds faces should first touch base with patrollers.

FREESTYLERS The park consists of half-a-dozen hits, including a reasonable table top and a short spine.

CARVERS After a grooming Upper Thruway and Upper Parkway are sweet, steep runs. Cloudspin and Skyward were the sites for the men's and women's Olympic downhill courses and are dream speed runs.

MOUNTAIN FOOD The best food is served in the Mixing Bowl Food Court in the main Base Lodge. The Cloudspin Lounge and Deli serves hot dogs and nachos. Boule's Bistro mid-mountain is the fast food, hot drink option.

HAZARDS AND RULES The pipe-smoking patrollers like everybody off the slopes promptly when the lifts close and that includes those wanting to session the park at day's end.

ABOUT TOWN

Lake Placid, service town to Whiteface, has hosted some fairly large parties, most notably the winter Olympics in '32 and '80. The main street sits just off the shores of Mirror Lake with the town's namesake a couple of miles north. Hotels and lodges are adorned with fairy lights that make for a surreal feel when it snows. As you would expect from a town that has coped with the Olympic circus twice, Lake Placid has plenty of hotels, restaurants and bars.

ACCOMMODATION The Mirror Lake Inn is the grandest hotel in town; prices range from $94 to $222 per person per night depending on the season — Tel: 518-523 2544. Cheaper options include the Prague Motor Inn with rooms from $40 — Tel: 518-523 3410, and the Alpine Air Motel which starts at $32 per person per night — Tel: 518-523 9261. Bunk beds cost $25 at the Adirondak Loj — Tel: 518-523 3441. For package deals, call Central Reservations — Tel: 1-800-447 5224.

FOOD At the Alpine Cellar you will be served bags of sauerkraut and lengths of bratwurst with lashings of German beer. Ask for the Van Gough ear burger at the Artist's Café on the Mirror Lake shorefront.

NIGHTLIFE The Cloudspin Bar in the Base Lodge is a great way to get the low-down on the key venues in Lake Placid. The cover charge at Christy's covers all your drinks on a Wednesday night. For moshing with ski-heads go to Mud Puddles or Roomers in the middle of town.

OTHER ACTIVITIES Luge rides, horse-riding, the Olympic Museum, bobsled rides, dogsled rides, tubing.

THANKS TO Dirk Gowans for his life-saving hospitality, Tim McCormack, Jason Strickland and Ben Green.

SNOWBOARD TRIPS

LOW PRESSURE travel

SURF TRIPS

LOW PRESSURE

THE LOW PRESSURE GROUP Unit 21, Pall Mall Deposit, 124-128 Barlby Road, London W10 6BL
Tel/Fax: +44 (0)181 960 1916 **Email**: mail@lowpressure.demon.co.uk **Web**: www.lowpressure.demon.co.uk

VERMONT

STATE INFORMATION

Population: 562,758
Time: Eastern Standard Time: GMT minus 5 hours
Capital City: Montpelier
Area: 9609 sq miles (24,775 sq km)

VISITOR INFORMATION SOURCES

Vermont State Department of Tourism and Marketing:
Tel: 802-828 3237
Fax: 802-828 3233
Web site: http://www.travel-vermont.com
E-mail: tourwebmaster@gate.dca.state.vt.us

Vermont Chamber of Commerce:
Tel: 802-223 3443
Fax: 802-229 4581
E-mail: vtchamr@together.net
Web site: http://www.vtchamber.com

GETTING AROUND

Main airports: Burlington International —
Tel: 802-863 2874, Rutland State — Tel: 802-773 3348
Train: Amtrak — Tel: 802-879 7298
Bus: Greyhound — Tel: 802-864 6811,
Vermont Transit — Tel: 802-864 6811
Road conditions: Tel: 802-828 2648 or
1-800-429 7623.
Speed limits: The speed limit is 50 mph (80 kmph) on
state highways and 65 mph (104 kmph) on the interstate.

INTRODUCTION

Snowboarding's history is entrenched in Vermont: the state was the birthplace of the US Open, the very first snowboard school and one of snowboarding's oldest brands — Burton. Vermont resorts were the first in North America to open their doors to snowboarding and have built their reputations on wicked service and facilities. Over the last thirty years, Vermont riders have worshipped their cult figures, developed the industry and raised a second generation of dedicated offspring. You can find die-hard conservative residents behind the doors of the clapboard houses and white spired churches, but the Vermonters you'll be riding with are the quiet believers who know their roots as well as their backyards — and they'll welcome you with open mitts.

Mike Montanaro, Stowe **Photo:** Gary Land

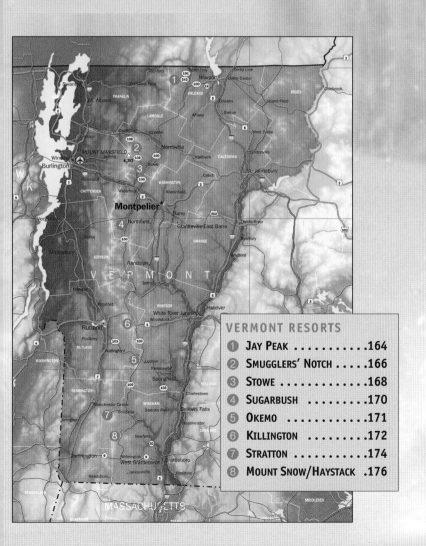

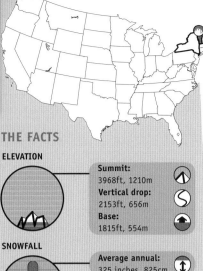

THE FACTS

ELEVATION

Summit:
3968ft, 1210m
Vertical drop:
2153ft, 656m
Base:
1815ft, 554m

SNOWFALL

Average annual:
325 inches, 825cm

Snow-making:
75%

AREA

Total area:
350 acres, 141ha

Advanced: 40%
Intermediate: 40%
Beginner: 20%

SEASON

Mid-November — late April

COMMUNICATIONS

Snow report: Tel: 802-988 2611
Web site: http://www.jaypeakresort.com
E-mail: jaypeak@together.net
Mountain information:
Tel: 802-988 2611 or 1-800-451 4449
Jay Peak Area Association:
Tel: 802-988 2259

LIFTS AND TICKETS

Number of lifts:
1 aerial tramway, 4 chairlifts, 2 T-bars
Lift pass prices:
1/2 day: $30
1 day: $40
Multi-day: $165 (5 days)
Season: $600
Other ticketing information:
Mont Saint Sauver, Mont Avila, Ski Morin Heights, Mont Gabriel and Mont Olympia resorts are all located between 40 and 50 miles (70 to 90 kilometres) north-west of Montreal in Saint Sauveur and Morin Heights villages. For reciprocity deals — Tel: 514-227 4671 or 514-871 0101.

SNOWBOARD SHOPS

The Snow Job — Tel: 802-988 4464

SNOWBOARD SCHOOL

Jay Peak Snowboard School
Tel: 802-988 2611
Special Learn to Snowboard packages are available for $29 including gear, lifts and a lesson.

Jay Peak

ON THE MOUNTAIN

Sitting just below the Canadian border, Jay Peak is renowned for its forested faces and abundant snowfall record; this resort gets more snow than any other eastern resort. The trails are a combination of traditional New England twisters and more recently developed open runways, however a recent glading programme has also opened up good tree riding areas. Vermont's only aerial tram keeps queues short on the main peak and the Jet Chair looks after those riding the smaller, but by no means less challenging, eastern mountain.

SNOW CONDITIONS Situated at the northern tip of the Green Mountains, Jay Peak is the first high elevation land-mass that storms hit as they move north-east. Storms from the east stall at the Canadian Maritimes and spin directly into Jay's path, bringing more snow. The resort has over 30 powder days in a good season.

FREERIDERS The diversity of the freeriding captivates those who ride here. Natural quarterpipes and halfpipes such as Canyon Land are found all over. The tree riding is extensive; in between the trails are 18 designated glades. The largest is the Everglades, measuring over one and a quarter miles (nearly two and a half kilometres). Riders wanting the best of both worlds can run the Jet, entering and exiting the trees to skier's right. The Haynes and UN trails offer similar opportunities. Skier's right of the Aerial Tramway, Green Beret has great ledges and bowls.

FREESTYLERS If you keep your eyes open, the whole mountain is overflowing with natural hits. When the pipe eventually calls, head over to the Interstate trail where you'll find Jay's low tech effort. It sits permanently on the trail directly below the Aerial Tramway and is looked after by the groomers, but life in the pipe is never the same after you've tasted the Dragon. There isn't a designated funpark but there are God-made structures till kingdom come.

CARVERS Can Am is a straight, wide run. If you hang a left at its entrance, you'll find River Quai, a run with a demanding top section and a fast, furious run-out.

MOUNTAIN FOOD The Tram Haus Cafeteria and the International Restaurant are the sole sustenance providers; they could serve pickled moose and it would go. Moose meat fans will, however, have to settle for the usual burgers and fries at the Tram Haus. The International Restaurant has a larger menu and live music after 8.00pm on Fridays and Saturdays. Expect to spend $10 on lunch and twice as much on dinner.

HAZARDS AND RULES No leash hassles here.

ABOUT TOWN

Jay is a blink-and-you'll-miss-it type of township; it's a speck on the landscape. The town is five miles (eight kilometres) down the road from the resort and was purpose-built to provide the obligatory amenities. The pace of life is slow and rural, however the surrounding villages of Montgomery, Westfield, Newport, Troy and North Troy offer more choices within a ten mile (16 kilometre) radius of Jay itself.

ACCOMMODATION Hotel Jay is as close as you'll ever get to living on the lift line. It has 48 spacious rooms, a jacuzzi and saunas. A two day package, including lift passes, lodging and meals, starts from $299 for two people. Slopeside condos include the Stoney Path Condos from $299 per week for a one bedroom condo and Mountainside Studios, similarly priced. In the surrounding areas, there is an abundance of country inns. The Black Lantern Inn is ten miles (16 kilometres) away in Montgomery Village; prices start at $45, and the Schnee Hutte is only a few minutes drive from the resort; prices start from $65. Central Reservations — Tel: 802-988 2611 or 1-800-451 4449.

FOOD For delicious clams, mussel-loaded pasta dishes and a real comfort zone, head to Hotel Jay. Dining further afield means hitting the highway to any of the surrounding hamlets. The Belfry, four miles (six kilometres) west on Route 242, is an old school house with old school food in a homely atmosphere. On the five mile (eight kilometre) drive toward Montgomery, you'll find the welcoming Jay Village Inn and Restaurant. Montgomery's main street has two main eateries, JR's and Lemoine's, which serve steak ribs and chicken meals. It's a similar distance in the other direction to Buon Amici, serving Italian food in North Troy.

NIGHTLIFE Once the sun sets, heads are hitting pillows at Jay. A good live act playing at the International Restaurant may lure a few heads who are prepared to miss freshies. The Golden Eagle Lounge pours beer until 1.00am but if it's a club scene you're after, look further south as this place is strictly business: sleep, eat, ride, repeat.

OTHER ACTIVITIES Snowmobiling, scrabble.

THANKS TO Conrad Klefos.

1

Opposite — A Jeff Brushie powder turn **Photo:** Gary Land
Top — **Photo:** Henry Georgi **Courtesy:** Jay Peak
Bottom — **Courtesy:** Jay Peak

GETTING THERE
By air: Delta Airlines fly into Burlington International Airport — Tel: 1-800-221 1212. A van transfer is available for hotel and condo guests. The transfer takes 90 minutes and costs $20 — Tel: 1-800-221 1212.
By train: The Amtrak Vermonter goes to Saint Albans, a 45 minute drive from Jay Peak.
By bus: Vermont Transit serves nearby Newport from all major New England points.
By car: From Boston: Take Interstate 93 north to Interstate 91, from Exit 26 follow Route 5 to Route 14 to Route 100. Head to Route 101 north and then follow Route 242 west.
From New York City: Use Interstate 95 to connect with Interstate 91 and follow directions above.

Smugglers' Notch

THE FACTS

ELEVATION

Summit:
3640ft, 1110m
Vertical drop:
2610ft, 793m
Base:
1030ft, 314m

SNOWFALL

Average annual:
272 inches, 691cm

Snow-making:
57%

AREA

Total area:
996 acres, 402ha

Advanced: 23%
Intermediate: 56%
Beginner: 21%

SEASON

Mid-November — mid-April

COMMUNICATIONS

Snow report: Tel: 802-644 1111
Web site: http://www.smuggs.com
E-mail: smuggs@smuggs.com
Mountain information:
Tel: 802-644 8851 or 1-800-451 8752
Tel: 0-800-89 7159 (toll free Europe)
Smugglers' Notch Chamber of Commerce:
Tel: 802-644 2239

LIFTS AND TICKETS

Number of lifts:
5 chairlifts, 3 surface lifts
Lift pass prices:
1/2 day: $30-$32
1 day: $38
Multi-day: $166 (5 day)
Season: $279 (purchased early season)
Other ticketing information:
The Club Smugglers' multi-day ticket allows access
to Stowe Mountain for one day.

SNOWBOARD SHOPS

No School Snowboard Shop — Tel: 802-644 5853
Route 108, Jeffersonville.

SNOWBOARD SCHOOL

Peter Ingvoldstad's Snow Sport University
Tel: 802-644 8851
The Snow Sport Uni has doubled its snowboard
instructing staff in the past year and is established
as one of the best learning centres in the East.
Night-riding lessons are offered.

ON THE MOUNTAIN

The three peaks of Smugglers' Notch sit on the horizon as if it was an Olympic podium; Madonna Mountain occupies the gold medal spot, Sterling Peak gets the silver and Morse Mountain wins the bronze. From the summit of Madonna Mountain, you have a bevy of runs that belie the resort's family image. Between the runs are large sections of accessible tree riding terrain; you have to look hard for openings off the trails and are best advised to follow the locals who can guide you through the back side drops. Close ties with neighbouring Stowe Mountain mean that visitors are encouraged to hike Snuffy's Trail, the route which links the two mountains. Check with patrollers as to whether Stowe's Spruce Lift is running, or you'll face a good 40 minute hitch back around the mountain. The antiquated Smugglers' lift system is a drawback; it would be worse if the place frequently crowded out but luckily it doesn't.

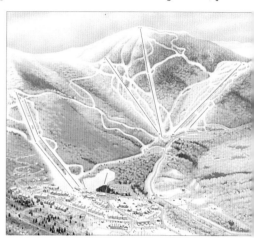

SNOW CONDITIONS The early season base is left ungroomed until the contours have developed around the stumps and boulders. Once the snow-making kicks in and the snowcats get on the job, Smugglers' cover is kept in good shape throughout the season.

FREERIDERS Upper Liftline on Madonna Mountain offers the steepest gradient. Granite slabs are exposed and riders sometimes take precarious leaps of faith larger than they had intended. Cliff drops of 15 to 30 feet (five to nine metres) can be sought out in the trees but you must have a guide. Hiking the Long Trail towards Madonna Mountain from the top of the Sterling Lift can be a haul, but the drops into the powder chutes from the ridge make it worthwhile. Smugglers' has a reputation for great snowfalls and the tree riding makes it a wooded paradise. The woods are also a great sheltering spot when the wind whips across the summit. The open trail policy means that riders can explore anywhere within the boundaries.

FREESTYLERS The terrain park, sculpted by snowboard guru Tom Vickery and his crew, is located under the Madonna 2 Chair. What it lacks in numbers of hits, it makes up for in size and shape. A new park is planned for the '97-'98 season which will have a dozen hits with a halfpipe at the bottom of MacPherson's run.

CARVERS Chilicoot Upper and Lower are the favourites for carvers. Steep and wide, FIS is good for a blast; try the upper section after recent grooming.

HAZARDS AND RULES Leashless riders are everywhere. If you want to invert in the park, watch out for the vigilant patrollers and park staff.

Smugglers' Notch

ABOUT TOWN

The resort village at Smugglers' Notch is geared toward the total family experience. Sitting at the base of Morse Mountain, it's a modern let's-get-together touchy-feelie complex that has enough restaurants, shops and take-away eateries to keep residents happy. The condos can sleep up to 2000 people and there's an indoor swimming pool, a recreation centre and bulletin boards loaded with ideas for the kids. You'll see craft shops and the Brewski Pub on the way down the road to Jeffersonville.

ACCOMMODATION Most of those who ride Smugglers' stay in the village condos. Great packages are available. The Snowboarders' No-Frills deal offers a five bedroom condo sleeping ten for $260 for three days or $510 for a week. Call Central Reservations — Tel: 1-800-451 8752 or 0800-89-7159 (toll free in Europe).

FOOD The wise take provisions into the village from the Grand Union Supermarket in Stowe and make use of their condo's full kitchen facilities. The forgetful are catered for by the Green Mountain Café and Bakery and the Country Grocery Store and Deli. In the resort village, the Hearth and Candle Restaurant has an extensive bill of foods. The Mountain Grille serves standard steak, fish and chicken. If you're after a pizza, try the Snowsnake Pizzeria with free delivery — Tel: 802-644 1142. Across the road from the resort, Bandito's has Mexican food. The ever-popular Jana's Cupboard, down the hill at Jeffersonville, has mains for around $10. For Vermont country ambiance, try Kelly's Old Gristmill.

NIGHTLIFE Sedate. For a brew or two, the Brewski at the village gates plays great tunes and is a mellow place for a game of pool. If you get snowed-in and cabin-fevered make the 40 minute drive to the brighter lights of Stowe, otherwise it's early nights and early rises.

OTHER ACTIVITIES The resort is hell-bent on complimenting snowsports with other activities, but they are usually family-orientated affairs like rubber-tube sliding and volleyball. The Nordic Ski Centre has ice-skating, an indoor swimming pool and hot-tubs.

THANKS TO Barbara Thomke, Tom Vickery.

②

Opposite — **Courtesy:** Smugglers' Notch Tourist Board
Top — **Courtesy:** Smugglers' Notch Tourist Board
Middle left — Brewskis at Smugglers' Notch **Photo:** Gina Dempster
Middle right — **Courtesy:** Smugglers' Notch Tourist Board

GETTING THERE
By air: Direct flights to Burlington International Airport, 30 miles (48 kilometres) away, are available with Delta's Business Express — Tel: 1-800-221 1212. A shuttle service is available and must be confirmed with the resort 48 hours in advance.
By train: Amtrak provides a service from New York City and Albany to Essex Junction. Bus transfers are available from Essex Junction.
By car: Take note! Route 108 between Stowe and Smugglers' is closed from mid-October to mid-May.

THE FACTS

ELEVATION

Summit:
4393ft, 1339m
Vertical drop:
2360ft, 720m
Base:
2360ft, 719m

SNOWFALL

Average annual:
260 inches, 660cm

Snow-making:
73%

AREA

Total area:
480 acres, 193ha

Advanced: 25%
Intermediate: 59%
Beginner: 16%

SEASON
Mid-November — late April

COMMUNICATIONS
Snow report: Tel: 802-253 3600
Web site: http://www.stoweinfo.com/saa
E-mail: stowevtusa@aol.com
Mountain information:
Tel: 802-253 3000
Stowe Area Association
Tel: 802-253 7321

LIFTS AND TICKETS
Number of lifts:
1 gondola, 1 high-speed quad, 7 chairlifts,
2 platter pulls
Lift pass prices:
1/2 day: $34
1 day: $48
Multi-day: $200 (5 days)
Season: $850-$975
Other ticketing information:
Two and three day passes allow a day's riding at
Smuggler's Notch. A restricted mid-week season
pass costs $575 to $675.

SNOWBOARD SHOPS
Snowboard Addic — Tel: 802-253 2996
Mountain Road, Stowe. Billed as the premier board
shop, this place comes up with the goods and has
excellent tuning. FREE hot dogs on Fridays shows
they're also compassionate.
Woodie's Snowboards — Tel: 802-253 4593,
Mountain Road, Stowe. On a par with Addic without
the hot dogs, check them for late season deals.
Boots n' Boards — Tel: 802-253 4225
Rentals, sales and service.

SNOWBOARD SCHOOL
Stowe Ski and Snowboard School
Tel: 802-253 3000 or 1-800-253-4SKI
Stowe for Starters costs $70 for a Spruce Peak lift
pass, rental and four hours of coaching. A 20
minute intensive Quick Trick workshop costs $15.

Stowe

ON THE MOUNTAIN

At 4393 feet (1339 metres), Mount Mansfield is the highest peak in Vermont. Since the first trails were cut in the '30s, it has been one of the state's pre-eminent resorts. Stretching over three faces and the valleys in between, Stowe delivers demanding terrain. An abundance of waterfall cliffs and tree riding on the north-facing slopes makes them the most challenging freeriding areas. The western face plays host to the gondola and its hard boot disciples while freestylers hang out in the pipe above the gondola base. Spruce Peak, to the south, works best after a dump, otherwise it's purely intermediate terrain. You can ride to neighbouring Smugglers' Notch over Snuffy's Trail.

SNOW CONDITIONS Mount Mansfield is east of Lake Champlain and the great lakes which means that the mountain is the recipient of relatively heavy falls of water-laden snow. Occasional gusty winds make warm layers the safest clothing bet.

FREERIDERS Upper Lord, Lower Haystack and Hayride all have good rolls and banks on either side. The Three Amigos Glades are well-spaced, allowing a fast run through the trees. From the top of the Gondolier trail on Mount Mansfield, explore the stream bed to skier's right where there are plenty of natural obstacles. The legendary front four runs of Goat, Starr, National and Liftline are also attention grabbers for freeriders. The top sections can lose their cover and the narrow, icy entrance may cause a few to balk. Make it through and you are treated to fast, demanding run-outs.

FREESTYLERS There are four parks but Lower Lord, Lower Tyro and Easy Street are for beginners and intermediate freestylers. The most demanding terrain park, Jungle, is located at Lower Standard. All the necessary elements are well-constructed and well-maintained with rail slides and barrels. The halfpipe is sweet but questionably positioned at the bottom of the gondola; it needs it's own lift.

CARVERS Wide cruisers from the top of the gondola back to the base allow plenty of room to maneuver, though you'll need to have your slalom skills down pat when it gets crowded. Centerline, Middle Lord and Standard have a consistent pitch — after a couple of orientation runs you will be treating it like a luge. Try the warm-up runs on Spruce for a change of scenery.

MOUNTAIN FOOD There are Base Lodges at all three base areas which have a variety of food on offer from sandwiches to burgers. The Cliff House Restaurant on Mount Mansfield has a great view and gourmet food. The Octagon Cafeteria, at the top of the Four Runner Quad, serves the the usual café stuff.

HAZARDS AND RULES No leash laws.

EVENTS AND COMPETITIONS Stowe holds a National Women's Ski and Snowboard festival in January. Around the same time, they hold the Dummy Big Air and a winter carnival.

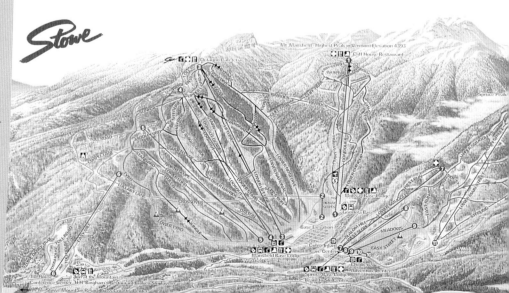

ABOUT TOWN

This quintessential Vermont township has history and charm oozing from every nook and cranny. There are over 60 restaurants in town, including excellent beer bars and lodging establishments. The glare of modern trading has been avoided with strict sign-posting laws; McD's golden arches are only three feet high! Stowe prides itself on its presentation and welcoming nature. Look hard enough however, and you will find down-to-earth grittiness behind the scenes.

ACCOMMODATION Stowe's bed base stretches from the township up the mountain road to the slopes; there's limited slopeside accommodation here. Options include the Golden Eagle Resort with rooms, apartments and condos starting from $79 per person per night — Tel: 802-253 4811. The Inn at the Mountain occupies a pristine spot toward the top of the mountain road; prices start from $145 per person per night — Tel: 802-253 4754. The Stoweflake is a costs $156 for two nights per person — Tel: 802-253 7355. Condo and accommodation agents include: Rentals at Stowe Co. — Tel: 802-253 9786, Simoneau Realty — Tel: 802-253 4623, All Season Rentals — Tel: 802-253 7353, and Stowe Country Rental Co. — Tel: 802-253 8132. Central Reservations — Tel: 802-253 7321 or 1-800-24 STOWE.

FOOD Stowe has a wide selection of food from traditional pancakes at the Scandinavia Lodge to succulent steaks at Gracie's Restaurant. The Bagel Shop in the Baggy Knees complex is a good stop for breakfast; it's on your right heading up the mountain road. After riding, head to Pickwick's Pub where the major drawcard is free end-of-the-day nibbles. For mid-range meals, Miguel's has a complete Mexican menu and the Whip serves up some mean S&M (salad and meat). Pull up a stool in the slung-back bar at the Shed and drink beer brewed on the premises. The Pie in the Sky delivers pizza to your room — Tel: 802-253 5100.

NIGHTLIFE Depending on what vibe you're after, it's a matter of mood that determines where you'll wind up in an evening. The Matterhorn draws the college crowd and rocks when its rammed and sucks when its hollow. Plastic cups are standard issue. The Shed's front bar is always humming with current sounds. Tucked away in the heart of Stowe is a late bar called the Back Bar. It has two pool tables and twisted, Bud-drinking regulars. The Rusty Nail Nightclub on the mountain road rocks with live bands, great dancing and local colour.

OTHER ACTIVITIES For those who blade there's a path winding around Stowe's perimeter. Rentals are available at Shaw's General Store and other sports shops.

THANKS TO Valerie Rochon, Dick Collins (who is riding well into his 70s), Rusty Starner and his cohort bad heads.

Opposite — Mike Montanaro **Photo:** Gary Land
Top — Mike Montanaro **Photo:** Gary Land
Bottom — The Chin **Photo:** Gary Land

③

GETTING THERE

By air: It's a 40 minute drive from Burlington International Airport, serviced by all the major carriers including Delta Airlines — Tel: 1-800-221 2121. Bus transfers are available.

By train: Amtrak's Vermonter travels daily from Washington, Philadelphia, New York City and Hartford, stopping at Waterbury 15 minutes from Stowe. The round trip costs $40 from Hartford and $94 from New York City — Tel: 802-256 7321 or 1-800-24-STOWE.

By car: From Boston, take Interstate 93 north to Concord. Pick up Interstate 89 north to Exit 10 and take Route 100 north to Stowe Village. Turn left onto Route 108 for the last six miles (nine kilometres).

Getting around: Stowe has a slick trolley and bus system which runs people around and up the mountain. It runs seven days a week from 8.00am till 10.00pm and costs $1 per ride — Tel: 802-253 7585.

Sugarbush

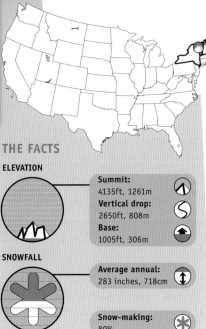

THE FACTS

ELEVATION

Summit:
4135ft, 1261m
Vertical drop:
2650ft, 808m
Base:
1005ft, 306m

SNOWFALL

Average annual:
283 inches, 718cm

Snow-making:
80%

AREA

Total area:
432 acres, 174ha

Advanced: 32%
Intermediate: 46%
Beginner: 22%

SEASON
Late October — early May

COMMUNICATIONS
Snow report: Tel: 802-583 SNOW
Web site: http://www.sugarbush.com
E-mail: info@sugarch
Mountain information:
Tel: 802-583 2381 or 1-800-53-SUGAR

LIFTS AND TICKETS
Number of lifts:
4 high-speed quads, 10 chairlifts, 4 surface lifts
Lift pass prices:
1/2 day: $30
1 day $37
Multi-day: $252 (6 days), $150 (off season)
Season: $925
Other ticketing information:
See Sunday River review p.190 for American Skiing
Company transferable deals.

SNOWBOARD SHOPS
Ride On! — Tel: 802-583 2381 ext. 473
Located in the Valley House Lodge, the shop
features top name equipment and clothing.
Mad Mountain Snowboards — Tel: 802-496 7433
Junction of Route 17 and Route 100.

SNOWBOARD SCHOOL
Sugarbush Snowboard School — Tel: 802-583 2381
Sugarbush offers a high level of snowboard
instruction, including a Guaranteed-Learn-to-Ride
programme costing $45 for rentals, clinics and lift
access. If you can't get down the mountain after a
two hour clinic, they'll give you the next one free.

GETTING THERE
By air: Sugarbush is 45 minutes from Burlington
International Airport which is serviced by Delta
Airlines — Tel: 1-800 221 1212.
By train: Amtrak's Vermonter travels daily from
Washington DC, Philadelphia, New York, and
Hartford to Waterbury which is only 20 minutes
from Sugarbush. The Ethan Allen Express travels
daily to Rutland with a shuttle transfer to
Sugarbush.
By bus: Vermont Transit run daily to Waterbury.
By car: From Boston, take Interstate 89 north to
Exit 9 and head south on Route 100B to Route 100.

ON THE MOUNTAIN

The American Skiing Company has made some changes to Sugarbush since its takeover, like
building seven new lifts. These advances compliment a trail system designed 35 years ago and
which remains largely unchanged since. Sugarbush is divided into two distinct territories: Mount
Ellen and Lincoln Peak. The Slide Brook Express Quad links the two peaks and riders can rip from
boundary to boundary. The Slide Brook Express Quad spans the Slide Brook Basin which is not
served by lift, although there are guided tours through this great back-country area.

SNOW CONDITIONS When the warm, wet air streaming in from the south-east meets the cold north-west
winds, the snow falls hard. Daily dumps of two and a half feet (one metre) have been recorded. Mount Ellen
and Lincoln Peak have a northerly aspect, keeping their snow in good nick.

FREERIDERS Castlerock Peak is the catch-cry for those wanting rushes. It's dubbed 'old school' terrain
because of its ungroomed, tight and bendy New England trails. Liftline, Rumble and Middle Earth trails are
notorious for steepness and bumps. Off the saddle between Castlerock and Lincoln Peak, steep chutes run
down either side of the central rockband. Break off the Paradise trail onto Lincoln Peak's upper face and
meet the trees. The powder stashes are phenomenal and the rugged contours hold goodies like stumps, rocks
and ledges. The 20 acres (five
hectares) of intermediate level terrain
on Gadd Peak have been cleared of
brush and there has been selective
tree thinning. The Black Diamond and
FIS runs are the short, steep
highlights on Mount Ellen.

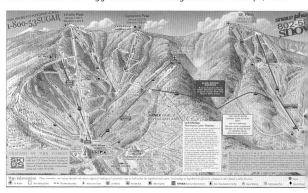

FREESTYLERS Seth Miller is the local
pro who helped develop the Mountain
Rage Snow Park. It's well-maintained
and located skier's left of the Spring
Fling Chair. The halfpipe is sculpted
by the new Pipe Dragon and sits just
above the Valley House Lodge.

CARVERS Those of a hard boot bent tend to hang out at Mount Ellen where the trails seem a little wider.
The steep, narrow trails at Sugarbush can bump up, so head to the groomed, cruisy trails of the mid-section.

MOUNTAIN FOOD The Mountain Lodge at the southern base area has a number of breakfast and lunchtime
options. Gate House Lodge Cafeteria has similar food and more room to eat in. The Valley House Lodge
houses the Mushroom Restaurant, the Valley House Cafeteria and the Wunderbar.

ABOUT TOWN

Mad River Valley, or 'the Valley' to friends, is home to Sugarbush Resort Village and the
supporting townships of Waitsfield, Warren and Fayston. The village provides all the essentials
and the surrounding hamlets are home to friendly, unpretentious locals who remain low key at
all times. Take the right-hand turn at the bottom of the access road to get to Warren.
Waitsfield lies in the opposite direction, heading north on Route 100.

ACCOMMODATION The Sugarbush Inn's main lodge is a grand affair; prices start at $79 per person per night
— Tel: 802-583 3333. The Powderhound Lodge on the Sugarbush access road has super functional units and
an excellent breakfast. B&B options start from $92 for a double room — Tel: 802-496 5100 or 1-800-548
4022. The resort offers packages with lodging and lift tickets from $69 off season. Central Reservations —
Tel: 802-583 3333 or 1-800-537 8427.

FOOD Chez Henri is a well-respected restaurant in Sugarbush Village. Down the access road lies Miguel's
Stowe Away with a full Mexican menu. The Common Man Restaurant, on the German Flats Road, has casual
family dining for under $20. On the way to Waitsfield, John Egan's Big World Pub and Grill serve great food
and their own brews.

NIGHTLIFE The Blue Tooth on the access road is a party den that hosts live bands and encourages tourists to
jump around. Gallagher's is much in the same vein. The Back Room is the late night venue in the resort village
which comes fully equipped with pool tables, dance music and microbrewed beer.

OTHER ACTIVITIES Ice-skating, hiking around the Green Mountains, sleigh rides and tubing.

THANKS TO Scott Campbell.

Okemo

ON THE MOUNTAIN

Okemo's commitment to snowboarding can not be faulted. With a huge halfpipe and a funpark equipped with its own surface lift and a 600 watt sound system to boot, it's easy to see how Okemo has earned its snowboarder friendly status. Freeriding is served equally well by sweet New England runs dotted with chutes, berms and whales, particularly around the tops of the South Face and Glade Peak Quad. Many believe the Upper Mountain and the South Face are the only areas worth riding but you only need to ride Exhibition or Heaven's Gate on a deep day to get another perspective.

THE FACTS

ELEVATION

Summit: 3441ft, 1050m	
Vertical drop: 2247ft, 685m	
Base: 1194ft, 334m	

SNOWFALL

Average annual: 153 inches, 388cm

Snow-making: 95%

AREA

Total area: 458 acres, 185ha

Advanced: 20%
Intermediate: 50%
Beginner: 30%

SEASON
November — April

COMMUNICATIONS
Web site: http://www.okemo.com
E-mail: okemo@ludl.tds.net
Mountain information:
Tel: 802-228 4041
Ludlow Chamber of Commerce:
Tel: 802-228 5830

LIFTS AND TICKETS
Number of lifts:
2 high-speed quads, 8 chairlifts, 3 draglifts
Lift pass prices:
1/2 day: $33, $37 (weekends and holidays)
1 day: $46, $50 (weekends and holidays)
Multi-day: $241 (6 days)
Season: $1010-$1100
Other ticketing information:
Okemo and Stratton have a reciprocal multi-day pass; ride three or more days at one area and get one free day at the other. There are rumours of a joint season pass.

SNOWBOARD SHOPS
The Pit — Tel: 802-228 2001
A large store with brand boards and boots.
Northern Ski Works — Tel: 802-672 5515
Rentals, services and repairs.

SNOWBOARD SCHOOL
Okemo Snowboard School — Tel: 802-228 4041
The school offers adult snowboard camps from $339 for three days.

GETTING THERE
By air: Connections can be made from Newark International Airport (New Jersey) to Rutland; 25 miles (40 kilometres from Ludlow.
By train: The Ethan Allen trains runs from NYC's Penn Station to Rutland — Tel: 1-800-USA-RAIL.
By bus: Vermont Transit Bus Lines stop in Ludlow — Tel: 802-773 2774.
By car: From New York City, take Interstate 91 north to Exit 6, then head north on Route 103 for 25 miles (40 kilometres) to Ludlow.

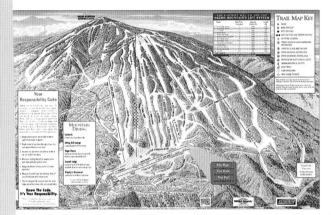

SNOW CONDITIONS Okemo hypes its snow-making prowess with just cause, as the resort blows enough snow to keep the trails covered until spring.

FREERIDERS Freeriding at Okemo means keeping your eyes open and hitting all man-made and weather-made obstacles as they appear. Work with what's available and make the most of the winding runs with their nice roll-overs. You'll find riders sessioning the hits under the South Face Quad on Wild Thing. Cut off mid-way to your left and head into the Forest Bump woods. The trees are well-spaced so go at speed.

FREESTYLERS Did we mention that Okemo has a superb 420 foot (128 metre) halfpipe and a funpark equipped with its own surface lift and a 600 watt sound system to boot already? These have to be the resort's highlights and both the park and pipe are well-maintained. Riders spend their whole day sessioning here.

CARVERS Okemo made its name in the '80s on the strength of its snow-making and grooming. Carvers will have a ball on the majority of the upper mountain runs including Defiance, Upper World Cup and Upper Chief. The Solitude Express Quad delivers riders to the top of Exhibition in double-quick time and the fast, straight descent will mean many thigh-burning runs. While a number of the intermediate runs do have well-groomed surfaces, this doesn't make up for the low gradient and riders may get bored. Double Diamond and Outrage are popular and have better pitches.

MOUNTAIN FOOD At the Base Lodge café you can get coffee and cookies for a couple of bucks. The Sitting Bull Lounge plays host to the lunchtime hordes. The nachos are the best by at $5 for a jumbo-sized portion.

HAZARDS AND RULES Speed warnings are planted all over the mountain and they work (if you hit them). Okemo staff will pull passes for poaching out-of-bounds. Inverted moves also get a big no-no.

EVENTS AND COMPETITIONS USASA events, ISF Pro Tour, JibFEST.

ABOUT TOWN

An obvious intermingling of life-styles pervades Ludlow, at the bottom of Okemo's Mountain Road. The rural town has welcomed the snow folk into their parlour but they haven't changed their own ways. You'll see plenty of baggily clad, body-pierced youths hanging at the snowboard shops, next door to the DIY store where Mr Jones still buys his pails of herbicide.

ACCOMMODATION Kettlebrook has the lowest slopeside rates; two people can stay mid-week in a one bedroom condo for $55 each. Central Reservations — Tel: 802-228 5571 or 1-800-78 OKEMO.

FOOD Priorities Restaurant is the main on-mountain dining option and it's well-patronised. At the Black River Brewhouse, shepherd's pie and nachos are washed down with Tom's quality brews. Spanky's at Cavendish Point lives up to its name, but it's a five mile (eight kilometre) drive on Route 103 to Proctorville. There's fine dining to be had at Nikki's and the Governor's Inn, both on the main street of Ludlow.

NIGHTLIFE On the mountain, The Loft is a converted three story barn where you can down a cold beer at the day's end. In town, Savannah's has live music including blues jams. The Black River Brewhouse serves wicked brews — we recommend 'blind faith'.

OTHER ACTIVITIES Sampling the local brews.

THANKS TO Pam Cruikshank, Matt Beck, Gordon Robbins.

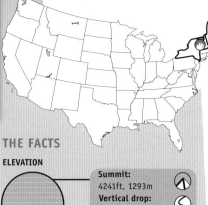

THE FACTS

ELEVATION

Summit:
4241ft, 1293m
Vertical drop:
3150ft, 960m
Base:
1065ft, 324m

SNOWFALL

Average annual:
250 inches, 635cm

Snow-making:
72%

AREA

Total area:
1200 acres, 484ha

Advanced: 32%
Intermediate: 32%
Beginner: 36%

SEASON
Mid-October — early June

COMMUNICATIONS
Snow report: Tel: 802-422 3261
Web site: http://www.killington.com
E-mail: info@killington
Mountain information:
Tel: 802-422 3333 or 1-800-621 MTNS
Rutland Region Chamber of Commerce:
Tel: 802-773 4181

LIFTS AND TICKETS
Number of lifts:
1 gondola, 6 high-speed quads, 17 chairlifts,
8 surface lifts
Lift pass prices:
1/2 day: $39
1 day: $48
Multi-day: $273 (7 days in the next 12 months)
Season: $1250
Other ticketing information:
See Sunday River review p.190 for interchangeable
ticket information.

SNOWBOARD SHOPS
Ride On! — Tel: 802-228 3344
On-mountain snowboard shops located at
Killington, Snowshed and Bear Base Lodges.
Season pass holders get $200 credit to spend.
Darkside Snowboards — Tel: 802-422 8600

SNOWBOARD SCHOOL
Killington Snowboard School
Tel: 1-800-621-MTNS
Separate clinics are available for women.

Killington

ON THE MOUNTAIN

Say it again: Killington is the Beast of the East. It's a mantra that has been chanted over the years and still rings true today. The seven peaks of Killington are home to a stack of statistics that burn most other eastern resorts outright. Lifts, snow-making, length of season and far-flung terrain are some of Killington's claims to fame. On the other hand, the resort's size can be as much a hindrance as a help as it's easy to get tangled in the long traversing trails intersected by more orthodox downhill runs. Killington Peak has the majority of expert terrain, although Bear Mountain has its own challenges and two new quads. The Skyeship is a luxury, eight passenger gondola with a sound system that transports riders from US Route 4 to the summit of Skye Peak in 12 minutes.

SNOW CONDITIONS They rave about the snow although it's more to do with the quantity produced and stockpiled than the amount of powder days you can expect. Over the last ten years, the season has averaged 244 days but by the end of the season, snow is more of a concept than a reality.

FREERIDERS Bear Mountain has some great lines to drop but bump-riding skills are needed before attempting the Outer Limits run. Overlooking Bear Mountain, Skye Peak's Vertigo and Needle's Eye are steep chutes which level out. Looking up the North Basin from Killington Road, you can see Rams Head and Snowdon Mountain from west to east, both beginner to intermediate level areas. Snowdon has a couple of steep runs, Northstar and Conclusion, and challenging tree riding in the Low Rider zone. For a tree warm-up, try the new Squeeze Play fusion zone on Rams Head. Moving further west to Killington Peak, ride the Canyon Quad and drop left from the top into the Big Dipper Glades. For a short steep run that gives up great snow banks, take East Glade or Rime to access East Fall. Dropping skier's right of the Canyon Quad Chair, you're greeted by a bevy of double black diamonds.

Another gladed zone, Julio, separates Skye and Killington Peaks on the way to the Superstar Express Quad. Skye Lark and Bittersweet both allow fast descents. Those into long, cruisy soul sessions might head for Sunrise Mountain or the longer runs on Skye Peak. If you take on the ten mile (16 kilometre) Juggernaut cat-track, be prepared to skate or walk some of the way.

FREESTYLERS The twin-tip crew migrate between the park on Bear Mountain and a couple of halfpipes constructed at the base of Snowdon Mountain. The pro pipe has 12 foot (four metre) walls while its smaller sibling has no vert at all. Both are maintained by a Pipe Dragon. Bear Mountain houses the Snowboard Park with approach runs from the top of the Bear Mountain Quad. The park is a straight strip loaded with hits of varying size, quality and difficulty. The direct fall-line means an unobscured view of riders below. Wild Fire and Bear Trap are as much fun as the park itself.

CARVERS A streak of shimmering white beckons carvers to Killington Peak. The bottom section can bump up and the double fall-line to skier's right is treacherous on icy days.

MOUNTAIN FOOD With seven base areas you won't be lost for somewhere to lunch on the mountain. Most riders will find themselves at the Bear Mountain Base Lodge or the main Killington Base Lodge. Both have stock eats.

HAZARDS AND RULES Newcomers to the mountain have to pick paths wisely or face long, flat traverses. It's called 'pipe etiquette' rather than rules: Killington want riders 'to wear leashes, to keep your distance in the pipe and to refrain from foul language.'

NEW
Teaching Mini Pipe
A pipe built for first-time vert riders.
Developmental Programs
Training for Freestyle and Alpine
Signature Pipes and Parks
To guarantee quality terrain
Family Center
Learn-to-Ride clinics and complete
rental fleet for younger snowboarders

Killingt
NORTH BASIN VI
SKYE PEAK
SNOWDON MOUNTAIN

• Halfpipe only ticket: $20
• Tunes & JIBURRITOS
  at The Pipe on weekends
  and holidays

ABOUT TOWN

The Killington Access Road is a highway by day and by night. When the sun's up, an ants' trail of vehicles delivers visitors to the slopes. When dusk comes, diners and revellers pick their way between the condos, bars and restaurants that line the way. It's quite a haul along Route 4 to the town of Woodstock and the 30 minute drive is only necessary if you need provisions from the Grand Union Supermarket. Everything else can be found on the Access Road. Tune into the local radio station WEBK as it will tell you everything that's going on in town (and who with).

ACCOMMODATION Condos such as the Fall Line complex start at two nights per person for $92. The Pinnacle has two nights per person for $62 and the Sunset Motel starts from $40 for two nights. Dorm rooms cost $35 at the Turn of the River Lodge. To book any of the above, contact Killington Central Reservations — Tel: 1-800-372 2007.

FOOD The Outback is the favourite spot with half price specials before 6.00pm which lure in the aprés crowd and malnourished boarders. The Outback has wicked pizza meals with free tunes — that's board tunes not vinyl. Ppepper's Bar and Grill (sic) next door is a '50s-styled number with '90s sounds piped in from the local radio station WEBK upstairs. It serves large pasta meals and the usual burgers and fries. The Wobbly Barn, built in '63 out of spare parts, has created a cult following. The barn is a conspicuous structure, as is its sister spot, the Picklebarrel, down the road.

NIGHTLIFE The Killington Access Road has been likened to the infamous Bourban Street in New Orleans, not because it's a notorious red light district but because of the infectious party spirit that is always festering. All tribes are catered to here, from London rave heads in search of a dance floor to students wanting frozen T-shirt competitions. If you know the stretch like the back of your hand, head out to the Inn at Long Trail and McGrath's Irish Pub on Route 4, Sherburne Pass.

OTHER ACTIVITIES Snowshoe tours, snowmobile tours, ice-skating.

THANKS TO Kim Armstrong, Jungle Jane and WEBK for the CD prize.

Top left — **Photo:** Gary Johnson
Top right — **Photo:** Gary Land
Middle — Chris Novak **Photo:** Gary Land
Bottom — Adam Moran **Photo:** Gary Land

6

GETTING THERE

By air: Killington Travel Service have fly/drive packages with Continental or US Air — Tel: 802-770 7800 or 802-747 4419.

By train: Amtrak's Ethan Allen Express travels from New York City's Penn Station to Rutland with transfers to Killington. The round trip costs $100 and takes about five hours. Two days' boarding with two nights' accommodation and a rail ticket costs $299 — Tel: 1-800-621 MTNS.

By car: From Boston: Take Interstate 93 to just south of Concord and exit onto Interstate 89 north. Follow US Route 4 west to Killington.
From New York City: Take Connecticut Turnpike (Interstate 95) onto Interstate 91 north and turn off at Exit 6 for Rutland. Follow Route 103 onto Route 100 and head north to Route 4 west to Killington.

THE FACTS

ELEVATION

Summit:
3875ft, 1181m
Vertical drop:
2003ft, 610m
Base:
1872ft, 571m

SNOWFALL

Average annual:
180 inches, 457cm

Snow-making:
80%

AREA

Total area:
544 acres, 219ha

Advanced: 28%
Intermediate: 37%
Beginner: 35%

SEASON
Mid-November — May

COMMUNICATIONS
Snow report: Tel: 1-802-297 4211
Web site: http://www.stratton.com
E-mail: skistratton@intrawest.com
Mountain information:
Tel: 802-297 2200 or 1-800-STRATTON
Manchester Chamber of Commerce:
Tel: 802-362 2100

LIFTS AND TICKETS
Number of lifts:
1 gondola, 1 six-passenger high-speed chairlift,
8 chairlifts, 2 surface lifts
Lift pass prices:
1/2 day: $39
1 day: $44, $49 (weekends and holidays)
Multi-day: $179 (6 days)
Season: $975-$1050
Other ticketing information:
A three day plus lift pass allows you one day's
riding at Okemo. The Frequent Skier Card costs $39
and saves $10 to $17 every day except holidays.

SNOWBOARD SHOPS
Syd and Dusty's — Tel: 802-297 4323
Located in Stratton Mountain Village. The shop has
hellish end of season sales, especially in clothing
lines, but you can pick up ex-rental stock dirt
cheap too.
Pipe Dreams — Tel: 802-297 4323
Stratton Mountain Village.
Pressure Drop Shop — Tel: 802-297 3457
Opposite Stratton access road on Route 11,
Bondville. You'll find a better selection of goodies
up at the Stratton stores but the odd steal can be
tracked down here too.

SNOWBOARD SCHOOL
Stratton Snowboard School — Tel: 1-800-STRATTON
They offer newcomer programmes, weekend EZ
Rider lessons, coaching, camps, race training,
seasonal programmes and women's snowboard
holidays. The Beginners' Three Pack includes lifts,
lessons and rental for three days; prices from $45.

Stratton

ON THE MOUNTAIN

Stratton has major kudos as one of the first resorts to open its lifts and trails to snowboarding back in '83, and later as home to the world's first snowboarding school. Stratton Mountain rides bigger than its 544 acres (219 hectares) suggest due to the cobweb of trails that fan out from the summit. Mix and match them and you can ride different lines all day. The mountain's solid reputation is based on its reliable cover, immaculately groomed trails and tree riding. The front face is served by the East's only six seater high-speed lift, and while it only runs to the mid-mountain station, it eases the queue pressure on the gondola beside it. Stratton hosts the annual US Open when 10,000 of the faithful descend upon the place, hoping to catch a glimpse of Terje busting ten feet out of the manicured pipe or Jim Rippey flying 30 feet overhead in the big air comp. You can session the pipe when it's over but they grind the giant ramp away for obvious reasons.

SNOW CONDITIONS Like all the low altitude resorts in the East, Stratton doesn't rely on nature and supplements its cover with snow-making.

FREERIDERS The woods on Stratton hold the key to the essential freeriding terrain. Skier's right of Polar Bear lies Trees for All, a tight run that must be followed to the end unless you want to bush-whack through dense underbrush back out onto the trail. Look for the signpost at the entrance or you will miss the run as it's completely hidden from the trail. Skier's left of Polar Bear, Trees Release Me is much the same again but with the added value of rocky drops and a few emergency exits that lead onto the Grizzly Bear and Polar Bear trails.

Left of Freefall, mid-way down the Kidderbrook Chair, the trees are more open allowing more snow to blow in. You can cut in and out from the Freefall trail and hit some decent stumps and fallen trees. Local knowledge is invaluable if you want to find the secret stashes, as local riders work at manicuring the glades over the summer months. One spot can be found off Kidderbrook run, on the left-hand side before the Freefall trail. Enter and follow the gully to the stream bed before being spat out onto the middle of Bear Down.

FREESTYLERS The two terrain parks are located on Lower Down Easter and East Meadow; both contain spines, table tops and fairly big hits. Daniel Webster is a beginners' park for sorting out simple tricks. Showcase Park houses the world-class halfpipe used for the US Open. It has a number of hits including a kicker with three angled approaches, meaning crossed-up flight paths and the chance of a mid-air collision.

CARVERS Upper Standard, at the top of the North American Lift, has wide, immaculately groomed runs with a consistent pitch and a few rolls. Follow the fall-line here. The upper section of Liftline is a must if it's not mogulled and the lower reaches are always groomed to perfection.

MOUNTAIN FOOD The Base Lodge café has all the usuals. The bland food is hot and hearty and you'll have a large crew of lunchtime companions. The latest addition is The Roost; the room is a bit cavernous when one man and his amp is blasting out 'Me and Bobby McGee', but if you concentrate on the $1 basket of chicken wings, you'll win over. Mid-mountain and the summit have cafés; the food is all similar and costs a quick $10 if you missed breakfast.

HAZARDS AND RULES No leash Nazis here.

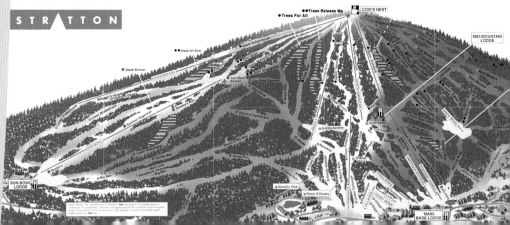

STRATTON

Stratton

ABOUT TOWN

Heavyweight Stratton owners Intrawest are well-versed in the field of resort transformation, having successfully boosted Whistler/Blackcomb and others into the upper echelons. Their emphasis is on creating an alpine feel by working the village into the focal point of resort activities. It's now glitz and clamour; chocolate shops and jewelry stores jostle for space with the snowboard dens, and the well-heeled eat bagels with the dread-locked.

ACCOMMODATION Two to five day lift and lodging packages cost $49-$99 per day. Birkenhaus Condominiums start from $170 for a one bedroom condo per night and from $350 for a four bedroom condo — Tel: 802-787 2886 or 1-800-STRATTON.

FOOD Condophiles should bring supplies with them or stock up at the Grand Union in Manchester, 20 miles (32 kilometres) from Stratton. Most of the resort's hotels welcome non-house guests for lunch and dinner. The Liftline Lodge serves a mean black bean soup for $3. The Birkenhaus, across the way, upholds a reputation for fine dining and can blow your budget to pieces if you like good food.

In the village itself, Mulberry Street was once a favourite haunt of lifties and instructors. Now that it's jumped aboard the cigar lounge boom, the old clientele have cooled off but still drop by to take advantage of their generously topped pizzas. Mulligan's, down the lane, also serve pub food in the middle level bar with more formal dining options in the restaurant above. Otherwise try the ethnic cuisine at the Inn at Bear Creek or the more straight-forward food at the Outback at Winhall River, both on Route 30.

NIGHTLIFE At the day's end, head for the bars in the Base Lodge and you may be treated to some good live sounds and the low-down on what the evening has in store. If you hang around the mountain, you will invariably end up at Mulligan's for a round of pool or two. Solid tunes and a good crowd means nights can start and finish here. Head to Bondville for late night grooving (OK — till

2.00am on Fridays and Sundays and 1.00am on Saturdays, thanks to Vermont's religiously influenced licensing laws). Local ska, reggae, hip-hop and rap artists perform for all they're worth and regularly crank the crowd. If it's the weekend mountain crowd you're after, try the Red Fox Inn where the patrons are as mainstream as the tunes.

OTHER ACTIVITIES Mountain-biking.

THANKS TO Dave Rathburn, Bernie Simms, Myra Foster.

GETTING THERE

By air: Albany Airport is 90 minutes from Manchester. It's a further 20 miles (32 kilometres) to Stratton.
By bus: Brattleboro is the nearest Greyhound stop. Manchester Taxis run a shuttle the last 40 miles (70 kilometres) to the resort — Tel: 802-362 4118.
By car: From Boston: Take Route 2 west to Interstate 91, then head north to Exit 2 and on to Route 30 north. Drive 38 miles (61 kilometres) north to Bondville.
From New York City: Take Interstate 95 north to New Haven, Vermont, then follow Interstate 91 north to Brattleboro, Exit 2. From there, as above.
Getting around: Stratton runs a shuttle service — Tel: 802-297 2200.

Opposite — Opening day **Photo:** Gary Land
Top left — Sergio Bartrina **Photo:** Nils
Top Right — Sebu **Photo:** Nils

Mount Snow Haystack

THE FACTS

ELEVATION

Summit:
3600ft, 1098m
Vertical drop:
1700ft, 518m
Base:
1900ft, 579m

SNOWFALL

Average annual:
155 inches, 394cm

Snow-making:
85%

AREA

Total area:
767 acres, 309ha

Advanced: 20%
Intermediate: 60%
Beginner: 20%

SEASON
Early November — early May

COMMUNICATIONS
Snow report: Tel: 802-464 2151
Web site: http://www.mountsnow.com
E-mail: mtsnow@mountsnow.com
Mountain information:
Tel: 802-464 3333 or 1-800-245-SNOW

LIFTS AND TICKETS
Number of lifts:
2 high-speed quads, 18 chairlifts, 4 surface lifts
Lift pass prices:
1/2 day: $32, $33-$34 (weekends and holidays)
1 day: $45, $47 (weekends and holidays)
Multi-day: $252 (6 days)
Season: $1050
Other ticketing information:
See Sunday River review p.190 for American Skiing
Company transferable deals.

SNOWBOARD SHOPS
Ride On! — Tel: 802-464 3333
A friendly crew who will allow you to use their
tools to do repairs, if you ask nicely.
Mountain Riders — Tel: 802-464 2222
On the Mount Snow Access Road.

SNOWBOARD SCHOOL
Ride On! — Tel: 802-464 3333
The Guaranteed Learn to Ride programme costs $50
for lifts, rentals and lessons.

GETTING THERE
By air: The closest major airports are Bradley
International Airport in Hartford and Logan
International Airport in Boston. For transfers to
Mount Snow — Tel: 1-800-245-SNOW.
By train: The Amtrak Vermonter runs to
Brattleboro and the Ethan Allen Express services
Rensselaer and Albany — Tel: 1-800-872 7245.
By bus: Vermont Transit and Greyhound both
service Brattleboro.
By car: From Boston, take Route 2 west to
Interstate 91 and follow it north to Brattleboro.
From there, head west on Route 9 to Wilmington.
Getting around: Shuttle around for free on the
Moover. For return shuttles to Brattleboro —
Tel: 1-800-451 4443.

ON THE MOUNTAIN

Mount Snow and Haystack joined forces a couple of seasons ago; the marriage means the resort now tops the East for numbers of lifts and only Killington has more trails. The two mountains remain unconnected by lift but now the American Skiing Company have taken the reins, there is talk of something similar to the linking quad at Sugarbush being installed here. At the moment, a ten minute bus ride connects the two resorts. Mount Snow's most challenging terrain lies on the North Face where the trails are steeper and the glades more testing. The Main Mountain has good intermediate and beginner cruising terrain. On the opposite east-facing side, Carinthia Face magnetises riders with the Gut halfpipe at the bottom. Haystack Mountain has moderate terrain with a few outstanding runs in the Witches and the glades surrounding them.

HAYSTACK

This is a rendering only. Actual conditions at Mount Snow and Haystack will vary.

SNOW CONDITIONS One of the American Skiing Company's first priorities was to tweak the snow-making facilities to 85 per cent coverage, an increase of 40 per cent. This is still relatively low for an eastern resort, most of which have 97 to 100 per cent snow-making.

FREERIDERS A favourite local stash is Olympic on the North Face, with its natural rollers and jumps. Overbrook has natural park features with hits of all sizes. Uncle's is a good trail especially when it's closed, but of course poaching is not allowed at Mount Snow. The best tree riding is found in the steeps of the Trials but don't go too far left towards the lake or you'll be hiking back out.

FREESTYLERS Mount Snow had the first park on the East Coast and still creates 'styler heaven with Un Blanco Gulch; it usually has at least 25 elements to session. Next to the Gulch is the world-class 400 foot (122 metre) halfpipe. Nicknamed the Gut, the pipe is situated mid-way down the fast, new Canyon Quad, so riders can get plenty of shots at it. It's maintained by Pipe Dragon and has huge floodlights for night-riding. The freestyle arena is known as Planet 9 and is situated at the base of the slope so you can see what's going on from the Carinthia Base Lodge.

CARVERS Long John and the trails on the Carinthia slopes are long cruisers favoured by local carvers and freeriders alike. Other choices for constant pitch corduroy are Chute on the North Face and Exhibition on Main Mountain. On Mount Haystack, the best bets are Merlin and Wizard. For a longer run, take Avalanche to the bottom or veer off mid-way to Needle.

MOUNT SNOW

SUNBROOK
(SEE INSET)

NORTH FACE
(SEE INSET)

CARINTHIA

MAIN M

MOUNTAIN FOOD The main Base Lodge is where you will find most lunchtime eateries. Spread over four floors, the lodge can accommodate large lunchtime crowds, even in bad weather. Cuzzin's makes a mean ham sandwich. The Planet 9 Lodge serves standard fries, burgers and hot drinks.

HAZARDS AND RULES The management take a dim view of inverted moves and snowboard park rangers monitor the park all day.

EVENTS AND COMPETITIONS The American Pro Snowboard Series has cash prizes for GS, slalom and halfpipe, and a large rock concert to boot — Tel: 802-464 3333 or 1-800-245 SNOW for dates. Mount Snow also USASA events, a Boardercross series, and the Huck Off series.

ABOUT TOWN

West Dover and Wilmington are the main service providers, sitting about five and 20 miles (eight and 32 kilometres) away respectively from the resort on Route 100. Wilmington is the larger of the two and if you can't find what you're after (it would have to be obscure), then it's a trip east to Brattleboro or on to Bennington. The collection of condos at the mountain base have no late night facilities and most visitors head out to Route 100 and the joints along the wayside.

ACCOMMODATION Snow Lake Lodge is within walking distance of the nearest lift and has everything you could ever wish for; prices start from $69.95 — Tel: 802-464 7788 or 1-800-451 4211. Condos clustered at the mountain base account for the rest of the resort's slopeside accommodation. Along Route 100 towards West Dover and beyond to Wilmington, you find more condos, B&Bs and country inns. Central Reservations — Tel: 1-800-254-SNOW.

FOOD Try either of Dot's Restaurants in West Dover and Wilmington for breakfast. The French-toasted sunflower bread with cream cheese and fresh berries is awesome and like the other dishes, costs around $5. In West Dover, Julie's Café is casual but classy; try their spicy south-western mains and pasta dishes spiked with chipolti peppers. Poncho's Wreck in downtown Wilmington has killer guacamole and nachos. The house vinaigrette is the best in the land.

NIGHTLIFE Mount Snow is a party place whose reputation precedes it. All over the East, you will hear stories raving about the scene. You can find Cuzzin's Bar on the mountain by the queues of well-dressed New Yorkers waiting to see Bruce Jacques, the one-man band who plays at the weekends. The Snow Barn is a perennial favourite with both locals and visiting New Yorkers. It's also a good place for the inside line on house parties. Deacon's Den is a mini-music hall that has all the paraphenalia (wagon wheel, moose-head thang) indicating that this is a down-home bar. It's a friendly, amped-up atmosphere, especially after the annual Saint Paddy's Day wet T-shirt competition.

OTHER ACTIVITIES Snowmobile tours, golf.

THANKS TO Melissa Gullotti, Jason Evans, Joey Sonntag.

Mount Snow/Haystack ⑧

Main picture — Fabien Rohrer **Photo:** Gary Land

Photo: Peter Mathis
Rider: Dani Kiwi Meier

TANKER 192

BASE

www.rad-air..com

NEW HAMPSHIRE

STATE INFORMATION

Population: 1,162,481
Time: Eastern Standard Time = GMT minus 5 hours
Capital city: Concord
Area: 8992 sq miles (23,199 sqkm)

VISITOR INFORMATION SOURCES

New Hampshire Office of Travel and Tourism:
Tel: 603-271 2665
Fax: 603-271 2629
Web site: http://www.visitnh.gov

GETTING AROUND

Main airports: Manchester — Tel: 603-624 6539,
Portland International Jetport — Tel: 207-772 0690
By train: Amtrak — Tel: 1-800-872 7245
By bus: Vermont Transit — Tel: 1-800-552 8737,
Greyhound — Tel: 603-436 0168
Road conditions: Tel: 603-627 4266
Speed limits: The limit is between 55 and 65 mph
(88 and 104 kmph) as posted.

NEW HAMPSHIRE RESORTS

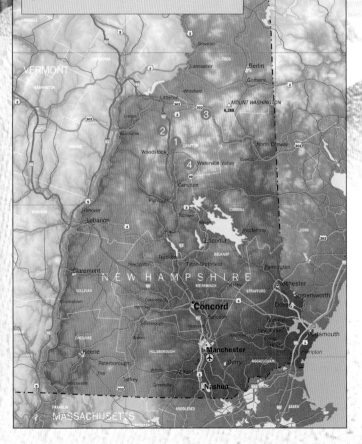

INTRODUCTION

The rugged relief of the White Mountains is imposing from a distance and even more so when you travel through the narrow valleys that punctuate them. Glaciers carved the notches allowing access through the ranges, and undaunted by the sheer granite faces, the settlers did the rest. In terms of riding, New Hampshire still has a rough-hewn feel with plenty of back-country; old logging trails wind their way in and out of some of the gnarliest tree riding in North America. Snowboarder's have imported radical pipe and park constructions at Loon Mountain and Waterville Valley; these resorts have issued the challenge to the rest of New England and it won't be long before they too will be chasing the Pipe Dragon. The riders here are a dedicated bunch of bums and students in the Tom Sims' mould who skip class to go riding.

Brian Knoxx, Waterville Valley **Photo:** Gary Land

THE FACTS

ELEVATION

Summit:
3050ft, 930m
Vertical drop:
2100ft, 640m
Base:
950ft, 290m

SNOWFALL

Average annual:
115 inches, 292cm

Snow-making:
97%

AREA

Total area:
250 acres, 101ha

Advanced: 16%
Intermediate: 64%
Beginner: 20%

SEASON

Mid-November — early May

COMMUNICATIONS

Snow report: Tel: 603-745 8100
Web site: http://www.loonmtn.com
E-mail: info@loonmtn.com
Mountain information:
Tel: 603-745 8111
Fax: 603-745 8214
Lincoln Woodstock Chamber of Commerce:
Tel: 1-800-227 4191

LIFTS AND TICKETS

Number of lifts:
1 high-speed quad, 1 gondola, 5 chairlifts, 1 pony tow
Lift pass prices:
1/2 day: $26, $32 (weekends)
1 day $38, $45 (weekends)
Multi-day: $110 (3 days), $139 (weekends)
Season: $800-$1000
Other ticketing information:
The Great White Mountain Pass Book is a discount coupon book for Loon, Cannon and Bretton Woods. It costs $240 and the 60 coupons offer up to 25 per cent off the daily rate — Tel: 1-800-232 2972. Passes at Loon, Bretton Woods and Cannon are interchangeable; pick up a credit voucher at guest services before 12.00pm.

SNOWBOARD SHOPS

Lahouts' Snowboard Shop — Tel: 603-745 6970
Jarred Derosier is the man to talk to here with a good selection of boards and March sale bargains.
Mothership Snowboards — Tel: 603-745 6597
Rentals and the like.
Village Snowboard Lincoln — Tel: 603-745 8852
Rentals and repairs.

SNOWBOARD SCHOOL

Loon Mountain Snowboarding School
Tel: 603-745 6281 ext. 5691
Their 1-2-3 Learn to Ride package starts from $55 for a two hour lesson, an Oxygen board and a lift ticket.

Loon Mountain

ON THE MOUNTAIN

Loon Mountain founder Sherman Adams accumulated 40 years of local knowledge before he started on his resort-building venture. He chose the mountain for its sheltered north-easterly aspect and its proximity to the then newly established highway, and today both factors still serve the mountain well. The front face between the South Ridge and the North Peak is home to the gondola and the quad and is a focal point for visitors. The main '97-'98 development is the cutting of new trails on the South Mountain which will increase rideable acreage. Loon has a bed base that outstrips the mountain's uphill capacity, and the mountain can crowd out and even sell out on occasion.

SNOW CONDITIONS Snow-making covers 97 per cent of the mountain. Guns translate into snow cover, even in the unpredictable East where winter storms can wash away a month's worth of base in days.

FREERIDERS When it dumps, East Basin is the magnet that pulls riders in. Banks form along the tree lines on Triple Trouble and Big Dipper and are well worth shredding. Upper Walking Boss on North Peak is good but gets tracked early in powder conditions. A well-travelled line at Loon takes in Upper Flying Fox or Upper Picked Rock before dropping into the funpark and back to the base of the gondola. The South Mountain has recently had trails cut as part of the Loon 2000 expansion. It's not serviced by lifts yet nor is there any snow-making system in place but the radical ride it raw.

FREESTYLERS Loon Mountain Park on the Lower Flying Fox trail is big, and we mean really big. The funpark has 18 elements and takes in seven per cent of the mountain's total rideable terrain. The kickers are large, especially the beast at the bottom of the run. It has a landing hill measuring 150 feet (45 metres) top to bottom and is equipped with two hits. The right-hand one will throw you about 40 feet (12 metres) and the other about 25 feet (eight metres). The pipe is also a monster. It measures 375 feet (114 metres) in length and has ten foot (three metre) walls pushed into shape by a Pipe Dragon. Riders can take in the pipe at the top of the park and then a series of smaller hits before the behemoth at the bottom. Park manager Steve Ash promises even bigger things to come.

CARVERS The whole of the East Basin attracts the hard-heads as it offers steep trails; the most demanding is Angel Street. On the west side, Upper Rumrunner to Coolidge Street has nice rolls and straight, wide tear-away run-outs.

MOUNTAIN FOOD The Summit Lodge at the top of Gondola Peak has great views and food from 9.30am. For breakfast, barbecue lunches and lounging on the sundeck, head to Camp III. At the base there's a variety of places to eat. In the Octagon Base Lodge, the Food Court has pre-cooked food under hot lamps and cold refried chips — they'll refry the refries if you ask.

HAZARDS AND RULES Leash laws are not enforced. The park is patrolled but the hits themselves make the rules.

EVENTS AND COMPETITIONS Regular freestyle competitions run throughout the season — Tel: 603-745 8852.

Loon Mountain

ABOUT TOWN

Lincoln and North Woodstock townships sit a couple of miles apart and together provide the bulk of the services for Loon Mountain, Cannon Mountain and to a lesser degree, Waterville Valley and Bretton Woods. The Kancamangus Highway connects the two towns and a drive either west or east will reveal New Hampshire's landscape at its finest. There are theatres, mini-malls and sports shops to burn, as well as all the major chains including Rite-Aide, Burger King and McD's. Both towns were well-established logging havens until the timber industry hit the doledrums in the '60s and the tourist industry took over. As both summer and winter tourist numbers have increased, the townships have prospered but have maintained their rural roots and flavour.

ACCOMMODATION The Mountain Club at Loon has two restaurants and an industrial strength hot-tub literally located on the trail. The place simply rules; prices from $109 — Tel: 1-800-229 STAY. Another large hotel is The Mill at Loon Mountain; double rooms cost $95 — Tel: 1-800-654 6183. Parker's Motel in North Lincoln will suit the budget-minded traveller at $50 per person per night. Condominiums and private townhouses can be rented through the Loon Reservation Service — Tel: 1-800-745 5666. Central Reservations — Tel: 1-800-227 4149.

FOOD The mainstay restaurants in North Woodstock are Truant's Taverne and Woodstock Station. Both serve unhealthily large portions of everything — it's a multi-ethnic haven. Appetisers and mains are reasonably priced at around $10-$15. The Clement Room offers quality dining in a more formal setting and the Chalet Restaurant down the street has lobster meal specials running all season. North Woodstock is also well-equipped with drive-by eateries; the most popular are the Roadkill Café and Able's Candy and Ice-Cream Shop. Peg's Family Restaurant deserves a special mention on the strength of its pancakes alone.

In Lincoln the key spots for filling food are Gordi's Fish and Steak House and the Common Man, both situated on the Kancamangus Highway which runs through the centre of town. At the Mountain Club on Loon, the Granite Grill has basic bar food while Rachel's has a comprehensive menu. Lincoln has a Grand Union for those of a cut-lunch bent, otherwise there are loads of sit-in or take-away lunch bars on the main drag.

NIGHTLIFE The Bunyan Room at the Octagon Lounge next to the gondola is a good place for a drink. Cold beer is served at the Blue Ox (known as Babes) inside the Governor's Lodge at the West Basin. Later, catch live sounds at the Granite Grill or head back into North Woodstock and engage in the world's shortest pub crawl. Cross the road between the Woodstock Station and Truant's Taverne as the mood takes you. Free pizza and chicken wings at Gordis' happy hour means the place buzzes with people nursing their pints between slices. During mid-season you'll be rubbing shoulders with visitors but locals come out of hibernation in spring, ready for the mud season.

OTHER ACTIVITIES Snowmobiling.

THANKS TO Steve Ash, Chris St. Don, Mike Baker, Preston Strout, Jarred and the lads at Lahouts, Janel McDonald, Dick, Karen Pendoly and Helen Anzouni.

Top — **Photo:** Gary Johnson
Inset — **Photo:** Gary Johnson
Bottom — Zach Diamond going big **Photo:** Gary Land

GETTING THERE

By air: Logan International Airport is a two and a half hour drive on Interstate 93. Delta Airlines use Manchester as a port, 90 minutes from Loon — Tel: 1-800-221 1212.
By car: Thrifty Car Rental is Loon's official service with low rates from either Boston or Manchester airports — Tel: 1-800-227 4191.
From Boston: Take Interstate 93 to Exit 32 for Lincoln; it's a two hour drive.
From New York City: Take Interstate 684 north to Interstate 84 east, then to Interstate 290 in Worcester, Massachusetts. Follow Interstate 290 east to Interstate 495 north, turn onto Interstate 93 north and take Exit 32 for Lincoln.

Cannon Mountain

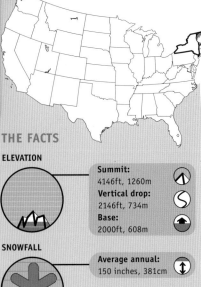

THE FACTS

ELEVATION

Summit:
4146ft, 1260m
Vertical drop:
2146ft, 734m
Base:
2000ft, 608m

SNOWFALL

Average annual:
150 inches, 381cm

Snow-making:
95%

AREA

Total area:
163 acres, 65ha

Advanced: 23%
Intermediate: 51%
Beginner: 16%

SEASON
Mid-November — April

COMMUNICATIONS
Snow report: Tel: 603-823 5563 or 1-800-552 1234
Web site: http://www.skinh.com
E-mail: info@skinh.com
Mountain information:
Tel: 603-823 5563
Franconia Chamber of Commerce:
Tel: 603-823 5661 or 1-800-237 9007

LIFTS AND TICKETS
Number of lifts:
1 passenger tram, 1 quad, 3 chairlifts, 1 surface lift
Lift pass prices:
1/2 day: N/A
1 day $28, $37 (weekends and holidays)
Multi-day: $90 (3 days)
Season: N/A
Other ticketing information:
Two adults ride for $28 on Tuesdays and Thursdays.
Student passes cost $20 mid-week. Save $5-$10 on
a day pass by showing yesterday's lift pass. See
Loon review p.180 for shared ticket information.

SNOWBOARD SHOPS
See Loon review p.180.

SNOWBOARD SCHOOL
Cannon Mountain Snowboard School
Tel: 603-823 8521
Learn to Snowboard for the Fun of It is a series of
three one day programmes that will get you
snowboarding for $35 a day.

GETTING THERE
By air: Logan International Airport is a straight
two and a half hour drive along Interstate 93.
By bus: Lincoln and Woodstock have a shuttle
service and taxi — Tel: 1-800-WE-SKI93.
By car: From Boston: Take Interstate 93 to the
Parkway Exit for the Visitor's Centre, Parkway Exit
Two for Tramway Lift or Exit Three.

Cannon Mountain

ON THE MOUNTAIN

Steep, narrow and twisted — that's Cannon Mountain. The resort has commanded respect for over 60 years and the runs visible from Interstate 93, such as Paulie's Folly and Avalanche, continue to do just that. The views from the Mittersaal Saddle of the Presidential Range remind you that you're in New Hampshire's heartland. Give-aways as to the age of this resort are the old double chairs and a close-knit, predominantly ski community who return season after season. As more riders are being introduced to the mountain, the demographics continue to even up. As far as constructing funparks goes, Cannon has fallen behind its neighbours but those who ride here tend to be looking for New England's rugged experience.

SNOW CONDITIONS Although Cannon is the tallest mountain in the Ski 93 conglomerate, it still relies heavily on snow-making. Much of the snow can be blown off the trails and into the trees (the best area to head for when it's windy), leaving exposed icy patches, particularly on the front face.

FREERIDERS The Taft Slalom path is a fast, banked number that should be followed onto Upper and Middle Ravine. Cut across the front face and pick up any of the much touted front five runs: Paulie's Folly, Avalanche, Zoomer, Rocket and Gary's. The Mittersal terrain is not marked on the trail map but it's definitely worth checking out. This used to be the site of an old ski pulley lift; the saplings and scrub are poking up but the trail is still visible. To get there, take Taft Slalom from the summit to the junction with Upper Hardscrabble. Unbuckle and walk five to ten minutes along the ridge line to the former exit ramp where you will see the old bull-wheel house and lift shack. Stay skier's right and spill out at the Peabody Lift. The usual back-country rules apply, and the same goes if you wish to explore the back side of Cannon Mountain.

FREESTYLERS It's not a huge priority at Cannon but a funpark has been constructed on the Peabody trail.

CARVERS Profile is the widest, steepest run and quite a few turns can be laid out before you hit the bottom of the Cannonball Express Quad. It's usually uncrowded so plenty of runs are guaranteed. The Upper, Middle and Lower Cannon combo is a run that will make your legs burn.

MOUNTAIN FOOD Food and drink are available at the Tram Valley Station, the Peabody Lounge and the Mountain Station.

HAZARDS AND RULES The mountain's compact nature and watchful patrollers means poaching could result in the pulling of your pass. They're casual on leash rules.

ABOUT TOWN

Franconia is the quintessential sleepy, little hollow. All the necessary stores and facilities are available and the neighbouring townships of Bethlehem and Sugarhill offer more options. Franconia is principally a lodging village and Cannon locals tend to travel into Lincoln or North Woodstock for a big night out.

ACCOMMODATION Country Inns offer a full range of accommodation including B&B, lodges and campgrounds — Tel: 1-800-906 5292. The two most prominent hotels in town are Hillwinds — Tel: 1-800-906 5292, priced from $27.50 per person per night, and the Franconia Inn — Tel: 1-800-473 5299, priced from $49 per person per night. Central Reservations — Tel: 603-823 5661 or 1-800-237 9007.

FOOD There are small-scale grocery stores and take-away joints like Cannonball Pizza who do subs and grinders (sandwiches and rolls). Jerry Garcia is dead but his bread lives on at the Grateful Bread, a patisserie with homebakes.

NIGHTLIFE If you're up for pool and a low key tone, the Dutch Treat Restaurant and Sports Bar beckons. Anything louder and it's the backroads to Lincoln.

OTHER ACTIVITIES The New England Ski Museum.

THANKS TO Ellen Chandler and the Vozzella crew.

For more About Town, see the Loon review p.180.

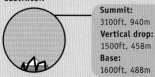

Bretton Woods

THE FACTS

ELEVATION

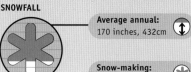

Summit:
3100ft, 940m
Vertical drop:
1500ft, 458m
Base:
1600ft, 488m

SNOWFALL

Average annual:
170 inches, 432cm

Snow-making:
98%

AREA

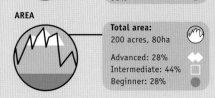

Total area:
200 acres, 80ha

Advanced: 28%
Intermediate: 44%
Beginner: 28%

SEASON

Mid-December — mid-April

COMMUNICATIONS

Web site: http://www.brettonwoods.com
E-mail: skibw@brettonwoods.com
Mountain information:
Tel: 603-278 5000 or 1-800-232 2972

LIFTS AND TICKETS

Number of lifts:
1 high-speed quad, 3 chairlifts,1 surface lift
Lift pass prices:
1/2 day: $23, $24-$29 (weekends and holidays)
1 day: $31, $38 (weekends and holidays)
Multi-day: $80 (3 days)
Season: $630
Other ticketing information:
Night-riding happens in the weekends and holidays
from 4.00pm to 10.00pm; tickets cost $12. See
Loon review p.180 for shared ticket information.

SNOWBOARD SHOPS

Bretton Woods' Rental Shop
Tel: 603-846 5560

SNOWBOARD SCHOOL

Bretton Woods' Snowboard School
Tel: 603-278 5000 or 1-800-232 2972
Group lessons cost $20, private lessons cost $40
and quick tip privates cost $25. Beginner packages
include rental equipment, T-bar ticket and a lesson
for $38.

GETTING THERE

By air: Logan International Airport and Portland
International Jetport are the closest major airports
to Bretton Woods.
By bus: There is no direct bus transportation.
By car: From Boston: Take Interstate 93 north to
Exit 3, Route 3N, onto Route 302 east.
Alternatively take Interstate 95 north to Route 16
north and onto Route 302 west.
From Portland: Take Route 302 west directly to
Bretton Woods.

ON THE MOUNTAIN

Bretton Woods is built to be carved; it has wide open trails and miles of immaculately groomed corduroy fanning out from a single peak. The pitch is not steep but it is consistent and allows riders to paint no-slip grooves all over the mountain. The trails have been ostensibly designed to allow for family cruising, and the mountain layout directs everyone back to the lifts which lie in close proximity to each other. This means less traversing; kids won't get lost and neither will the first-time visitor.

SNOW CONDITIONS The mountain is sheltered and has only been closed once in living memory because of high winds.

FREERIDERS Extensive glading efforts in recent years have meant an increase in the volume of expert-rated terrain. Riders had been using the West Glade for years before the resort recognised the potential and thinned out the area to make the tree riding even better. They have also weeded out the new Black Forest Glade to create 25 acres (ten hectares) of similar lines on the opposite side of the mountain. For more orthodox freeriding, head skier's right from the summit down Zealand and into Darby's Drop. Otherwise head skier's right from the bottom of Zealand, following the rolls and fall-aways leading into Deception Bowl. Watch out for the bumps in the top section and don't get caught plodding on the sedate run-out back to the Bethlehem Express Quad.

FREESTYLERS There is a 400 foot (120 metre) halfpipe, innovatively named Half Pipe, which is well-maintained and regularly sessioned by the locals. Although there's plenty of space for flat-landing tricks and learning to ride switch, there's no funpark to speak of.

CARVERS Bretton's Wood and Range View are long trails; the latter is dotted with tree islands to weave around. Skiers leave the banks on the sides of these trails alone and it's your duty to shred them. Bigger Ben to Big Ben is a popular run serviced by the Bethlehem Express Quad which means more vertical quicker.

MOUNTAIN FOOD The Top o' Quad Restaurant at the top of the Bethlehem Express Quad has food as good as the views with lunch and dinner menus. The Base Lodge is a standard mountain lodge; it has a large open fire, plenty of space for family groups and bar stools for solo mountaineers.

HAZARDS AND RULES A relaxed attitude rules all round.

ABOUT TOWN

The resort is situated on the doorstep of Mount Washington in the valley of the same name. There are a smattering of small towns in the valley: Lincoln and North Woodstock are the major service providers 20 miles (32 kilometres) away. Besides the spectacular, century-old Mount Washington Hotel which was the scene of the famous World War II Bretton Woods Agreement, there's a variety of accommodation, a few eateries and service stations. Visitors to Bretton Woods may choose to stay in Lincoln or North Woodstock which both have 'big city' extravagances such as movie theatres and more restaurants.

ACCOMMODATION Twin Mountain is about five miles (eight kilometres) away. The Pleasant View is a good place to stay; prices range from $34 to $130 — Tel: 603-846 5560 or 1-800-662 9613. Ten to 15 miles (16 to 25 kilometres) further afield in Bethlehem, Franconia or Sugar Hill, an overnight stay can cost as little as $39 per person in one of the roadside B&Bs. Contact Bretton Woods Lodging Agents — Tel: 603-278 1000 or 1-800-258 0330, or Ski 93 Central Reservations — Tel: 1-800-WE SKI 93.

FOOD Though it might not seem so at first glance, there are a number of dining options within a reasonable distance of the resort. Restaurants are dotted along Route 302 and Route 16, the well-beaten path between the resort and North Conway. Variations on the ever popular meat, fish and chicken grill abound. Further south to Conway, you will find Café Noche, Johnathon's Seafood and the Alpenglow Grill where a vegetarian fettucine goes for $9.95 and grilled stuffed beef costs $14.95.

NIGHTLIFE Night-riding from the Top o' the Quad is about it.

OTHER ACTIVITIES Snowmobiling.

THANKS TO Herb Boynton, Ben Wilcox, Karen Finogle.

Waterville Valley

THE FACTS

ELEVATION

Summit:
4004ft, 1222m
Vertical drop:
2020ft, 616m
Base:
1984ft, 605m

SNOWFALL

Average annual:
140 inches, 355cm

Snow-making:
96%

AREA

Total area:
270 acres, 109ha

Advanced: 20% ◆
Intermediate: 60% ☐
Beginner: 20% ●

SEASON

Early November — late April

COMMUNICATIONS

Web site: http://www.waterville.com
E-mail: info@waterville.com
Mountain information:
Tel: 603-236 8311
Fax: 603-236 4344
Chamber of Commerce:
Tel: 1-800-468 8311
Tel: 0-800-969 394 (toll free from Europe)

LIFTS AND TICKETS

Number of lifts:
1 high-speed quad, 7 chairlifts, 4 surface lifts
Lift pass prices:
1/2 day: $27
1 day $37, $44 (holidays)
Multi-day: $155 (5 days)
Season: N/A
Other ticketing information:
Waterville passes will be valid at Booth Creek Resorts in the '97-'98 season. Student tickets cost $25 mid-week and $30 in the weekend (with a valid college ID).

SNOWBOARD SHOPS

Planx — Tel: 603-236 8311
Located next to the Base Lodge, Planx offers a full line of retail equipment, clothing and accessories.

SNOWBOARD SCHOOL

Waterville Valley Snowboard School
Tel: 603-236 8311 ext. 3136
Register at the Ski School desk in the Base Lodge. Beginners' packages, including rental, lift tickets and lessons, start from $49. New for '97-'98 is the Waterville Valley women's clinic in February.

ON THE MOUNTAIN

Waterville Valley was designed in the '60s by Tom Corcoran and he could not have chosen a more picturesque spot. Mount Tecumseh sits amid lush New Hampshire evergreens; snowboarding has taken root here, particularly since the birth of the Boneyard Snowboard Park five seasons ago. Waterville Valley now has four terrain parks and a Pipe Dragon which keeps the new halfpipe in tip-top shape. The '96-'97 season saw the shortening of the high-speed quad, formerly plagued by closure. There is also a new high-speed quad on the Valley Run for the '97-'98 season.

SNOW CONDITIONS Waterville Valley boosts the natural snow base with 100 per cent snow-making. The short summit steeps are very exposed to wind, and the snow often gets blasted off the open trails into cushy drifts near the trees.

FREERIDERS From the Schwendi Hutte, riders can access the parallel Gemma and Ciao runs; both have a consistent pitch and a serious launching pad at their apex. When they're not closed, the Wild Weld Glades that sit off Lower Bobby's Run have great tree riding. The walls on the Oblivion cat-track are good for banked turns and have been unofficially named the Walls of Justice. Go skier's left at the top of the White Peak Express Quad into Tangent, a tight trail that fills up on a deep day.

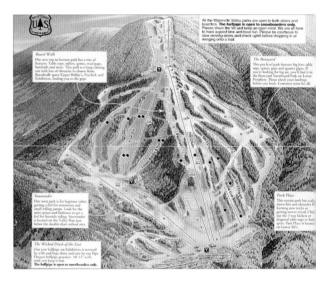

FREESTYLERS 'Stylers are well looked after at Waterville Valley with the choice of four parks: Board Walk, Boneyard, Snowonder and Park Place. Both Snowonder and Park Place are beginner/intermediate areas for training and improving. Board Walk meanders through Upper Bobby's Run and Psyched. It's long and cruisy with table tops, hand rails, rollers, spines and road gaps. Boneyard on Lower Periphery is the pro-level park, loaded with spines, gaps and quarterpipes. It also features a hanger-style hut where riders can warm up and view those sessioning outside on closed-circuit television. The Wicked Ditch of the East is a new halfpipe located above the Base Lodge on Exhibition. It's ten to 12 foot (three to four metre) walls are maintained regularly by a Pipe Dragon.

CARVERS True Grit is the run with the best pitch but maximum radius turns will intersect the mogul field on the left. Utter Abandon and Upper Sel's Choice provide adequate carving terrain.

MOUNTAIN FOOD If you're a family person, the mid-mountain Sunnyside Up café is a great place to go. Schwendi Hutte has lunch on the sundeck and great deli sandwiches. Try the Base Lodge café for breakfasts, Mexican, grills and whatever else is on the daily menu. On the third floor of the Base Lodge, there is the World Cup Bar and Grill for the full sit-down burger meal.

HAZARDS AND RULES There's no obvious policing of leash rules. Those riding the parks and pipes should do so with respect to others or pay in pain.

EVENTS AND COMPETITIONS Each season Waterville kisses winter on the lips with the Grand Opening Jam in their early season park. Later on, they host the BoarderCross and Snowman Jams. To party while you ride, don't miss the fourth annual Boneyard Spring Fling in April. This two day funpark and pipe event attracts the best riders in New England.

Waterville Valley

ABOUT TOWN

You can't get lost at Waterville Valley as all the action is focused around the Town Square in the resort village, a couple of miles down the access road. Shuttle buses run potential revellers and the family-minded to the village and the bulk of local accommodation. The Square is walking distance away and has the requisite restaurants, bars and convenience stores. It feels very new but welcoming nonetheless, thanks to the spectacular surrounding scenery.

ACCOMMODATION Waterville Valley has a 2500 bed base comprised of country inns, condos, lodges and hotels. Off the mountain, a B&B will cost you between $45-$90 with hotels, motels and condos in the same bracket. Waterville Estates Condos offer rooms for $35 per person on a six share basis — Tel: 1-800-222 5064. Waterville Valley Lodging are the agents for accommodation in the valley — Tel: 1-800-468 2553.

FOOD The main attraction must be the Schwendi Hutte, if only for the novel way that diners are delivered to the mid-station restaurant. A specially designed snowcat people-carrier ferries patrons into Chef Jack's domain. There's a selection of gourmet meat and fish dishes. The Hutte seats only 12 at a time so reserve early — Tel: 603-236 8311 ext. 3000. Legends 1291, a rock n' roll sports bar, combines themes with an easy mix of eating, drinking and grooving. Chilli Peppers is close by and has cheap beer at $1.75 for a pint. The place has a chilled-out atmosphere and the food is served in generous spicy-hot portions.

NIGHTLIFE Nightlife is centered around the eating houses with the Legends DJ on sounds duty till the later hours. Some will choose to travel up to Lincoln and North Woodstock for more party options — beware of black ice on the interstate.

OTHER ACTIVITIES Ice-skating at the newly refrigerated rink. The facility, adjacent to the Town Square, is also equipped with a climbing wall. Pack your skateboard and head down to the NuWave indoor skatepark in Laconia, 30 miles (48 kilometres) away.

THANKS TO Matt Gormley and Phil Smith.

Opposite — Avrid Swanson **Photo:** Ed Sawyer **Courtesy:** Waterville Valley
Top — Brian Knox **Photo:** Ed Sawyer **Courtesy:** Waterville Valley
Bottom — Steve Hunt **Photo:** Gary Land

GETTING THERE

By air: Logan International Airport is 130 miles (208 kilometres) away from Waterville Valley. The nearest airport is Manchester, 70 miles (112 kilometres) away, and is serviced by Delta's Business Express — Tel: 1-800-221 1212.
By bus: Lincoln and Woodstock have a shuttle service and taxi but most travel to the resort by car.
By car: From Boston: Take Interstate 93 north to Exit 28, then drive 11 miles (18 kilometres) on Route 49 to the resort village. The trip takes two hours.
From New York City: Take Interstate 91 to Interstate 84, then follow Mass Turnpike to Interstate 290 and onto Interstate 495. Keep heading north on Route 3 to Interstate 93 and turn off at Exit 28.

MAINE

STATE INFORMATION

Population: 1,200,000
Time: Eastern Standard Time = GMT minus 5 hours
Capital city: Augusta
Area: 33,215 sq miles (85694 sqkm)

VISITOR INFORMATION SOURCES
Department of Tourism:
Tel: 207-623 0363
Fax: 207-623 0388
Web site: http://www.mainetourism.com

GETTING AROUND
Main airport: Portland International Jetport —
Tel: 207-772 0690
By train: Amtrak — Tel: 1-800-872 7245
By bus: Greyhound — Tel: 207-772 6587
Road conditions: Tel: 1-800-649 5071
Speed limits: The maximum speed on the road is
65 mph (104 kmph).

MAINE RESORTS
1 **SUGARLOAF**........ 188
2 **SUNDAY RIVER**...... 190

INTRODUCTION

Maine is not all moose watching and lobster shelling. Within Maine's vast forests of pine, spruce and fir, riders are ripping. Logging trucks share the highways with 4x4 family ski-wagons and the odd rusted up Saab, all with quivers of snowboards strapped to the roof. This epitomises the snowboard scene in Maine. Crews of hard-core skaters ride the concrete in the tiny towns dotted throughout the state's interior during the summer months, and rule the mountains in the winter. Sunday River and Sugarloaf are the state's mainstay resorts and are two of the East's finest. Those at Sunday River occasionally gripe at their guinea pig status, as the resort is the flagship for the American Skiing Company and all their test-drives are tried out here first. Changes are normally for the best and others are quick to follow suit.

Main Picture — Courtesy: Sunday River

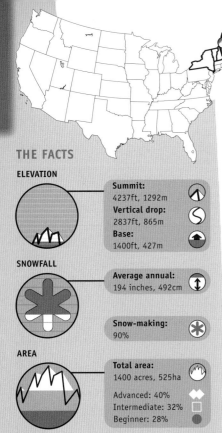

THE FACTS

ELEVATION

Summit:
4237ft, 1292m
Vertical drop:
2837ft, 865m
Base:
1400ft, 427m

SNOWFALL

Average annual:
194 inches, 492cm

Snow-making:
90%

AREA

Total area:
1400 acres, 525ha

Advanced: 40%
Intermediate: 32%
Beginner: 28%

SEASON

Late October — May

COMMUNICATIONS

Snow report: Tel: 207-237 2000 or 207-237 6808
Web site: http://www.sugarloaf.com
E-mail: info@sugarloaf.com
Mountain information:
Tel: 207-237 2000 or 1-800-THE LOAF

LIFTS AND TICKETS

Number of lifts:
1 gondola, 2 high-speed quads, 11 chairlifts,
1 surface lift
Lift pass prices:
1/2 day: $34, $31 (13-18yrs)
1 day: $46, $41 (13-18yrs)
Multi-day: $211 (5 days), $195 (13-18yrs)
Season: $895 (pre-season)
Other ticketing information:
See Sunday River review p.192 for American Skiing
Company transferable deals.

SNOWBOARD SHOPS

Ride on! — Tel: 207-237 2000
Rentals and services at the Base Lodge.

SNOWBOARD SCHOOL

Perfect Turn — Tel: 1-800-THE LOAF
Group lessons start from $25. Learn to Ride
packages, including lift tickets, equipment and
lessons, start from $50.

Sugarloaf

ON THE MOUNTAIN

The Longfellow Mountains sit adjacent to the Bigelow Mountains and the two ranges contribute six of the ten 4000 foot (1216 metre) peaks in Maine. Sugarloaf is the second highest peak in the state. The marketers have tagged Sugarloaf 'one big mother', and the mountain is certainly is that. The feature that first impresses is the tree-barren summit, serviced by the new Timberline Quad. Trails splay down the mountain and create a criss-cross pattern of traditional New England paths and broader, speed-inducing motorways. Sugarloaf's boundary to boundary policy means all the terrain is fair game and this makes an already big mountain bigger.

SNOW CONDITIONS High altitude, a north-facing aspect, and the most northerly latitude of any East Coast resort adds up to a high natural snowfall that lasts well into the season.

FREERIDERS From the top of the new Timberline Quad, hit the Binder ridge run, cut off-trail into the woods and re-enter about 50 yards (40 metres) further down the trail. The run is loaded with kickers and powder banks. Double Bitter is narrower than the parallel Tote Road, so it fills up on powder days. The Snowfields runs are great when there's enough good snow and the wind isn't blowing, otherwise they're the preserve of skiers who like to slide on ice. The best glades are found off King's Landing or ask a local to show you the Broccoli Gardens. Ripsaw, Bubblecuffer and Upper Winter's Way are rarely groomed and have natural obstacles and hits. Watch for beginners when exiting King Pine Bowl.

FREESTYLERS The halfpipe is awesome. It's 500 feet by 30 feet (152 metres by nine metres) and boasts 12 foot (three and a half metre) walls. Crazy Eddy upkeeps the park, grooming it daily with a Pipe Dragon. The pipe is above the seven acre (two and a half hectare) terrain park which has plenty of gaps, boardercross banks and table tops to huck. The configuration is altered regularly to keep the hucksters guessing.

CARVERS Tote Road is used by riders as an ideal warm-up run as it's a wide open cruiser with a few rolls. King's Landing is much the same but steeper, and a few of the whales will throw you far. If you turn off Tote Road onto Competition Hill, Skidder or Upper Narrow Gauge, be prepared to encounter ski racers including US team members — potential for trouble.

HAZARDS AND RULES You are not supposed to ride the groomer access road between Tote Road and Scoot but some do after a dump and some have passes pulled. No leash hassles here.

EVENTS AND COMPETITIONS The biggest snowboarding event at Sugarloaf is the US Snowboard Grand Prix, an Olympic qualifying event. They also host the US National Freestyle and National Alpine Championships. The Boarderfest features a big air event, halfpipe competition and boardercross.

1

ABOUT TOWN

Sugarloaf Village is situated at the end of the Carrabasset Valley. It's definitely off the beaten track and for that reason the resort has been well-planned. The village is centred around the Base Lodge, flanked by the impressive Sugarloaf Mountain Hotel, the Gondola Village and the Sugarloaf Inn. A little further down the road is the Sports and Fitness Centre. In between the community buildings lie the condos, the majority of which are hidden away behind fir trees. The self-sufficient complex means trips into the nearest town of Kingfield, some 15 miles (24 kilometres) away, can be limited if not avoided altogether.

ACCOMMODATION Of the 9600 beds available, 7500 are located at the resort village with the rest in and around Kingfield. The resort has a number of lodging packages including the Reggae Ski Week with lift tickets, lessons, lodging and health club privileges from $69.95 mid-week or $89.95 in the weekends. The Sugarloaf Mountain Hotel is for those who need the trappings of cable television and fully equipped kitchens; rooms go for $100-$220 — Tel: 207-237 2222. The Sugarloaf Inn is less lavish and rooms cost $120-$152 — Tel: 207-237 2000. The board-to-door Gondola Village at the bottom of the Gondola trail by the Whiffle Quad has more accommodation options; a three bedroom condo starts from $243. On-mountain reservations — Tel: 1-800-843 5623 or 1-800-THE LOAF. Off-mountain reservations — Tel: 1-800-843 2732 or 1-800-THE AREA.

FOOD The Double Diamond Restaurant at the Sugarloaf Mountain Hotel is popular with both house guests and visitors, as is the Seasons Restaurant at the Sugarloaf Inn. Geppetto's has a greenhouse out back, a new slant on the garden bar concept. A cosy front bar caters for the overspill. The Bag and Kettle is the spot for quick eats at the end of the day or a casual burger and fries dinner. A good quarter of a mile down the road are the Porter House for fine dining and the Carrabasset Valley Yacht Club for a laid-back, fireside atmosphere.

NIGHTLIFE Nightlife is restricted by the resort's isolated location although visiting live acts do have a tidy venue at the Widowmaker. Otherwise it's party at the restaurants after dinner or bed.

OTHER ACTIVITIES Ice fishing, snowmobiling dogsledding, snowshoeing, ice-skating. Guest services — Tel: 207-237 6939.

THANKS TO Heather Smith, Mark Latti and Jake Kilberth at Ride On!

Top — **Courtesy:** Sugarloaf

GETTING THERE

By air: The closest airport is Portland International Jetport. A shuttle transfer costs $90 a round trip — Tel: 207-237 2000 or 1-800-THE LOAF.
By car: From Boston, take Interstate 95 to Portland and then the Maine Turnpike to Exit 12. Follow Route 4 north through Farmington and pick up Route 27 to Kingfield and Sugarloaf.
Getting around: A shuttle service runs regularly.

Sunday River

THE FACTS

ELEVATION

Summit:
3140ft, 958m
Vertical drop:
2340ft, 713m
Base:
800ft, 244m

SNOWFALL

Average annual:
155 inches, 393cm

Snow-making:
92%

AREA

Total area:
645 acres, 260ha

Advanced: 38%
Intermediate: 36%
Beginner: 26%

SEASON
Mid-October — late May

COMMUNICATIONS
Snow report: Tel: 207-824 5200
Web site: http://www.sundayriver.com
E-mail: snowtalk@sundayriver.com
Mountain information:
Tel: 207-824 3000 or 1-800-543 2SKI
Bethel Area Chamber of Commerce:
Tel: 207-824 3585

LIFTS AND TICKETS
Number of lifts:
4 high-speed quads, 15 chairlifts, 2 surface lifts
Lift pass prices:
1/2 day: $34
1 day: $46
Multi-day: $212 (5 days)
Season: $1150, $925 (before October 14)
Other ticketing information:
The Magnificent 7 Pass costs $273 for seven days
boarding at any combination of the American
Skiing Company resorts and is valid for one year.
The seven resorts are Sunday River, Pico,
Killington, Mount Snow, Sugarbush, Attitash and
Sugarloaf. An All-Mountain Season Pass costs
$1099 pre-season and the Edge frequent skier
programme applies to all seven resorts — Tel:
1-800-621-MTNS for more details on
interchangeable programmes.

SNOWBOARD SHOPS
Ride On! — Tel: 207-824 3000
The focal point for all riders is the shop south of
the Ridge Base Lodge.

SNOWBOARD SCHOOL
Sunday River Snowboard School
Tel: 207-824 3000
The Perfect Turn Programme offers lessons from
$25 for a group lesson or $55 for a private clinic.

ON THE MOUNTAIN

Eight interconnected peaks, state-of-the-art snow-making and an efficient lift system that boasts no less than nine quads are the distinguishing features of Sunday River. Expanding westward over recent years, the resort has been prepared to experiment with trail design as the gladed Oz and Jordan Bowl areas show. Terrain and lift development seem to have always kept one step ahead of increasing numbers on the mountain. Even now with nearly 600,000 visitors a season, the queues are light and trails relatively uncrowded.

SNOW CONDITIONS Comprehensive snow-making and a dependable water supply have allowed the resort to expand across neighbouring mountains; such is the effectiveness of the system that it seems Sunday River could stretch even further and confidently maintain cover. The resort's northerly latitude makes up for its low altitude.

FREERIDERS The Chutzpah and Hardball glades on White Cap Peak are demanding and freeriders can get similar thrills further west around Oz and Jordan Bowl. Revolutionary for the eastern mountains, Blind Ambition is a wide, gladed run parallel to Excalibur and Rogue Angel in Jordan Bowl. Oz pushes the idea further with a mix of gladed trails and wider runs with tree islands dotted throughout. The most recent gladed creation is the Flyin' Monkey, between the Cyclone and Emerald City trails. The Celestial glades on Aurora Peak are a paradise after a snowfall, as are the Airglow and Black Hole runs which both require a fair degree of respect. You'll find the resort's largest tree riding area on Barker Mountain where the trees in Last Tango grow tighter as you descend. You have an out if the going gets too tough; head skier's right onto the Right Stuff trail.

FREESTYLERS The lighted halfpipe is where the kids gravitate after the lifts have stopped running. It's located on the Tempest Trail on White Cap Mountain and is kept in good nick by a Pipe Dragon. Sunday River have steered away from large 'boarder only' funparks, electing instead to scatter all the usual elements around the resort. The rationale is that skiers and boarders will assimilate (ever see a skier ride a spine?) and 'snowboard ghettos' will be eliminated. The mini-parks stretch from White Cap Mountain to Aurora Peak and you'll find table tops, quarterpipes, spines and ramps. These hits are sculpted by the new Kassbohrer halfpipe blade, the first of its kind in North America.

CARVERS The terrain here is a pretty picture for carve-heads. The winding, snail-trail patterns of the older New England resorts have been superseeded by super highways like White Heat, Right Stuff and Downdraft. North Peak's Escapade and Grand Rapids are less steep but also well-suited for carvers.

MOUNTAIN FOOD The South Ridge Base Lodge has a Food Court that is tops for breakfast with freshly baked muffins and pastries and good lunchtime fodder. Barker Mountain Base Lodge has a cafeteria as does White Cap Lodge. Neither one is as tasty as the Food Court but the food does the trick.

HAZARDS AND RULES The patrollers like to know what's going on, so if you build a hit on trail (as many do), save hassles by having a word with them and they'll be cool.

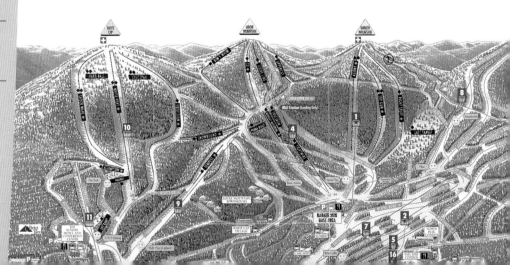

Sunday River

ABOUT TOWN

Sunday River resort lies six miles (ten kilometres) north of Bethel, the main service town. Bethel is a typical New England township with grand historical buildings. The austere ambience is being offset, not in a bad way, by the development of the town's new facilities. The train station complex has a four-screen movie theatre with a new restaurant and you can expect more of the same in the near future. Many visitors choose to spend their entire stay on the mountain for a couple of reasons: the road into town can be treacherous and the amenities on the mountain cater for all needs.

ACCOMMODATION The Summit Hotel has double rooms from $109 — Tel: 802-824 3500. Across the road are the Snow Cap Inn and the Snow Cap Ski Dorm, both offering affordable lodgings that are well-patronised; prices for a double room start from $110 and dorms start from $25-$35. Call the Summit Hotel for reservations. Hundreds of condos are scattered throughout the resort. Again, most are functional rather than funky but their proximity to the lifts more than makes amends. Central Reservations — Tel: 1-800-543 2754.

FOOD Dining out at Sunday River means either eating on the mountain, heading to Bethel or settling for the Brew Pub on Route 2. The slopeside favourite must be Legend's Restaurant which occupies a large ground floor space in the Summit Hotel. Filling meals are served at the South Ridge Base Lodge. The Walsh and Hill Trading Company serve steaks and salads in low key surroundings. On Bethel's main street, the Sudbury Inn has forged a reputation as one of the best in town. The budget conscious are likely to opt for Sud's Pub, crouched downstairs with a cosy, familiar feel. Other options on Bethel's main street are Mother's, Skidder's Pub and the highly touted Matterhorn.

NIGHTLIFE Things tend to wind up fairly early in this neck of the woods, so it makes sense to start early. If there's nothing happening at the Bumps Bar in the White Cap Lodge, then chances are it's a Tuesday evening or everyone's down at the Brew Pub on Route 2. Aim for the Backstage Bar in Bethel if you're up for pool.

OTHER ACTIVITIES Ice-skating, tubing, cross-country skiing, snowshoeing, sleigh rides and a video arcade.

THANKS TO Kathleen Willis, Michael Bertie, Drew at Sunday River TV, Christine Johnson.

Opposite — Surfin' at the Sunday River Slush Cup **Courtesy:** Sunday River

Top — Night-riding **Courtesy:** Sunday River

GETTING THERE

By air: Portland International Jetport is a 90 minute drive away.
By bus: There is no bus service to the greater Sunday River area.
By car: From Boston and New York City: Take Interstate 95 north to Portland, follow the Maine Turnpike north to Exit 11 and then pick up Route 26 north to Bethel. From Montreal: Take Autoroute 10 east to Route 55 south which becomes Route 91 in Vermont. Head south to Saint Johnsbury and pick up Route 2 east to Bethel.

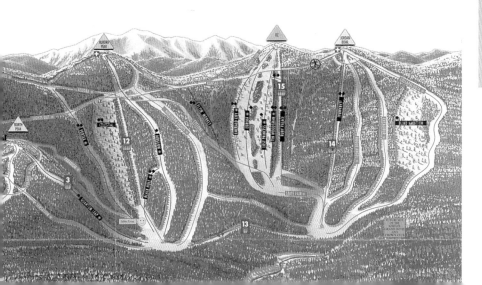

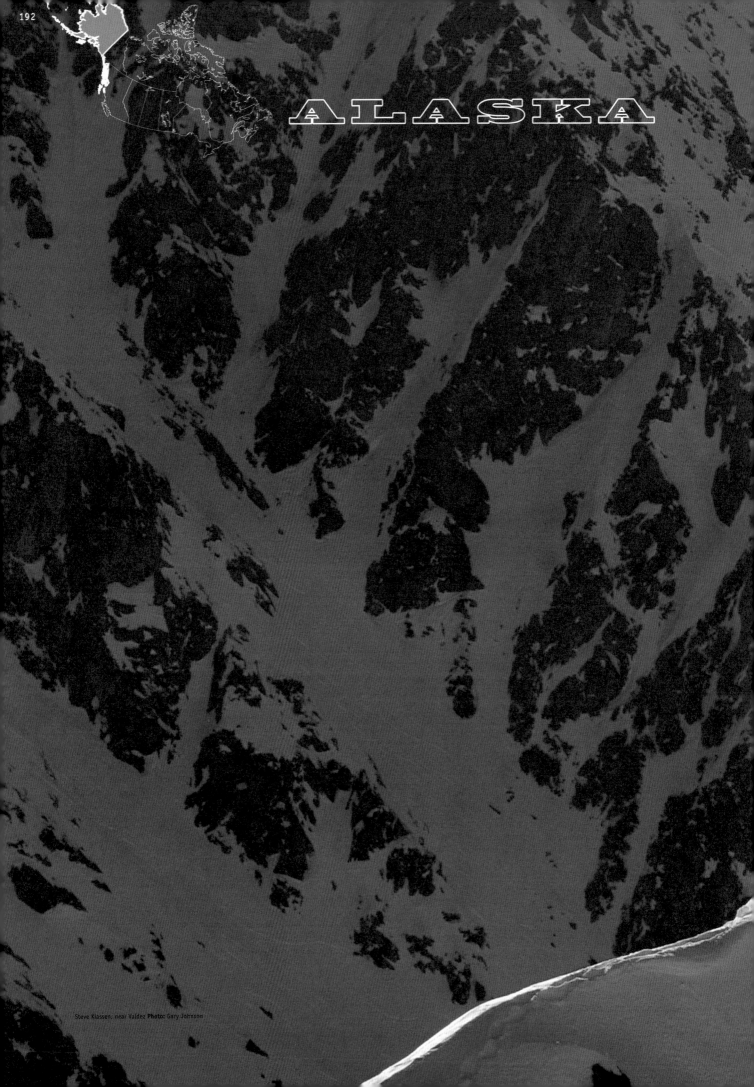

ALASKA

Steve Klassen, near Valdez **Photo:** Gary Johnson

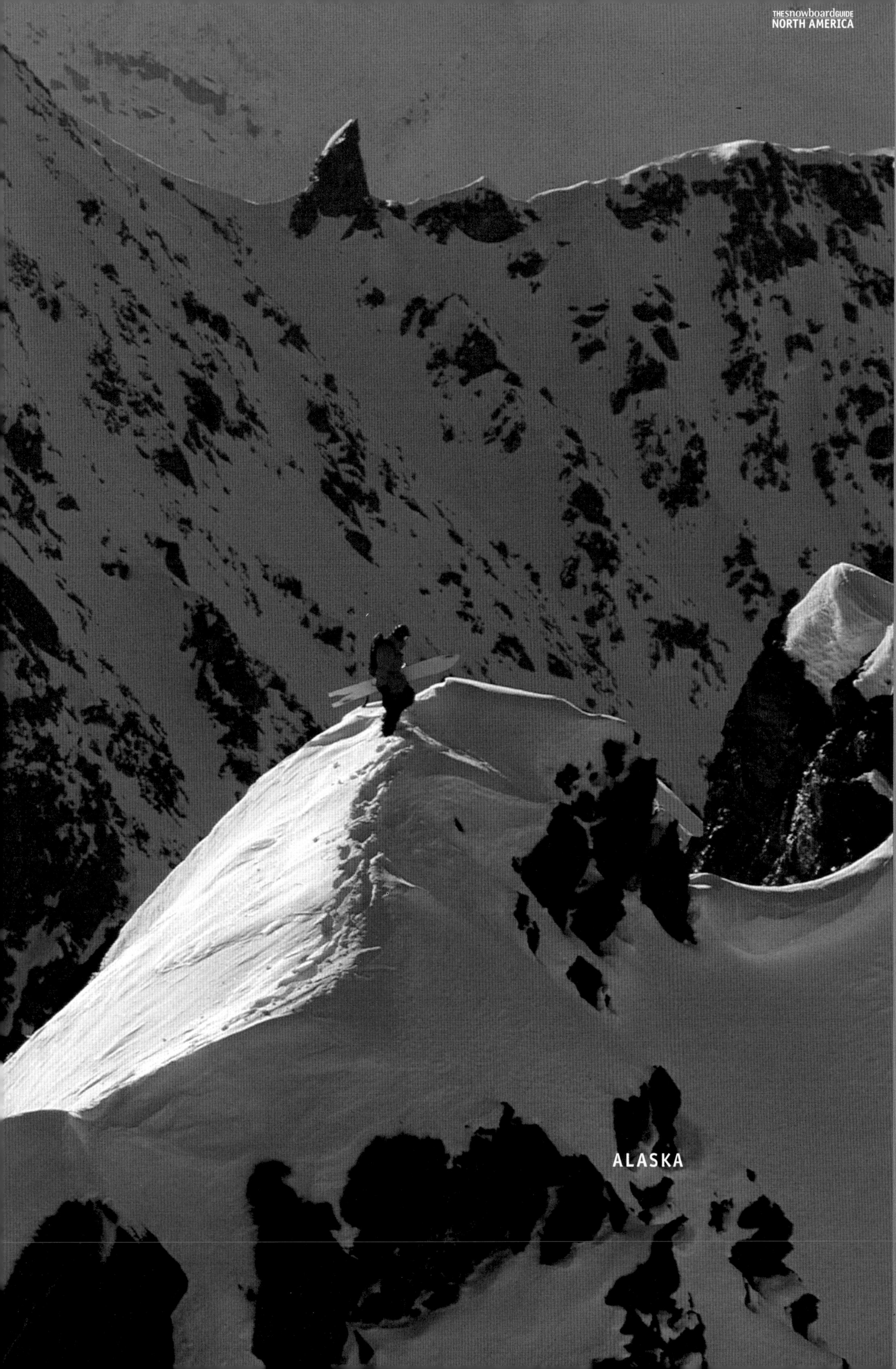

ALASKA

196

ALASKA

STATE INFORMATION

Population: 599,200
Time: Pacific Standard Time = GMT minus 8 hours
Capital city: Juneau
Area: 586,412 sq miles (1,512,943 sqkm)

VISITOR INFORMATION SOURCES

Alaska Wilderness Tourism Association:
Tel: 907-463 3038
Fax: 907-463 3280
E-mail: awrta@alaska.net
Web site: http://www.alaska.net/~awrta

GETTING AROUND

Main airport: Anchorage — Tel: 907-274 3531
By train: Alaska Railroad Corporation — Tel: 907-265 2323 or 1-800-544 0552
By bus: Seward Bus Line — Tel: 907-224 3608
Road conditions: Alaska Travel Hotline — Tel: 1-900-407 2222
Speed limits: You can drive up to 75 mph (120 kmph).

Opposite — Adam Hostetter, between a rock and a hard place
Photo: Greg von Doersten

Right — Frost heaves, Alaska roads **Photo:** Tim Rainger

THE ALASKAN HIGHWAY

The Alaskan Highway, sometimes referred to as the Alcan, is a two lane road that winds and rolls across the wilderness. It runs 1520 miles (2464 kilometres) through Canada and Alaska from Dawson's Creek, British Columbia, through Yukon territory to Fairbanks, Alaska, and is open and maintained year-round. The road was built in eight months in '42 to supply a land route for equipment and supplies by the US Army, and is still considered an engineering marvel. There are few steep grades except between Fort Nelson and Watson Lake, where the road crosses the Rocky Mountains. The road is asphalt, its condition ranging from poor to excellent; watch for frost heaves at all times. It's advisable to drive slowly in affected sections to avoid breaking an axle. Gas, food and lodging is found between 20 and 50 miles (80 kilometres) on average, but the longest stretch without services is about 100 miles (160 kilometres).

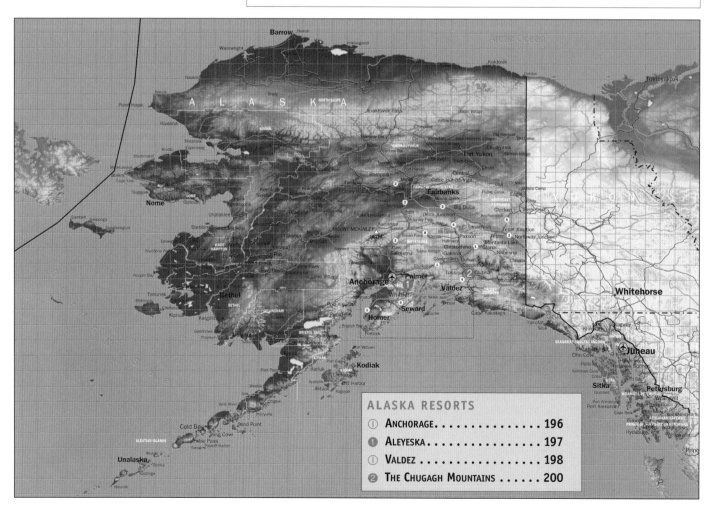

ALASKA RESORTS

INTRODUCTION

The wild west of 1880s America fringed the length of the Rockies from Colorado to British Columbia. It represented a frontier of kinds; a thin line between the relentless march of European civilisation and a hitherto wild, untamed region. Alaska is North America's remaining frontier and in many ways akin to the wild west of old. Alaskan rules are different to those further south and are less stringently enforced — as you'll hear: 'Alaska rules because there are none.'

Five per cent of the land-mass is comprised of glaciers and the raddest riding is found on the sharp, steep terrain which has been gorged out by these ice-masses, and further deformed by earthquakes. You can snowboard in many parts of Alaska year-round if you're prepared to hike, but the main commercial focus for riders are Valdez and Aleyeska. While Aleyeska is a small destination resort of some repute, Valdez offers a completely different experience via helicopter, light plane and now snowcat. The Thompson Pass received nearly 75 feet (23 metres) of snow in '64 and the area has a yearly average that's way higher than other North American resorts. Owing to the low elevation of many of the most ridden peaks and their proximity to the ocean, the snow tends to stick to seemingly impossible slopes. Despite rather harrowing evidence to the contrary, there are few killer grizzlies, not everyone is a Vietnam vet and not all the terrain is on 50 degree slopes.

Anchorage

Anchorage

THE FACTS

VISITOR INFORMATION SOURCES
Anchorage Visitor's Centre — Tel: 907-274 3531.

GETTING THERE
By air: If you're going to Valdez or Aleyeska, Anchorage is the first stop for all planes from the US or Canada. Delta Airlines fly to Anchorage — Tel: 1-800-221 1212.
By sea: BC Ferries provide a vehicle and passenger service between Port Hardy on Vancouver Island, Canada and Prince Rupert, via Haines and Juneau — Tel: 604-386 3431.

VEHICLE RENTAL
If you're renting a car or a van from Anchorage, there are a few options ranging from rent-a-wreck cars to luxury RV vehicles capable of housing, feeding and sleeping five or more people. It all depends on the size of your group, the depth of your wallet and what you're planning to do. Some motorhome companies to try are: The Great Alaskan Holidays — Tel: 907-248 7777 or 1-888-225 2752, ABC Motorhome Rentals (located at Anchorage International Airport) — Tel: 907-279 2000, Alaska Panorama — Tel: 907-562 1401, Clippership Motorhome Rentals — Tel: 907-562 7051 and Go Alaska — Tel: 907-248 7784. For car rental call Arctic Rent-a-Car — Tel: 907-561 2990, Denali Cars — Tel: 907-276 1230, Rent-a-Wreck — Tel: 907-562 5499, Pay-less Car Rental — Tel: 907-243 3616 or Dollar Rent-a-Car — Tel: 907-248 5388 or 1-800-800 400.

ABOUT TOWN

Anchorage and the Kenai Peninsular make up an area known as South Central. In '95 Anchorage's population broke the 250,000 mark for the first time, making it about half the entire state population. Anchorage is the kick-off point to stock-up and get prepared to venture further into Alaska's wild terrain.

ACCOMMODATION Accommodation is available at over 70 hotels and 100 B&Bs. The Day's Inn is central and mid-priced at $68 per night — Tel: 907-276 7226. The Red Ram Motel is pretty cheap costing between $45 and $70 a night. Even cheaper accommodation can be found at either Anchorage Hostelling International with dorm beds from $15 a night — Tel: 907-276 3635, or the International Backpackers' Inn and Hostel with dorm beds from $12-$15. For other options, contact the Visitor's Centre — Tel: 907-274 3531.

FOOD The 'in' place is the Moose Tooth, which serves up gourmet pizza and microbrews. The best Thai food in town is found at the Thai Kitchen. It's a small place with enticing, spicy smells wafting up from the Thai grocery store in the front; the tiny restaurant is out the back with five or six tables. For a wholefood kick, the Middle Way Café sits beside camping giant REI. You can choose from a menu of gabanza beans, humus and all the healthy standards. If you need to get a feel for what's happening on the snowboard scene, the Roosevelt Café is the hang-out complete with a Seattle-grunge crew. They sell beer and have the occasional live band.

NIGHTLIFE To get a feel for Anchorage, head to the Pioneer Bar downtown on 4th Ave. It's not as rough as some of the other downtown bars, but still has a colourful local scene. The crowd is young and hip, and the place rocks from 9.00pm till 2.00am. The place has pool tables and an old junkie juke-box. The Bird Creek Brewery tour on Thursday or Friday costs $5, and you get tickets for three freshly brewed pints. A pint normally costs $3-$4 in this city, so the brewery is a good way to get a head start on the weekend. Anchorage isn't a big clubbing destination but the Wave has DJs spinning tunes for a mixed gay and straight crowd.

THANKS TO Chris Miller and Mary Carol.

SNOWBOARD SHOPS
Boarderline Snowboard Shop
Tel: 907-562 7972 (Anchorage)
You'd be foolish to come through Anchorage and not pass by the Liska brothers' snowboard shop at 5011 Arctic Boulevard. They have all the info you could want as well as additional shops in Gridwood and Juneau.

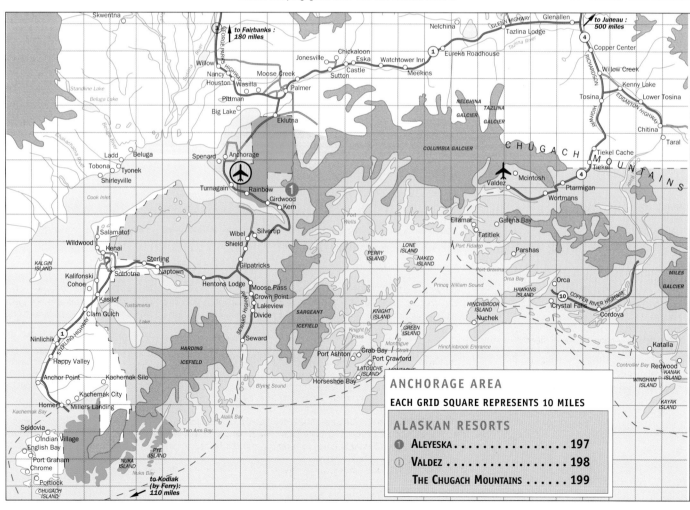

ANCHORAGE AREA
EACH GRID SQUARE REPRESENTS 10 MILES

Aleyeska

Aleyeska

Aleyeska

THE FACTS

ELEVATION

Summit:
2750ft, 838m
Vertical drop:
2500ft, 762m
Base:
250ft, 76m

SNOWFALL

Average annual:
583 inches, 1480cm

Snow-making:
12%

AREA

Total area:
786 acres, 317ha

Advanced: 17%
Intermediate: 71%
Beginner: 12%

SEASON
Mid-November — mid-April

COMMUNICATIONS
Snow report: Tel: 970-754 7669
Mountain information:
Tel: 907-754 2285
Fax: 907-754 2200

LIFTS AND TICKETS
Number of lifts:
1 high-speed quad, 6 chairlifts, 1 aerial tram
Lift pass prices:
1/2 day: $27, $21 (14-17yrs)
1 day: $39, $24 (14-17yrs)
Multi-day: $60 (2 days)
Season pass: $925
Other ticketing information:
Night-riding happens on Fridays and Saturdays
from 4.30pm to 9.30pm. A night ticket costs $16.

SNOWBOARD SHOPS
World Cup Sports — Tel: 907-783 2282

SNOWBOARD SCHOOL
Aleyeska Ski School — Tel: 907-754 2285
Group lessons include a two hour class, rental
equipment and lift tickets from $40 for a beginner
and $60 for intermediate to advanced riders.

GETTING THERE FROM ANCHORAGE
By air: Anchorage International Airport provides
transfers; book through guest services at a cost of
$25 one-way.
By car: Aleyeska is 40 miles (64 km) south-east of
Anchorage on the stunning Seward Highway.
Getting around: The resort offers a free shuttle
between the Westin Aleyeska Prince Hotel and the
base of the ski area near the Day Lodge. You don't
need a car as the village centre is near the carpark.

ON THE MOUNTAIN

Aleyeska is an Aleut Indian word meaning 'great land of white to the east', and is the origin of
the name Alaska. Travelling east from Anchorage is half the buzz; the drive along the Seward
Highway around the Turnagain Arm is wild. On one side of the road, huge ice floes heave up out
of the sea like ocean liners, and on the other mountains thrust up towards the sky. Aleyeska
resort reflects these extremes; the base sits at sea level, while the upper reaches are well
beyond the tree line. The mountain is a series of ridges and bowls with the outer areas
consisting of steep open slopes, chutes and gullies. Opened in the '96-'97 season, the North
Face of Mount Aleyeska consists of more than 300 acres (120 hectares) of double black
diamond terrain, offering hard-core powderhounds a naturally segregated playground. Glacier
Bowl is another radical area, home to the World Extreme preliminary trials.

SNOW CONDITIONS As the mountain is at sea level, Aleyeska is actually not as cold as you'd expect; day
temperatures are warmer than Colorado. The resort is sometimes prone to wet snow and coastal fog.

FREERIDERS Aleyeska has plenty of hits, natural pipes and steeps. From the top of the mountain, you can
plunder the North Face and ride the Tram back up. The North Face is a great area for big mountain carving,
or head for the Far Side trail, which has some nice, natural halfpipes. When conditions allow and the areas
are open, the best in-bounds hiking is found on the Headwall, Chilkoot Ridge or Glacier Bowl. For great
stashes of pow, take the High Traverse over to the double black diamond slopes of Max's. Check their open
status first: the steep terrain is prone to avalanche. The South Face has some great runs, particularly the
steeps and trees off Lolo's and Gear Jammer. For natural pipes and jumps, Silvertip is a choice run.

FREESTYLERS In addition to the natural terrain features, the resort has a new Glacier Reef Terrain Park at
the top of Chairlift 6 near the bottom of Glacier Bowl. There is good air to be had off the berms, table tops
and quarter hits. Natural hits lurk on Mighty Mite and Trapline, skier's right of the Spirit Quad. The South
Face also has some great terrain; Mambo and Denali have hits and kickers off the banks all the way down.

CARVERS Aleyeska has long, groomed runs with a consistent fall-line conducive to carving. A wicked leg-
burner starts with Silvertip down to Runaway, and onto Upper and Lower Race trails. Main Street funnels
down to Ego Flats and Klondick for a long-haul fest, which shreds nearly the entire vertical of the mountain.

MOUNTAIN FOOD If you're up the mountain and ravenous, the Glacier Express in the Upper Tram Terminal
has snacks, soups and burgers. The Seven Glacier Restaurant in the same building has classy food and
radical views — it's open on Fridays and Saturdays for dinner. The Sitzmark Bar near the base of Chair 3 has
après-ski shenanigans, beer and live entertainment.

HAZARDS AND RULES Fast or reckless riding is punished by pass-pulling. Entering the in-bounds terrain
from outside the boundary is illegal.

EVENTS AND COMPETITIONS Aleyeska hosts the Alaska Extreme Skiing and Snowboarding Trial, a qualifier
for the real thing in Valdez.

ABOUT TOWN

Aleyeska Resort was the site of one of Alaska's first gold strikes. It has preserved some of its
frontier charm: pick-up trucks out-number four wheel drives and most restaurants serve up
reindeer burgers and feisty caribou steaks. Tourism is the town's focus, and with a small
population of 1000 people, faces will become familiar after a couple of days.

ACCOMMODATION The Westin Aleyeska Prince Hotel is a 307 room deluxe, chateau-style hotel. Packages include
lift tickets for $29 — Tel: 907-754 1111. There are several B&Bs, as well as condos which can be rented from Aleyeska
Accommodations — Tel: 907-783 2000 or the Aleyeska Booking Company — Tel: 907-783 4386. If you plan to stay
in Anchorage, the Chamber of Commerce can give you information on lodgings — Tel: 907-272 2401.

FOOD The Westin Aleyeska Prince Hotel has several restaurants including the Pond Café and the Katsura
Teppanyaki, a Japanese steakhouse serving fresh seafood and grilled steaks. The Bake Shop near the base of
Chair 3 has all-you-can-eat soups served with fresh rolls — in the evenings it's a good place for a beer. Pizza,
hamburgers, pasta and nightly specials are served up at the Chair 5 Restaurant in the Girdwood town centre.
The Double Musky restaurant on Crow Creek Mine Road is an excellent choice for Cajun cookery.

NIGHTLIFE The Sitzmark Bar, near the base of Chair 3, is an ideal après hang-out with live entertainment in
the weekends, a pool table and game room. Max's, on Crow Creek Mine Road, has live bands and a grooving
dance floor. Chair 5 Restaurant has pool tables and cold beers.

OTHER ACTIVITIES Ice-skating, winter glacier and wildlife cruises, sight-seeing, snowmobiling.

THANKS TO Alison Knox.

VALDEZ
CHAMBE
VISITOR'S PARK
ONLY

CHEVRON MISSISSIPPI

HELENKA B

Valdez

ABOUT TOWN

The current population of Valdez is 10,000 and the town has a good range of services and facilities for such an out-of-it place. You'll find half-a-dozen hotels, a few bars, restaurants, cafés, and tackle and bait shops.

ACCOMMODATION There are five hotels operating in Valdez along with over 40 B&Bs. The Totem Inn is the slightly beat-up heart of the snowboard scene. It's exactly how you expected it would be, with super friendly, unassuming staff and a kitchen that knocks out wicked cooked breakfasts, as well as a range of traditional lunches and dinners by the fire. There are usually a lot of long, slow hours to kill in between riding sessions and not surprisingly the bar is well-propped up all night. The pinball machine also takes a hammering. Cheap, clean rooms cost $59 per person per night — Tel: 907-835 4443. The Downtown B&B is probably the cheapest place to stay; it has a kitchen and other facilities for $40-$60 a night — Tel: 907-935 5406. Valdez Visitor's Bureau — Tel: 907-835 835 2984 or 1-800-770 5954.

FOOD The Valdez Café features seafood specials, vegetarian delights and baked desserts. On the main street, the Fu Kung does fine sushi among other Chinese dishes. The supermarket is handy if you're self catering or need lunch supplies. Oscar's does unreal breakfasts; try the fruit and nut pancakes, or the big bacon and egg fry up.

NIGHTLIFE Very little really... what there is revolves around drinking and eating your way through long, Arctic spring evenings.

OTHER ACTIVITIES Valdez Harbour Boat and Tackle rentals, on the main pier, hire boats, rods and tackle for excursions into the sound. Red snapper, halibut and cod are out there all year, with the first king salmon coming in mid-May — Tel: 907-835 5002. The indoor driving range is a good laugh.

THANKS TO Tom Thibedeau, Doug Brewer, Dave the Wave, and Dave Lee for their insanely kind co-operation; Danny for his soulful guiding, Nik Perata for total attitude.

All photos: Tim Rainger

LEGEND

Jeff Galbraith, Senior Editor of Snowboarder, has described Valdez as 'a town without pity'. The town has, over the years, been both blessed and cursed.

It's original strategic importance was as Alaska's northern-most ice-free port. Gold-mining and timber-milling were key money-spinners for 50 years earlier this century, and the fisheries industry was also immensely valuable, reaching its peak in the '40s when nearly ten million salmon were pulled out of the Pacific annually. Valdez was confirmed as the terminus of the All Alaska Pipeline on July 17, '73, when Spiro Agnew cast the deciding vote in congress two weeks before resigning office on corruption charges. Bypassing existing environmental legislation, this umbilical cord connects Valdez to the largest oil field in North America, 801 miles (1281 kilometres) north. When the pipeline opened in 1977, Valdez went from being an insignificant coastal town to the fourth busiest port in the US, and the largest in terms of oil tonnage.

Two major disasters have struck Valdez in the last 25 years. In an extreme twist of the odds, both happened on a Good Friday. The first occurred on March 27, '64, when an earthquake measuring a staggering 9.2 on the Richter scale caused a massive section of the American plate to lurch up and over the Pacific plate. The shock waves were felt for 500,000 square miles (1,295,000 square kilometres) and 100,000 square miles (259,000 square kilometres) of land were deformed. The death toll stood at 133 people, 33 of them killed in Valdez. Nearby Montague Island in Prince William Sound was raised over 35 feet (11 metres), Chenega Island was uplifted five feet and shifted 52 feet (16 metres) to the south. Tidal waves up to 170 feet (52 metres), caused by undersea landslides, destroyed the Valdez harbour and several other towns in the sound. After the earthquake, Valdez relocated five miles (eight kilometres) west.

Alarm bells for the second catastrophe began ringing a decade in advance, but the oil consortiums and congress blindly failed to heed the repeated warnings of conservationists and local fishermen. When the Exxon Valdez steamed into Queen Charlotte Sound on Good Friday, March 24, '89, and ripped her guts open on Bligh Reef, Valdez hit the world news in full technicolour. While Exxon and the world sat and watched for three days, 11.2 million gallons (50.9 million litres) of crude Prudhoe oil drifted in a slick through the sound and out into the Gulf of Alaska. The initial clean-up took five months and involved 11,000 people, 1,100 boats and 100 light aircraft and choppers. The fiasco ended with a $100 million clean-up bill and a $900 million civil claim pending against Exxon, payable to the state and federal governments.

GETTING THERE

By air: You can fly from Anchorage to Valdez but it's spendy — Tel: 970-276 7234 or 1-800-276 7234.
By sea: For information about how to get to Valdez by sea call the Alaska Marine Highway Ferry System — Tel: 907-235 8449 or 1-800-323 5757.
By bus: There's no public transport in the winter; the easiest way to get around is by hitching.
By car: The route from Anchorage is a 304 mile (486 kilometre) asphalt road with nearly continuous frost heaves. It's kept open all year-round.

THE FACTS

VISITOR INFORMATION SOURCES

Valdez Visitor's Bureau:
Tel: 907-835 2984 or 1-800-770 5954
E-mail: valdez@alaska.net

ALASKA BACK-COUNTRY ADVENTURES (ABA)

Tel: 907-835 5608
E-mail: bcountry@ptialaska.net.

ABA is the longest running, and most established heli-operation, remaining the carrier of choice of the King of the Hill extreme competition. Doug Brewer and Tom Thibedeau fly snow-planes and choppers in the Thompson Pass, about 30 miles (48 kilometres) from Valdez. ABA consider themselves an aerial taxi with a mandatory guide service, but stress they don't just service extreme terrain. The operational centre is a cluster of portable housing, with Tom's big motorhome parked next door. There are no facilities other than basic toilets and a few drinks. The billing system they employ uses chips costing $65 for one heli flight. They only run full choppers and won't fly incomplete groups so jockeying for places is a bit of an art. You see lonesome cowboys cruising the carparks and bars, approaching groups in an effort to score a spare seat. The record number of runs in a day is 19, held by the notorious Richie Fowler. The plane is cheaper than the chopper ($35 per lift) and can land you in unreal, open powder bowls with mellow descents of up to 3000 vertical feet (984 metres).

TSAINA LODGE

Tel: 907-835 3500

Tsaina Lodge, located a few miles further from Valdez, is now the centre of operations for Doug Coombes, aka 'the Grand Coomba', who used to be the head guide at ABA in its early days. It's a top-end place to stay and is skier-orientated due to Doug's legendary reputation as an extreme skier.

H2O HELI ADVENTURES

Tel: 1-800-578-HELI

H2O Heli Adventures are run by Dean Cummings. They fly A-Stars and specialise in the coastal peaks near Valdez. H2O also offer sea kayaking, ice-climbing and river kayaking trips.

OTHER GUIDING SERVICES

Valdez Heliski Guides — Tel: 907-835 4528

The Chugach Mountains

The story of heliboarding is directly linked to the disastrous Exxon Valdez oil spill of '89. The massive clean-up operation involved an assorted crew of adventurous and enterprising folk: Chet Simmons, Michal Cozad and Tom Thibedeau among them. When the operation started slowing down, they went skiing. Cozad bought the Tsaina Lodge to rennovate into a ski lodge, and Simmons flew the ops into the Chugach Mountains around Thompson Pass.

In a bid to get international press and paying customers to his lodge, Cozad and local girl Shannon Loveland got together in May, '90 to promote a new invitation only event, the World Extreme Ski Contest. By the time the competition was completed, a new Mecca had been established and soon everybody worth their salt wanted to prove themselves in Alaska. The first snowboard event was held in '93, and the following year Nik Perata took over what became riding's extreme world comp, the King of the Hill. The presence of such a huge pool of talent around these competitions undoubtedly gave birth to the thriving back-country industry, which has grown up around spring freeriding in the Thompson Pass. The Thompson Pass was the first epicentre; operations are now springing up in other areas near Valdez with choppers flying into ranges like The Books and even further afield. Valdez is now an annual pilgrimage for a rapidly diversifying clientele of skiers and snowboarders, and what started off as a very specialised adventure for an extreme few, has been significantly broadened in appeal.

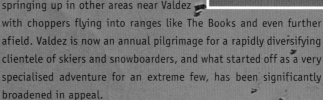

There's no escape from the vastness of the place, however, you don't have to be a Steve Klassen to enjoy the riding. Glaciers, steep terrain and huge snowfalls equals a certain amount of danger. Guides minimise the risk, but you can't take it away. The season has long daylight hours, mellow temperatures and fresh powder that's perfectly timed to kick in just as it's all disintegrating into slush and ice in the Lower 48.

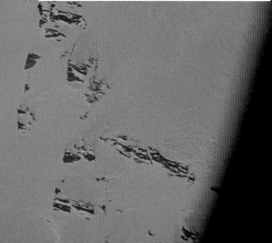

Main picture — Photo: Tim Rainger
First inset — Nik Perata **Photo:** Tim Rainger
Second inset — King of the Hill artwork **Photo:** Tim Rainger
Third inset — Queen of the Hill, Julie Zell **Photo:** Greg Von Doersten
Fourth inset — ABA heli-mechanic **Photo:** Tim Rainger
Fifth inset — ABA heli-port **Photo:** Tim Rainger

HOT TIPS

- **Camping**: Tenting is a common occurrence, despite the glacial locations. ABA allow you to camp near their heli port. There's also a campsite in town.
- **Hitch:** It's easy from Valdez.
- **Campervans:** If you're with a crew of four or more, a campervan is a good call. Being with a crew is also an advantage for organising lifts.
- **Pick your crew**: Knowledge of the strengths and weaknesses of the people you're riding with is crucial. It's obviously

better if the group is at a similar level.
- **Boards:** Don't even think about bringing a short board unless you're contemplating building kickers.
- **Safety:** To get on a plane or chopper you'll need a transceiver, a climbing harness and ideally a shovel and probe. ABA have some spares, but you should own your own harness at least. The sports' store was running out of sizes by mid-April so buy one at home.
- **Snowplanes:** Planes are half the price of a heli-chip and offer unreal riding.

Opposite — Michele Taggart **Photo:** Mark Gallup

Top left — Camping for the season at ABA **Photo:** Tim Rainger

Top right — ABA snowplane **Photo:** Tim Rainger

Bottom — Pepe Shouen **Photo:** Tim Rainger

Blue

TODD FRANZEN AND JASON FORD   PHOTOS : JEFF CURTES

(800) 948-3196

TODD FRANZEN

SALOMON

CANADA

BC backcountry **Photo:** Tim Rainger

BRITISH COLUMBIA

STATE INFORMANTION

Population: 3,764,000
Time: Pacific Standard Time = GMT minus 8 hours
Capital city: Vancouver
Area: 947,796 sqkm (588,960 sq miles)

VISITOR INFORMATION SOURCES

Super Natural British Columbia:
Tel: 250-387 1642 or 1-800-663 6000
Web site: http://www.tbc.gov.bc.ca

GETTING AROUND

Main airports: Vancouver International Airport — Tel: 604-276 6373
By train: BC Rail — Tel: 604-984 5246 or 1-800 663 8238, VIA Rail Canada — Tel: 1-800-561 8630
By bus: BC Transit — Tel: 604-521 0400 or 250-385 2551
Road conditions: Tel: 1-900 451 4997
Greater Vancouver — Tel: 604-299 9000 or Kelowna — Tel: 250-861 2929
Speed limits: The speed limit ranges between 90 and 100 kmph (55 and 60 mph).

INTRODUCTION

British Columbia is four times the size of the Great Britain. Within its vast regions are some of North America's most respected monuntain ranges: the Monashees, the Cariboos, the Selkirks, the Purcells and the MacDonald Range. These backbones contain a bunch of varied resorts, including the North America's most visited, Whistler Blackcomb. Around Vancouver city, the resorts of Grouse, Cypress and Mount Washington keep the city kids hucking and training for forays into the wild interior. This hard-core turf has been home to noted riders such as Craig Kelly, Omar Lundie, Brian Savard, Kevin Young and legions of others.

Opposite — Brian Savard, Revelstoke **Photo:** Mark Gallup

Right — Road signs **Photo:** Tim Rainger

BRITISH COLUMBIA'S RESORTS

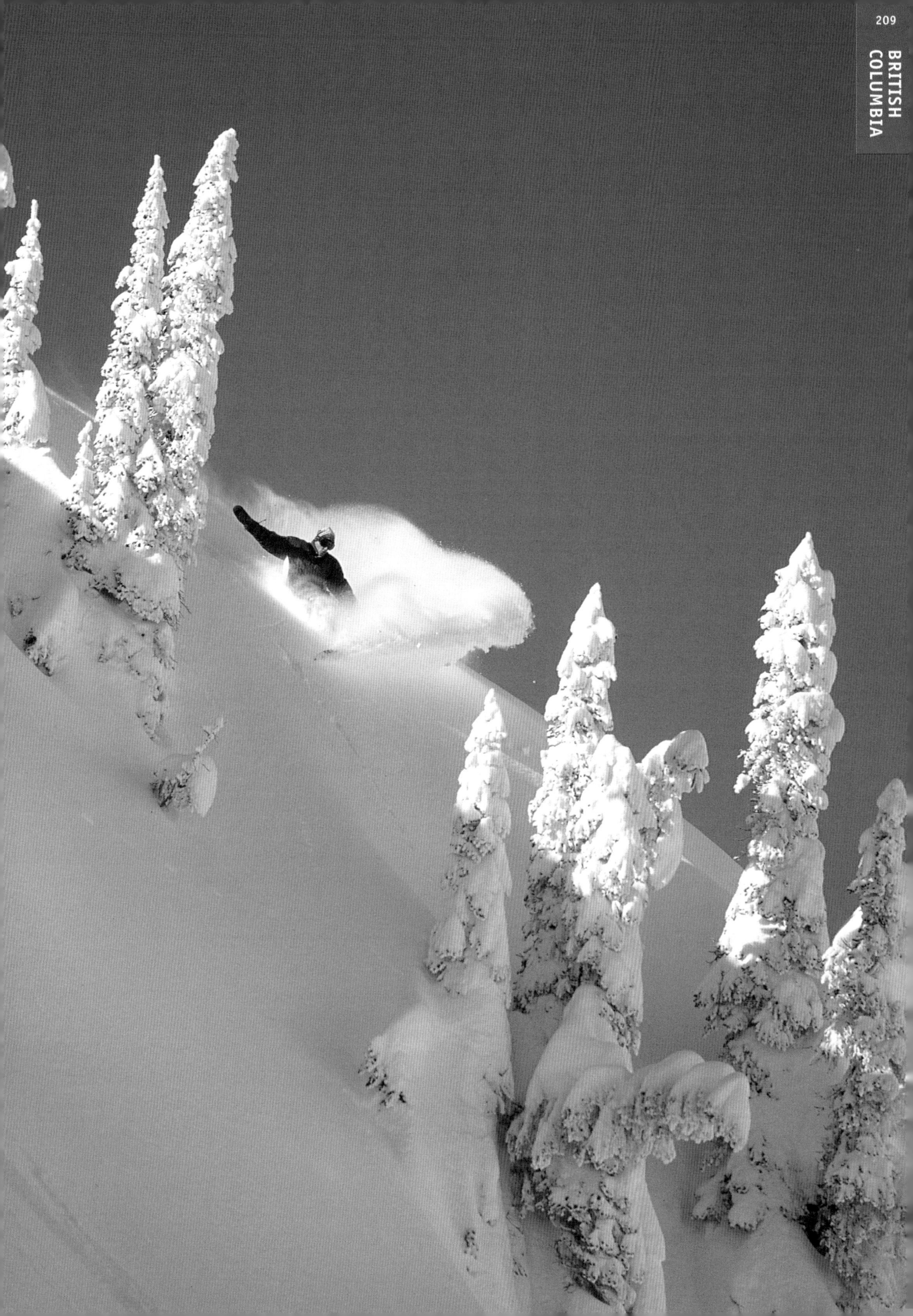

Mount Washington

THE FACTS

ELEVATION

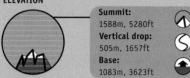

Summit:
1588m, 5280ft
Vertical drop:
505m, 1657ft
Base:
1083m, 3623ft

SNOWFALL

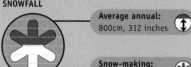

Average annual:
800cm, 312 inches

Snow-making:
None

AREA

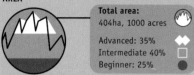

Total area:
404ha, 1000 acres

Advanced: 35%
Intermediate 40%
Beginner: 25%

SEASON
Early December — mid-April

COMMUNICATIONS
Snow report: Tel: 250-338 1515 or 250-657 2734
Web site: http://www.vquest.com/alpine/
E-mail: alpine@vquest.com
Mountain information:
Tel: 250-338 1386
Fax: 250-338 5795
Vancouver information centre:
Tel: 250-657 3275

LIFTS AND TICKETS
Number of lifts:
5 chairlifts, 1 poma, 1 handle tow
Lift pass prices*:
1/2 day: $23.50
1 day: $36
Multi-day: $162 (5 days)
Season: $825
Other ticketing information:
* Prices do not include GST or the BC21 Road
Improvement Levy which adds an extra $2 to every
adult day pass. The season pass is a book of 25 day
passes.

SNOWBOARD SHOPS
Ski Tak Hut — Tel: 250-334 2537
Board and ski specialists.

SNOWBOARD SCHOOL
Mount Washington Snowboard School
Tel: 250-338 1386
A huge, friendly staff make Mount Washington an
ideal place to learn. From beginner to advanced
racing techniques, you'll find it all including new
adult snowboard camps in '97-'98.

ON THE MOUNTAIN

With its bald top and snow-covered firs, Mount Washington is a freakish sight in the middle of a mild, lush Pacific island. Used mostly by locals, it is known throughout the province as a teaching mountain but also has some rad terrain to satisfy advanced riders. Its isolation lends a peaceful vibe to the riding with nothing around but a provincial park and more mountains. It has a large park and halfpipe among the glades, and chutes and bowls which trap plenty of snow. With a good lift system and excellent trail organisation, day-trippers and seasonal visitors will find it's a great all-round hill to ride.

SNOW CONDITIONS Mount Washington and its neighbouring coastal range are the first defence of Vancouver Island against the systems which spew buckets of snow in autumn and early winter. Clouds and swells hit the West Coast and unload over the mountains, giving an average snowfall of eight metres (26 feet). Windy conditions occasionally form cornices and can enclose the upper tree line in a thick crust. Unlike the mainland North Shore, Mount Washington has a decent altitude which keeps the snow cold and light.

FREERIDERS The best place to be for first tracks after an island dump is up the Blue Chair and down the Powder Face. It's a black diamond run but tilts to double black without warning. After a few big turns, choose one of the tight boundary runs: Boundary, Farout or Raven, all packed with rocks and stumps for high-speed launching. It's an academic blue run down Easy Rider for a tedious transfer back to the Blue Chair via the Red Chair for round two. For more vertical per hour, stick next to the Hawk trail by the Blue Chair for similar but busier terrain. The most hospitable glade riding are the trees between the runs marked Schum's Delight and Fletcher's Challenge. These are pitched for an advanced rider with a nice clearing halfway down — lay out some fat ones before diving back into the lips, humps and timber. Rumours of new lifts in the near future should alleviate some of the weekend crowd mayhem.

FREESTYLERS The large snowboard park has table tops and spines with a nice big quarterpipe at the end. All this is set within the natural lie of the land and is well-maintained by hands on shovels and rakes. The pipe is dragoned and usually kept to competition standards; locals put it to constant use. With the focus on providing proper training facilities, it won't be long before another Brian Savard hits the big time from Mount Washington.

CARVERS The grooming team leave consistently perfect trails. There are long, sweeping runs with rollers and good steeps making the majority of Mount Washington into a dragstrip. Whiskey Jack, beneath the Whiskey Jack Chair, is a great, wide boulevard. Head to Linton's Loop and follow Rainbow to the base of the Sunrise Quad. Ride the Sunrise Quad and blast down the frozen rollercoaster of Fletcher's Challenge or Fantastic for a full plummet. Pay attention to merging traffic coming from your right where the Rainbow and Fantastic trails funnel into the quad base.

MOUNTAIN FOOD The cafeteria in the Day Lodge does great hot breakfasts and lunches and has daily specials. There's also an indoor picnic area where BYO brown-bags are welcome. For fair-weather picnics, there's an outdoor area below the Whiskey Jack Chair serving barbecue grills. Also in the Day Lodge, the Whiskey Jack Lounge is a sports enthusiast's dream with larger than life screens and a good selection of microbrews and pub food.

HAZARDS AND RULES The steeps to skier's right of the Blue Chair can be hazardous to inexperienced tree riders; further right of that it's base jump time. They will yank your pass and kick your arse for going one inch past that boundary.

EVENTS AND COMPETITIONS Try all the new products free during the Demo Daze in early December. 6D Clothing has a popular slopeside in April and the resort big air comps are also a big hit in springtime.

Mount Washington

ABOUT TOWN

A 30 minute drive from Mount Washington's resort village is the fully-fledged, groovy town of Courtney. It sits on the edge of the Strait of Georgia which separates Vancouver Island from the mainland, and the pace of life is slower despite the proximity of the large island cities of Nanaimo and Victoria. Fishing, logging and tourism are the valley's main breadwinners so the locals are good at making outsiders feel welcome. The town is entertaining with bars offering live music, comedy and sports. Being a coastal town, there's plenty of fresh seafood and fresh air to prepare you for fresh tracks.

ACCOMMODATION For B&Bs, condos, chalets and other options in Mount Washington Village, call Mile High Accommodations — Tel: 1-800-699 6499, or Mount Washington Chalets; priced from $85 per night mid-week — Tel: 250-658 5533. Mountain Resort Accommodations also offer on-mountain hotel bookings — Tel: 1-800-370 1403. There is a sprawling RV park with all the hook-ups next to the lifts; prices start at $25.75. Central Reservations have a long list of private owners who rent out chalets and condos and can cater for big parties; the cheapest cost $85 per night for a one bedroom unit. Central Reservations — Tel: 250-334 5703.

In Courtney, the Washington Inn is a cheap, popular choice; prices for a double with a couch start at $70 a night — Tel: 250-338 5441. Also in Courtney, the Arbutus Hotel has clean, convenient rooms and a door-to-lift shuttle service to Mount Washington. Facilities include a coffee shop, restaurant, lounge, pub, hot-tub, sauna, off-track betting and a cold beer and wine store; prices start at $59 for a double — Tel: 250-334 3121. Comox Valley Tourist Information — Tel: 250-334 3242.

FOOD For excellent take-away sandwiches, go to one of Subway's four chain stores. Vegetarians will love Bar None Café which has tasty food with fresh juices and great cappuccinos. The Black Fin Pub has a varied menu, beers and views of the Beaufort Range, Comox Glacier and Bayne's Sound. For Mexican food, the Mex Café and Pub has a family atmosphere with darts, pool and a big screen. Most of the pubs have good meals available. Another hit with locals is the Atlas Café and its sister joint, Orbit's Pizza.

NIGHTLIFE Aprés-ski and weekend nights go off at the Whiskey Jack Lounge at the base of the mountain. The large room is packed with every boarder in the vicinity getting liquored up to live music. There's also a good selection of snacks, draught beers and friendly staff. In Courtney, the Loft is a big barn masquerading as a club which features live music and a huge selection of on-tap draught beers. The DJ at the Mex, next door to the Loft, kicks out rock n'roll, pool and darts. Good pub grub is served till late. The Arbutus Pub is good for entertainment with comedy nights and live bands — listen to the tales of locals and legends.

OTHER ACTIVITIES Surfing on the West Coast, kayaking, fishing, diving, whale-watching. To find surf, go south from Courtney on Highway 19 to Parksville and then follow Highway 4 to Tofino. There's a good break at Long Beach.

THANKS TO Erin Keam, Steve Downing, Leanne Mercer.

Top — Getting there **Photo:** Tim King
Middle left — **Photo:** Tim King
Middle — Top of the Blue, opening day **Photo:** Phillip Stone
Courtesy: Mount Washington
Middle right — **Photo:** Tim King

GETTING THERE

By air: Vancouver is the nearest international airport, or you can fly with Air BC or Canadian to the Comox Valley Airport.
By boat: From Vancouver either take a ferry from Horseshoe Bay in West Vancouver or Tsawassen, south of Vancouver. It takes 90 minutes to reach the cities of either Victoria or Nanaimo — Tel: 1-800-663 3721.
By bus: You can take a bus from Victoria or Nanaimo and transfer by shuttle to the Mount Washington resort. Grayline — Tel: 250-388 5248.
By rail: From Victoria there is a train service to Courtney with VIA Rail — Tel: 1-800-561 8630 or call Travelworld in Victoria — Tel: 250-382 3121.
By car: The Comox Valley is 100 kilometres (60 miles) north of Nanaimo. Mount Washington is 25 kilometres (17 miles) west of the Comox Valley along Highway 19 around the edge of the Strait of Georgia.
Getting around: Part of Mount Washington Village can only be accessed by foot or by the Village Snowcat Service; price $19 per trip — Tel: 250-334 5706.

Cypress Bowl

THE FACTS

ELEVATION

Summit:
1448m, 4750ft
Vertical drop:
533m, 1750ft
Base:
915m, 3000ft

SNOWFALL

Average annual:
350cm, 138 inches

Snow-making:
None

AREA

Total area:
52ha, 128 acres
Advanced: 40%
Intermediate: 37%
Beginner: 23%

SEASON
December — April

COMMUNICATIONS
Snow reports: Tel: 604-926 6007 or 604-878 9229
Web site: http://www.cypressbowl.com
E-mail: cypressb@istar.cd
Mountain information:
Tel/Fax: 604-926 5612

LIFTS AND TICKETS
Number of lifts:
4 chairlifts, 2 T-bars
Lift pass prices*:
1/2 day: $23
1 day: $31, $26 (13-18yrs)
Multi-day: $217 (book of 8 passes)
Season pass: $495
Other ticketing information:
*Prices don't include GST. Off-mountain ticket sales cost $23 for a day pass. Season pass holders will receive 50 per cent off tickets to Apex, Big White, Mount Washington and Fernie Alpine Resorts.

SNOWBOARD SHOPS
Cypress Mountain Shop — Tel: 604-878 9229
This shop has the works. Buy an unlimited $28 wax card for the season. B+B: $25
Vertical Addiction — Tel: 604-872 2999
The shop is boarder-owned with good quality staff.

SNOWBOARD SCHOOL
Cypress Snowboard School — Tel: 604-926 5346
Week long adult classes cost $289 including rentals or $219 with your own gear. It includes five two hour lessons, lift tickets and a pass for one night a week for the entire season.

GETTING THERE
By bus: A shuttle bus runs between Horseshoe Bay, Park Royal South in West Vancouver and the mountain — Tel: 604-878 9229. It goes every 90 minutes on week days and every hour in the weekend; prices from $7 a round trip or $56 for a book of ten tickets.
By car: Cypress Bowl is a 20 minute drive from the city. Head through Stanley Park into West Vancouver and drive west on Highway 1 to the Cypress Provincial Park Exit.

ON THE MOUNTAIN

Cypress Bowl is situated on the steep, west-facing slopes of Cypress Provincial Park, overlooking Vancouver city and the Strait of Georgia beyond to Vancouver Island. The ski area is made up of two peaks: Black Mountain and Mount Strachan. Mount Stachan is the higher peak with more challenging and varied terrain. Although small by Canada's standards, the mountain is well thought-out and is a great place to learn or improve on. All the runs flow together and there's no need to traverse. Boarders are treated right with a pipe and park on Mount Strachan and a permanent boardercross course on Black Mountain. Only 20 minutes from downtown Vancouver, it's a popular mountain with night-riding doubling as evening entertainment for the city kids. While cruising these slopes, take time to look skyward during January and February as Canadian bald eagles are a common sight above the cypress trees.

SNOW CONDITIONS The low altitude summit warms up early and morning riding is more consistent, although the heavy, wet afternoon slush can be fun. The peaks face each other making a bowl which is a good trap for incoming Pacific storms. The bowl offers good wind protection and it's a hot bed of action — T-shirts are normal pipe attire even in January and February. It's a good idea to bring an extra pair of gloves and spring pants.

FREERIDERS After a fresh snowfall, freeriders will want to stay high and explore Mount Strachan. The trees between Top Gun and the south face boundary are the most challenging with nice steeps and a few small cliffs. Humpty Dumpty and the area just to the east also have good, if somewhat short, freeriding. Under the Sunrise Chair, the Waterfalls and Slash offer steep thrills and stump jumping without the crowds. Intermediates will love Halfpipe and Lower Bowen, both serviced by the Midway Chair. On the south side of Black Mountain, try the ridge between Panorama and Windjammer.

FREESTYLERS At Black Mountain there are several well-shaped natural kickers beneath the chair and a boardercross course. There is a decent handmade halfpipe and funpark halfway down Mount Strachan, directly beneath the Sunrise Chair. The funpark has half-a-dozen heavily used hits including a spine, a gap and a long, sloping table top. The snow softens up in the afternoon making landings more bearable than in the early morning or evening. A good slopestyle and quarterpipe training arena awaits and the floodlights mean that it can be used till 10.00pm.

CARVERS The well-groomed, wide trails are ideal for carving. Beginners will find gentle rollers beneath the Sunrise Chair or try Collins boundary run on Mount Strachan. Speed freaks can take T-33 from the Sky Chair onto Horizon for the best burn to the bottom. Panorama to Windjammer, and Trumpeter to Upper Fork are also good runs for the learned on Black Mountain.

MOUNTAIN FOOD Beside the carpark at the base of the mountain, there is a cafeteria which offers daily specials on hot and cold breakfasts and lunches. A lunch room with vending machines and a large patio provide for BYO budgets. The bar lounge opens from 12.00am through till 10.00pm and serves good pub grub with a choice of draught beers.

HAZARDS AND RULES Leashes are mandatory. There are deadly cliffs in the out of bounds areas so take heed.

EVENTS AND COMPETITIONS All three North Shore resorts (Cypress, Grouse and Forbidden Plateau) host big air events for glory and a few nice prizes. Several slalom races are held here each season, organised by the snowboard school and local shops. Kokanee sponsor a mid-season boardercross which is open to the public.

Vancouver

GETTING THERE

By air: Vancouver has an international airport which has flights from all over North America and the Pacific Rim. Delta Airlines have regular connections — Tel: 1-800-221 1212.

ABOUT TOWN

With a population of over one million, Vancouver is positioned on the edge of the Pacific Rim and is a favourite for outdoor enthusiasts. It is one of the few cities in the world where you can play golf, scuba dive and snowboard all in one day, and the inhabitants pride themselves on being sports fanatics despite the frequent rain showers. The city is a collection of vibrant sectors which cater to all lifestyles and desires. There's a strong hippy and health food culture with some of the best bookshops on the coast. Granville Island is the place to buy fresh seafood, produce and artisan handicrafts. Boutiques, clubs and Indian art shops are found down in Gas Town. There are skate parks in this area too — just call in at a skate shop for an update on local events. If it's a dull day, take a hike around Stanley Park in the middle of the city.

ACCOMMODATION

The closest lodging to the slopes is the Capilano Inn, a basic, comfortable Best Western starting at $100 per night for a double room, or with kitchens for $12 extra — Tel: 604-271 8280. The Coach House Inn in North Vancouver has double rooms from $65 per night — Tel: 604-985 3111 or 1-800-663 2500. The Fraser Arms next to the airport on West Marine Drive has cheap, clean rooms for $45 per night — Tel: 604-261-2499. Vancouver Hostelling International has beds from $17.50 — Tel: 604-684 4565 and Hostelling International has cheaper beds from $15 — Tel: 604-224 3208. North Vancouver Central Reservations — Tel: 604-987 4488, Vancouver Richmond Tourist Office — Tel: 604-271 8280.

FOOD

In Vancouver you can eat whatever kind of food you like, whenever you want it. Davie Boulevard has trendy cafés and eateries with healthy delis and vegetarian restaurants close by. There are falafels, samosa stands and plenty of oriental restaurants. For a light lunch or fresh groceries on Granville Island, go to the market under the Granville Street bridge. The Round Table in Richmond is the best place for a slice of pizza; Pizzarillos on Burrard Ave is pretty good too. The Wazubee Café on Commercial Drive has cheapish dishes that are as funky as the decor. Doll and Penny's Diner on Davie Boulevard never closes and is a good place to eat, drink coffee and sober up.

VANcouver **Photo:** Tim King

NIGHTLIFE For a full run-down on what's going on, read the free Georgia Straits. Try the Chameleon downstairs at 801 Georgia Ave for dancing and stiff drinks. All types of music blare nightly in Gas Town. The Town Pump is the spot for alternative and heavy sounds. Davie Boulevard is great for cafés, clubs and meandering — the possibilities are unlimited and drinks average $4.

OTHER ACTIVITIES You name it. On the mountain you can go tobogganing, tubing, cross-county skiing, snowshoeing and telemarking — Tel: 604-922 0825.

THANKS TO Steve Downing, Michelle, Kaya, Gerald, Gary, Priska, Moss Tomlinson, Sarah Koo, Kara Sieverwight, Serena Vaillancourt, Robert at the Ski and Snowboard School.

THE VANCOUVER AREA

EACH GRID SQUARE REPRESENTS 10 MILES

[Map of the Vancouver area showing British Columbia and Washington, with locations including Port Hardy, Courtenay, Comox, Campbell River, Nanaimo, Victoria, North Vancouver, Vancouver, Pemberton, Garibaldi, White Rock, Bellingham, and routes to Seattle, Kelowna, and Port Hardy.]

Grouse Mountain

THE FACTS

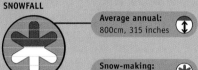

ELEVATION

Summit:
1250m, 4100ft
Vertical drop:
366m, 1210ft
Base:
854m, 2900ft

SNOWFALL

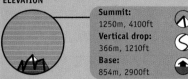

Average annual:
800cm, 315 inches

Snow-making:
50%

AREA

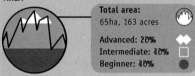

Total area:
65ha, 163 acres
Advanced: 20%
Intermediate: 40%
Beginner: 40%

SEASON
Late November — April

COMMUNICATIONS
Snow report: Tel: 604-986 6262
Mountain information:
Tel: 604-980 9311
Fax: 604-984 6360

LIFTS AND TICKETS
Number of lifts:
2 tramways, 4 chairlifts, 2 T-bars, 4 rope tows
Lift day prices*:
1/2 day: N/A
1 day: $19 (week days), $25 (weekends)
Multi-day: $99 (5 days)
Season: N/A
* GST included.

SNOWBOARD SHOPS
The Board Room — Tel: 604-985 9669
They have everything but snow.

SNOWBOARD SCHOOL
Grouse Mountain Snowboard School
Tel: 604-980 9311
Lessons for beginners through to advanced riders.

GETTING THERE FROM VANCOUVER
By bus: Take the Vancouver city bus 232/236 direct to the Grouse Mountain base station; the round trip costs about $2 — Tel: 604-521 0400.
By car: From North Vancouver take the Marine Drive Exit onto Capilano Road and follow it five kilometres (three miles) to the Skyway base.

ON THE MOUNTAIN

Being up on Grouse Mountain is like being in a Vancouver city neighbourhood park; the Skyride base is just 20 minutes from downtown Vancouver and it's a seven minute ride from the base to the top of the mountain. The feeling you get from riding towards a sprawling city is mesmerising, especially at night when trail lights blaze till 10.00pm. This is a great learning and training resort with one of the largest snowboard schools in North America. Colossal, inspirational sculptures created with chain-saws decorate the lift area and slopes.

SNOW CONDITIONS Grouse receives the most snow on the North Shore. It comes in the form of a fat eight metre (28 foot) layer of heavy snow with occasional light powder days. Due to the low altitude, the snowpack can warm up quickly.

FREERIDERS The trees beneath the Blueberry and Inferno Chairs tend to preserve the powder pockets. The back side runs from the Peak Chair offer the most challenging terrain; Devil's Advocate and Purgatory have large rocks and drops which launch you back to the Inferno Chair. There is a natural halfpipe called the Coffin on account of its steep walls, and a fun dogleg beneath the Blueberry Chair on Deliverance. These are best ridden before noon as they tend to get tracked out and look like a minefield after the battalion of skiers have charged through.

FREESTYLERS A decent 100 metre (300 foot) pipe has been designed and up-kept by the resort's snowboard director Jay Balmer and his brother Shawn, both of whom are ripping boarders and skaters. The Enchanted Kingdom funpark above the pipe is also well-maintained. A sound system cranks the jams at the pipe making it easier to get up and practice on the table tops, gaps, spines and boxes.

CARVERS For good carving, stay near the edges of all the blue and black runs as moguls form in the middle. Get there early morning or early evening for the best combing effects. Beginners will be comfortable on the runs of Centennial and Expo. Those craving white knuckles should stick to the Inferno and Peak Chairs.

MOUNTAIN FOOD Above the Blueberry Chair, Beaver Tails is a great place for a sweet treat and a hot chocolate. In the Main Lodge, the cafeteria has big muffins for breakfast and a basic $5-$7 lunch. A large wood-burning fireplace in the main foyer makes it a nice place to warm up while lunching on your picnic. Bar 98 has filling bar foods and vegetarian dishes; meals are priced from $7-$12 and the view is wicked. If riders want a feast at night, head down the hall to the Grouse Nest Restaurant.

HAZARDS AND RULES Leashes are a must. Stay within the boundaries or lose your lift ticket and face a fine for trespassing, particularly in the Capilano watershed area.

EVENTS AND COMPETITIONS A seasonal big air and boardercross competition.

NIGHTLIFE Bar 98 is open until 11.00pm and peaks with happy hour drink specials during the aprés-ski period. Sample some of the many microbrews, then head for the big city lights.

OTHER ACTIVITIES There are heli-tours (sight-seeing only) at the mid-station and free 20 minute Kodak films at the Theatre in the Sky.

THANKS TO Ken, Jay, Shawn Balmer, Steve and Michelle Downing, Leigh Tynen.

For more About Town, see Vancouver review p.213.

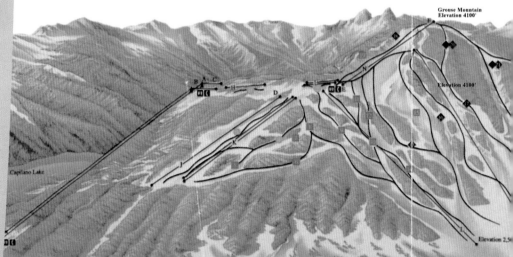

Grouse Mountain
Elevation 4100'

Grouse Mountain

③

Top — Pipe training **Photo:** Tim King

Bottom left — Chainsaw carving **Photo:** Tim King

Bottom middle — Jay Balmer, Director **Photo:** Tim King

Bottom right — Snowboarding carves its place in history in the Grouse's Nest foyer **Photo:** Mike MacWatt

THE FACTS

SNOWFALL

Average annual:
914cm, 360 inches

Snow-making:
Extensive

AREA

Total area:
2832ha, 6998 acres

Advanced: 25%
Intermediate: 55%
Beginner: 20%

LIFTS AND TICKETS

Lift pass prices*:
1/2 day: $42, $34 (13-18yrs)
1 day: $52, $42 (13-18yrs)
Multi-day: $265 (dual mountain for 5 days)
Season: $1325 (dual mountain), $1069 (Whistler)
Other ticketing information:
*GST not included. Tickets are valid for both ski areas.
A BCTV BC Ski Card saves on money on every lift pass,
with the first day and every following seventh day

WHISTLER FACTS

ELEVATION

Summit:
2182m, 7160ft
Vertical drop:
1530m, 5020ft
Base:
675m, 2214ft

COMMUNICATIONS

Snow report: Tel: 604-932 4191
Web site: http://www.whistler-mountain.com
E-mail: whistler@whistler.net
Mountain information:
Tel: 604-932 3434 or 1-888-588 3434
Fax: 604-938 9174
Number of lifts:
2 gondolas, 3 high-speed quads, 4 chairlifts,
2 T-bars, 2 handle-tows, 1 platter lift

BLACKCOMB FACTS

ELEVATION

Summit:
2284m, 7494ft
Vertical Drop:
1609m, 5280ft
Base:
675m, 2214ft

COMMUNICATIONS

Snow report: Tel: 604-932 4211
Web site: http://www.blackcomb.com
E-mail: blackcomb@whistler.net
Mountain information:
Tel: 604-938 7703 or 1-800-766 0449
Fax: 604-938 7527
Number of lifts:
1 gondola, 6 high-speed quads, 3 chairlifts,
2 T-bars, 3 handle-tows, 1 platter lift

Whistler Blackcomb

ON THE MOUNTAIN

The sheer amount of terrain between Whistler and Blackcomb puts the duo into a league of their own. From the top of Whistler Mountain's high alpine Peak Chair or Blackcomb Mountain's Horstman T-bar, the choices are mind-boggling. Glorious sickness awaits on these two mountains: 200 plus trails, three glaciers and 12 bowls, not to mention tons of wind lips, cornices, boulders and hundreds of acres of trees — all combined with the biggest vertical drop in North America. From Blackcomb you get great views of Whistler Mountain, Whistler Village and the majestic Overlord and Spearhead Glaciers of the Great Beyond, while from the top of Whistler you can see the Black Tusk and Mount Garibaldi.

Whistler and Blackcomb resorts have walked a tightrope of co-operation in recent years, sharing a base area, a reputation and marketing campaigns but being run by completely different owners. Blackcomb belong to Intrawest whereas Whistler was family managed in the old-school skiing way. But with a merger in '96-'97 which added Whistler to the Intrawest stable of Tremblant, Panorama, Stratton, Snowshoe, Mammoth and Copper Mountain things are changing. The claim is that both Whistler and Blackcomb will retain their individual character; Whistler specialises in high alpine bowls and glades with a traditional ski focus whereas Blackcomb is renown for its glacier-grooved steeps and a trendier, younger crowd.

SNOW CONDITIONS The weather is a wildly mixed bag of meteorological tricks due to the coastal orographic effect. Sitting less than 80 kilometres (50 miles) from the sea, just east of where warm and cold ocean currents collide, this area has consistent dumps of both wet and dry snow. Snow accumulates heavily on all slopes depending on the wind direction; prevailing westerlies can fill the bowls with deep fluff. Occasionally thermal inversions occur making the top layer of the snowpack warmer and heavier, adding to avalanche danger. It's best to bring a change of gloves and dress in layers for when the weather pulls one of its not so practical jokes.

BACK-COUNTRY OPTIONS Some of the world's best heliboarding takes place here with many companies covering thousands of square kilometres. Town and Country Heliboarding are a snowboard-only company; trips start from $300-$400 per person. They cover a vertical drop of 2500 metres to 3100 metres (8000 feet to 10,000 feet) in three runs. A freeride package with six runs of 4300 metres to 5800 metres (5,000 feet to 20,000 feet) is also available for die-hards with too much money and not enough time to boot-track. Powder boards can be rented for $20. For more information — Tel: 604-938 2927 or E-mail: tc-heli@snozone.com,

Whistler Snowmobile Guided Tours take snowboarders into the back-country. They're located in the Deer Lodge — Tel: 604-932 4086. Other companies include Whistler Heliskiing — Tel: 604-932 4105, Mountain Helisports — Tel: 604-932 2070, Tyax Heliskiing — Tel: 604-932 7007 and Black Tusk Helicopter —Tel: 604-898 4800.

Whistler/Blackcomb ④

HAZARDS AND RULES An average of 15 people die each year (mostly out of bounds) in the Whistler-Blackcomb area so it's important to take an Ortovox transceiver and all the rest of the kit. Pay attention to the flashing lights which signal high risk areas and go with someone who knows the back-country traps.

EVENTS AND COMPETITIONS Airwalk sponsors weekly halfpipe and slopestyle competitions for small prizes, points count towards a seasonal total. It takes place at Blackcomb and is open to all; register in the Blackcomb Day Lodge at the ski school desk. Every April Whistler rolls out the carpet for the World Ski and Snowboard Festival. Westbeach hold their classic halfpipe jam and invitational big air under the stars. The Kokanee North American Boardercross Championships bring out many awesome shredders. Also worth checking out from the terraces at Christine's is the Couloir Extreme race and the World Big Foot Comp. The Grundig FIS Snowboard World Cup features GS, halfpipe and Super-G events.

Top left — Sergio **Photo:** Nils

Main picture — Dustin Varga and Tom Burt **Photo:** Chris Murray

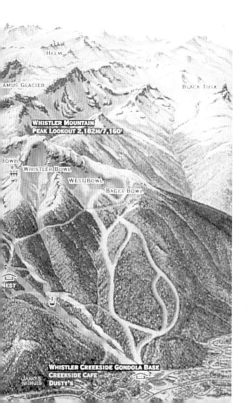

WHISTLER

FREERIDERS Whistler has even more bowls than Blackcomb and more freaks looking to snake first tracks. Luckily there are so many choices that you'll get your share if you can keep up with the frantic pace. The Harmony Express Quad accesses nice cruisers in the Symphony and Harmony Bowls. Skier's left of the Harmony Express Quad, the Drop is the steeper of these cruisy runs. After a dump, head for Surprise under the Peak Chair where there are nice rocks and ridges to huck from.

Follow the ridge skier's left from Whistler Peak to drop the 20 metre (60 foot) cliffs known locally as Air Jordan. When the top opens, go skier's right from the peak around to the monster rush runs, Couloir and Cirque which drop into the Glacier Bowl. Down the face of Whistler Bowl, Doom and Gloom and High Shoulder challenge experts with steeps, spines and cliffs. Stay on top of the ridge to Highway 86 then cut into the double blacks of West Bowl for extreme freeriding down a quick 800 metre (2000 foot) vertical. For the best glades, cut across Highway 86 at the bottom of West Bowl into Big Timber and Peak to Creek. This winding creek bed run takes you down to the Creekside Gondola. For other great timber stashes, ask a local to show you International Trees and the Shooting Galley.

FREESTYLERS Both Whistler and Blackcomb have two impeccably dragoned pipes open from November to mid-April. Whistler's pipes are located at each

end of the Green Express Quad Chair; the best is the competition standard Nintendo pipe set in a permanent structure. The Nintendo Snowboard Park has the full collection of berms, spines, banks, table tops and quarterpipes.

CARVERS Beginners will have a blast on the extra-wide slopes of the Olympic area. Those who have carving down to an art should try the combined Upper and Lower Dave Murray Downhill runs, beginning above the Orange Chair and finishing up at Creekside. Intermediates might want to advance onto the lesser used Seppo's beneath the Black Chair, or the longer undulating Franz's to Lower Franz's down to Creekside. Intermediate and advanced edgers will get heel-to-toe satisfaction from the Boundary Piste and Harmony Ridge runs, both complete circuits of the Harmony Express Quad. From Peak Chair, lay out arcs along Highway 86 around the West Bowl boundary.

MOUNTAIN FOOD The Roundhouse serves a variety of hot food and is famous for its super burritos called Roundhouse Wraps, a good deal at $7. For cafeteria food or barbecues, Pika's terrace at the top of Whistler Mountain is the place to refuel and meet mates but it can get crowded. For a quieter lunch of fresh sushi, go upstairs and enjoy the view. Raven's Mountain Deli at the top of Creekside Gondola has good soups, hot lunches and a wide selection of sandwiches made to order.

④

Whistler Blackcomb
CONTINUED...

BLACKCOMB

FREERIDERS Locals race for freshies by taking the Glacier Express Quad or the 7th Heaven Express Quad and traversing skier's right to Spanky's Ladder and the trio of Garnet, Ruby and Diamond Bowls. These are super scary steeps where occasionally limb and life are lost. The traverse from Garnet Bowl is seriously exposed and once you point down into Diamond Bowl, your eyes will water behind your goggles. An alternative is to head up the Showcase T-bar to the entrance of Blackcomb Glacier where you can drop the barrel-like Blowhole. From here you can hike 50 metres (162 feet) to possibly the world's most filmed jump, the legendary Wind Lip. Hike further up the glacier to the shoulder and drop the chutes off Spearhead into the Great Beyond. These areas deserve extra respect and full off-trail kit. All of the above runs funnel down to the five kilometre (three mile) Blackcomb Glacier Road which returns you to the Excelerator Quad.

Another sick route is to head skier's left from the 7th Heaven Express Quad and traverse the narrow ridge to Couloir Extreme and Big Bang for a hell drop into Jersey Cream Bowl. As these slopes become tracked out, some head for the huge quarterpipe to skier's right of the 7th Heaven Express Quad while others go skier's left to some sweet glades below Zhiggy's Meadow. For more great tree cruising, the Crystal Chair gives access to quick, bumpy runs which exit onto the Blackcomb Glacier Road.

FREESTYLERS Blackcomb's main Fate Pipe above the Solar Coaster Express Quad is the pick. The place is packed with grommets and pros, some of whom don't always give a proper "dropping" call so expect some close calls, particularly at weekends. Summer camps take place on the Blackcomb Glacier where pipes are built from June till mid-August. The Kokanee Snowboard Park is outstanding. It has every conceivable jump and obstacle configuration you could wish for. Each hit is graded by difficulty and marked accordingly. The grooming is maintained to the same high standards as the immaculate pipes. You can ride the park as part of a circuit starting with the Fate Pipe and back to the Solar Coaster Express Quad via the black diamond charger Freefall. Park fanatics can take the Catskinner Chair which services the length of the pipe and park only.

CARVERS Beginners can see the whole mountain by taking the Crystal Traverse down to Crystal Road, ending with Green Line back down to the base of the Wizard Express Quad. From the Crystal Chair, Rock n'Roll and Ridge Runner will give intermediates a rush similiar to Buzz Cut and Expresso under the Excelerator Quad. For a longer burn with occasional bumps, head down Springboard under the lift line of the Solar Coaster Express Quad. A more undulating run from the same lift is Choker down to Slingshot and onto Lower Gear Jammer. 'Liftee's pick' is posted at the lifts, naming the daily groomed runs and the lift to take to get you there.

MOUNTAIN FOOD The Rendezvous Mountain Grill and Christine's at the top of the Solar Coaster Express Quad have daily hot meal specials and are popular. Beaver Tail's speciality are deep-fried dough-balls with your choice of sweet or savoury pizza toppings. Crystal Hut is a nice place to dry out and have a bowl of chilli or a huge salad. For a great view and grilled burgers, try the terrace of Horstman Hut on a sunny day. All places on both mountains serve junk food.

ABOUT TOWN

Whistler is a sprawling town jammed with more boarders than any other Canadian resort. The town is a conglomeration of several separate developments: Whistler Village, at the base of Whistler Mountain, Village North, a ten minute walk from the lifts, Upper Village, at the base of Blackcomb Mountain and Creekside, at the base of the Creekside Gondola. Whistler Village is the cobblestoned gondola base area stretching to the Village Square where the freaks chill. Whistler Village melds into Village North where you'll find the Town Plaza and the Market Place, a five minute walk from Village Square. The Market Place is where the locals shop; winding streets, walking paths and courtyards link the hundreds of shops and homes in chaotic harmony. It's a vast, cosmopolitan community and Intrawest's mega-dollars have made Whistler into Canada's fastest growing municipality.

Whistler is nearly stretched to its limit as far as land use is concerned but they are expanding further up the hill and back towards Creekside, poised for the next big commercial boom following the Whistler-Blackcomb merger. Looking sometimes more like a street party than a town, there's always a good vibe in Whistler with rich tourists and dregs living and partying peacefully together. The town is a dream come true for shoppers but it's also a great place to meet or watch other nomads and drink coffee and beer.

GETTING THERE

By air: All the major Canadian and American airlines fly into Vancouver International Airport, including Delta Airlines — Tel: 1-800-221 1212. If you're flying out of Vancouver, there's a $10 Airport Improvement fee for North American flights and a $15 fee for international flights. Scheduled and charter flights go direct to Whistler from Vancouver and Seattle — Tel: 604-664 5625. Drive through Vancouver from the airport and head north on the Sea to Sky Highway 99 for an awesomely beautiful two hour drive.
By bus: Maverick buses run five times daily from the downtown Vancouver bus depot; a one-way ticket costs $17 — Tel: 604-662 8051. Perimeter buses run seven times daily from Vancouver International Airport; a one-way ticket costs $45 — Tel: 604-266 5386.
By train: BC Rail offers a daily service between North Vancouver and Whistler with one morning departure to Whistler and one return evening trip; prices from $29 one-way including a meal.
By car: From Seattle take Interstate 5 to the US border, then head to Highway 99 through Vancouver and north for 120 kilometres (75 miles) to Whistler. For road information — Tel: 604-664 5625.
Getting around: Everything is walkable but hitchers do well too. A community ski bus runs frequently between Whistler Village and Creekside with stops clearly posted on the main routes — Tel: 604-932 4020.

ACCOMMODATION As Whistler attracts nearly one and a half million visitors annually, the infrastructure is well set-up. The region has more slopeside accommodation than any other mountain resort in Canada. There are 102 hotels, condos and B&Bs offering a total of 3560 rooms. We'd be crazy to start recommending specific places but here is a handful of options. Listel Whistler Hotel is a mid-priced palace in the heart of it all, just seconds from the gondola — Tel: 604-932 1133. Pinnacle's International Resort in Whistler Village is also worth the extra money as it has stylish rooms with fireplaces and balconies starting from $150 — Tel: 604-938 3218. For the best, Chateau Whistler would satisfy the Trumps — Tel: 1-800-441 1414.

Cheaper options include the Fireside Lodge — Tel: 604-932 4545 and the UBC Lodge — Tel: 604-932 6604; both have beds from $20 per night. For tight budgets, Whistler has a youth hostel with 30 beds priced at $17.50 per night — Tel: 604-932 549. Central Reservations — Tel: 604-664 5625 or 1-800-WHISTLER or book through their website: http://www.whistler.travel.bc.ca.

FOOD Whistler has over 100 restaurants, lounges and bars with food. For pub stuff, the Longhorn and Cinnamon Bear are always fun. In the Royal Bank building on Whistler Way, there are a number of places to eat including Café Escondido serving excellent, hot Mexican food, and fast food outlets like Misty Mountain Pizzas, Subway, A&W and McDonald's. Auntie Em's serves home-cooked Eastern European specials in the Market Place. For the best cookies and baked goods, visit the Cookie Co. next to Mountain Riders. The Kypryiakis Greek Restaurant is also highly recommended. The Crab Shack has seafood and a big screen TV for sports fans. Thai, Chinese, Japanese, German and French are also easy to find. Check the local papers for specials if you're on a budget, or shop at the one-stop food store in the Market Place.

NIGHTLIFE Whistler is a rocking town and party-heads will be well and truly plastered with choices. The local Sea and Sky radio station, announces all the parties, live music schedules, movies and mayhem several times daily. The Pique, a free local paper, also has the latest on what's going down. Located in the Village Square, the Liquor Store is a good place to start. After riding try Merlin's at the base of Blackcomb, a favourite aprés shred for boarders and live music venue with wacky bands. For a more chilled-out atmosphere, the Cinnamon Bear in the Delta Resort has a sporty aprés crowd with pool tables and great shooters. The Whistler crowd hit the sundecks of the Longhorn Saloon for a cool one or half-dozen. The Saloon has a good mix of live and spun music along with pool tables, darts and non-stop action videos.

If naked ladies and beer are your thing, head to the Boot on Tuesday and Wednesday nights. Buffalo Bill's is a western tourist bar with 30-something rock n' roll and beer. Tommy Africa's, downstairs across from the Village Square grocery store, has blasting jams and snowboard videos. For late night booty-shaking, head to the Rogue Wolf, a new dance club with an entry price tag and a good mix of tunes. The Savage Beagle grooves to house, hip-hop and trance.

OTHER ACTIVITIES Paragliding, paintball, rafting, in-line skating, climbing, mountaineering, heli-biking and working out.

THANKS TO Tara Woolley, Marci Fear, Jillian Dunagan, Penny Wright, Darren Walsh, Regi and friends and everyone named dude.

Opposite top — Tom Burt **Photo:** Chris Murray
Opposite bottom — **Photo:** Randy Lincks **Courtesy:** Blackcomb
Top right — Whistler and Blackcomb Mountains **Photo:** Randy Lincks
Courtesy: Whister Resort Association

THE FACTS
SNOWBOARD SHOPS

Mountain Riders — Tel: 604-932 3659
Rentals, sales, service. They have a cool staff of riders and are right next to the lifts in Whistler Village.
Showcase Snowboard Shop — Tel: 604-938 7720
The shop carries a full line of boards, boots and clothing and is located directly behind the Longhorn Pub in the Carelton Lodge.
Westbeach — Tel: 604-932 2523
Their staff of riders in the Market Place are helpful and do a lot for the local scene. They offer tons of hard-core store stuff for snowboarders and skaters.

SNOWBOARD SCHOOL

Blackcomb Mountain Snowboard School
Tel: 604-938 7720 or 1-800-766 0449 ext. 20
Whistler Mountain Snowboard School
Tel: 604-932 3434 or 1-888-588 3434
The Learn to Ride programme starts from $75 a day including lift ticket, lesson and equipment. They also offer ARC camps which include personalised instruction in alpine, freestyle, gate training and freeriding as well as video analysis, equipment and the rest. There's also a similar Oxygen two day camp; prices for ARC are $180 and for Oxygen are $160 plus GST.
Camp of Champions
The two day camps are taught by local pros such as Swatch pro-rider Omar Lundi, Todd Slosher, Wes Makepeace and Brian Savard. The camp includes breakfast, video analysis and perks; prices from $195.
Craig Kelly's World Camp — Tel: 360-599 1258
Learn to style the summer pipe and park, improve your slopestyle and carving technique and get back-county freeride tips from the guru himself.

Sun Peaks

THE FACTS

ELEVATION

Summit:
2077m, 6810ft
Vertical drop:
900m, 2951ft
Base:
1177m, 3859ft

SNOWFALL

Average annual:
449cm, 177 inches

Snow-making:
11%

AREA

Total area:
444ha, 1096 acres

Advanced: 22%
Intermediate: 54%
Beginner: 24%

SEASON

Late November — mid-April

COMMUNICATIONS

Snow report:
Tel: 250-578 7232 (Kamloops)
Tel: 604-290 0754 (Vancouver)
Web site: http://sunpeaksresort.com
E-mail: info@sunpeaksresort.com
Mountain information:
Tel: 250-578 7842 or 1-800-807 3257
Fax: 250-578 7843

LIFTS AND TICKETS

Number of lifts:
2 high-speed quads, 2 chairlifts, 1 T-bar, 1 platter
Lift pass prices*:
1/2 day: $32, $28 (under 18yrs)
1 day: $41, $36 (under 18yrs)
6 days: $228, $198 (under 18yrs)
Season: $679, $599 (under 18yrs)
Other ticketing information:
* GST included. Combined packages with Silver Star and Whistler are on offer — Tel: 1-800-807 3257.

SNOWBOARD SHOPS

Oronge Ltd. — Tel: 250-851 8799
Run by boarders for boarders in Kamloops, the shop has sales, service and rental deals. B+B: $20.

SNOWBOARD SCHOOL

Sun Peaks Snowboard School — Tel: 250-578 7222
Located in the Day Lodge. Advanced riders can get tips from World Cup rider Brett Tippie and beginners can take advantage of the all-inclusive full day lesson, lunch and rental packages starting from $66.

ON THE MOUNTAIN

Mount Tod and its surrounding peaks are situated in a sparsely populated region just north of Kamloops. Mount Tod was purchased in '92 by Nippon Cable who have invested more than $75 million bringing in a new lift system, grooming equipment, on-mountain accommodation and eateries. The locals still call the ski area Tod Mountain after pioneer fur trader John Tod but unfortunately Tod means 'death' in German and the marketing gurus thought Sun Peaks was a more welcoming name. The hospitality and friendliness of the resort staff compliment the terrain, and with investment plans underway, Sun Peaks will be ensured a placing among Canada's top resorts in years to come.

SNOW CONDITIONS Sun Peaks is fed by prevailing south-westerly Pacific storms producing acres of light powder. The slopes and wooded areas receive an average of four and a half metres (15 feet) of snow per season which usually lasts until mid-April.

FREERIDERS With a vast acreage of ungroomed terrain such as West Bowl, Crystal Bowl and the glades around the Head Walls, Sun Peaks has some wicked freeriding. Greenhorns can progress along snowboarding's exponential learning curve on the Five Mile trail which starts at the Top of the World — believe it! The more challenging Seven Mile road is another of the Peaks' long runs. Don't forget the powder runs like Expo, Chief and Chute, all a short hike from the Top of the World. Riders will find some nice glades between the runs off the Sunburst Chair.

FREESTYLERS The 914 metre (3000 foot) snowboard park is accessed from the Sundance Express Quad. From the top of Sunrise trail, head skier's left to an opening in the trees; you'll find a selection of small hits leading through a cleared path into the ungroomed terrain before the park entrance. Starting at the top of the pipe, you are led into a nicely transitioned banked slalom run that's perfect for boardercross training. Head onto a series of varying hits and slopestyle terrain if you're still the right way up. Either drop into the novice halfpipe or collect more air time from the surrounding jumps before re-entry on to the Sundance trail.

CARVERS Carvers will not be disappointed with the jumbo cord trails. Take the Sundance Express Quad up the Sundance Ridge and you'll have a choice of lanes through walls of trees: try Sunrise, Sun Catcher or Grannie Greene's. Freecarvers can lay-back at speed on either side of the Sunburst Express Quad.

MOUNTAIN FOOD The Sunburst Lodge at the top of the Sunburst Express Quad has a great terrace plus an indoor barbecue and cafeteria. This is the only mid-mountain stop-off, otherwise it's down to the lodges at the village or the Burfield Base.

HAZARDS AND RULES Sun Peaks has an open-minded attitude to the back-country as most of it will be accessible within the next five years.

EVENTS AND COMPETITIONS The '97-'98 events include the FIS Grundig Snowboard World Cup, the Nancy Greene Downhill Invitation, the weekly Sun Peaks Challenge Race (Super G), the Kokanee Kross Snowboard Series and Velocity Challenge. The Spring Carnival Slush Cup is an end-of-season event.

Opposite — **Photo:** Tim King
Top — **Photo:** Mike MacWatt
Bottom — **Photo:** Mike MacWatt

ABOUT TOWN

Sun Peaks resort is the town. Despite being small, it is well-planned with a village atmosphere. The nightlife is restricted by the lack of bars and clubs, although '97-'98 will see the opening of new venues for eating, drinking and dancing. There is no grocery or liquor store so self-caterers and room-partyers should stock up before leaving the highway. Meeting people won't be a problem as you'll soon know everyone after a few drinks at Macker's, Masa's or the Burfield. Getting home isn't a problem either as most places are within walking or board-to-door distances.

ACCOMMODATION For slopeside accommodation, Nancy Greene's Cahilty Lodge can't be beaten — Tel: 1-800-244 8424. The Stumbock Sun Peaks Lodge — Tel: 1-800-333 9112 and Four Points Sundance Lodge — Tel: 1-800-483 2888 also have slopeside beds. There is a youth hostel at

Kamloops, a 45 minute drive from the resort. Other accommodation includes the Fathers' Country Inn at $42.50 per night per person — Tel: 1-800-578 7322 and Burfield Chalets which start at $80 per night — Tel: 1-800-811 4588. Chalets can be as low as $145 per person per week at the Brookside Chalets — Tel: 1-800-811 4588 to a loftier $250 for a three bedroom place with loft at the Wolf's Den — Tel: 1-888-553 5566. To get a run-down of what's on offer, contact Central Reservations — Tel: 1-800-807 3257.

FOOD Macker's at Nancy Greene's offers a sumptuous breakfast buffet, a fat lunch menu and a wide variety of evening meals, all at reasonable prices. The best Euro-style breakfast is served at the Stumbock. Lunch time is busy at Masa's Bar and Grill and features soups, salads, burgers and sandwiches. Next to Masa's is Bottom's which has a casual pub atmosphere with great food. The barbecue ribs are so good that if you need a knife to eat them, Bottom's will pay for your meal. For the budget-minded, Bento's will certainly fill the

gap — try the giant cinnamon rolls. The Café Soleil's tempting aroma of fresh coffee, tea and pastries will draw you in for a quick fix. On Wednesday and Thursday evenings you can venture up to the Sunburst Lodge for torch-light barbecues and $20 fondue feasts.

NIGHTLIFE If you're starting early, Macker's is a great place to watch the sun go down. A two minute walk takes you to the small but merry Stumbock Bar, or head to Masa's Bar where most people meet up at the end of the day. Masa's has live bands at the weekends, a disco and a large selection of beers, spirits and bar meals. The Burfield is another place to relax with a cool beer.

OTHER ACTIVITIES The sports centre has a swimming pool, fitness centre and lighted outdoor skating. Snowmobile tours — Tel: 250-578 5484.

THANKS TO Al Raine and Nancy Greene, Mike Duggan, Chris Nicolson, Scott and the Macker's crew, Rae Beilman and all the local riders.

(5)

GETTING THERE
By air: From Vancouver and Calgary, it's a four to eight hour drive respectively. There is a domestic airport in Kamloops serviced daily from Vancouver, Kelowna, Calgary and Edmonton.
By bus: Greyhound has a service to Kamloops — Tel: 1-800-661 8747.
By car: It's a short 53 kilometre (31 mile) drive from Kamloops north on Highway 5. Take the Heffley Creek Exit and follow the signs for a half hour scenic drive to the village. Even though the roads are well-maintained, chains may be necessary during storms.
Getting around: The village of Sun Peaks is very centralised and most people walk or board to the lifts, restaurants and hotel rooms. There is a shuttle bus that will transport guests who are staying in chalets situated further from the lifts. For a ride, call Sun Star Shuttle — Tel: 250-319 3539.

Silver Star

THE FACTS

ELEVATION

Summit:
1915m, 6280ft
Vertical drop:
760m, 2491ft
Base:
1155m, 3780ft

SNOWFALL

Average annual:
570cm, 224 inches

Snow-making:
None

AREA

Total area:
909ha, 2250 acres

Advanced: 30%
Intermediate: 50%
Beginner: 20%

SEASON
Mid-November — mid-April

COMMUNICATIONS
Snow reports:
Tel: 250-542 1745 (Vernon)
Tel: 250-860 7827 (Kelowna)
Tel: 250-832 1181
Web site: http://www.silverstarmtn.com
E-mail: star@junction.net
Mountain information:
Tel: 250-542 0224 or 1-800-663 4431
Fax: 250-542 1236

LIFTS AND TICKETS
Number of lifts:
3 high-speed quads, 2 chairlifts, 2 T-bars,
1 beginner tow
Lift pass prices*:
1/2 day: $30
1 day: $45
Multi-day: $195 (5 days)
Season: $660
Other ticketing information:
* GST included. Night-riding is open from Tuesday
till Saturday, 3.30pm to 9.00pm and is included
free in a three day plus multi-day pass. At the
beginning and end of the season, riders can board
free in selected weeks.

SNOWBOARD SHOPS
Brian James Ski and Sport — Tel: 250-558 6065
B+B: $37.
Jim Attridge Centre — Tel: 250-542 1515
Full sales, service and rental.

SNOWBOARD SCHOOL
Silver Star Snowboard School — Tel: 250-558 6065
Hi-Season Camps from $240 include five lessons,
lift pass and video analysis.

ON THE MOUNTAIN

Silver Star is a family mountain; kids are left to play with the other kids while Ma and Pa head for their respective favourites. Riders will have a good time though as much of the better terrain is left alone and there are plenty of hidden treasures lurking beneath the mellow surface. The sub-alpine mountain has plenty of tree runs and a wide variety of pitches, including some challenging slopes on the north face and in the Vance Creek area.

SNOW CONDITIONS The mountain receives an average of five to six metres (18 feet) of snow each season. The back bowls and chutes on the Putnam Creek face tend to collect deeper powder than the windier Vance Creek face.

FREERIDERS There are a number of black diamond runs on the Vance Creek side with good powder in amongst the trees. Try out Attridge Face, Ridge Run, Moon Beam, Out Back and Fast Back. Hard-core riders are better off on the Putnam Creek side which has longer, steeper and tighter slopes. Warm up on Caliper Ridge then head for Doggnog and Headwall. Chute 5 has killer airs and you can speed faster than a free-falling bungy-jumper. For steep, natural halfpipes, spines and cliff drops, head over to Where's Bob or Free Fall. Ride the Holy Smokes for a quick drop (named after the burnt-out pines) through an S-shaped valley and down to Spirit Bowl.

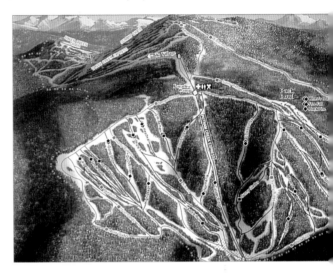

FREESTYLERS There is a hand-shaped intermediate pipe, just above the funpark on the south face. There are rumours of a Pipe Dragon in the air which would improve the present pipe to competition standards. Silver Star has a respectable one hectare (two and a half acre) funpark but unfortunately it is serviced by the slow Yellow Chair. Marked hits help you regulate the risks and build up confidence in your slopestyle technique.

CARVERS If you want to lay down some serious trenches, head up the Summit Chair and drop the Eldorado blue to green. Head back up the Putnam Creek Express Quad to Paradise Camp and take Bergerstrasse to Gypsy Queen and Judo's Run. On the south face, try Milky Way to the junction with Exhibition and all down the way to the Vance Creek Express Quad lift line. If you can still stand up after this carving test, slice the tight, winding Little Dipper or Whiskey Jack.

MOUNTAIN FOOD The one stop on the Putnam Creek face is the Paradise Camp. There's an outdoor patio and indoor dining area with all your favourite savoury grills. The Day Lodge at the base area has the usual foods.

HAZARDS AND RULES Leashes are mandatory. Watch out for merging double black runs on the north face.

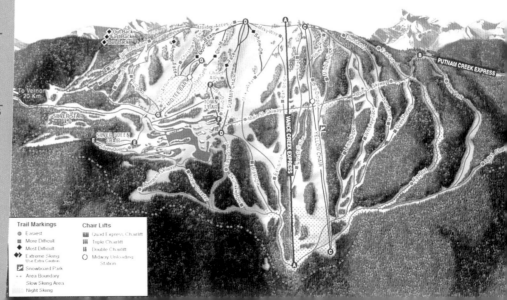

Silver Star

ABOUT TOWN

Silver Star Mountain Resort is the Disneyland of British Columbia. The streets resemble a kitsch western film-set painted by Lewis Carrol on drugs. The buildings are imitation late Victorian and the gas-lit street lamps and absence of traffic give it an old-world feeling. The town of Vernon is 20 kilometres (13 miles) away and has tons of movie theatres, bowling alleys, clubs and restaurants.

ACCOMMODATION There are seven hotels and over 50 vacation homes at Silver Star Mountain Resort with slopeside access. The Vance Creek Hotel comes recommended and has rooms which sleep four people; prices start from $100 per night or from $135 with a kitchenette. The Kickwillie Inn can sleep up to eight people per room for $150 per night. Central Reservations — Tel: 1-800-663 4431. If you want more information on staying in Vernon — Tel: 1-800-665-795, E-mail: verntour@junction.net or check out the net: http://www.vernontourism.com. B&Bs include Wray's B&B from $65 per night for a double room — Tel: 250-545 9821, and Willy's Ranch from $50 per night for a double room — Tel: 250-542 0617. The hard-core can hang out at the Swan Lake RV Park for $18 a hook-up — Tel: 250-545 2300.

FOOD In Putnam Station Hotel, the Craigellachie Dining Room, has great lunches including buffalo-sized burgers. Lucciano's Trattoria has awesome pizza, pasta and seafood in a Mediterranean atmosphere. For sandwiches and deli food, the Lord Aberdeen Hotel has a general grocery and liquor store. Bugaboo's Bakery has speciality breads and pastries, hot chocolates and cappuccinos. There are loads of choices in Vernon. If you head downtown, the Han Mongolian Barbecue does a wicked oriental stir-fry. Vegetarians will relish the organic cuisine at Lebens and Italian fanatics will enjoy eating out at Intermezzo. For other choices, ask for the North Okanagan Visitor's Guide — Tel: 250-542 1415.

NIGHTLIFE The Vance Creek Saloon has live music, pool, video games and a good atmosphere in a rowdy western setting; wear your cowboy boots. The Cellar Lounge in the Putnam Station Hotel is a cosy, fireside wine bar. Many of the locals head back to Vernon to party in the down-home pubs.

OTHER ACTIVITIES Tubing in the tube town beside the Silver Queen Chair. Sleigh rides, ice-skating, snowmobiling.

THANKS TO Darren and Drew Neilson.

6

Top — Silver Star Town **Photo:** Mike MacWatt

Bottom — Cody Ralph **Photo:** Mike MacWatt

GETTING THERE

By air: The closest domestic airport is Kelowna. The scheduled shuttle service from the airport to Vernon takes one hour and costs $15. You can also book shuttles straight to the resort costing $38 return for four people — Tel: 604-542 6119.

By bus: Greyhound buses stop at Silver Star Mountain Resort — Tel: 1-800-663 4431.

By car: Connect with Highway 97 to Vernon and follow 48th Ave to Silver Star.

Getting around: If you're staying in the village, everything is within walking distance.

Panorama

THE FACTS

ELEVATION

Summit:
2379m, 7800ft
Vertical drop:
1220m, 4000ft
Base:
1159m, 3800ft

SNOWFALL

Average annual:
300cm, 118 inches

Snow-making:
50%

AREA

Total area:
800ha, 2000 acres

Advanced: 25%
Intermediate: 55%
Beginner: 20%

SEASON
Mid-November — April

COMMUNICATIONS
Snow report: Tel: 250-342 6941
Web site: http://www.panoramaresort.com
E-mail: paninfo@panoramaresort.com
Mountain information:
Tel: 250-342 6941 or 1-800-663 2929

LIFTS AND TICKETS
Number of lifts:
4 chairlifts, 2 T-bars, 1 handle tow, 1 poma
Lift pass prices*:
1/2 day: 33.65
1 day: $42.06
Multi-day: $152.34 (5 days)
Season: $599
Other ticketing information:
* GST not included. A student (18-24yrs) season pass costs $419.

SNOWBOARD SHOPS
Big Deals — Tel: 250-342 6941
B+B: $30.

SNOWBOARD SCHOOL
Panorama Snowboard School — Tel: 250-342 6941
Small but focused, the school was named the best ski and snowboard school in Canada for two seasons. Three hour group lessons cost $69 and specialist one hour lessons cost $19.

ON THE MOUNTAIN

Quietly tucked away in the Purcell Mountains on the eastern fringe of the Rockies, Panorama is a bit of a surprise. Large and steep, Panorama has a low profile among the riding scene and a small accommodation threshold which means that most mornings you can ride the lifts with 30 or 40 chairs between people. The mountain splits horizontally by degree of difficulty; everything above the Horizon Chair is intense whereas the terrain below it is mellow. All the trails are kept to a high standard. For the '97-'98 season, another 162 hectares (400 acres) of black diamond and blue terrain will added to the Extreme Dream Zone, the main freeriding area.

SNOW CONDITIONS The north and north-west exposures around the mountain keep Panorama's snow in good condition, so the low figures don't really tell the full story.

BACK-COUNTRY OPTIONS They're pretty mellow about out of bounds behaviour, but don't be tempted by the daily chop-chop-chop of RK Helis unless you're a novice — it's a play-school.

FREERIDERS The Extreme Dream Zone includes most of the double blacks serviced by the Summit T-bar. It is comprised of a series of steep, short shots with light tree cover and some good drops skier's right of the Summit T-bar. Skier's left of World Cup Way, the short, steep Champagne Chute often holds powder longest and will give amateur riders a taste of the extreme potential around them. Café and Latté are two radical lines that could send you running for your mother. Most people funnel down through Trigger instead of riding here, and you'll often find good fresh if you head away from the middle lines.

As far as the rest of the mountain goes, the Upper Bowl is open with soft snow and some unreal hits. The Sunbird lift line trail is awesome in powder with steep drops, little cliffs and the like. For a 30 degree tree run, try out the Black Door. Hideaway also has some intense tree lines. The lower half of the mountain holds bowl riding, tree riding and an even spread of blue, black and green trails, all of which are groomed close to perfection.

FREESTYLERS There's a good funpark with half-a-dozen hits, designed and built by Steve Saunders. Whiskey Jack has a bundle of hits on the sides of the trail. Horseshoe has tons of rollers with hits on the sides.

CARVERS Panorama has won Ski Magazine awards for grooming and given the continuous gradient and uncluttered runs, it's an unreal place to carve. The Fritz is super fun.

MOUNTAIN FOOD The Cappuccino Hut at the top of the Horizon Chair is a nice place to snack on big sausages or steak sandwiches during the day. Everything else is found at the Day Lodge and Pine Inn.

HAZARDS AND RULES Take a guide if you hike off the back; there's also a good hike out at the bottom. Check with the ski patrol to see what the conditions are like before you go. Take note that out of bounds rescues are billed to the rescuee.

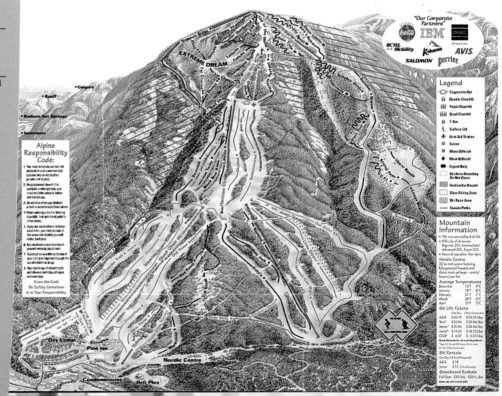

Panorama

ABOUT TOWN

Panorama is located only two hours south-west of Banff and the drive through the Banff and Kootenay National Parks is one of the most spectacular in the world. There is a small village on the mountain plus a large lodging complex. Everyone who works in the village is unbelievably friendly — it's said to be company policy to weed out the grumpy ones. Whatever their secret, it's well done because the end result is a refreshingly warm and welcoming environment.

If you find yourself wanting more, Invermere is 15 minutes away. Originally called Copper City by the first owner in 1890, the town changed its name to Invermere ('inver' means at the mouth, and 'mere' means lake in Gaelic). It's a nice town of 2000 people and has a picturesque lake, a river and lots of craft stores — almost like a mini-Banff. Check out the movie theatre featuring shag-pile carpet on the walls and model airplanes on the roof — it's a beauty.

ACCOMMODATION Not a lot of choices at present, though this will undoubtedly change with two new hotels under construction for the '97-'98 season. The Horsethief Lodge has double rooms from $127 per night. There is also the Pine Inn Hotel and the Toby Creek Lodge; prices start at $92. Lodging and lift packages are available. Special packages in January start from $119 per person for three nights and two days mid-week. All enquires and telephone contacts via Central Reservations — Tel: 250-342 6941 or 1-800-663 2929.

FOOD The T-bar and Grill is the most popular food stop with the locals — it's a kind of pub with a grill restaurant; meals cost around $7-$10. The locals party hard and it's hard to avoid joining in. The Starbird Family Dining Room and Lounge is much as the name suggests. They have a mid-priced menu and an awesome $15 buffet but their pizzas are downright bad. The food is healthy but not exceptional. Toby Creek has great food but you pay for it. In Invermere, the Blue Dog is a super nice café serving delicious soup and muffins. Also in Invermere, Strands has fine dining. For something different, the Black Forest cooks Bavarian dishes and the Oriental Palace makes a mean stir-fry.

NIGHTLIFE At Panorama, the Glacier is a small club open till 2.00am with sketchy DJs and an assortment of live acts. Monday is jam night, Wednesday features live bands and of course the weekends wail. The Jackpine Pub serves jugs of beer in mountaineer-themed decor.

OTHER ACTIVITIES Snowmobiling, dogsled rides, free sleigh rides and skating.

THANKS TO Ken Wilder, Bonnie Bavin, Shelagh Bridgewater, Brian Lyall and Mike Faucham.

GETTING THERE

By air: Calgary International Airport is the principal gateway serving all major carriers including Delta Airlines — Tel: 1-800-221 1212.
By bus: Greyhound go from Calgary and the trip costs $35 one-way — Tel: 1-800-663 2929.
By car: Drive past Banff from Calgary and turn south off the Trans-Canada Highway 1 onto Highway 93 towards Radium Hot Springs. Travel south on Highway 93/95 for ten kilometres (six miles) to Invermere. Panorama is 18 kilometres (11 miles) west of Invermere.

⑦

Top — The Summit **Photo:** Tim Rainger
Bottom — Steve Saunders launching out of the funpark **Photo:** Tim Rainger

Big White

8

THE FACTS

ELEVATION

Summit:
2286m, 7500ft
Vertical drop:
777m, 2550ft
Base:
1508m, 4950ft

SNOWFALL

Average annual:
750cm, 295 inches

Snow-making:
None

AREA

Total area:
840ha, 2075 acres

Advanced: 26%
Intermediate: 56%
Beginner: 18%

SEASON
Mid-November — mid-April

COMMUNICATIONS
Snow report: Tel: 250-765 7669 or 1-900-451 4997
Web site: http://www.bigwhite.com
E-mail: bigwhite@silk.net
Mountain information:
Tel: 250-765 3101
Fax: 250-765 8200

LIFTS AND TICKETS
Number of lifts:
4 high-speed quads, 3 chairlifts, 1 platter lift,
1 T-bar, 1 handle tow
Lift pass prices*:
1/2 day: $34, $28 (13-18 yrs)
1 day: $45, $37 (13-18 yrs)
Multi-day: $234 (6 days), $192 (13-18 yrs)
Season: $300-$400
Other ticketing information:
* GST included. Night-riding is open from 5.00pm
to 9.00pm, Tuesday to Saturday costs $16.

SNOWBOARD SHOPS
There are no snowboard shops in Big White, but
there are a couple in Kelowna:
Island Snow — Tel: 250-763 1338
Rentals and the rest.
540 Skate and Snowboard — Tel: 250-765 5403
Core store with the gear.

SNOWBOARD SCHOOL
Big White Snowboard School — Tel: 250-765 3101
The Learn to Snowboard package starts from
$54.95 and includes rentals, a two hour lesson,
and a ticket for the Plaza Lift.

ON THE MOUNTAIN

Big White is an understatement: Monster White is closer to the truth. It has an uncrowded, cruisy attitude that is local, laid-back and geared towards utilising the mountain to the fullest. It's difficult to get lost because the runs are clearly marked and the well thought-out lift system enables riders to access the best terrain. The '96-'97 season saw Big White open up a former locals' haven of glades and groomed terrain known as the Westridge area. After a dump the area is heaven; the 'snow ghosts' or snow-encrusted pines give a spooky, other-worldly feeling and the pow provides the heavenly bit.

SNOW CONDITIONS An average of around seven and a half metres (25 feet) of snow buries Big White each season. The front side has a southerly aspect which catches the sun while Westridge has a westerly aspect.

FREERIDERS The newly opened Westridge area has a gladed bowl which has the best powder after a dump. The Alpine T-bar on the south face gets you to the Enchanted Forest. The Cliff and the wide open Parachute Bowl are for those who like mixing speed with big airs and powder. This area has the highest elevation and freshies can be found for days. Similarly, the Falcon Chair accesses great bowl riding with plenty of wind lips, chutes and (with a short hike) more tree runs through the Falcon Glades. Continuing down towards the Powder Triple Chair, surf-stylers can ride the frozen waves of the Corkscrew, Flagpole and Dragon Glades.

FREESTYLERS The two pipes and park are products of noted rider Flynn Seddon, six-year veteran of the World Cup circuit and co-ordinator for the Canadian Nationals, and his creative and dedicated group of shapers. Both pipes are found on the south face. The steeper of the two is on Speculation while the easier pipe is on Freeway. Beneath the Bullet Express Chair, the funpark has the goods. It's an excellent slopestyle training ground and is well-maintained. Freestylers will definitely not be disappointed with the park, pipes and a serious selection of naturally formed mountain hits.

CARVERS This is charging heaven for hard-booters. Euro-stylers in search of a speed rush need look no further than Big White for immaculately groomed runs of marathon distance. The Ridge Rocket, Bullet and Black Forest Express Quads service virtually all the best runs, like the wide intermediates of Perfection, Paradise and Exhibition. Cougar Alley is sure to keep you grinning insanely. Beginners will enjoy Lower Sun Run and Highway 33. The longest run at Big White is seven kilometres (four miles) from the top of the Alpine T-bar to the base of the Westridge area.

MOUNTAIN FOOD The Loose Moose is the highest restaurant on the hill and is boardable from all the runs between the Ridge Rocket and Bullet Express Quads; it has a huge selection of snacks, salads, burgers and beverages for the famished. Raakel's, on the lower section of the Perfection trail, has a real boarder vibe and matching menu. The Alpine Centre and the Ridge Day Lodge also have cafeterias while the new Westridge Warming Chalet has vending machines for snacks and beverages.

HAZARDS AND RULES Leashes are mandatory.

EVENTS AND COMPETITIONS The Canadian and North American Snowboard Championships are scheduled to be held here in the '97-'98 season.

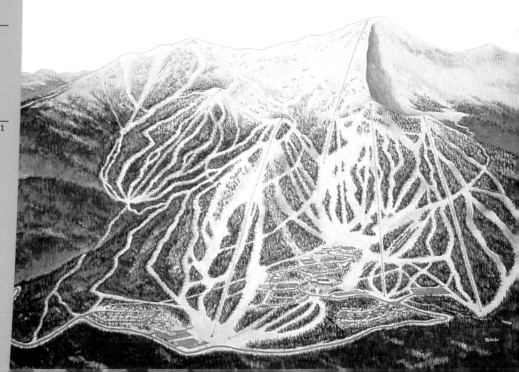

ABOUT TOWN

Big White is a welcoming, self-sufficient community which has everything within walking distance — remember to pack boots to wade through the powder. With a population of over 100,000, Kelowna is a 45 minute drive from Big White and boasts the largest shopping centre east of Vancouver as well as a a wide selection of cafés, restaurants, bars and clubs. The population apparently includes the Ogopogo, a sea-monster allegedly resident in Lake Okanagan. Rumour has it that this is the Loch Ness Monster's holiday home.

ACCOMMODATION One of the best deals is the Whitefoot Lodge at $59 per night; the room price includes a lift ticket, an indoor hot-tub, sauna, restaurant, grocery, liquor store and indoor parking. Built into a massive rock, the Rock House is popular and it's essential to book early — Tel: 250-861 4754. In Kelowna, packages including lift tickets and hot breakfasts start from $49 per night at the Best Western — Tel: 1-800-860 1212. Ask about their packages with lodging, lifts and lessons thrown in. Book through Central Reservations — Tel: 250-765 8888 or 1-800-663 2772 or their web site: bwcenres@silk.net.

FOOD There are only a few choices for food but they cover most budgets and tastebuds. Snowshoe Sam's has great food all day including epic breakfasts. Raakel's has barbecues, nachos, music, beer and sundeck seating. Tokyo Tom's serves sushi and oriental favourites. Beano's Coffee Parlour in the new Village Centre is the place for great coffee to start the day.

NIGHTLIFE Snowshoe Sam's offers drink and munchie specials. A good mix of people end up on the dance floor and there's a games room on the main floor upstairs. For excellent live music, a fun atmosphere and party-sized food servings, try Raakel's. The Loose Moose Tap and Grill has a huge drink selection, a cool dance floor with a cat-track DJ booth, a snowboard simulator and good food.

OTHER ACTIVITIES Ice-skating, cross-country trails, snowmobile tours — Tel: 250-765 8888.

THANKS TO Flynn Seddon, Wayne and Houston (from the Avalanche Rescue Team), Neil and Brian for showing us some fine tree runs.

8

Top — Big Grey **Photo:** Mike MacWatt

Bottom — **Photo:** Jim Baker **Courtesy:** Big White

GETTING THERE

By air: Kelowna has the nearest domestic airport, 45 minutes from Big White. A shuttle bus goes daily to Big White from the airport but reservations are required; price $55 return. Contact Central Reservations.

By bus: A bus goes from Kelowna on Friday, Saturday, Sunday and holidays; prices from $15 return, $11 one-way — Tel: 250-765 3101.

By car: Kelowna is 483 kilometres (293 miles) from Vancouver via Highway 97C. For road conditions — Tel: 1-900-451 4997.

Getting around: There are shuttles from Kelowna up to the resort. Car drivers should note that there are no gas stations so fill up before leaving the highway or take a spare tank.

Kimberley

9

THE FACTS

ELEVATION

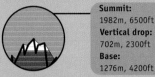

Summit:
1982m, 6500ft
Vertical drop:
702m, 2300ft
Base:
1276m, 4200ft

SNOWFALL

Average annual:
275cm, 110 inches

Snow-making:
62%

AREA

Total area:
484ha, 1200 acres

Advanced: 20%
Intermediate: 60%
Beginner: 20%

SEASON

Mid-December — April

COMMUNICATIONS

Snow report: Tel: 250-427 7332
Web site: http://www.kimberleyski.info-pages.com
Mountain information:
Tel: 250-427 4881
Fax: 250-427 3927

LIFTS AND TICKETS

Number of lifts:
3 chairlifts, 1 T-bar, 2 handle tows
Lift pass prices*:
1/2 day: $27
1 day: $35
Multi-day: $147 (5 days)
Season: $425-$595
Other ticketing information:
* Prices include GST. There is night-riding beside
the Maverick T-bar from 5.30pm to 9.30pm,
Christmas till mid-March. All multi-day tickets
include night-riding.

SNOWBOARD SHOPS

Boarder's Choice — Tel: 250-489 4568
The local specialist store in Cranbrook, about 30
kilometres (20 miles) from Kimberley.
Gerick's — Tel: 250-426 6171
Also in Cranbrook.

SNOWBOARD SCHOOL

Kimberley Ski School — Tel: 250-427 4881
The price for the First Timer package is $39.95
which includes a 90 minute group lesson, rental
and a rope tow pass.

ON THE MOUNTAIN

Kimberley is a small, family-focused resort with trails etched tightly into its forests. There are two main areas to ride; the first is the lower mountain accessed by the Rosa Chair, the Maverick T-bar and the Buckhorn Chair. The runs that fan out and down to the base area make up the bulk of the terrain. With most of the resort's black diamond runs, the second broad area spreads out from the top of the Easter Triple Chair. During the '98-'99 season, Kimberley is introducing a new T-bar directly below Twist in the North Bowl which will open up 35 per cent more terrain and increase the vertical on the existing runs in the bowl by 518 vertical metres (1700 feet).

SNOW CONDITIONS Facing south-east, Kimberly catches the sun. The orientation and the low altitude mean that it's great when it snows but the slopes get baked pretty quickly.

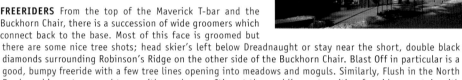

BACK-COUNTRY OPTIONS Columbia Valley Adventures organise full back-country packages: snowcats and heliboarding, snowmobiles, dogsleds, transportation and accommodation. These guys will get you where you want to be for the amount of money you want to spend and they are well-recommended — Tel: 604-427 2570 or 1-800-615 5565.

FREERIDERS From the top of the Maverick T-bar and the Buckhorn Chair, there is a succession of wide groomers which connect back to the base. Most of this face is groomed but there are some nice tree shots; head skier's left below Dreadnaught or stay near the short, double black diamonds surrounding Robinson's Ridge on the other side of the Buckhorn Chair. Blast Off in particular is a good, bumpy freeride with a few tree lines opening into meadows and moguls. Similarly, Flush in the North Bowl combines steeps and trees with good snow. It's not the world's most exciting freeride mountain with no open bowls and a high percentage of tight trees surrounding the 47 motorway trails.

FREESTYLERS Not a huge commitment to the man-made stuff in '96-'97. There is a small, handmade halfpipe which locals' say is good to train in. The half-a-dozen intermediate hits are located under the Rosa Chair in the Rosa Terrain Park. The best hit is a medium-sized gap jump which launches you from a buried VW hippy bus. There's also an aerial ski jump above the Day Lodge which is good for big air training.

CARVERS Kimberley is best suited to carvers. Midnight, Main and Rosa are the best maintained and groomed, though most of the groomers can be charged full-throttle without too much fear of intersecting cat-tracks and other unwelcome speed reducers. Otherwise it's nice and wide with lots of space on the blues, though scary moguls can form on the blacks.

MOUNTAIN FOOD Krug Stube lounge in the North Star Centre is a quiet place to eat with excellent burgers, fries, pasta and soup. For similar fare, try the Day Lodge café on the main level. If you're really hungry, eat at Mingle's Grill.

HAZARDS AND RULES Beware the tight trees.

EVENTS AND COMPETITIONS There's a spring splash festival with fun races, mountain bike races and a slush pool finale.

ABOUT TOWN

Kimberley is a small town with about 6500 inhabitants, a couple of bars and several restaurants. It's named after the African diamond mining town but the minerals here are less glamourous: ore, lead and zinc. It's now known as the Bavarian town of the Rockies, a reputation manifested in some fairly crude architectural styles, Bavarian names and events like huge accordion parties and the July Fest which celebrate beer-drinking and om-pah-pah music. In Platzl, a pedestrian-only part of Kimberley's downtown, you'll find the world's largest cuckoo clock, hand-painted fire-hydrants, decorated foot-bridges and other lovingly thought-out details which add to the Bavarian kitschness. Cranbrook, 30 kilometres (20 miles) from Kimberley, has about 20,000 inhabitants. It is predominantly a logging town with some nightlife and a couple of snowboard stores.

ACCOMMODATION There are a few options just below the lift base. The Mountain Edge condos are compact units with fireplaces, TV and shared jacuzzis; prices are around $80 a night for two people. The Budget B&B is also reasonably priced from $46 a night; if you stay three nights, the third night is free. The Mountain Recreation Centre has the cheapest accommodation; RV and camping sites start from $16 — Tel: 1-800-667 0871.

FOOD Zante's serve good Greek food; the restaurant is low-priced and dishes up large helpings. Chef Bernard's is a popular European restaurant. For something further up the price scale, try the Bavarian Gasthaus. Real German food is served at the Bauernhaus. The owner dismantled the 350 year-old building, shipped it over from Germany and rebuilt it here. Cowboys and the Rocky Mountain Restaurant in Marysville Hotel are both inexpensive places with standard food.

NIGHTLIFE The pub Sullivan's gets busy in the early evenings and weekends. It has jukeboxes, the occasional live music act, pool tables, meals and is open till 2.00am. The 5.00pm happy hour on

Opposite — Kimberley town **Photo:** Tim King

Top — Happy Hans, town mascot **Courtesy:** Kimberley

Bottom — **Photo:** Tim Rainger

Fridays includes free finger-food. Hotel Kimberley is the late night party bar; bands play on Thursday, Friday and Saturday nights.

OTHER ACTIVITIES Drinking, practising the accordion and memorising irregular German verbs.

THANKS TO Shannon Harrison, Mike Bradford, Steve Norton at Columbia Valley Adventures, Duff Boyd at Raven's Roost.

9

GETTING THERE

By air: Cranbrook has the nearest local airport, a 30 kilometre (20 mile) drive from Kimberley. Shuttle services to Kimberley are available during the ski season; just inform your hotel of your arrival and departure times.

By bus: Daily Greyhound services arrive from Calgary at noon each day and from Vancouver on Tuesday through to Saturday.

By car: From Calgary it's about a four hour drive. Take Highway 1 west to Highway 95 south, and then Highway 95A to Kimberley.

Getting around: It's a few miles from town to the mountain base so it's useful to have a car, although hitching is possible.

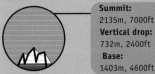

Island Lake Lodge

THE FACTS

ELEVATION

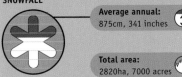

Summit:
2135m, 7000ft
Vertical drop:
732m, 2400ft
Base:
1403m, 4600ft

SNOWFALL

Average annual:
875cm, 341 inches

Total area:
2820ha, 7000 acres

SEASON

Mid-December — late March
The season is broken into bookable slots of three or four days.

COMMUNICATIONS

E-mail: islandk@mail.elkvalley.net
Mountain information:
Tel: 250-423 3700 or 1-888-4-CATSKI
Fax: 250-423 4055

LIFTS AND PRICES

Number of lifts:
3 Piston Bully snowcats
Prices*:
3 days: $1161 or $1290
4 days: $1548 or $1720
6 days: $2205 or $2460
1 week: $2575 or $2805
Other ticketing information:
*GST not included. Prices are for seven to ten guided runs a day and include food and accommodation with shared facilities. The variation in cost depends on when you go in the season. If you want more private accommodation, you can fork out an extra $45 per night and stay in the new Red Eagle Lodge which has its own kitchen and living area.

GETTING THERE

By air: Daily flights on either Air BC or Canadian Airlines can be made into Cranbrook, one hour from the lodge. Pick-ups can be arranged from Cranbrook for $100 return, or from Calgary and Kalispell for $250 return.
By car: Island Lake Lodge is nine kilometres (six miles) away from Fernie Alpine Resorts. See Fernie review p.232.
Getting around: The lodge is a 45 minute snowcat drive from the carpark. Arrival time is 6.15pm on the night before and departure time is 5.30pm on the last day of boarding. If you want to go to town for the evening, snowmobiles are the only mode of transportation.

ON THE MOUNTAIN

Island Lake Lodge rules. No matter what criteria you name, Island Lake rates 11 out of 10. It's a 2820 hectare (7000 acre) freeriders' playground set in the heart of the Canadian Rockies. Serviced by a fleet of snowcats and guides, the terrain will completely blow your mind. Not only is the snow consistently epic, but the terrain encompasses the entire spectrum from insanely steep chutes and long, natural halfpipes through to gladed cliffs, natural hits and rollers. The good bowl riding and beautiful tree riding through old cedars will bring a virgin buzz reminiscent of your first ever powder day. As Craig Kelly himself says: "Island Lake is my favourite place to ride. The variety of terrain and the quality of the snow is an unparalleled combination that I have seen nowhere else." His small shareholding in the lodge hardly makes him an impartial judge, but it's the old 'I liked it so much I bought the company' story. In many ways, putting your money down is the ultimate sign of faith. Other notable shareholders include film-maker Warren Miller and extreme skier Scott Schmidt.

FREERIDERS After a healthy breakfast, guests are split into teams of up to 12 people with two guides and driven to the first drop-off at around 762 metres (2400 feet) above the lodge. The guides point out the best lines down. All dangers are analysed, a collective decision is reached and the lead guide kicks off. Each member of the group rides their own line with the stragglers being swept up by the second guide acting as a tail gunner. The cat picks you up from a pre-arranged meeting point and then it's back up again. Lunch is on an 'as you want it' basis with big crates of sandwiches, fruit, cakes, chocolate bars and coffee available all day in the cab of the cat. Each team packs in between six and ten runs depending on the group's ability.

On a typical day, you'd start a good run well above the tree line. The peaks and ridges above the bowls get as steep as you want and there are a massive array of super extreme lines, many accessed by short hikes and climbs. Below the peaks, the terrain opens out into a series of glorious bowls before hitting the tree line. In low light, fog or snowstorms, the protected options include the back side trees which remain beautifully defined even in pretty atrocious conditions.

FOOD AND ACCOMMODATION All visitors used to stay in the hand-built tamarack log lodge which sleeps 36 people in simple shared rooms. The Red Eagle Lodge is a new facility offering more private accommodation with ensuite bathrooms. This is not budget riding but once you make the exchange into Canadian dollars, it gets that much more affordable.

Dinner and breakfast are served in the Main Lodge in a super relaxed atmosphere. Next to the dining tables, big sofas surround a huge, river-stone fireplace which is the focus of the evening's entertainment. The bar is conveniently just an arm's reach away but a few quiet ones is all most people indulge in. Partying is low on the priority list; the clientele are generally here to ride and ski, so it's early to bed and early to rise. The additional conveniences include hot air boot-dryers, a fully equipped workshop and jacuzzi on the balcony which makes Island Lake Lodge for the freeride community what Tavarua Island is for the surfing community — paradise with all the extras.

Island Lake Lodge

10

Opposite top — The lodge **Photo:** Tim Rainger
Opposite bottom — Panorama **Photo:** Tim Rainger
Main picture — Shannon Melhuse with lodge in background **Photo:** Mark Gallup
Top inset — **Photo:** Tim Rainger
Bottom inset — Javier Pioccacini **Photo:** Tim Rainger

Fernie Alpine Resorts

ON THE MOUNTAIN

Fernie Alpine Resorts occupies a couple of bowls and ridge lines chopped out of the east side of the saw-toothed Lizard Range. It's a mountain with a huge variety of terrain and a very healthy snowfall and yet for all the talk you hear about Fernie, few people clog the mountain. It has terrain of a similar quality to Island Lake Lodge but is lift-serviced instead of cat-serviced.

Lake Louise recently purchased Fernie and there are major developments planned for the '98-'99 season including a new high-speed quad from the base to the top of Timber Bowl and another from mid-Timber Bowl to White Pass. The present acreage will be nearly doubled, opening up three new bowls called Currie, Timber and Siberia. Snowcat riding will take place in the '97-'98 season in the areas cut for the anticipated lifts and will cost around $195 a day.

Griz, the legendary man of the mountains, is the local snow God. The story goes that he sleeps in bear caves in summer and shoots powder from his hunting rifle in winter. Fernie hosts a festival every February to pick the crustiest guy in town to be Griz for the next year.

SNOW CONDITIONS Fernie faces east to north-east but when it snows here it snows big, often up to ten metres (35 feet) per season. December and January are way cold which translates into superb snow conditions. Fernie sits at the cross-roads of east-west and north-south valley chains and consequently gets hit by big storms which by-pass the Kootenay region.

FREERIDERS It's hard to pick specific runs because the whole mountain is extremely rideable and entertaining. Currie Bowl is presently unserviced by lifts but can be reached by a short hike. Traverse skier's right from Face Lift above Lizard Bowl and hump up the saddle. Lizard Bowl is a big, open area skier's right of the top two lifts which is awesome with fresh pow. There's a wide variety of pitches with some big hits, short steep chutes, little trees and a nice natural pipe near the Freeway trail.

Going skier's left from the top of either Face Lift or the Boomerang Chair, you hit Cedar Bowl. The north-facing ridge drops into the bowl which holds some nice gullies and natural halfpipes with good snow. Lightly spaced trees fringe the bowl and are also enjoyable. Below Cedar Bowl is the area called King Fir which fades into the trees below Cedar Ridge and holds some 37-40 degree powder stashes between the trees. On a good powder day, ride the upper mountain lifts as the quad is slow and often has queues.

FREESTYLERS There are two funparks; the best one is Deer Park built below the Deer Chair. It's remodelled and changed quite regularly so we can't really make a comment on specific features. Bambi Park has a halfpipe as well. Both parks are built out of earth pre-season but the '96-'97 snowfall exceeded the expectations of the builders and flattened many of their features. There's a well-known gap jump at the head of Blueberry.

CARVERS The groomers like Bear and Northridge dropping off North Ridge are steep as all hell and can be perfect corduroy in the morning. There's also a world-class Super-G run, a speed fiend's dream.

MOUNTAIN FOOD Gabriella's Pasta Restaurant at the base serves excelelnt Italian cuisine. Big portions go for reasonable prices like $5.95 for meatball sandwiches. The Bear's Den is a small food concession; prices are the same but there's less variety.

HAZARDS AND RULES Skiers have to stay out of the halfpipe and park. Leashes are obligatory.

THE FACTS

ELEVATION

Summit:
1794m, 5900ft
Vertical drop:
731m, 2400ft
Base:
1066m, 3500ft

SNOWFALL

Average annual:
875cm, 345 inches

Snow-making:
Minimal

AREA

Total area:
405ha, 1000 acres

Advanced: 30%
Intermediate: 40%
Beginner: 30%

SEASON

Early December — mid-April

COMMUNICATIONS

Snow report: Tel: 250-423 3555
Web site: http://www.rockies.net/~fsv
E-mail: fsv@elkvalley.net
Mountain information:
Tel: 250-423 4655
Fax: 250-426 6644
Fernie Chamber of Commerce:
Tel: 250-423 6868
Fax: 250-423 3811

LIFTS AND TICKETS

Number of lifts:
1 high-speed quad, 2 chairlifts, 2 T-bars, 1 handle tow, 1 platter lift
Lift pass prices*:
1/2 day: $29, $22 (13-18yrs)
1 day: $36, $28 (13-18yrs)
Multi-day: $192 (6 days)
Season: $510, $330 (13-18yrs)
Other ticketing information:
*GST included. A month pass costs $299. Early purchase season passes cost $420.

SNOWBOARD SHOPS

Frozen Ocean — Tel: 250-423 3042
Run by Napoleon Champagne and the crew, the shop is in an old house down by the Seven Eleven on Highway 3.

SNOWBOARD SCHOOL

Adventure Shop Snowboard School
Tel: 250-423 3515
First Timer package (lift, lesson, rental) costs $45.

Fernie Alpine Resorts

ABOUT TOWN

Fernie has been around for about a century and though now a town of 5000 people, it still retains a rough-hewn feel. Unfortunately many of the earliest buildings were erased in the fire which swept through several blocks of the town in 1903. Legend has it that this and subsequent disasters were the workings of a curse placed on the valley by a local Indian chief, as revenge for the philandering miner James Fernie's ill-treatment of his daughter. Fernie was more obsessed by the source of the coal around her neck than by her and a curse was cast; the valley would 'suffer from fire, flood, strife and discord; all will finally die from fire and water.' Another fire totally destroyed Fernie in 1908 and the valley has been plagued by spring floods throughout its history. The curse was lifted in '64 by Chief Red Eagle of the Tobacco Plains Tribe in the interests of protecting the new Highway 3.

ACCOMMODATION If you choose to stay on the mountain, the Griz Inn Sports Hotel and Condominiums is the obvious choice. It's cheap, friendly and right at the lift base with a good sundeck and bar. A one bedroom unit sleeping four starts from $165 — Tel: 250-423 9221 or 1-800-661 0118. In Fernie itself, there is a fairly wide spread of low cost motels, a few hotels and B&Bs. The Mountain Inn B&B costs $50-$120 a night — Tel: 250-423 3754. Wildflower B&B is another good place to stay with clean, non-smoking rooms from

$45 a single and $55 a double — Tel: 250-432 6484. The cheapest option in town is the Fernie International Hostel and Motel; a dorm bed goes from $12 and a single room from $29.95. There is a shared kitchen and a free pancake breakfast — Tel: 250-423 6811. Individual homes from Fernie Mountain Properties sleep eight to 12 people; prices start from $285 per night for three nights — Tel: 250-423 9286. Central Reservations — Tel: 250-423 9284 or 1-888-754 7325.

FOOD Rip and Richard's Eatery by the bridge specialises in south-western cuisine; their great pizzas are made in a wood-burning oven. They probably stay open the latest in town but that's only till 9.30pm or 10.00pm if it's a big night. Nearby Lil' Richies has good breakfast specials and 'great blizzard' ice-cream. Rocky's Family Restaurant on Highway 3 east of Fernie serves up stir-fries, salad, Ukrainian and Italian food. Antonio's Restaurant in the Cedar Lodge specialises in prime ribs and salad. Country Tyme Natural Foods has a bakery, cappuccino bar and vegetarian café. It doubles up as a holistic centre and also has remedies and bodycare products.

NIGHTLIFE Evening and night entertainment is very pub oriented with occasional live music. First beers off the mountain are at the Day Lodge Bar at the base of the lifts. The Northern Hotel is one of the main-stays with a random selection of rock, jazz and blues bands. The Royal Rockin' Bar is just that, a bit of a dive but it can rock. All the traditional pub games from pool to football can be played at the Park Place Bar and Grill. A non-alcoholic option is Jamocha's Coffee House and Bagel Co. which has coffee machines steaming until 10.00pm.

OTHER ACTIVITIES Curling, ice-skating, coal-mine tours, snowmobiling and moonlight rides with East Kootenay Snowmobile Rentals and Tours — Tel: 250-423 3883 and Fernie Wilderness Adventures —

Tel: 250-423 3883. The Chamber of Commerce has free trail maps and BC Trailpasses for $50; funds support back-country rescues and grooming.

THANKS TO Muriel McLeod, Heiko Socher, Mark Ballard and Cindy, Napoleon Champagne and the Frozen Ocean crew.

GETTING THERE

By air: The nearest airport is Cranbrook, just over an hour's scenic drive away with daily flights from Vancouver and Calgary. Fernie Alpine Resorts operate a shuttle for package skiers out of Calgary from Friday to Sunday and daily out of Cranbrook on mid-afternoon flights. Shuttles can be scheduled to carry 11 people from Calgary airport for $268 — Tel: 250-423 4408. Local accommodations also provide airport shuttles.
By bus: Greyhound offers a twice daily service to Fernie — Tel: 1-800-661 8747.
By car: Fernie is located in the south-east corner of BC on Crows Nest Highway 3, approximately 60 kilometres (40 miles) from the Alberta and US borders.
Getting around: If you're staying in Fernie, the $2 Ski Shuttle goes up to the resort during ski hours and in the evening if required — Tel: 250-423 4408.

11

Opposite — Stephen Whelan at Currie Bowl **Photo:** Nolen Oayda
Top — 'Welcome to Fernie' — road sign on highway **Photo:** Tim Rainger
Bottom — Looking downtown at 7.30am on a crisp, spring Saturday morning with Fernie Alpine Resort in the background **Photo:** Tim Rainger

Red Mountain

THE FACTS

ELEVATION

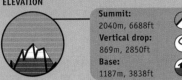

Summit:
2040m, 6688ft
Vertical drop:
869m, 2850ft
Base:
1187m, 3838ft

SNOWFALL

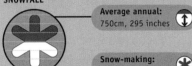

Average annual:
750cm, 295 inches

Snow-making:
Zip

AREA

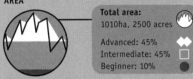

Total area:
1010ha, 2500 acres

Advanced: 45%
Intermediate: 45%
Beginner: 10%

SEASON
Early December — early April

COMMUNICATIONS
Snow report:
Tel: 250-362 5500 (Rossland) or 509-459 6000
Web site: http://www.ski-red.com
E-mail: redmtn.@awinc.com
Mountain information:
Tel: 250-362 7384
Fax: 250-362 5833
Rossland Chamber of Commerce:
Tel: 250-362 566
Fax: 250-362 5399

LIFTS AND TICKETS
Number of lifts:
4 chairlifts, 1 T-bar
Lift pass prices:
1/2 day: $30
1 day: $39
Multi-day: $198 (6 days)
Season: $525, $380 (13-18yrs)
Other ticketing information:
The Red Mountain BC Ski Card gives you two free
days and discounts each day you ride. The card can
be used at Whistler and Silver Star.

SNOWBOARD SHOPS
Powder Hound — Tel: 604-362 5311
In Rossland, this shops has the works.
Le Roi's Sports — Tel: 250-362 7124
At the base of the mountain.

SNOWBOARD SCHOOL
Red Mountain Snowboard School
Tel: 250-362 7115 or 1-800-663 0105

ON THE MOUNTAIN

In the south of the Monashee Mountains, Red Mountain ski area overlooks the town of Rossland. Encompassing Red Mountain and Granite Mountain, its 1010 hectares (2500 acres) of groomed runs, natural glades and incredible back-country hiking make it comparable to terrain usually accessed by helicopter. This could be the answer as to why the town and mountains have such a laid-back, ride-hard vibe — it's contagious. Advanced boarders from all over Canada stop off at Red in search of ungroomed, hidden treasures.

SNOW CONDITIONS Red Mountain has the lower altitude of the two mountains and the snow is mostly groomed and packed powder. Granite Mountain has more terrain left ungroomed and the high elevation preserves light snow until the end of the season.

FREERIDERS The Long Squaw is a five mile (eight kilometre) trail down Granite Mountain which has beginners feeling advanced after their first run and helps orientate other levels of riders. Advanced riders can try the black diamond Powder Fields and Pale Face on skier's right of the Motherlode Chair. From the top of the Paradise Chair, the options are spread to the boundary with runs like Southside Road and Meadows. If you're experienced and feeling fit, traverse past Paradise Lodge and hike to the flat top of Mount Roberts for some of the best freeriding around. The faces of Granite Mountain offer the lot: rocks, drops, chutes, wind lips and trees.

FREESTYLERS Jibophiles will excel everywhere. The Rhythm Method halfpipe is medium-sized and located next to the T-bar beneath Red's Face. Traversing along Boardwalk will take you to the funpark. Machine-groomed with long table tops, boxes, pyramids and spines, this park makes a good training ground for the mountain's plentiful and more challenging natural airs. Try the challenging runs on Granite Mountain like Roots, Cambodia and Waterfall.

CARVERS The Long Squaw is pure corduroy joy. A few of the 83 trails to recommend are Towers of Red, directly beneath the Red Chair, Upper Back Trail and Face of Red; get into a tuck position to speed back to the Base Lodge. Ruby Tuesday, Doug's Run and Maggie's Farm are the best for strong riders whereas Gambler, Southern Bell and Southside Road are challenging for novice and intermediate edge-to-edgers.

MOUNTAIN FOOD The cafeteria and Rafter's Bar and Grill have tex-mex at decent prices and hazardously cheap pitchers of beer. The terraces at the Paradise Lodge serve hot-dog sandwiches and the country's best chocolate-chip cookies.

HAZARDS AND RULES Leashes are mandatory. There are many obvious big air opportunities but check for rocks if you don't know the area. Avalanche warnings are posted for riders to follow not flaunt. When you head back-country, travel in fully prepared groups (with shovels, probes and Ortovox) and use the patrol sign-out board at the top of Long Squaw.

RED MOUNTAIN
ROSSLAND, BRITISH COLUMBIA

Red Mountain

ABOUT TOWN

Rossland is a charming gold-rush town settled in 1897 with a wide main street and shops crammed down either side. The horses have been replaced by four-by-four pick-ups but that's about as sophisticated as it gets. It's a mountaineer's dream and all at a stress-free prices. The locals are friendly and if there's a house party going on, they're sure to make you feel welcome. They are isolated from the big ski scene and are probably better off without it.

Opposite — **Photo:** Mike MacWatt
Top — **Photo:** Mike MacWatt
Bottom — Jamie Rizzoto **Photo:** Mike MacWatt

ACCOMMODATION The Scotsman Motel has clean, comfortable rooms from $38 as well as a fully licensed restaurant serving mountainous breakfasts — Tel: 250-362 7364. The Uplander is Rossland's answer to the Ritz; it's a full service three star hotel with rates starting at $55 for a single — Tel: 250-362 7375. Just 200 metres (400 yards) from the Granite Chair, Red Mountain Cabins are a bargain at $33 — Tel: 250-362 9000. The Mountain Shadow Hostel in downtown Rossland is well-equipped and costs around $17 — Tel: 250-362 7160. Central Reservations — Tel: 250-362 7700 or 1-800-663 0105.

FOOD Healthy breakfast feasts at the Sunrise Café and the Swiss Family Restaurant at the Scotsman Motel will keep you going until lunchtime, and the bakery next door makes great breads, muffins and

pastries. For a pricier, first class meal, the Uplander serves the best selection of steaks, seafood and pastas. If you're vegetarian, try Elmer's Café for reasonable food and a congenial atmosphere. The budget-minded can DIY from the Rossland grocery store.

NIGHTLIFE Rossland's nightlife is limited but healthy. The Flying Steam Shovel has beer, snacks and pool tables with service until 1.00am. The pub in the Uplander has more pool tables, a giant screen playing surf and snow flicks and bar food. It rocks every Friday and Saturday night with live music.

OTHER ACTIVITIES Snowmobiling, cross-country skiing, curling and an Aquatic Centre in Trail.

THANKS TO Scat Peterson, Dott the Scott, Travys.

12

GETTING THERE
By air: Twice daily flights go from Vancouver, Calgary and Edmonton to Castlegar with Mountain Air or Time Air. The pre-arranged airport shuttle costs $10 — Tel: 604-368 6666.
By bus: Greyhound have a daily service to Rossland on the east-west route — Tel: 1-800-661 8747.
By car: Red Mountain is situated just two miles (three kilometres) north-west of Rossland. Drive two hours north from Spokane, Washington on Highway 25.
Getting around: Take the daily City Transit Bus from the town to Red Mountain during the winter.

ALBERTA

STATE INFORMANTION
Population: 2,774,512
Time: Mountain West = GMT minus 7 hours
Capital city: Edmonton
Area: 661,185 sqkm (255,303 sq miles)

VISITOR INFORMATION SOURCES
Alberta Tourism:
Tel: 1-800-661 8888, Fax: 403-427 0867
Web site: http://www.atp.ab.ca

GETTING AROUND
Main airports: Edmonton International Airport — Tel: 403-890 4350, Calgary — Tel: 403-735 1372
By train: VIA Rail — Tel: 506-857 9830 or 1-800-561 8630
By bus: Greyhound Bus Lines — Tel: 403-265 9111 or 1-800 561 8630, Red Arrow — Tel: 403-424 3339
Road conditions: Tel: 403-246 5853
Speed limit: The speed limit is 100 kmph (60 mph) on the highways.

INTRODUCTION
Driving from Edmonton or Calgary to Banff National Park is an experience in itself; the stunning scenery, and the wild emptiness of it all could almost make you crash your car. It's pure, untouched territory, and the same goes for most of the riding. Banff National Park has three resorts within its confines: Lake Louise, Sunshine Village and Banff Mount Norquay. Further afield, Marmot Basin near Jasper is even more remote and it takes a true nature freak to make the rewarding pilgrimage. Party heads will be unlikely to make it past the Banff town limits because all their needs will be met by the wicked riding and non-stop nightlife.

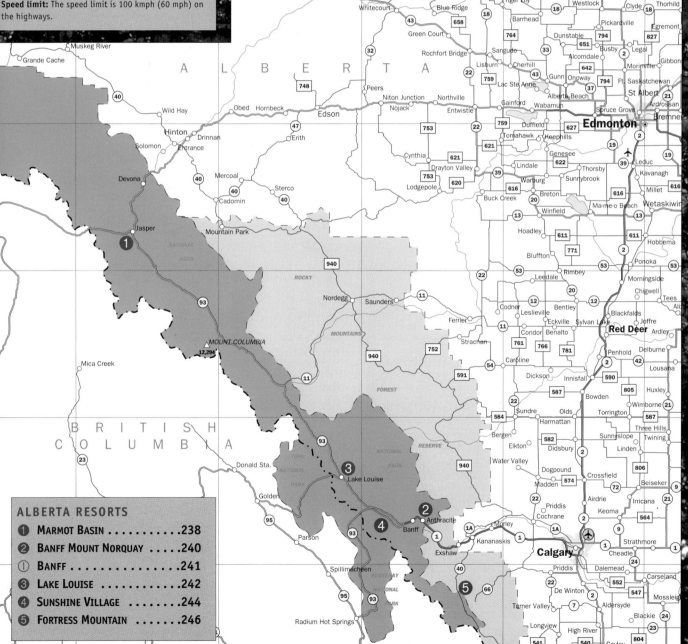

ALBERTA RESORTS

Marmot Basin

ON THE MOUNTAIN

Marmot Basin sits within Jasper National Park, the largest park in the Canadian Rockies. A spectacular three hour drive from Banff, Marmot Basin takes an extra bit of effort to reach but it's worth it for the isolation, the stunning scenery and the wildlife. Winter is the uncrowded off season as the hoards come during summer. The scenery is unbelievable; if you're driving don't forget to watch the road as the incredible scenery will have your mouth agape. As far as the terrain goes, the alpine bowls and uncrowded tree-lined trails of Marmot Basin make it a true frontier outpost for the travelling boarder. Remember that the ski area is a part of a national park and respect the abundant wildlife who don't appreciate your litter, cigarette ends and toilet paper, particularly in the summer after the snow has gone.

SNOW CONDITIONS Marmot's high elevation and bowl shape ensures a stash of dry powder which provides good ground cover until April. Because of its northerly latitude, Marmot Basin is cold so dress warmly.

FREERIDERS The best runs can only be hiked but lifts are being extended for the '97-'98 season although the plans have yet to be confirmed. Freeriders will enjoy the challenges of the Peak Run steeps and the great powder through open trees at Eagle East. For blasting turns in powder, Thunder Bowl is the place to ride but beware the cat-track. For advanced riders, the Rock Gardens provide a good variety of drops and trees. In the future more good powder runs will be lift-serviced on the Cornice boundary. Molly's Ridge, accessed by the long, challenging T-bar, is a charged-up run with a cornice and small cliffs for advanced jumpers. If you plan to jump, probe the landings first as it is blasted occasionally and large bits of debris accumulate.

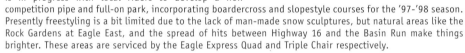

FREESTYLERS The present pipe is a non-vert, small volume effort perfect for the complete novice. Planning is in progress with local riders to develop a new competition pipe and full-on park, incorporating boardercross and slopestyle courses for the '97-'98 season. Presently freestyling is a bit limited due to the lack of man-made snow sculptures, but natural areas like the Rock Gardens at Eagle East, and the spread of hits between Highway 16 and the Basin Run make things brighter. These areas are serviced by the Eagle Express Quad and Triple Chair respectively.

CARVERS This is very much a carvers' paradise with well-groomed trails and an excellent spread of varied pitches. Spillway, Lift Line and Dromedary have the steepest pitches. If you're not quite ready for black diamonds, hit the mellower runs like Lower Dromedary and Tranquilliser. For the hard and fast, take the Caribou Chair and ride Exhibition and Keifer's Dream. Big chicane bends and rollers feature on S-turn and Paradise but be aware of tree-dwelling freeriders dropping in and merging trails.

MOUNTAIN FOOD If you missed breakfast, the Paradise Chalet is a good start to the day and the traverse from the top of the Eagle Express Quad is sure to wake you up. The cafeteria and lounge serve up freshly cooked meals and bar snacks all day. The sun-blessed balcony off the upstairs eating area looks up the basin to the top of the resort and is a good lunchtime spot. The Lower Chalet also offers a well-priced menu to suit all taste-buds with decor that may trigger flash-backs to your school canteen.

HAZARDS AND RULES Leashes are not required but they still have the 'one leg out' law made up by some non-snowboarding idiot.

EVENTS AND COMPETITIONS The New Ground Snowboard Cup is held in the spring.

THE FACTS

ELEVATION

Summit:
2601m, 8534ft
Vertical drop:
897m, 2944ft,
Base:
1704m, 5590ft

SNOWFALL

Average annual:
400cm, 158 inches

Snow-making:
None

AREA

Total area:
400ha, 1000 acres,

Advanced: 30%
Intermediate: 35%
Beginner: 35%

SEASON
Late November — late April

COMMUNICATIONS
Snow report: Tel: 403-488 2422 or 403-488 5909
E-mail: brrode@tetusplanet.net
Mountain information:
Tel: 403-852 3816
Fax: 403-852 3533
Jasper National Park:
Tel: 403-852 66161

LIFTS AND TICKETS
Number of lifts:
5 chairlifts, 2 T-bars, 1 surface lift
Lift pass prices*:
1/2 day: $34
1 day: $39
Multi-day: $195 (5 days)
Season: $512
Other ticketing information:
* Prices include GST. Season pass prices vary from $384 for an adult pass purchased in July to $544 for a pass purchased after November.

SNOWBOARD SHOPS
Freewheel — Tel: 403-852 3898
The shop rents boards, boots, and safety equipment and has facilities for service and repairs. Downstairs they rent and sell crampons, ice-axes and mountain gear.

SNOWBOARD SCHOOL
Alpine Sports Centre — Tel: 403-852 3816
The school offers all-inclusive packages for beginners from $45 or five day packages with video analysis, two hour lessons and a concluding fun competition from $96.

Marmot Basin

ABOUT TOWN

Although the area is isolated, the amenities are excellent. The information centre and banks are all centrally positioned. There are a number of eateries and more importantly, a couple of great places to drink and spin your own discs. It's easy to get around the village on foot although you may be accompanied by wandering elk and other forms of wildlife pacing the pavement. Slightly further from the town you'll see wild bighorn sheep, coyotes, moose, wolves and the odd lynx.

ACCOMMODATION There are a number of similarly priced lodges in Jasper but the pick of the bunch are the Tonquin Inn and the Maligne Lodge. Both are run by ex-Olympic freestyle ski champion Rick Bowie and his wife Karen Decor — they know everyone and everything in the area. The Tonquin Inn has spacious rooms

sleeping two to four people with kitchens and fireplaces priced from $84. Deluxe executive suites sleep three to six people and include a full kitchen, fireplace and private sauna for $139. There is also a pool, spa baths, sauna and gym — Tel: 1-800-661 1315. The Maligne Lodge offers the same standard

of accommodation but the prices are even more affordable. Jasper Central Reservations can tell you about other options — Tel: 403-852 5488.

FOOD There is nothing particularly exotic about Jasper's food but there are plenty of places to eat. The Prime Rib Village in the Tonquin Inn has seriously good steaks and exceptional seafood. For breakfasts, lunches, tasty bakes and soups in a smoke-free environment, Nick's Bar is the place to go. Miss Italia Ristorante has authentic Italian cuisine with homemade pasta, pizza, desserts and a take-away service — Tel: 403-852 4002. The North Face also does good pizzas. Tokyo Tom's in Jasper has a sushi bar and serves Japanese cuisine as well as steak and seafood dishes. If you've missed out on fame and fortune (OK — it's been a disadvantage being tone-deaf), they also have a karaoke machine.

NIGHTLIFE Pete's Bar and Grill has just about everything for board-heads. The local jam night is Tuesday and anyone who wants to go up and spin discs can contribute to the groove. The crowd is friendly and although there isn't a dance floor as such, the place rocks. The bar has live music, pool, darts, food and a big screen TV showing boarding and Beavis and Butthead videos. Atha B's pub also has live bands and a busy atmosphere with a good vibe and food of a similar resonance — it's another drinking and dancing joint. Incorporated in the same building is O'Sheas' Restaurant and Sports Lounge with pub dining and a big screen TV. In the Sawridge Hotel on the north side of Jasper, Champs is surrounded by motels and private accommodation — Tel: 1-800-661 6427.

OTHER ACTIVITIES Maligne ice tours take a two to three hour look at what amazing artworks nature can create. Tours cost $22 and depart daily — Tel: 403-852 3370.

THANKS TO Brian Rode, Buddah the Truck, Seb and Josee, Justin and Seabasss, Sotirios Korogonas and Pete's Club Crew: Mike Olsen, Curtis Bowen and Norman Pelletier.

Top left — Photo: Mike MacWatt
Top right — Frozen waterfall on the Maligne Ice Tour Photo: Mike MacWatt
Middle — The Tonquin Inn
Panoramic — Glorious Rockies rulin' Photo: Mike MacWatt

1

GETTING THERE

By air: There is a choice of international airports including Edmonton, Calgary or Vancouver. Edmonton is the closest, three hours east of Jasper by car.
By train: Jasper has a train service which connects with Edmonton and Vancouver. Trainspotters will appreciate the '50s art-deco style — Tel: 1-800 561 8630.
By bus: Greyhound Canada operate daily services from Edmonton, Kamloops, Vancouver and Prince George. Information is available from their web site — http://www.greyhound.co. or Tel: 1-800-661 8747.
By car: This has to be the most spectacular entrance of all. The scenery from Banff to Jasper is incredible; visitors drive though the mountain ranges of the Rockies and three national parks on Highway 93. From Edmonton take the Yellowhead Highway 16.
Getting around: The ski area is several kilometres away from the town and lodging area, and it's serviced by bus. The resort also provides a daily shuttle service to Marmot Basin from most major hotels in town. Departures leave three times daily.

THE FACTS

ELEVATION

Summit:
2133m, 6996ft
Vertical drop:
503m, 1650ft
Base:
1636m, 5366ft

SNOWFALL

Average annual:
300cm, 120 inches

Snow-making:
90%

AREA

Total area:
66ha, 162 acres

Advanced: 44%
Intermediate: 45%
Beginner: 11%

SEASON

Early December — mid-April

COMMUNICATIONS

Snow report: Tel: 403-762 4421
E-mail: rocote@banff.net
Mountain information:
Tel: 403-762 4421
Fax: 403-762 8133

LIFTS AND TICKETS

Number of lifts:
1 high-speed quad, 3 chairlifts, 2 surface lifts
Lift pass prices*:
1/2 day: $27 morning, $25 afternoon
1 day: $33
Multi-day: N/A
Season: N/A
Other ticketing information:
*Prices include GST. A Tri-Area multi-day pass
includes all three Banff ski areas (Banff Mount
Norquay, Sunshine Village and Lake Louise) and a
free shuttle service up to the slopes. Passes are
valid from three to 14 days; the price for six days
is $303. The resort offers night-riding from 4.00pm
to 9.00pm for $19. A restricted ticket to the
Cascade pipe and park costs $23.

SNOWBOARD SHOPS

See Banff review opposite.

SNOWBOARD SCHOOL

Unlimited Snowboard School — Tel: 403-762 4421
The Discover Boarding package includes a
restricted lift ticket, a two hour lesson and rental
for $35.

Banff Mount Norquay

ON THE MOUNTAIN

Mount Norquay sits beside Cascade Mountain overlooking the busy town of Banff. From the top
of the North American Chair, the panoramic view of the Rockies and the valley floor below
spreads out before you. It's a small but convenient
resort which offers its best terrain to the freestyle
and carving fraternities.

SNOW CONDITIONS Like the other mountains around Banff,
Norquay receives a snowfall that lasts. Sunlight hours are
short and the air is dry and cold, especially in December and
January. Storms move in from the west but Banff's area also
gets hit from the north and south.

FREERIDERS If the avalanche zones are active, freeriding is
almost non-existent. The favoured choices are the small tree
clusters between the Spirit Chair and Mystic Express Quad,
and the double black diamond Gun Run.

FREESTYLERS Minutes from downtown Banff, Norquay is a
good training ground for local and travelling boarders to
improve their pipe technique and big air skills. Just above the
Day Lodge, the funpark and pipe are accessed by the Cascade
Chair. The pipe is regularly serviced by Norquay's own Dragon,
and provides near perfect transitions and a gradient suitable
for all comers. On exiting the pipe, you ride into the grand
funpark of clean, well-shaped table tops and quarter banks,
sticking up like pyramids amongst dunes. For the ultimate
agility test, try the monster mogul fields either side of the
North American Chair.

Pipe and park **Photo:** Tim King

CARVERS Designed by skiers for skiers, Norquay has lots of well-groomed, narrow trails. Off the Mystic
Express Quad you'll find some nice, straight black runs like Black Magic and Ka Poof. Intermediates have the
choice of virtually half the trails on the mountain. Try wide Excalibur or Knight Flight. Everyone will find a
run to suit them off the Spirit Chair and although the runs are quite short, they're perfect for warming up.

MOUNTAIN FOOD The Norquay Lodge is a licensed snack bar at the base of the North American Chair but it
is only open on weekends and holidays. The newly constructed Cascade Lodge, opposite the ticket and rental
shop at the end of the main carpark, is open seven days a week. A well-run deli and cafeteria serve a mid-
priced menu to suit all tastes. The Lone Pine Pub and Restaurant upstairs could keep you off the hill longer
than you planned with live music, healthy food and table service.

HAZARDS AND RULES If conditions are sketchy, avoid the arse-kicking moguls on the Lone Pine trail.

For About Town, see Banff review opposite.

Banff

THE FACTS

COMMUNICATION

Banff Visitor Information Centre:
Tel: 403-762 0270
Fax: 403-762 8163
E-mail: skitherealrockies@atpt.com

SNOWBOARD SHOPS

Rude Boys — Tel: 403-762 8480
For service, boards, rental and the like. Rude Boys is entirely owned and run by local boarders. It's a good place to hang out before and after boarding.
Monod Sports — Tel: 403-762 4571
Monod Sports is more race-orientated and specialises in alpine and freeride boards.

GETTING THERE

By air: Calgary International Airport is a 90 minute drive east of Banff.
By bus: A regular bus service is available from Calgary Airport to Banff and Lake Louise on either Brewster or Laidlaw Transportation; prices are $32 one-way to Banff and $37 one-way to Lake Louise.
By car: Banff is 128 kilometres (80 miles) west of Calgary along the all-weather, four lane Highway 1.
Getting around: Many hotels in Banff offer free shuttles around town.

Top — Banff **Photo:** Mike MacWatt
Bottom — View of the township **Photo:** Mike MacWatt

ABOUT TOWN

Just one look at these jagged peaks and forests and you'll admit that you'd have to span the globe to find a more beautiful landscape than that of Banff National Park. Founded in 1877, Banff was Canada's first National Park. It was set up to entice tourists to explore the glacial back-country and bathe in the natural hot springs of the Banff Springs Hotel, a 15 minute walk from the park gate. With such extensive terrain looming beyond day-trip capabilities, it wasn't long till the first lifts transformed the peaks around Banff Park into a vast playground for well-to-do skiers.

Today the park contains three resorts: **Sunshine Village**, **Banff Mount Norquay** and **Lake Louise**. These three make up more than 2430 hectares (6000 acres) of Canada's highest lift-serviced boarding. They are tucked away in the awesome ranges which line the 64 kilometre (39 mile) Trans-Canada Highway from Banff to Lake Louise. If you need to get out of the tourist scene for a breather, check out the small but laid-back scenes of **Fortress** and **Marmot Basin**.

The town of Banff lies about ten minutes from the east gates of the park in the beautiful Bow Valley. The winter sports industry thrives here and the town is always buzzing. Being a frontier resort, elk graze around the town so watch what you're putting your feet in and avoid the females. It's a year-round town and the cost of living can be kept down as there are all the usual outlets and supermarkets. Banff is understandably crowded in high season but the vibe is always friendly.

ACCOMMODATION There are over 120 places offering beds in Banff but there's also a friendly crowd of seasoners who may help you out with rented accommodation if you're on skid row. Banff Youth Hostel is situated three kilometres (two miles) outside Banff on Tunnel Road. It has dorms and private rooms from $30 — Tel: 403-762 6204 or 1-800-363 0096. The Youth Mountain Lodge (YMCA) also has dorms and private rooms for under $20, as well as cheap daily meals in their café. It's a two minute walk downtown — Tel: 403-762 3560 or 1-800-813 4138.

For an inexpensive B&B, try the rustic, non-smoking Blue Mountain Lodge just a few minutes from central Banff — Tel: 403-762 5134. The Banff Voyager Inn Motel is reasonably priced and offers a sauna, whirlpool and restaurant within walking distance of town — Tel: 403-762 3301 or 1-800-879 1991. If money is no problem, check into the legendary Banff Springs Hotel. Overlooking the town of Banff, the hotel has 817 rooms. Their luxurious list of treats include a heath and beauty spa, sports training facilities, body therapy, indoor and outdoor pools, mini-golf and over 50 shops — Tel: 403-762 2211 or 1-800-441 4141. Central Reservations — Tel: 403-762 0270.

FOOD Waddaya want? Banff has it all. To kick the day off, start with breakfast at Melissa's. One of the locals' favourite eateries is the Rose and Crown which is undoubtedly the best place in town for hot wings and aprés-ski snacks. For Swiss-Italian dishes from $10 a main, try Ticino's where waiters wear strange versions of Swiss national dress. Steaks and hearty pub food are served at Buffalo Bill's across Banff Ave from the Rose and Crown. Aardvark's, around the corner on Caribou Street, serve a quick slice of pizza, sandwiches or veggie food until 3.00am. There are also plenty of Asian and Indian restaurants, sushi and fondue bars, European cafés and excellent coffee shops.

NIGHTLIFE Aprés-ski hits Banff in a wave at around 4.00pm and goes hard until about 6.00pm when people go out to eat to sober up. After 10.00pm most riders drown their thirsts at one of the many clubs. The Rose and Crown has a popular pool and games room with a cranking juke box on one side and a live music stage on the other. The bands are usually alternative and the crowd is laid-back. The Barberry Coast is another live venue on Banff Ave, open till 2.00am for moshing or glass tapping.

The biggest and most popular DJ driven dance club is Silver City (or Syphilis City as it's affectionately known by locals). The amorous crowd gets pretty raucous at Wild Bill's Legendary Saloon where headline bands such as Fishbone kick it out. For brews and cues, King Edward's Billiards Hall sits above the pricey Hard Rock Café on Banff Ave. Altogether there are over 100 places on the Banff drinking roster, all within crawling distance.

OTHER ACTIVITIES On a rainy day the Whyte Museum of the Rockies on Bear Ave is an interesting way to spend a couple of hours. There are plenty of gift shops and art galleries; the most interesting are the fossil houses with tons of fascinating dead things. Otherwise go dogsledding with Mountain Mushers — Tel: 403-762 3647 or horse-back riding — Tel: 403-762 4551.

THANKS TO Janice Belsher, Rude Boys, Silly Rabbit, Norm, Elise, Phil, Rob, Evan, the Compton Crew at the Purple Porch and the Back House Boys.

Lake Louise

THE FACTS

ELEVATION

Summit:
2672m, 8765ft
Vertical drop:
1010m, 3315ft
Base:
1662m, 5450ft

SNOWFALL

Average annual:
360cm, 140 inches

Snow-making:
40%

AREA

Total area:
1656ha, 4100 acres

Advanced: 30%
Intermediate: 45%
Beginner: 25%

SEASON

Early November — mid-May

COMMUNICATIONS

Snow report: Tel: 403-244 6665
Web site: http://skilouise.softnc.com/louise.html
E-mail: vertical@skilouise.com
Mountain information:
Tel: 403-522 3555 or 1-800-258 7669
Fax: 403-522 2095

LIFTS AND TICKETS

Number of lifts:
2 high-speed quads, 6 chairlifts, 1 T-bar, 1 platter
lift, 1 children's rope tow
Lift pass prices:*
1/2 day: $35.51
1 day: $42.06
Multi-day: $194.86 (5 out of 7 days)
Season: $699, $419 (13-25yrs)
Other ticketing information:
*Prices do not include GST. When you purchase a
Lake Louise Plus Card for $50, you ski free on your
first day and save $12 on every subsequent day lift
pass purchased. Plus Card holders also receive a $7
discount at Nakiska, Fortress and Wintergreen. For
the Tri-Area multi-day pass, see Banff Mount
Norquay review p.240.

SNOWBOARD SHOPS

See Banff review p.241.

SNOWBOARD SCHOOL

The School — Tel: 403-522 1333
The Discovery Lesson costs $46 and includes a lift
pass, a half day group lesson and rental. Also
offered is a five day programme with three hour
instruction, guiding, fun races, video filming, lift
line priority and a beer and nachos reception; the
whole package costs $154. Christmas and Easter
camps feature coaching from pro-riders, video
analysis and T-shirts; prices from $200 for a week.

ON THE MOUNTAIN

You'll be immediately awestruck by the enormity and beauty of Lake Louise. The mountain is divided into three areas: the Front Side/South Face, the Back Bowls and the Larch Area. The Back Bowls hold some of the best riding and hiking anyone could wish for. It's a great chance to get loose with no trees to jump out and hit you in the face, but watch out for the permanently closed avalanche areas around the cliff bands at the top of Mount Whitehorn and between the summits of the Paradise Triple Chair and the Top of the World Quad. If you're not a hiker by nature, Lake Louise will soon cure your lethargy when you realise what you're missing out on. The ungroomed terrain on the Front Side extends down to the base area through the wisely thinned out trees under the Olympic Chair. The Larch Area has more glades and carving trails with the tempting Wolverine Ridge and Purple Bowl just a staunch hike away over the ridge.

FREERIDERS The variety of freeriding is virtually endless given the vast expanse of the Back Bowls and out of bounds areas. Front Side favourites among beginners and intermediates are Wiwaxy, Deer Run and Eagle Meadows. There are top quality runs for all levels in the Larch Area, including some great tree riding. If you are happy among the trees, the Eagle Chair on the Front Side will introduce you to some of the finest tree lines around Upper Meadowlark. Otherwise traverse skier's left to the Ptarmigan Glades or head down to STM, Eagle Poma and Eagle Trees. While ascending the Top of the World Express, choose your line right or left to Mirkwood and Tickety Chute for a steep fast run. If you're exploring the popular out of bounds areas such as Pipestone, Vortex or past West Bowl to the Maintenance Chutes, be sure to ride with a guide and check with the ski patrollers in the area. Should visibility become poor or the winds pick up, avoid lifts A, M and G. Dropping into the Back Bowls at the top of Summit Platter, Ridge Run and Whitehorn are both awesome but potentially treacherous — don't be tempted unless you're 100 per cent confident. For avalanche forecasts — Tel: 403-522 3833.

FREESTYLERS Take the Olympic Chair up and follow Wrong Turn to the base of Summit Platter. The halfpipe there is well-shaped and well-maintained and leads into the Evian Snowboard Park. Transitions are near perfect and hits are nicely spaced for a flowing run which emerges from the natural glade area onto Wiwaxy trail. Despite being a bit too short, the park is a fun place to ride especially on windy days.

CARVERS Most south-facing blue and green runs are groomed daily. Wiwaxy is a long, winding green trail which tends to be busy. If this is the case and your board craves more speed, opt for the Men's Downhill. Meadowlark and Cameron Way are two of the Front Side's best G-force runs. The wide open Larch Run is the ultimate and will test the best of you, or take the easy route down Lookout and check out the incredible scenery. Both these runs are found in the Larch Area; head up the Friendly Giant Chair and the Eagle Chair, and then across to the Ptarmigan Chair.

MOUNTAIN FOOD The base area is served by the Whiskyjack Lodge. It has a variety of food from excellent hot and cold buffets in the Northface Restaurant to soups, sandwiches and other snacks at the Deli Corner. The café is a bit pricey for what you get and should only be visited if you're ravenous.

HAZARDS AND RULES Leashes are not required. Avalanche information is posted in the Whiskyjack Lodge, near customer services. It is legal to leave the ski area boundary but you do so at your own risk.

Lake Louise

ABOUT TOWN

The village has evolved around the train station and the five star Chateau Lake Louise. The train station is now defunct for passenger service but the Chateau is as majestic as ever. Development is heavily regulated by the National Parks Service and consequently Lake Louise is a small collection of sparse lodges and gas stations surrounding Samson Mall.

It has all the basics such as cafés, a grocery store, a liquor store, a laundromat, bus depot, car rental and a bakery.

ACCOMMODATION The Chateau Lake Louise is the pinnacle of Lake Louise accommodation with 515 rooms within the restaurant, shopping and relaxation complex. Even with a $65 million restoration, the Chateau is surprisingly affordable, especially for groups — Tel: 1-800-441 1414. The Lake Louise Inn has a comfortable selection of well-equipped apartments suited to all tastes and budgets. A bar and nightclub are located underneath the Inn — Tel: 403-544 3791. Castle Mountain Village sits in Bow Valley mid-way on the 30 minute drive from Lake Louise to Banff; individual chalets for two to six people start from under $50 — Tel: 403-522 3511. The International Youth Hostel in Lake Louise has excellent facilities including a veggie café, five bedroom dorms, double rooms and a library. It's often booked out so call first — Tel: 403-522 2200. Central Reservations — Tel: 403-256 8473.

FOOD Lake Louise Station Restaurant offers affordable evening meals in the old station house and rail cars. Laggan's Mountain Bakery and Delicatessen is the first choice for breakfast or snacks, serving take-away or sit-in coffee, fresh baking, soups and sandwiches. Frankie's Pizza and Pasta at the Lake Louise Inn, and the Village Bar and Grill in Samson Mall are ideal places to line your stomach before a night out. Also in the mall, Bee-Line is a quick take-away joint for pizza, burgers or nachos. Best value for money meals are found at the International Youth Hostel café on Village Road.

NIGHTLIFE Below the Lake Louise Inn, Charlie Two's attracts an energetic crowd. Test your physical and mental dexterity on the TV quizzes, pool table or on the dance floor where cool DJs play the right sounds. Beer, cocktails and table service are topped off by the Lake's best wings; it goes mad on Tuesday and Friday. Saturday night at the Stables by the Chateau and Sunday at the Lake Louise Bar and Grill end the week on a high note. Providing someone is willing to drive, Banff is an excellent option — it's only half an hour away and the party scene is well worth checking out.

OTHER ACTIVITIES Canadian Rockies Icefield Tours — Tel: 403-762 8252.

THANKS TO Janice Belsher, John Shea, Dave Holland and Sarah Geddes.

For more About Town, see Banff review p.241.

Opposite — Hugh Fraser **Photo:** Mark Gallup

Top — The Chateau Lake Louise **Courtesy:** CP Hotels

Middle — Jason Lowe at the Ptarmigan Upshoots **Photo:** Bill Marsh

GETTING THERE

By bus: There is a regular bus service from Banff and a ski bus from Calgary. For the Banff service — Tel: 403-762 9102 or 1-800-661 4946.
By car: Lake Louise is 40 minutes from Banff on Highway 1.
Getting around: The shuttle bus in the village operates from most hotels to the base of the ski lifts.

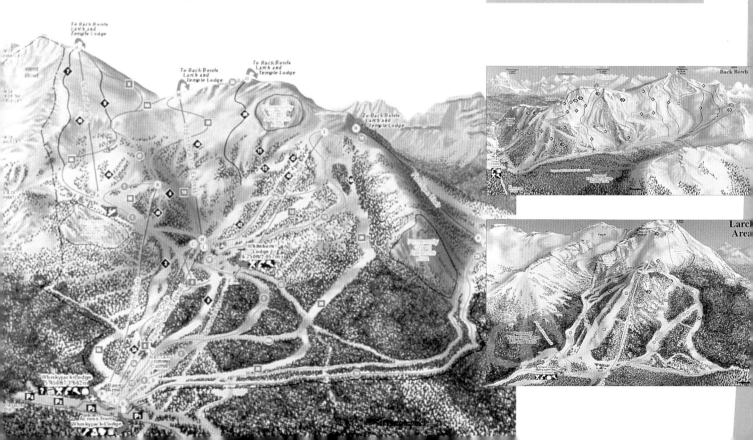

Sunshine Village

ON THE MOUNTAIN

The story goes that the resort was named in '28 when a party skiing from Shadow Lake to Mount Assiniboine were lost in heavy cloud and driving snow. Missing the Canadian Pacific Cabin, they stayed out all night and coming over Mount Standish the next morning, saw the cabin on a bluebird powder day and dubbed the area 'Sunshine Valley'. The resort has the highest base elevation of any Canadian ski resort and sits astride the Continental Divide which drops down east to the Atlantic and west to the Pacific. The ski area encompasses the original terrain of Lookout Mountain and Mount Standish, with the addition of Goat's Eye Mountain bringing more radical options. The truckloads of snow and wicked freeriding and natural terrain park on Mount Standish guarantees riders a blast here.

SNOW CONDITIONS Due to its height and location in a natural bowl, Sunshine is blessed with dry, light powder. It lies in the heart of the Bow Valley and is known for the consistent storms which heaps up a healthy ten to 15 metres (33 to 50 feet) of the white stuff each year. There are 195 days in an average season which extends well into May.

FREERIDERS Name your poison, it's all here. North of the Goat's Eye High-Speed Quad, Goatsucker Glade offers the most challenging, uninterrupted glade riding. If you want something hair-raising, try the famous Free Fall skier's right of Goatsucker. From the top of the Goat's Eye Quad, hike up and turn skier's left for some awesome double blacks. Head down into the large bowl between Goat's Eye Mountain and the Eagles for untracked snow and continue down into the trees. Long cruising glade runs are found skier's left of the Wawa T-bar, below the Day Lodge. Traverse for a couple of minutes, hike for five, then point downhill and enjoy the boardercross-style terrain down to the gondola mid-station. It's wise to take it easy until you know the area as there are a couple of hairy cliffs in this unpatrolled territory.

Mount Standish is a natural terrain park with plenty of hits and small cliff jumps. Off the Standish Chair, go skier's right to easier rolling trees and meadows. Otherwise go skier's left and hike for two minutes to access a long, steep ridge with a great run-out for powder huckers. For steep, wide open glades, try the runs between the Angel Quad and the Tee Pee Town Chair. Off the Angel Quad are are more good intermediate runs with some fun hits, trees, wind lips and rollers — keep your speed up and watch out for irritating flat bits and congestion near the bottom when exiting the trees.

FREESTYLERS The Kokanee Snowboard Park and the halfpipe cover the lower portion of Billy Goat's Gruff trail and much of Goatchicken Gulch trail. You can get there from the Wheeler Double Chair or the Fireweed T-bar via the Banff Ave trail. The pipe is dragoned weekly and has some interesting neighbours such as the Sphinx, a hit shaped after the Egyptian tourist trap. All the volcanoes, table tops, gaps and spines are marked for intermediate or advance jibbers.

CARVERS It's hard-boot heaven; trails are all maintained on a daily basis. On Goat's Eye, the three kilometre (two mile) tendon-tearing warm-up Sunshine Coast is marked blue but pitches to black. Wild Fire and Scapegoat are two extreme paths down Goat's Eye. On Lookout Mountain, follow the rolling fall-line Green Run to Angel's Flight. Anything under the Angel Quad and the Tee Pee Town Chair should have you ripping.

MOUNTAIN FOOD When you've spat out the last mouthful of pine needles, wade though ankle-deep peanut shells at Mad Trapper's for a jug with the crew and a cowboy snack. The Sunshine Day Lodge has it all from picnic areas and delis to prime rib buffets on the third floor. If you're after an enormous plate of cheap pasta, try the Alpine Grill or the Chimney Corner Lodge.

HAZARDS AND RULES Back-country hikers taking advantage of the open out of bounds policy should be especially careful as steep cliffs are never far away. For an up-date on back-country conditions, contact the Banff National Park Warden Service — Tel: 403-762 1460.

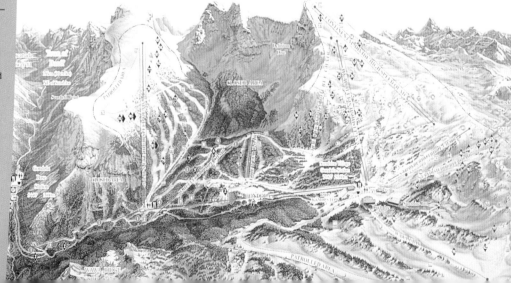

THE FACTS

ELEVATION

Summit:
2730m, 8954ft
Vertical drop:
1072m, 3514ft
Base:
1658m, 5440ft

SNOWFALL

Average annual:
1020cm, 408 inches

Snow-making:
No need!

AREA

Total area:
1283 ha, 3168 acres

Advanced: 35%
Intermediate: 45%
Beginner: 20%

SEASON
Mid-November — late May

COMMUNICATIONS
Snow report: Tel: 403-760-SNOW
Web site: http://www.skibanff.com
Mountain information:
Tel: 403-762 6500
Fax: 403-762 6513

LIFTS AND TICKETS
Number of lifts:
1 6-passenger gondola, 3 high-speed quads, 4 chairlifts, 2 T-bars, 2 beginner tows
Lift pass prices*:
1/2 day: $38, $30 (13-25yrs)
1 day: $45, $38 (13-25yrs)
Multi-day: N/A
Season: $699, $399 (mid-week only)
Other ticketing information:
*Prices include GST. For the Tri-Area multi-day pass, see Banff Mount Norquay review p.240.

SNOWBOARD SHOPS
Sunshine Ski and Sports — Tel: 403-762 6592
Two locations, one at the gondola base and one in Sunshine Village, offering professional service, repairs and readjustments. The staff are friendly and happy to impart their knowledge. B+B: $33.

SNOWBOARD SCHOOL
Sunshine Snowboard School — Tel: 403-762 6560
They offer the works from beginner to technical improvement classes with free lesson deals for those staying at the Sunshine Inn for five days or more. If you're a butt-crunching beginner, the Beginner Package offers a full lift pass, lesson and hire for $49.

4

ABOUT TOWN

Sunshine Village is a fun, plateau village with a collection of bars, restaurants and ski schools. The resort has an unusual transport system; the carpark is at the gondola base station in the valley and it's a scenic 30 minute ride up the gondola to Sunshine Village at the lift base area. The lifts to Lookout Mountain and Mount Standish run from Sunshine Village; sunbathing is second only to people hanging out and bragging about the best line they've discovered. The high-speed quad up Goat's Eye Mountain runs from the gondola mid-station.

With most people staying in Banff and the gondola closing at 6.00pm most nights (10.30pm on Fridays and Sundays), the nightlife in Sunshine Village is limited. Mad Trapper's Saloon stays open late some nights for ski-week events such as karaoke. If you want more night entertainment, you can ride down (on your board or in the gondola) to the carpark and drive 16 kilometres (ten miles) to the metropolis of Banff. If you miss the last gondola back to the village, you'll be dossing in the carpark for the night.

Top left — The Eagles **Photo:** Mike MacWatt
Top right— We didn't get his name, but this guy rips **Photo:** Tim King
Bottom — **Courtesy:** Sunshine Village Ski Resort

ACCOMMODATION For board-to-door convenience and a treat in relaxation, stay at the Sunshine Inn. Take a soak in their outdoor pool, have a few drinks in the Chimney Corner Lounge or eat at the superb Eagle's Nest Restaurant — Tel: 1-800-661 1676. Central Reservations — Tel: 403-762 5000 or 1-800-661 1676.

THANKS TO Ralph Scurfield, Maria Crump, Norm, Jay, Elise, Phil, Mike at Versa, Al Curry.

For more About Town, see Banff review p.241.

Sunshine Village

④

GETTING THERE
By air: Sunshine Village is 138 kilometres (86 miles) from Calgary International Airport.
By bus: There are coach services from Calgary Airport and downtown Calgary on Laidlaw — Tel: 403-762 9102 and Brewster — Tel: 403-762 8400.
By car: Banff is a 90 minute drive west of Calgary. Take the Sunshine Exit on the Trans-Canada Highway, eight kilometres (five miles) west of Banff.
Getting around: Sunshine Village is just 20 minutes west of Banff and 40 minutes east of Lake Louise. Many of the hotels in Banff and Lake Louise offer free shuttles around town and to the ski areas. If you are staying at the Sunshine Inn, speak sweetly to the reception staff about hopping on the staff bus for nights out in Banff.

Fortress Mountain

THE FACTS

ELEVATION

Summit:
2320m, 7610ft
Vertical drop:
280m, 918ft
Base:
2040m, 6692ft

SNOWFALL

Average annual:
635cm, 250 inches

Snow-making:
60%

AREA

Total area:
113ha, 328 acres

Advanced: 25%
Intermediate: 55%
Beginner: 20%

SEASON
Early November — late April

COMMUNICATIONS
Snow report: Tel: 403-245 4909
Mountain information:
Tel: 403-264 5825 or 403-591 7108
Fax: 403-591 7133

LIFTS AND TICKETS
Number of lifts:
3 chairlifts, 3 T-bars
Lift pass prices*:
1/2 day: $20
1 day: $28
Multi-day: $168
Season: $400
Other ticketing information:
* Prices include GST.

SNOWBOARD SHOPS
See Banff review p.241.

SNOWBOARD SCHOOL
Fortress Snowboard School — Tel: 403-591 7108
Offers beginner to advanced lessons.

ON THE MOUNTAIN

As you glance up this monolith from the base station, the ski area is dwarfed by the massive craggy rocks which look like the crazy ramparts of a giant fortress. The layout of the front side is striking but its glades, groomed runs, styling halfpipe and freestyle ski jumps are only the front line of a large battalion of awesome runs. On the other side of the ridge, the back side presents hundreds of off-trail possibilities. A new double chair is planned for the '97-'98 season opening up more back side potential and eliminating the long traverse to the Farside Chair. The resort has a relaxed attitude towards the official boundaries which makes it easy to enjoy the expansive, high back-country.

SNOW CONDITIONS Fortress is located in the same storm path as Sunshine Village so it's also a magnet for monster dumps. Being in a bowl ensures that all slopes get loaded, but the cornices and lips form mostly on the north faces due to the southern direction of the storms.

BACK-COUNTRY OPTIONS The resort plans to offer snowcat powder days for the '97-'98 season; prices start at $195 for a full day including lunch or at $110 for a half day — Tel: 403-591 7108.

FREERIDERS Tree-freaks will enjoy the front side glades of Palisade Park and Fourth Chutes. On the back side, there are great lines through glades, natural halfpipes, wind lips and powder-choked meadows. Intermediates will learn to groove through the weeded trees of Wall Street, Roller Coaster and Enchanted Forest, to skier's left of the Backside Chair on the ski area boundary. Advanced riders should head skier's right of the Backside Chair towards the Backside Glades and Tight Pride 1 and 2 where a fallen forest of burnt-out trees offers plenty to slash and bust. After a fresh snowfall, powder-hogs will enjoy Devil's Gulch. Pick your own natural halfpipe in the lower half of the run. The most attractive face is that of the Fortress itself. Although out of bounds, it is worth the easy 15 minute hike up the shoulder from the top of the Farside Chair and you'll be guaranteed first tracks all day long. Ride with the locals and approach with the same caution as any avalanche risk zone. Just a short hike out of bounds, skier's left of the Canadian Chair, you can't help but be drawn to two fat, natural halfpipes which are endowed with four metre (13 foot) cornice drop-ins.

FREESTYLERS A well-maintained halfpipe, serviced by a Pipe Dragon, ensures that freestylers will be shooting a top-class pipe. It's located between Chutes 2 and 3 on the front side. There is no man-made funpark but Fortress is a collection of natural pipes, quarters and airs.

CARVERS Friar's Tuck and Chutes 1 and 2 stay mostly mogul free and offer well-groomed, quick runs on the front side. Watch out for the big, entrenched moguls on Watch Me. On the back side, Show Off and Sorcerer are two nice warm-ups while the Jolly Jester offers the longest burn back to the Farside Chair and the Curved T-bar North.

MOUNTAIN FOOD The cafeteria in the Day Lodge has basic junk food and sandwiches. The Fireside Lodge offers a better selection of hot meals and colossal nachos platters.

HAZARDS AND RULES It's a long, tedious traverse to the Farside Chair but there are rumours of a new chair which will save your calves.

EVENTS AND COMPETITIONS The Devil's Gulch Snowboard Weekend in March goes wild with live music and local parties.

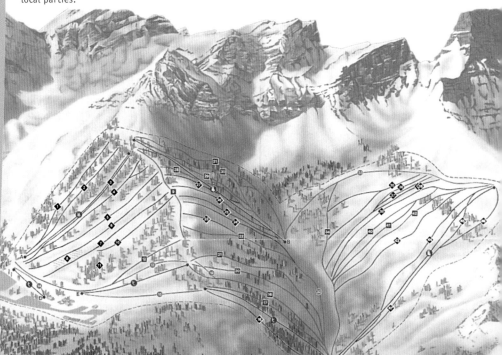

Fortress Mountain

ABOUT TOWN

Sitting in a picturesque valley, Kananaskis Village was originally developed for the '88 winter Olympics. It's a half hour drive from the mountain and has a fair selection of good dining areas, bars and souvenir shops. Most guests here are up-market cross-country and downhill skiers heading to the trails of Nakiska. Banff is a 90 minute drive north-west and Canmore is 45 minutes away.

ACCOMMODATION One of the Canadian Pacific favourites is the Kananaskis Lodge. For $147 you get two nights' lodging and two days' lift tickets. For full accommodation packages — Tel: 1-800-258 7669. Fortress Mountain Hotel offers similar deals for just $118 — Tel: 1-800-258 7669. The on-mountain, board-to-door Fortress chalets sleep up to ten people; prices from $150 mid-week or $200 weekends and holidays. Bring your own bedding — Tel: 403-591 7108. Otherwise head to the Country Ribbon Creek Hostel at Kananaskis where beds cost $12 a night — Tel: 403-762 4122. The cheapest option is camping in the parking lot; it costs $5 a night with camping hook-ups or $75 a month with power. Central Reservations — Tel: 403-591 7108.

FOOD Cafeteria dining is found around a huge central fireplace at the Fortress Day Lodge. They serve good basic meals in the Fireside Lounge which has a sports TV and a mellow groove. Evening dining is limited to seven restaurants in Kananaskis Village. Bread-dipping takes place at Brady's Market fondue sessions. The Inn Restaurant at the Kananaskis Inn has good breakfasts and a big sundeck with a great view of the steeps. The Big Horn Lounge serves pub snacks while the Geezer Rock and Country Band keep everyone jiving. There's a small, expensive grocery store or a Shell Petrol Stop for the essentials.

NIGHTLIFE The watering hole of choice is Woody's Pub in the Kananaskis Inn. Western grub and pub snacks make up the menu and some good alternative and classic rock bands top the marquee which can go off come midnight — Tel: 403-591 7500 for the latest billings. The Fireside Lounge in the Lodge is a great place to swill down drinks and spin yarns with locals and tourists. Canmore has occasional live music and special party nights. Try the camping area for alternative nightlife.

OTHER ACTIVITIES Chess, scrabble, Fortress Mountain has a trivial pursuit board.

THANKS TO Emile Cochand the Third.

For more About Town, see Banff review p.241.

Top — **Photo:** Bill Marsh

Main picture — The tracks of a content, unknown, solo rider **Photo:** Mike MacWatt

GETTING THERE

By air: Calgary International Airport is the closest.
By bus: There is a shuttle running daily from neighbouring Nakiska. This connects to Banff and Calgary via Brewster Transportation — Tel: 403-591 7711 ext. 4027. A proposed bus service will run from Banff and Canmore on selected days throughout the '97-'98 season.
By car: Head west from Calgary for 65 kilometres (39 miles) on Highway 1, then 40 kilometres (24 miles) south on Highway 40 past Kananaskis and follow the signs down Fortress Road. Fortress is 128 kilometres (80 miles) south-east of Banff.
Getting around: You'll need a car or snowshoes.

5

CIRCE BY GRAVES

Ride More Talk Less
DEMO TOUR

RIDE
snowboards

www.ridesnowboards.com
Demo Tour Hotline
425.222.6351

QUEBEC

STATE INFORMATION

Population: 7,000,000
Time: Eastern Standard Time = GMT minus 5 hours
Capital city: Montreal
Area: 648,899 sq miles (1,667,928 sq km)

VISITOR INFORMATION SOURCES

Quebec Tourist Board:
Tel: 1-800-63 7777
Fax: 514-864 3838
E-mail: info@tourisme.gouv.qc.ca
Web site: http://www.quebec_region.cuq.qc.ca

GETTING AROUND

Main airports: Mirabel — Tel: 514-476 3010, Dorval —
Tel: 514-633 3105
By train: VIA Rail — Tel: 1-800-361 5390, Amtrak —
Tel: 1-800-872 7245
By bus: Autocars Orléans Express — Tel: 514-395 4000,
Rout-Pass — Tel: 514-866 1000
Road conditions: Tel: 514-873 2605
Speed limit: The maximum speed limit is 60 mph
(100 kmph).

INTRODUCTION

Quebec is the largest province in Canada and one of the most diverse. The Laurentains and Appalachain Mountain Ranges offer some of the steepest terrain east of the Canadian Rockies, although the thick forest and relatively small mountains aren't geared towards backcountry riding. Quebec instead contributes to Canada's freestyle and racing squads, producing riders like Brett Carpenter who frequently mounts ISF podiums. The province has kept its' of old-world French charm, and if you like your haute cuisine, it's served up here in true French style but at half the price of Europe.

QUEBEC RESORTS

① **MONT TREMBLANT** **250**
② **MONT-SAINTE-ANNE** **252**

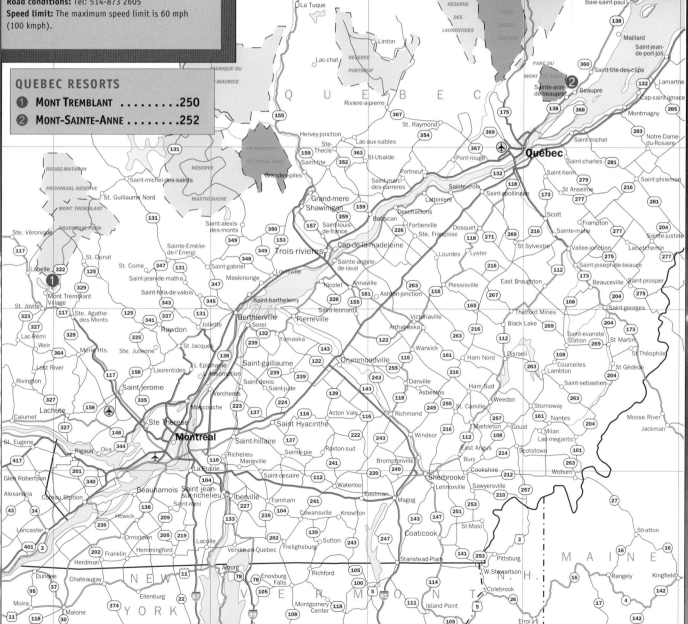

Mont Tremblant

THE FACTS

ELEVATION

Summit:
915m, 3001ft
Vertical drop:
650m, 2131ft
Base:
265m, 870ft

SNOWFALL

Average annual:
367cm, 144 inches

Snow-making:
74%

AREA

Total area:
203ha, 500 acres

Advanced: 50%
Intermediate: 30%
Beginner: 20%

SEASON

Mid-November — mid-May

COMMUNICATIONS

Snow report: Tel: 514-333 8936
Web site: http://www.tremblant.ca
E-mail: tremblant@odyssee.net
Mountain information:
Tel: 819-681 2000 or 1-800-461 8711
Fax: 819-681 5999

LIFTS AND TICKETS

Number of lifts:
1 gondola, 5 high-speed quads, 4 chairlifts, 1 T-bar
Lift pass prices*:
1/2 day: $35, $29 (13-17yrs)
1 day: $46, $37 (13-17yrs)
Multi-day: $252 (6 days), $198 (13-17yrs)
Season: Not available unless you're a resident.
Other ticketing information:
*Prices include GST. The Tremblant Max card offers discounts of up to $10 depending on the day of the week, and you receive one day's free boarding when you flick over your $39. Budget Rent-A-Car offers free one day passes with a weekend rental.

SNOWBOARD SHOPS

Adrenaline — Tel: 819-681 2000
All the kit.
Tremblant Ski Service — Tel: 819-681 3000
For great tune-ups and an on site pick-up service.

SNOWBOARD SCHOOL

Mont Tremblant Snowboard School
Tel: 819-681 3000 ext. 5666 or 1-888-ECOLE SKI
$57 buys a lift ticket, rental and a lesson or guide. Night school is also available for $10 including equipment. Snowboard weeks offer 14 hours of tuition in a class of six for $235 (tax and lift passes not included).

ON THE MOUNTAIN

The Algonquins called Mont Tremblant 'Manitou-Ewitchi-Saga' which means 'the mountain of the dread Manitou'. Manitou was their God of the Wilderness who would throw rocks and create storms if he got mad. Today the bars are the only things that rock, and storms are welcome as they sweep up the Saint-Lawrence seaway bringing snow. The area was revamped in '91 by Intrawest at a cost of $350 million. The mountain has a straight-forward layout; the trails are carved into the trees on both sides of a long east-west ridge. Take a Toblerone Bar and put six high-speed toothpicks on the front and back sides of the middle block, and you'll have a scale model of the ski area. The front (south) side base area is surrounded by up-market hotels and condos at 265 metres (870 feet); the back side base has a similar elevation but is limited to a carpark and Day Lodge. The mountain specialises in excellent, traditional Eastern carvers and glades which go off on the (occasional) powder day.

SNOW CONDITIONS Mont Tremblant sits in a snow belt where Atlantic storms ride up the Laurentians from the Saint-Lawrence seaway. Although Tremblant doesn't get the huge snowfalls of West Coast mountains, the latitude keeps the temperatures well down and the snow sticks. Grooming is an art form here but bullet-proof ice can be part of the package.

FREERIDERS The Edge and the adjoining glades on the western boundary of the back side are the best bets when conditions permit. Plenty of good-sized rocks, stumps and small cliffs can be found as you slalom through the glades of Emotion, Reaction and Sensation. Emotion is for advanced riders only as one false move in here and a family of woodpeckers will have to remove your corpse from the bark. Buzz and Windigo beneath the Expo Chair are also fun glades to freeride.

FREESTYLERS A 60 metre (196 foot) pipe is located on the front side under the Express Flying Mile Chairlift. Snow-making machines ensure it's always in working order although it's usually best in March and April. A kicking sound system keeps the rhythm up on the front side. The funpark has a well-maintained series of hits and slides. Beginners, jibber-manics and slopestylists will love it, particularly in the afternoons as it's south-facing and the snow softens up. Another pipe is planned at the Edge on the back side.

CARVERS A carvers' paradise! On the front side, the Express Tremblant Quad runs like a Grand Prix and Zig Zag, McCulloch and Ryan Haut to Ryan Bas will satisfy speed carvers. Take the ridge line trail La Crête, skier's right of the TGV Chair, and hang a left onto Alpin Haut and Beauvallon Haut for nice, wide groomers. On the back side, try the Beauchemin Haut trail for lovely, long turns through the trees. Géant or Coyote onto Devil's River under the Express Duncan Quad are both good for a blast. The Cossack and Expo double black diamond trails under the Expo Quad are best in the morning before they get mogulled out.

MOUNTAIN FOOD The only place on the top of Mont Tremblant is the Grand Manitou which serves good, cheap meals; $3.50 buys a hot-dog plate and drink. French cuisine is served at La Légende but expect to pay for it. La Légende also has a cafeteria and lunch box area for brown paper-baggers.

HAZARDS AND RULES Some of the green runs have long flats. Leash checks are rare but leashes are mandatory. It is actually illegal to catch air outside the park area or to ride with a walkman.

EVENTS AND COMPETITIONS Canadian Snowboard Freestyle Competition and Snowboard Canada Jam Tour.

Mont Tremblant

ABOUT TOWN

Tremblant is a popular resort for students from Toronto, Ottawa and Montreal. Entering the resort, you'll probably be accosted by the Tremblant version of Mickey Mouse, a stunt-caribou on a trike. The recent Intrawest developments of the '90s have given the town a Hollywood-set feel; new condos abound and techno-colour shops sell everything from trendy shoes to handicrafts. Mixed with the rustic buildings that the resort's founder Joe Ryan put up in the '30s, it's an eclectic scene. The resort has been pedestrianised in the centre and is small enough to walk the length of in two minutes. The Village du Tremblant is just a couple of minutes drive around the lake.

ACCOMMODATION Accommodation ranges from private B&Bs to hotels. A package deal from New York with flights, lift passes and lodging for three nights at the Marriott costs $425 per person.

Lodging prices start at around $28 per person a night at the smaller motels off the slopes. Three nights in a slopeside, one bedroom condo sleeping four at La Chouette starts at $494 plus tax. A one bedroom condo at Condolet and Apparthotel for three nights costs $267 plus tax. Book with Central Reservations — Tel: 1-800 567 6760.

FOOD On the south side of the Village du Mont Tremblant, the Petite D'Jeuner or Lorraine's will fuel you up for a good day's riding. Le Grand Manitou, on the mountain, and its sister restaurant in town serve a good variety of breakfasts and lunches. In the Plaza Saint-Bernard, Mexicali Rosa's has a great, affordable Mexican menu and drinks. Reserve in the morning — Tel: 819-681 2439. Le Shack has funky decor and good eats with live jazz in the evenings — it's the first place you see at the bottom of the hill.

Le Pizzateria serves snacks and pastas with a smile but for the best Italian outside of Florence, go to the Coco Pazzo. There is no grocery store in the resort proper but cheap take-away foods are an easy option. The closest supermarket is Bonchoix on Chemin Principal, the main street of the Village du Mont Tremblant. For an incredible French meal at half the price you'd pay in France, try Le Sauciére next door to the Bonchoix. It's expensive but good value. For a copy of the restaurant guide — Tel: 819-681 5500.

NIGHTLIFE The Caribou rocks; half the crowd rave in their ski or snowboard boots on the tables and some keep going till the bar shuts at 3.00am. For billiards, big screen videos and live rock bands, head ten paces east from the Caribou to the Café d' Epoque. El Diablo is a locals' roost with a micro-brewery. They have food all day including brunch; their speciality dishes are smoked meats. The sports channel plays on the TV or live music plays at the weekends. The streets are alive till the small morning hours.

OTHER ACTIVITIES Skating, cross-country skiing, snowmobiling, museums, art galleries and a double-screen cinema with French and English films for armchair entertainment. The Canadian Pacific Hotels have swimming pools and saunas.

THANKS TO Jimi Donkin, Luc Bombardier and Peter at Le Photo Shoppe, Yves Juneau and Isabelle, Jason and Jamie Troutman.

Top — **Courtesy:** Mont Tremblant
Bottom — **Photo:** Chaco Mohler

GETTING THERE

By air: The nearest airport and train stations are in Montreal. It's a 90 minute drive from Mirabel or Dorval Airports on Highway 15 and Route 117 to the resort. A ski shuttle runs from both airports and Montreal hotels for $27 one-way plus tax — Tel: 819-425 8681.

By bus: Take the Voyageur bus from the main terminal in Montreal — Tel: 819-842 2281. An occasional shuttle runs from Montreal's downtown bus terminal — Tel: 514-435 8899.

By car: From Montreal: Head north on Highway 15 and onto Route 117 to Saint Jovite, then follow the signs. From Quebec City: Take the main Highway 40 to Montreal and head north on Highway 15; the trip takes about three and a half hours.

Getting around: By foot, taxi or the local village bus.

Mont-Sainte-Anne

ON THE MOUNTAIN

Mont-Sainte-Anne has a great view overlooking the vast Saint-Lawrence seaway and town of Beaupré. Beginners will improve on the gentler north and west sides while the steeper south side is better for intermediates and advanced riders. Both the FIS and the ISF hold professional races down Mont-Sainte-Anne's pipes and trails and everyone indirectly wins from these competitions as the features are kept in tip-top shape. The hard-boot clan can celebrate the groomerhood with wide avenues and hard-core freeriders will love what's left ungroomed.

THE FACTS

ELEVATION

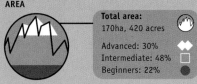

Summit:
800m, 2625ft
Vertical drop:
625m, 2050ft
Base:
175m, 575ft

SNOWFALL

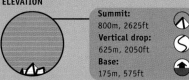

Average annual:
400cm, 180 inches

Snow-making:
85%

AREA

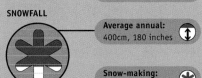

Total area:
170ha, 420 acres

Advanced: 30%
Intermediate: 48%
Beginners: 22%

SEASON
Mid-November — late April

COMMUNICATIONS
Snow report: Tel: 418-82 4579 SNOWLINE
Web site: http://www.mont-saint-anne.com
E-mail: info@mont-saint-anne.com
Mountain information:
Tel: 418-827 4561
Fax: 418-827 3121

LIFTS AND TICKETS
Number of lifts:
1 gondola, 2 high-speed quads, 4 chairlifts,
3 T-bars, 2 J-bars
Lift pass prices*:
1/2 day: $37, $31 (14-22yrs)
1 day: $43, $38 (14-22yrs)
Multi-day: $187 (5 out of 6 days)
Season: $780
Other ticketing information:
*GST included. Night-riding is offered from Tuesday to Saturday till 10.00pm. Night-riding and cross-country skiing is included on the multi-day pass. The computerised lift ticket system allows you to ride for a full week, a half day or any combination you want to dream up.

SNOWBOARD SHOPS
Chateau Mont-Sainte-Anne — Tel: 418-827 5211
For good, quick service the Chateau's team does waxing and tune-ups. The shop is the closest to the gondola base.
Sports Experts — Tel: 418-827 3708
On site at the base of the mountain.

SNOWBOARD SCHOOL
Mont-Sainte-Anne Snowboard School
Tel: 418-827 4561
Their competent staff will have even the most unco-ordinated up and turning with Learn to Ride packages including lesson, lift pass and rentals for $43. One hour private lessons for up to two people cost $46.

SNOW CONDITIONS The front line of these mountains are a natural catchment area for the storms travelling up the Saint-Lawrence seaway carrying heavy Atlantic clouds. The weather fronts pick up moisture from the river and transform the vapour masses into an average of four metres (13 feet) of snow each season. The wind and heavy traffic can quickly polish the front face to a bullet-proof icy glaze mid-season, so stock up on insurance and sharpen your edges.

FREERIDERS Many steeper runs on Mont-Sainte-Anne have staircase patterns, big rollers and are left ungroomed; Les Sept Chutes is the most challenging. Take on the natural slopestyle hits and wind-blown lips on the sides of Le Gros Vallon, La Montmorency and L'Espoir runs. Les Ilots offer the only glade riding in the area as the resort has very few trees which are thinly spread enough for intermediates to navigate. These trees are best first thing in the morning as they quickly fall victim to moguls.

FREESTYLERS The halfpipe is world-class and has hosted ISF and FIS events. There are loads of hits on the sides of the trails and creative riders will have a ball. Skate-stylers train and hang out at the Aire de Jeux Surf des Neiges (which translates into plain Snowboard Park). The first Pipe Dragon to roam Québec grooms this small, compact funpark and halfpipe.

CARVERS Mont-Sainte-Anne is essentially a carvers' mountain where some of Canada's fastest racers develop their skills. On the south slopes below La Tourmente High-Speed Quad, try L'Express. On the west face, La Crête has some great speed riding. If you want a leg-eraser, check out the the runs on the north face: L'Anore, La Première Neige or the faster L'Archipel.

MOUNTAIN FOOD The natural choice for breakfast is the aptly named Le Petite Dejeuner which serves good crêpes. For pizza and pasta next to a warm fire, head to the North Side Lodge. For simple cafeteria lunches, hearty soups, big cakes and muffins, riders can fill up at the Summit Lodge just below the gondola station.

HAZARDS AND RULES All snowboarders must have leashes. Venturing into the woods costs tickets but look for the two new gladed trails in the '97-'98 season which will let you chuck wood legally.

EVENTS AND COMPETITIONS Grundig FIS Snowboard World Cup in December '97.

Mont-Sainte-Anne

ABOUT TOWN

Mont-Sainte-Anne is a destination resort overlooking the majestic Saint-Lawrence seaway. The layout is geared for functionality and you will never find yourself more than one minute from anything you need. A five minutes drive from the mountain base, Beaupré is a modern strip of fast food chains and malls which retain a lingering old-world French style, particularly when it comes to food. Beaupré is also home to the factory where Atlantis, A-boards, Oxbow and other quality sticks are made. Quebéc City is only 30 minutes away so the mountain and satellite towns are over-run by city slickers in the weekends.

ACCOMMODATION Condo packages at Mont-Sainte-Anne including a weekend's lift tickets, lodging and one dinner start at $99 per person at the Village Touristique Mont-Sainte-Anne — Tel: 418-827 6666 or 1-800-463 7775. A five day, five night package at the Chalets Monmorency (a five minute walk to the lifts) starts from $340 per person — Tel: 418-826 2600 or 1-800-463 2612. Motels and B&Bs can be found a couple of miles away from the mountain in Beaupré and Sainte-Anne-de-Beaupré. A weekend package with dinner and breakfast at the Auberge du Fondeur costs $99 — Tel: 418-827 4561 or 1-800-463 1568. Rooms in private homes are available from $25 a night. If you have the money, the Chateau Mont-Sainte-Anne will give you a night to remember — Tel: 418-827 5211. For more information, contact Central Reservations — Tel: 418-827 5281 or 1-800-463 1568.

FOOD Besides the usual mèlange of take-outs and convenience stores, there are some top places to eat. Splash out at La Camarine, rated among the top ten restaurants in Québec for its nouveau French cuisine. The bistro L'Aiguille du Midi at the mountain base serves French food, and L'Aventure Mont-Sainte-Anne in Beaupré does a good barbecue and has a sundeck. La Biscotte deli in Mont-Sainte-Anne has lovely food, as does the

restaurant Chez Albert. It's set in a beautiful old building and has large, wood-oven pizzas. The Zig Zag Bar has a novel idea that will appeal to budget eaters; bring your own food and they'll supply fondue pots when you buy drinks. The cafeteria at the base of the resort serves a $6.50 hot lunch menu which includes a drink and dessert.

NIGHTLIFE The Zig Zag Bar is the place to be in Mont-Sainte-Anne. It has a funky atmosphere with a great happy hour — three beers for $5. You can shoot pool and dance to live bands or DJs on a peanut shell covered floor. For billiards and disco, head for L'Aventure Mont-Sainte-Anne in Beaupré.

The Chateau Mont-Sainte-Anne has a fireside bar which features live solo musicians and a free-for-all piano in the lounge. It's a popular place for students who having fed each other fondue at the Zig Zag Bar, go into the lounge for a fondle. If you want to hang with the scene in Québec City and dancing's your thing, go to the Chez Dagobert where you'll bump into plenty of thirsty skaters and boarders. It's situated in the Grand Allée district of old Quebec City which has many other trendy spots for clubbers.

OTHER ACTIVITIES The best pool and fitness centre is in the Val des Neiges condos. Dog-sledding, snowshoe tours, paragliding and cross-country skiing are also available. The Quebec City Winter Carnival celebrates the Mardi Gras season in the first two weeks of February.

THANKS TO Suzanne Roy, Florence Bourg, Michel Couture, the Mont-Sainte-Anne Ski Patrol and the Mont-Sainte-Anne Snowboard Club.

(2)

Top — **Photo:** Jean Sullivan **Courtesy:** Mont-Sainte-Anne
Middle — **Photo:** Jean Sullivan **Courtesy:** Mont-Sainte-Anne
Bottom — **Photo:** Jean Sullivan **Courtesy:** Mont-Sainte-Anne

GETTING THERE
By air: The nearest domestic airport is Québec City, 40 kilometres (25 miles) east of Mont-Sainte-Anne. Montreal is the nearest international airport, a further 213 kilometres (155 miles) east. Taxi transfers from Québec City cost $50 for up to six people in a cab. A daily shuttle runs from Québec City to Mont-Sainte-Anne and costs $18 for the round trip.
By bus: Orléans buses go from the Quebec Via Rail Terminal to a gas station in Beaupré; price $20 — Tel: 418-525 3000. From Beaupré take a mini-taxi for $6 to the resort.
By car: From Québec City, take Route 138 east via Montmorency Highway to Beaupré, then head north for five minutes on Route 360 to Mont-Sainte-Anne.
Getting around: Everything is within walking distance as Mont-Sainte-Anne is a self-sufficient community.

Summer Camps

Main picture — Team Windells, July '96 **Photo:** Tony Welch
Left — Colin Lentz, Timberline **Photo:** Gary Land
Right — Max Plozë, Windells' **Photo:** Tony Welch

WHAT IS IT?

The words 'summer' and 'snowboarding' seem a contradiction in terms, but take one high altitude volcano, drop it near the Pacific north-west, deposit 33 feet (11 metres) of snow each year, then chill. The possibilities become immediately clear. Enter Mount Hood, Oregon, or more specifically, the Palmer snowfield at Timberline. This wide expanse of year-round snow is home to no less than four major summer snowboard camps, with a couple of ski race camps chucked in for the mix.

Starting in June, there's a huge range of programmes, hosted by pro riders and coaches, all designed to improve your riding technique and style. Halfpipes and hits are spread right across Palmer, offering everyone

from beginners to shredders the chance to improve on their repertoire under the watchful eyes of the pros. The emphasis is undoubtedly on freestyling, though freeriders and carvers are offered specialised options.

Morning conditions can vary from fresh pow (if you're lucky), or a freshly groomed, crisp, hard surface. Afternoons mean slush, but they can be a good chance to put in some air time and utilise the soft landings. An endless array of other activities are offered, including skate ramps, wakeboarding, mountain-biking, whitewater rafting, river surfing, swimming, fishing, hiking, paintballing, and more. If you get bored, you'd have to be half dead.

MOUNT HOOD SNOWBOARD CAMP
Location: Mount Hood
Tel: 503-668 8322
Fax: 503-688 7986
Price: $1050 (a week)
Includes: Lodging, lessons, lift tickets.

ROCKY MOUNTAIN SNOWBOARD CAMP
Location: Winter Park, USA
Tel: 970-879 9059
Fax: 970-879 0775
E-mail: snowcamp@rockysnocamp.com
Web site: http://www.rockysnocamp.com
Price: $925 (a week)
Includes: Lodging, lessons, lift tickets.

CRAIG KELLY'S WORLD SNOWBOARD CAMP
Location: Blackcomb in Whistler, Canada
Tel/Fax: 360-5991258
Price: $975 (a week)
Includes: Board, lessons, lift tickets.

OREGON
WINDELL'S SNOWBOARD CAMP
Location: Timberline
Tel: 1-800-765 7669
E-mail: windcamp@teleport.com
Months: June, July, August
Price: £1015 (1 week)
Includes: Lodging, lessons, lift tickets.

HIGH CASCADE SNOWBOARD CAMP
Location: Mt Bachelor
Tel: 1-800-334 4272
Fax: 541-389 6371
E-mail: hcsc@teleport.com
Web site: http://ww.teleportcom/~hcsc
Months: May, June, July, August, September
Price: $1150 (a week)
Includes: Lodging, lessons, lift tickets.

Heliboarding

WHAT IS IT?

Jumping into a chopper with three or four friends, getting dropped off into the infinite silence of an empty range, then riding a couple of thousand vertical feet of untracked powder unquestionably rates as the ultimate freeride sensation. The heli angle adds a full throttle adrenaline burst to the experience, and the heli can land you in places that a cat never can. It is, by nature, the most spendy way to ride but there is a wide range of prices, and an equally broad range in value for money. It all depends on what you're looking to achieve. A few of the operators are completely paranoid of accidents and litigation laws, and consequently run on terrain not much steeper than a nursery slope. Avoid them at all costs unless you're a total powder novice. Others are known for their varied terrain and consider themselves aerial taxis. The best thing is to be up front about your ability, and the kind of experience you're after before booking.

PACIFIC

WASHINGTON
NORTH CASCADES HELISKIING
Tel 1-800-494-HELI
Prices: $420 (1 day), $1500 (3 days)
Includes: Guiding, food and a guarantee of 10,000 vertical feet (3050 metres).
Comment: Runs range from 1500 to 4000 feet (500 to 1300 metres), and they cover 300,000 acres (121,2000 hectares) in Okanogan National Forest, which means you won't stumble over your own tracks twice. If the weather's dire, never fear — they have a snowcat.

MOUNTAIN WEST

IDAHO
SUN VALLEY HELISKI
Tel: 1-800-872 3108
Fax: 208-726 6850
E-mail: svhali@sunvalley.net
Web site: http://www.destinationnw.com/svheliski
Prices: $475 (1 day)*
Other options: 'Club Vertical' starts at $1762 (one week) for lodging and 30,000 vertical feet (9150 metres).
Includes: The works; superb guides, food and safety equipment and 10,000 feet (3050 metres) of vert.
Comment: *The days are charged in vertical footage: the greater vert, the lower the rate.* '96-'97 marked SVH's thirtieth anniversary, so they have enough experience to know their white stuff. Keeping the groups and the guide-guest ratio small, their groups access over 750 square miles (1200 square kilometres) around the area. A typical run is around 3500 feet (1067 metres). To get to the steeps you have to prove you can ride and have a like-minded crew, but the intermediate terrain is fun, and the guides are snowboard friendly.

WYOMING
HIGH MOUNTAIN HELIS
Tel: 307-733 3274
Prices: $495 (1 day)
Includes: Six runs, an enormous lunch, safety equipment, guides and transfers.
Comment: High Mountain Helis cover some unreal terrain in the Teton Park, west of Jackson.

COLORADO
TELLURIDE HELI-TRAX
Tel: 970-728 4909
Fax: 970-728 6990
Web site: http://www.telluridemm.com
Prices: $525 (1 day)
Includes: Five runs, guiding, safety equipment and food.
Comment: Colorado's only heliskiing operation, and with a top landing exceeding 13,000 feet (400 metres) accesses North America's highest heliski terrain. Tailormade tours can be catered for.

UTAH
Wasatch Powderbird Guides
Tel: 801-742 2800
Fax: 801-742 2832
E-mail: skiwasatch@aol.com
Prices: N/A
Comment: A champagne-style operation that can be group booked to take you almost anywhere in the Wasatch Range. Powderbirds are consistently heavily booked due to the primo terrain and snow conditions.

ALASKA
ALASKA BACK-COUNTRY ADVENTURES
Tel: 907-835 5608
Fax: 907-283 9354
E-mail: bcountry@ptialaska.net
Prices: $65 per lift
Includes: One lift for one person as a minium of five people, plus mandatory guiding service.
Comment: Run by Tom Thibedeau, ABA were Alaska's original operation, and without a doubt reign supreme. The King of the Hill runs with them, and they'll take you anywhere you want to go. There's also the recent addition of a mandatory guiding service.

VALDEZ HELISKI GUIDES
Tel: 907-835 4528
Fax: 307-733 2686
E-mail: dougcoombs@blissnet.com
Prices: $490 (1 day)
Other options: With lodging, it costs an extra $65 per night (two people).
Includes: Six runs, lunch, equipment and guiding.
Comment: In the six runs you can cover 20,000 feet (6100 metres) vertical if you can take it. Run out of the Tsaina Lodge by Doug Coombs, these guys rule and will take you wherever you want to ride. It's slightly skier-orientated, but cool all the same.

VALDEZ H2O
Tel: 1-800-578 HELI
Fax: 505-661 2340
Prices: $460 (1 day), $1,500 (3 days, 4 nights)
Includes: Six runs, lunch, safety equipment and guiding.
Comment: Based out of a log cabin and flying in the Chugach Range, each run has a 2500 to 5000 feet (800 to 1500 metres) vertical drop. They also offer Mix-It-Up packages where you can alternate between cats, fixed-wing planes and helis. Run by Dean Cummings, H2O can also organise other activities such as kayaking, ice-climbing and rafting.

CANADA
BRITISH COLUMBIA

RK HELISKI PANORAMA INC.
Tel: 604-342 3889 or 1-800-661 6060
Fax: 604-342 3466
Prices: $399 (1 day)
Includes: 12 person helis, three descents, safety equipment, guiding and lunch.
Comment: If you have an independent head on your shoulders and like to ride hard we suggest that you try elsewhere. It's probably good for powder novices.

WHISTLER HELISKIING
Tel: 604-932 4105
Fax: 604-938 1225
Prices: $450 (1 day)*
Other options: Extra runs cost $50. They also do a Deluxe for $600 (1 day), $1800 (3 days), and a semi-private person package.
Includes: Base day is three runs, but you can do as many as you want. Lunch, safety equipment, ground transportation and snowboard guides are included.
Comment: *The vert is calculated by heli lift and the minimum is 2745 metres (9000 feet).* Whistler Heliskiing have been operating for over 15 years and have recently added a legendary Bell-407 to their usual Bell-212s. This beast climbs at 610 metres (2000 feet) a minute so you will be amping before you even start riding. They also have powder boards for hire at $30.

TOWN AND COUNTRY
Tel: 604-938 2927
E-mail: tc-heli@snozone.com
Web site: http://snozone.com/heli
Prices: $300-400 (1 day)*
Includes: Guiding, safety equipment, food and as much as you can take.
Comment: *For a vertical drop of 2500-3100 metres (8000-10,000 feet) in three runs.* These guys are the world's only snowboard specific heli operation. Co-ordinated by Paul Decarie of Whistler Heliskiing, they use the Bell-407 for a special freeride package for those with thighs and money to burn, offering a vert of up to 5800 metres (20,000 feet). T&C's accessible terrain is incredible — anything you want — they can drop you right in the thick of it so you can ride the most extreme lines, with guides who snowboard.

CANADIAN MOUNTAIN HOLIDAYS (CMH)
Tel: 1-800-661 0252 (all operations) or 1-800-663 0100 (CMH Kootenay only)
Fax: 403-762 5879 or 250-265 4447 (CMH Kootenay)
Prices: $2250 (3 days)*
Includes: Accommodation, meals and equipment.

Comment: CMH introduced helisking to BC in '65, and they now cover 11 areas with a combined terrain the size of Switzerland. This is the largest heliskiing operation in the world, and all areas except the recently acquired Kootenay are booked up a year and a half in advance. Having said that, most of their clients are not extreme — don't expect anything challenging.

TYAX LODGE HELISKIING
PO Box 1118, Vernon, BC V1T 6N4
Tel: 604-558 5379 or 1-800-667 4854
Fax: 604-558 5389
Prices: $1255-$1482 (2 days)
Includes: Two nights' accommodation at Tyax Mountain Lake Resort, meals and lodge facilities, 8800 metres (28,860 feet) of vertical and a return bus transfer from Vancouver or Whistler.
Comment: The seven day package offers a fat 30,000 metres (98,400 feet) of vertical, and the lodge has a sauna, outdoor jacuzzi and fitness centre, so you're really will be roughing it here.

Catriding

WHAT IS IT?

Catriding might be heliboarding's poorer cousin, but while it lacks some of the glam and excitement of a chopper, it usually offers way more vertical per day and a lot less stress. It's true that choppers can land in steeper terrain (though many of them often don't), but many of the companies, such as Island Lake Lodge, operate around some formidable terrain and suffer no shortage of steeps. Cats cost half as much as helis.

Cats are comfy to cruise in, too. The heated ones are best, and during your ten to 20 minute ascent you get to dry your goggles, catch your breath, have a snack or whatever. The gradients range from mellow to intense; discuss what you're after with the operators before you make your mind up.

PACIFIC
OREGON
MOUNT BAILEY SNOWCATS
Tel: 1-800-733 7593 or 541-793 3333
Fax: 541-793 3309
Web site: http://www.diamondlake.net
Prices: $200 (1 day)
Other options: They do two to five day packages at up to $800 for five days, and are more than happy to design and price special packages.
Includes: Guaranteed 15,000 feet (5000 metres) of vertical, guides (who snowboard), lunch, safety equipment and transportation.
Comment: These guys are one of the best, rated by many as the only 'real' back-country cat operation on the West Coast. From the drop off at the top of Mount Bailey, you are looking at 360 degrees of incredible terrain including spooky, wind-sculptured playgrounds to trees, bowls, avalanche chutes and anything else you could name. Look out for volcanic hot-holes, and bring collapsible poles!

MOUNTAIN WEST
COLORADO
STEAMBOAT POWDER CATS
Tel: 970-879 5188 or 1-800-288 0543
Web site: http://www.csn.net/ski.powdercats.html
Prices: $185 (1 day)
Includes: Lunch, transfers, safety equipment, guiding and four to five runs.
Comment: The terrain is not super extreme but the atmosphere but mellow. Owned and operated by Jupiter Jones and his very friendly family, it's ideally suited for intermediate riders. Good terrain and good snow.

ASPEN POWDER TOURS
Tel: 970-925 1220
Web site: http://www.skiaspen.com
Prices: $225 (1 day)
Includes: A gourmet lunch, guiding, safety equipment and six to eight runs in a heated ten-seater cat.
Comment: Opens up 1500 acres (400 hectares) on the back side of Aspen.

GRAND TARGHEE SNOWCAT
Tel: 307-353 2300 or 1-800-TARGHEE
E-mail: targhee@pdt.net
Web site: http://idahonews.com/targhee/powder/html
Price: $185-$216 (1 day)*
Includes: Lunch, eight to ten runs.
Comment: *The price is cheaper if you are resident in one of their lodgings.* The terrain is pretty mellow, but the cats open up 1,500 acres (400 hectares) of terrain.

MOUNT HOOD MEADOWS CAT SERVICES
Tel: 503-337 2222
Fax: 503-337 2217
Prices: $12 (1 ride)
Includes: A ride up an extra 1020 feet (335 metres).

IRWIN LODGE
Tel: 970-349 9800 or 1-888-GO-IRWIN
Fax: 970-349 9801
Prices: $209-$255 (1 day)
Includes: Three meals, accommodation, guiding, safety equipment, transfers and an average of 20,000 feet (6100 metres) vertical a day.
Comment: With 63 feet (20 metres) of snow a year and 2400 skiable acres (600 hectares), you won't be complaining much.

UTAH
POWDER MOUNTAIN CAT SKIING
Tel: 801-745 3772 or 801-745 3691
Prices: $90 (a transferable 12 punch pass)
Includes: Providing access to an extra 1200 acres (485 hectares) of primo terrain.
Comment: Operates Friday to Monday and doubles the acreage of this small resort. It's very cheap and flexible, if you're there for a few days.

ALASKA
ALASKA
GLACIER SNOWCAT TOURS
Tel: 907-373 3118 or 1-800-770 3118
Prices: $225 (1 day) or $440 (2 people)
Other options: They also do one to five day packages with accommodation starting at $575 for two people (one night, one day).
Includes: Accommodation packages include all meals, guiding, and ground transport on 1500 acres (606 hectares) with runs up to 2000 vertical feet (610 metres).

HATCHER PASS GLACIER SNOWCATS
Tel: 907 346 1276
Prices: $125 (1 day) $500 (5 days)
Includes: Guiding, equipment and absolutely unlimited vertical averaging at 16,000 feet (4880 metres), though the record is 27,000 feet (8235 metres).
Comment: Epic. With 1500 acres (606 hectares) to play in, you won't cross your own tracks even though they go till dark, or someone collapses. The guides are back-country, hard-core types and give you plenty of leeway — call them. They understand snowboarding.

CANADA
BRITISH COLUMBIA
ISLAND LAKE LODGE
Tel: 250-423 3700 or 1-888-4-CATSKI
Fax: 250-423 4055
Prices: $1161-$1290 (3 days)
Other options: Various packages are available in deluxe or standard accommodation.
Includes: Seven to ten guided runs a day, five star food and simple accommodation.
Comment: There is no better riding anywhere. It might not be as extreme as Alaska, but everything about the package is unreal, though not cheap. This is a freeride connisseur's heaven-on-earth with a vertical of 732 metres (2400 feet) per descent.

CAT POWDER SKIING INC.
Tel: 604-837 5151
Fax: 604-837 5111
Prices: $1125 (3 days)
Includes: Accommodation, meals, guides, safety equipment, local transportation and unlimited vertical.
Comment: Based on Mount MacKenzie. This is another quality operation offering riding up to 5500 metres (18,000 feet) of vertical every day.

SNO MUCH FUN CATSKIING INC.
Tel: 604-426 5303
Fax: 604-426 5567
Prices: $181.90 (1 day) or $161.50 (2 days and over)
Includes: Unlimited riding, guides, safety equipment, an endless lunch.
Comment: Averaging 3000 vertical metres (10,000 feet) of wilderness powder riding daily in awesome snow. Owned and operated by snowboarders, this place is as hard-core as you can get.

Main picture — Island Lake Lodge panorama **Photo:** Tim Rainger
Inset — Island Lake Cat **Photo:** Tim Rainger

THE stormrider GUIDE
europe

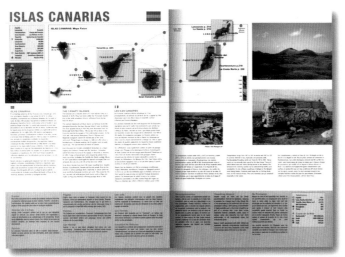

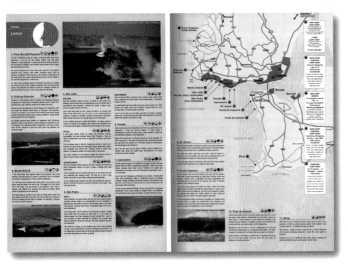

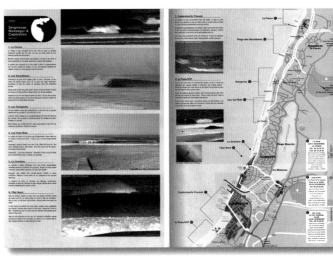

The only surf atlas covering the European coastline, completely revised since the highly successful first edition. Over 600 spots, from lava reefs to mellow beaches, are mapped and described with assistance from over 100 of Europe's leading surf personalities.

- **240 full colour pages** • **80 detailed double page road maps** • **Relief maps**
- **Over 300 photos** • **Includes Morocco, Northern Europe and the Med**

the lowdown

LOW PRESSURE

EUROPEAN SALES ENQUIRIES
THE LOW PRESSURE GROUP Unit 21, Pall Mall Deposit, 124-128 Barlby Road, London W10 6BL
Tel/Fax: +44 (0)181 960 1916 **Email:** mail@lowpressure.demon.co.uk **Web:** www.lowpressure.demon.co.uk

THEsnowboardGUIDE
europe

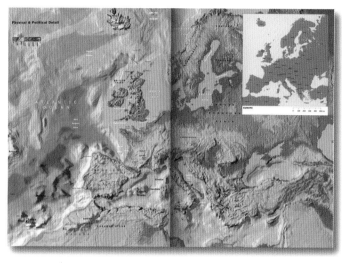

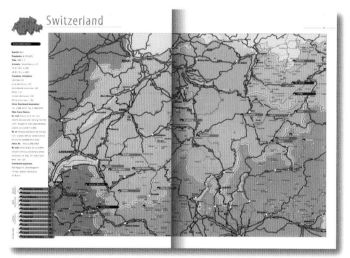

The only comprehensive guide to the mountains of western Europe, compiled specifically for snowboarders by a collection of Europe's leading riders and personalities. Over 80 resorts are described in detail, giving essential information on everything from the deepest powder runs to the best night out.

- **240 full colour pages** • **European road maps** • **Crucial travel information**
- **Lift pass facility information and piste maps** • **Over 300 incredible photos**

the lowdown

LOW PRESSURE

US SALES ENQUIRIES
BOARD WILD 3321 South East Hawthorne Boulevard, Portland, Oregon, 97214
Tel: (001) 503-238 0690 **Fax:** (001) 503-238 1965 **Web:** www.boardwild.com

it doesn't matter how you ride... just ride

LOW PRESSURE

THE LOW PRESSURE GROUP Unit 21, Pall Mall Deposit, 124-128 Barlby Road, London W10 6BL
Tel/Fax: +44 (0)181 960 1916 **Email**: mail@lowpressure.demon.co.uk **Web**: www.lowpressure.demon.co.uk

FURTHER READING

Baedeker USA, *Baedeker*

C. Leocha, 'Skiing America '97'

D.Brown, 'Bury my Heart at Wounded Knee', *Vintage*

D. Hanscom and A. Kelner, 'Wasatch Tours',
Wasatch Publishing 1993

J. & N. Lethcoe, 'A History of Prince William Sound, Alaska'

J. Humes & S. Wagstaff, 'Boarderlands: The Snowboarder's Guide to the West Coast', *HarperCollinsWest*

J. Kerouac, 'On the Road', *Penguin*

Jack London, 'The Jack London Reader', *Courage Classics*

N. Zimmerman, 'The American Southwest', *Fodor's Compass American Guides*

R. Enzel, 'The White Book of Ski Areas', *Inter Ski Services*

S. Lamb, 'The Smithsonian Guide to the Southern Rockies', *Random House*

'The Alaska Almanac', *Alaska Northwest Books*

'The Snowboard Guide: Europe,' *Low Pressure Publishing*

William Burroughs, 'Mountain Weather', *The Crowood Press*

FOCUSED
ON YOUR
FEET

BILLY SUMMERS   PHOTO: RUBEN SANCHEZ